S0-BSD-539

CARL A. RUDISILL LIBRARY
LENOIR-RHYNE COLLEGE

WAR MEMOIRS OF DAVID LLOYD GEORGE

1915–1916

By permission of the Imperial War Museum

THE FAMOUS KITCHENER POSTER WHICH WAS PLACARDED THROUGHOUT THE COUNTRY TO HELP IN RECRUITING KITCHENER'S ARMY

WAR MEMOIRS

of

DAVID LLOYD GEORGE

★ ★

1915-1916

WITH ILLUSTRATIONS

LITTLE, BROWN, AND COMPANY

BOSTON  1937

Published November, 1933
Reprinted November, 1933
Reprinted March, 1937

PRINTED IN THE UNITED STATES OF AMERICA

CONTENTS

WAR MEMOIRS OF DAVID LLOYD GEORGE

Lloyd George was the only member of the British Cabinet who remained continuously in office throughout the World War. He was Chancellor of the Exchequer at the outbreak of the War, then Minister of Munitions, later Secretary of State for War, and finally in December, 1916, he succeeded Asquith as Prime Minister and held that office until 1922. This fact alone makes his War Memoirs of the highest importance, for no book hitherto published on the War can present a record more consecutive, more sustained and more intimate than his.

The whole work is complete in six volumes. The first two volumes cover the events which led up to the outbreak of the War and the War years 1914–1916. In these two volumes Lloyd George shows conclusively how at every stage the civilian had to be brought in to amend the shortcomings of the military and he is unsparing in his criticism of the early conduct of the War. Instances of obstruction and shortsightedness are fully documented, and the chapter on the strategy of the War is an overwhelming indictment of the military mind.

ILLUSTRATIONS

WAR MEMOIRS OF DAVID LLOYD GEORGE

1915–1916

CHAPTER I

THE BALKANS AND THE SOMME

Eastern collapse suits the Westerners — Salonika army left without equipment and therefore impotent — Force too large for a garrison — Force too small for a campaign — Joffre's vacillations of policy — Joffre's visit to London in June, 1916 — Eloquence of Joffre — A cynical performance — Summary of my contribution to the discussion — Futility of an inadequate offensive — Meagre results of Somme offensive — The attrition argument fallacious — German man-power still abundant — My visit to the Somme front — Cavalry waiting for a break through — Death of Raymond Asquith — Minds clouded by battle smoke — Germans turn on Roumania — Roumanian weakness — My memorandum to the D.M.O. — Dangers on the Roumanian front — Measures to aid Roumania urged — Advantages to Germany of the Roumanian collapse — Allied losses heavier than German on the Somme.

THE whole strategic possibilities of the war for the Allies were changed by the Serbian collapse. The opportunities offered for a formidable movement against the Eastern flank of the Central Powers had been, if not entirely lost, at least made more difficult and doubtful. The constant allurement to amateur and other strategists of such a chance to divert troops from the Western charnel house was shut down. The General Staffs of France and Britain had not won *the* War, but they had won *their* war. The Dardanelles had been evacuated: the Balkans had been transferred from Allied to enemy hands: the road to the Danube, to Constantinople and the Black Sea had been finally blocked; Serbia had been wiped out; Russia was tottering to her fall; Roumania was isolated. What consummate strategy! The Germans had not been beaten, but the politicians had been thwarted. The Capital Letters were triumphant. They sang their chortling *Te Deums* from Chantilly to Whitehall. The

East with its opportunities, which were also temptations, was no more. Hail to the blood-red sun of the West!

It is true that forces which numerically appeared to be very powerful were sent to Salonika and there was every appearance of a formidable army of British, French, Serbians and Greeks, numbering in the aggregate hundreds of thousands, being assembled in that theatre. It was for all offensive purposes reduced to stagnation and impotence by an equipment so inadequate as to render this conglomerate army quite incapable of making any effective attack upon the enemy. The General Staffs were determined that all temptation to action must be removed from generals performing in that theatre. There were two possible uses to which the Salonika Expeditionary Force could be put. One was that it should be sufficiently strong to hold up the Bulgarians and a certain number of Austrian and German and Turkish troops, and to prevent them from being thrown on to other points where their accession might have been harmful and perhaps decisive. The plan would also have the effect of preventing the surly and suspicious King of Greece, who was only too sympathetic to the Germans, from throwing in his lot with them under the pretext that he could not resist the invasion of such a powerful force. As it was, he handed over Kavalla and a Greek division to the enemy as an offering to propitiate an idol he feared as well as adored. He might have given them the whole of the Greek Army had we not been there. For that purpose the force was much too large. If that was to be the sole purpose of the occupation of Salonika, the force was much too large and a smaller army well entrenched at Salonika, supported with an adequate quota of guns, would have answered equally well. It could easily have been reinforced by sea had there been an attack; there was no object in accumulating large forces there and providing them with powerful offensive armaments.

The second alternative was that we should have an army at Salonika, which could either have attacked the Turks on the right flank, cut their communications with Germany, and possibly captured their capital; or, on the other hand, stormed the defiles of the Balkans, broken through and defeated the Bulgarian Army, reëstablished relations with Roumania, and through Roumania with Russia; in fact, recreated the chance which had been lost through the fatal strategy of the early autumn of 1915. The fine achievement of the Serbian Army under General Misitsch later on, when it fought its way through to Monastir, proves that this was not outside the region of attainment by an army which was even moderately equipped with artillery and ammunition.

The military Chiefs pursued neither of these policies.

As I shall point out later on, the Salonika Army was left practically without any guns or ammunition which would have enabled it to bombard its way through the crudest defences in such a difficult terrain. It was camped on the malarial plains of the Struma and the Vardar for two years without being given the means of fighting its way to healthier ground. The British Staff were in favour of the first course and would have reduced the force to dimensions sufficient for the discharge of this rôle. The French Staff hesitated between the two. The argument between them went on for months. The French Commander-in-Chief, once an obdurate Westerner, now feigned conversion to some of the tenets of the Eastern faith. Here undoubtedly the reasons were political and personal. The influence of General Joffre in France had considerably diminished, owing to his failure to put the defences of Verdun in order for a whole month after he had been warned that an attack was impending. The autocratic authority which he once exerted and which up to that date was quite sufficient to intimidate Governments and to compel them, against their judgment, to conform to his stubborn will, had faded almost to vanishing point, since the German guns at Verdun had laid bare his limitations. The leading statesmen of France, including the President and the President of the Council, believed in attacking the enemy on the southeastern flank. In this they were supported — in fact they were acting on the suggestion of — the most gifted soldier in the French Army: General Gallieni.

General Joffre, therefore, in order to placate the men who for the first time had become his masters, deferred to their wishes about reinforcing the Salonika Front. It was his offering on the altar of the offended gods. The Moloch of the Western Front had been temporarily satiated. Some sacrifice might now be spared for the idols of the Elysée. General Joffre's influence had been strong enough to resist their plan when it would have been useful and perhaps decisive; but his authority was too weak to offer any effective opposition when the plan had ceased to have anything like the same value. This is one of the comic interludes which are woven into every tragedy.

Joffre came over to London on June 9th, 1916, to persuade the British Cabinet to join the French in strengthening the forces at Salonika. At that time the great offensive on the Somme had been agreed to by both Staffs and both Governments. I was one of the members of the Cabinet who accepted Lord Kitchener's view as to the futility of launching this attack. Lord Kitchener reluctantly withdrew his objections and the rest of us were overruled. The preparations were now far advanced. It was part of General Joffre's case that the offensive was essential in order to relieve the pressure on the French at Verdun. For the same reason we had been asked to take over a considerable sector of the Western Front hitherto occupied by French troops. The French needed every battalion they could spare for the defence of Verdun. It is one of the incomprehensible episodes of the war that the French Commander-in-Chief, the ruthless advocate of the "all for the West" policy, should at such a juncture come over to Britain to beg us to join the French in sending a considerable contingent of French and British soldiers to Salonika in order to launch a stage attack which must fail for lack of guns and ammunition.

At the Conference which was held in Downing Street, General Joffre presented his case with great force and eloquence. As to whether he was a good soldier or not, let others judge. Although I may not be competent to express an opinion I still hold one, and hold it strongly. As to his gifts as an orator, I feel that as an old Parliamentarian I am quite equal to forming a judgment, and quite entitled to state it. He was one of the most forceful and dramatic speakers I heard at any conference which I ever attended. But although on this occasion he spoke with all the outward visible manifestations of earnestness and sincerity, in voice, gesture, language, and facial expression, it was difficult to believe that he was convinced even by his own eloquence. He was urging an attack with forces devoid of the armament necessary to achieve their purpose, and he made no suggestion that the equipment should be strengthened up to the point of effectiveness. It was one of the most cynical performances I have ever listened to. Having regard to the inevitable loss of brave lives which would have been entailed in such a futile enterprise, it would have been wicked had it not been that he was relying upon our turning his proposal down. I realised that he did not mean business and that an offensive at Salonika unsupported by the necessary guns and ammunition must fail; I also knew that such a failure must discourage any future attempt under more favourable conditions.

Here is an official summary, taken down at the time, of the part I took in the discussion:

"Mr. Lloyd George said that he had always been in favour of an advance from Salonika, but that unless there was a fair chance of success he considered it fatal; and because the facts before him were not convincing that it would be successful, he, as a supporter of the principle of an advance, was doubtful. We had had a bad experience at the Dardanelles, where we lost about 200,000 men as well as prestige. Unless there was a reasonable chance of success he was entirely opposed to it. The facts given by our General Staff had not been seriously controverted by General Joffre to-day. To attack a good army, in strong positions, with only twenty-four French and six British heavy howitzers was very dangerous. General Joffre said that we should be keeping the enemy busy and quoted the Russians. But the Russians were occupying the attention of the Austrians, the Bulgarians were not helping anyone. If there was a fair chance of breaking right through and threatening the enemy's flank, the Roumanians might come in on our side. But General Joffre does not say there is this chance; he did not contemplate breaking through the Bulgarian lines — he was only thinking of comparatively trifling victories. To attempt the operation with inadequate strength was to discredit it. Sir Douglas Haig has in front of him very serious operations undertaken merely to relieve the pressure on France. This consideration had appeared conclusive to the War Committee, otherwise they were opposed to the offensive at the present time, considered purely as a military operation. The Ministry of Munitions were sending heavy guns to France, but nothing like what Sir Douglas Haig wanted, and therefore Sir Douglas Haig would prefer to undertake his operations later, when he was sure of a full supply of these guns. The test was whether General Joffre in these circumstances would like to see, say, fifty howitzers diverted from France to Salonika. Mr. Lloyd George said that he was as firm a believer in an eventual offensive from Salonika as M. Briand himself, and urged that we should not begin any advance from Salonika until we were quite ready, as an unsuccessful offensive would prejudice any further offensive on this flank. No Government after the failure would try it a second time. This indeed was the main reason for his opposition. The Allies were not yet equipped to defeat the Bulgarians — to say nothing of the possibility of Turkish opposition in addition."

So, much to the secret satisfaction of General Joffre, we turned our backs on Salonika and our faces once more to the Somme. It ranks with Verdun as one of the two bloodiest battles ever fought on this earth up to that date. The casualties on both sides were well over a million. It was not responsible for the failure of the German effort to capture Verdun. It was only an element in slackening up a German offensive which had already slowed down and was by now a practical and almost an acknowledged failure. The French Commander-in-Chief said in May that the Germans had already been beaten at Verdun. Had the battle continued to rage around the remaining forts which held up the German Army we could have helped to reinforce the hard-pressed French Army either by sending troops to the battle area or by taking over another sector of the French Front. The Somme campaign certainly did not save Russia. That great country was being rapidly driven by the German guns towards the maelstrom of anarchy. You could even then hear the roar of the waters. That is, we might have heard it had it not been for the thunders of the Somme. These deafened our ears and obscured our vision so that we could not perceive the approaching catastrophe in Russia and therefore did not take measures to avert it. One-third of the Somme guns and ammunition transferred in time to the banks of another river, the Dnieper, would have won a great victory for Russia and deferred the Revolution until after the war.

It is claimed that the Battle of the Somme destroyed the old German Army by killing off its best officers and men. It killed off far more of our best and of the French best.

The Battle of the Somme was fought by the volunteer armies raised in 1914 and 1915. These contained the choicest and best of our young manhood. The officers came mainly from our public schools and universities. Over 400,000 of our men fell in this bullheaded fight and the slaughter amongst our young officers was appalling. The "Official History of the War", writing of the first attack, says:

"For the disastrous loss of the finest manhood of the United Kingdom and Ireland there was only a small gain of ground to show. . . ."

Summing up the effect on the British Army of the whole battle it says:

"Munitions and the technique of their use improved, but never again was the spirit or the quality of the officers and men so high, nor the general state of the training, leading and, above all, discipline of the new British armies in France so good. The losses sustained were not only heavy but irreplaceable."

Had it not been for the inexplicable stupidity of the Germans in provoking a quarrel with America and bringing that mighty people into the war against them just as they had succeeded in eliminating another powerful foe — Russia — the Somme would not have saved us from the inextricable stalemate. I was not surprised to read in the British "Official History of the War" that M. Poincaré is reported to have said that the greatest of all French soldiers, General Foch, was opposed to the Somme offensive. When the results came to be summed up they reminded me of an observation made by Mr. Balfour when the project of this great offensive first came from the French Staff. He said: "The French are short of men; yet they want to do something which would reduce their numbers still more." At that time he was in favour of telling the French that we thought they were going to make a mistake.

Whilst the French generals and our own were reporting victory after victory against the German Army on the Western Front — whilst our Intelligence Departments at the front were assuring their Chiefs, and through them, their Governments at home, that five-sixths of the German divisions had been hammered to pulp and that the remaining divisions would soon be reduced to the same state, the German General Staff were detaching several divisions from the battle area in France and sending them to the Carpathians to join the Austrians and Bulgarians in an attack on Roumania. No one on the Allied side seemed to have anticipated this move — at least, no one made any plans to counter it, if and when it came. The whole mind of the Western strategists was concentrated on one or other of the hamlets along the Somme. They exaggerated the effect of every slight advance, and worked themselves into a belief that the Germans were so pulverised by these attacks that they had not the men, the guns, or the spirit to fight anywhere much longer. They were only waiting, with hand cupped to ear, for the crack which would signify the final break of the German barrier, and they were massing cavalry immediately behind the French and British battle line to complete the rout of the tattered remains of the German Army. This is no exaggeration of their illusions. I saw them at this moment of exaltation.

When the Battle of the Somme was being fought I traversed the front from Verdun to Ypres. With M. Albert Thomas I visited General Haig at his Headquarters and with him I drove to General Cavan's Headquarters to meet General Joffre. The latter and M. Thomas were anxious to secure a number of six-inch howitzers for the French Front. We had followed the advice given by the young French artillery officer at the Boulogne conference (described in the next chapter) and manufactured these howitzers on a great scale, with a view to concentrating a plunging fire to demolish the enemy trenches. The French had gone in more for the long-range gun, and they were short of howitzers.

When we reached General Cavan's quarters there was a heavy bombardment going on from our eight-inch howitzers assembled in the valley below, known to the soldiers as the Happy Valley. The roar of the guns beneath and the shrill "keen" of the shells overhead were deafening. We could hardly carry on a conversation. We found the noises were worse inside Lord Cavan's quarters than outside. After we had arranged the matter of the howitzers we got on to a general talk about the offensive. Both generals — Joffre and Haig — were elated with the successes already achieved. On my way to this rendezvous I had driven through squadrons of cavalry clattering proudly to the front. When I asked what they were for, Sir Douglas Haig explained they were brought up as near the front line as possible, so as to be ready to charge through the gap which was to be made by the Guards in the coming attack. The cavalry were to exploit the anticipated success and finish the German rout.

The Guards could be seen marching in a long column through the valley on their way to the front line preparatory to the attack. Raymond Asquith was amongst them. Before I reached Ypres I heard that the attack had failed and that the brilliant son of the British Prime Minister was amongst the fallen. When I ventured to express to General Joffre and Haig my doubts as to whether cavalry could ever operate successfully on a front bristling for miles behind the enemy line with barbed wire and machine guns, both generals fell ecstatically on me, and Joffre in particular explained that he expected the French cavalry to ride through the broken German lines on his front the following morning. You could hear the distant racket of the massed guns of France which were at that moment tearing a breach for the French horsemen. Just then a Press photographer, of whose presence we were all unaware, snapped us.

Photo. Imperial War Museum

M. ALBERT THOMAS (FRENCH MINISTER OF MUNITIONS), SIR DOUGLAS HAIG AND GENERAL JOFFRE IN EARNEST CONVERSATION WITH MR. LLOYD GEORGE DURING HIS VISIT TO THE SOMME FRONT

The conversation gave me an idea of the exaltation produced in brave men by a battle. They were quite incapable of looking beyond and around or even through the struggle just in front of them. That would have been all right had the Allied Governments been advised on the whole field of the war by independent advisers who were superior or equal in capacity and will power to these resolute soldiers, whose vision was clouded by the smoke of the battle in which they were engaged. But neither the French nor ourselves had military counsellors at the side of Ministers comparable in ability and force to Joffre, Foch, and Haig. General Gallieni had been a sick man for years and therefore did not possess sufficient vitality to enforce the advice which his genius counselled. Of Sir William Robertson I shall have something to say later on. A mistaken loyalty to Sir Douglas Haig fettered his common sense. The result was that the break through was postponed from victory to victory. We suffered enormous losses. Some of them were irreplaceable — in the case of officers and in the picked men who had joined the Kitchener armies in the first moments of enthusiasm. The Germans flaunted our wild onslaught on the Somme and advertised its failure by their Roumanian campaign. They marched to the Danube to celebrate and exploit their victorious repulse of the Allied armies on the Western stream. Mackensen crossed the great river from the Bulgarian side and marched on Bucharest. Falkenhayn's Army had already fallen like an avalanche from the Carpathian heights and overwhelmed the ill-equipped Roumanian armies on the plains. Roumania, with its oil and wheat, fell into German hands and thus months and years were added to the war.

Before the attack on Roumania came I was disturbed by news that was coming through from the Balkans, which indicated a movement on the part of Bulgaria against her Trans-Danubian neighbour. We had also received a disquieting memorandum from Colonel Thomson (afterwards Lord

Thomson), our military attaché at Bucharest, as to the equipment of the Roumanian Army. In guns and ammunition it was quite unequal to the armament which the forces of the Central Powers could easily spare for the attack. I spoke to one of the Military Staff at the War Office on the subject, but he tried to comfort me by assuring me that apart from the fact that the Germans had no troops or guns to spare from the Somme, where he said their losses in men and material were gigantic, it was getting too late for German action in Roumania, as snow would already have fallen on the Carpathians, and the passes were impervious to artillery. Moreover, he did not think much of Colonel Thomson or his report. I was not completely reassured and a day or two later I sent in to the Chief of the Imperial General Staff the following note:

"D.M.O.

"I have just seen the telegram announcing the declaration of War by Bulgaria against Roumania. This is an additional ground for the anxiety which I expressed to you on Saturday as to the possibilities in the immediate future in the Balkans. I then expressed some apprehension that Hindenburg, who has strong Eastern proclivities and has always been opposed to the concentration of Germanic forces in the West, would direct his attention to the crushing of Roumania, and that we ought to be thinking out every practicable plan for giving effective support to Roumania in the event of her being heavily attacked. We cannot afford another Serbian tragedy. We were warned early in 1915 that the Germans meant, in confederation with the Bulgars, to wipe Serbia out. In spite of the fact, when the attack came we had not even purchased a single mule to aid the Serbians through Salonika. The result was when our troops landed there, owing to lack of equipment and appropriate transport, they could not go inland and Serbia was crushed.

"I hope that we shall not allow the same catastrophe to befall Roumania through lack of timely forethought.

"There are four disquieting facts in the situation:

"1. Hindenburg's well-known Eastern inclinations.

"2. The declaration of War by Bulgaria against Roumania. "I cannot believe Ferdinand would have taken this risk where it was quite unnecessary unless he had received substantial guarantees of German assistance in the attack on Roumania.

"3. The slackening of the German attack on Verdun. Hindenburg will certainly give up this foolish attack at the earliest possible opportunity. The abandonment of this operation will release hundreds of heavy guns and hundreds of thousands of good troops. If in addition to this he were prepared gradually to give ground on the Somme, making us pay for it as he retires, he could transfer several more Divisions from the West to the East. He could give up four or five times as much ground as we have won during the past two months without surrendering any vital positions.[1]

"4. I can hardly think that the equipment of the Roumanian Army would enable it long to resist an attack from an Austro-Germanic-Bulgarian force, armed with hundreds of heavy guns and supplied with enormous quantities of heavy shell. The Roumanians are very scantily supplied with heavy guns and I doubt whether their supplies of ammunition are sufficient to enable them to get through a continuous fight lasting over several weeks.

"I therefore once more urge that the General Staff should carefully consider what action we could take in conjunction with France and Italy immediately to relieve the pressure on Roumania if a formidable attack developed against her. There may be nothing in my fears, but no harm could be done by being prepared for all contingencies.

D. LLOYD GEORGE.
4. 9. 16"

The Russians made a gallant effort to help the outnumbered and out-gunned Roumanian Army. But by Christ-

[1] I am entitled to point out that five months later the Germans actually adopted this plan and by doing so completely upset the strategy of the Nivelle offensive.

mas the greater part of Roumania was in the hands of the enemy. The Roumanian King was forced to an abject peace, and a country which had been a menace and a peril to the Central Powers became to them a fruitful source of much-needed supplies of oil and corn. Roumania and Serbia were both *hors de combat;* Greece had been neutralised, with the pro-German elements in its Government right on top. Three countries which between them could have thrown more than a million excellent soldiers into action on the side of the Allies had been eliminated from the calculations. The effort to save Roumania had finally exhausted the great strength of Russia. The Allied generals in contemplating the results of their strategy found refuge in grotesque computations of German losses on the Somme. They were placed at a million on the British Front alone. We were left to imagine what havoc the French had wrought with their guns. Our great offensive had failed in the avowed objective of a break through and we took refuge in statistics. Sir Douglas Haig had not achieved his strategic aim, but a distinguished academician more than made up for the failure by a great statistical triumph he achieved in one of the back rooms of the War Office. The learned professor was acting under the direction and on information supplied by the "Intelligence" Department of the War Office. Surely its officials never displayed greater intelligence than when they played up to the urgent need of the army chiefs for some symbol of victory. As a matter of fact we lost on our front 50 per cent. more men than the Germans did. The French casualties were not as heavy as ours but they also were heavier than the German losses.

Thus ended the third campaign of the Great War.

CHAPTER II

THE MINISTRY OF MUNITIONS: PRACTICAL ACHIEVEMENTS

War Office view of my duties — Its refusal to recognize changed conditions — Requirements of the new warfare — Decision to consult with leaders in the field — Conference at Boulogne — I meet General Du Cane — My first question — My second question — General arrangements to coördinate munition production — Artillery problems: Colonel Walch's views — Sabbath incongruity — General Du Cane widens his views — Sir John French makes an increased demand — My "Big Gun Programme" of August, 1915 — War Office informed — War Office indignation — My refusal to cancel orders — Lord Kitchener's memorandum — War Office cannot man the guns — Cabinet discussion — Fate of the Committee — General Sir Ivor Philipps's letter — Changed army views in 1916.

DURING a considerable part of the time occupied by the events described in the foregoing pages, my own departmental work was the development of our munition production. I have already told how, upon my appointment at the beginning of June, 1915, as Minister of Munitions, I proceeded to organise this new Department of State. I must now give some account of the work we were able to carry out during the thirteen months that I was responsible for its direction, until my translation to the War Office in July, 1916.

I shall not, of course, attempt to write a detailed history of the immense range of activities covered by the Ministry; but shall confine my notice to a few only of the developments of outstanding importance which took place during that period. They will serve as samples to illustrate the infinite variety of problems we were faced with, and the measure of success with which we achieved their solution.

1. The Gun Conference at Boulogne

When I undertook the official task of manufacturing munitions for the British Army, the War Office view of my duty was that my sole business was to comply with the demands which came from their Ordnance Department. Once I fulfilled these requisitions my statutory responsibility was, according to their interpretation, at an end. In a letter dated June 5th, 1915, from the War Office, detailing the relations between their Department and the Ministry of Munitions, it was laid down that "the duties of the new Department with regard to the supply of each kind of munitions will begin when the requirements of the War Office have been made known to it, as regards the kind, quantity, and quality of such munitions, and they will end when the delivery of such munitions has been made to the War Office."

I took a different and a much wider view of my responsibility. The rigid and hardened mentality of the War Office refused to bend or give to any facts that were not stale with age and chronicled in accepted military histories. They rejected all experience which they had not been taught during the training they received in the days of their remote youth. I had been driven by their stubborn attitude to the conclusion that if we waited until our Whitehall generals woke up to the realities it might be too late then to save the situation. For months the Commander-in-Chief in the field had called their attention to the difference between this war and any other war which had ever been waged before by the British or any other army, because of the unexpected substitution of siege warfare for the anticipated war of movement. This altered the munitions problem so far as cannon were concerned in at least three respects: (1) It called for guns and mortars of a much bigger calibre than any hitherto sent to the field; (2) It necessitated a quite unprecedented expenditure of shell; and (3) shrapnel, which was invaluable against masses of men moving in the open field or in searching out inadequate cover, became useless when the opposing troops were sheltering in a deep trench; and therefore the need of the army was for high explosive of the heaviest calibre to tear up wire and to crash into trenches and parapets. I had learned from the correspondence placed at my disposal by Sir John French that he had repeatedly urged this point of view upon Lord Kitchener. I, therefore, came to the conclusion that I had to take the risk of a personal initiative, not merely in methods adopted for executing orders which came from the War Office but in determining for myself what the needs of the Army were and in organising my programme accordingly.

Not having the training of a soldier, and having no personal knowledge of these matters beyond what I had acquired during the past few months by contact with French generals and British officers — and these talks were not adequate to enable me to formulate a detailed and reliable programme for guns, machine guns, and rifles — I decided to take immediate steps to consult with men of authority, and especially with men who had personal experience of the practical exigencies of the situation in the battlefield. It was useless to rely upon the Ordnance Department of the War Office. I was convinced that with them shrapnel was not a necessity of war but had become a point of honour. They felt that they could not desert it without a reflection upon their own prevision and patriotism. I decided, therefore, to go behind them to men who had first-hand knowledge of the actualities and requirements of the present war. This decision was reflected in the following note which I find amongst my papers:

"That a conference be arranged at the earliest moment between the French Military Authorities and M.M. (Minister of Munitions) on the one hand and the British Military Authorities and M.M. on the other with a view to arriving at a common basis for computing the number and calibres of guns and the quantity and natures of ammunition necessary to ensure the success of the next great offensive operation on the Western Front."

This turned out to be a momentous decision, for in the sequel it undoubtedly revolutionised the whole of our ideas as to the scale and character of the requirements of our Army. The conference was fixed for June 19th, 1915, at Boulogne. Before this conference I was confronted with a gun programme which even those who framed it afterwards admitted was quite unequal to the needs of the military situation. I decided to test its sufficiency by drawing upon the best experience available from the battle front. I made arrangements with M. Albert Thomas, who was organising munitions in France, for the attendance of representatives of the French artillery. I asked him to bring along not merely the official adviser of his Ministry on these matters, but also, if possible, someone from the front who had actual experience of the effect of both the French and German artillery with a view to ascertaining what kind of gun it would be most useful to manufacture, and in what proportions. Boulogne was crowded up to the attics and the only accommodation available for the conference was a frowsy room at a second-rate hotel; (later on in the war the whole hotel was completely demolished down to the cellars by a bomb). I had communicated with Sir John French and asked him to send his very best artillery expert to the conference. When I arrived at Boulogne I was met by General Du Cane, who had been sent as the Commander-in-Chief's representative. As I discovered at the time, and even more completely later on, he was a man of great intelligence, and what was even more important to me under these conditions, he was more accessible to the influence of fresh facts and new ideas than most men high up in his profession with whom I had business dealings. The French were not present at the first conference, but I had a full discussion with General Du Cane and handed to him the following note for consideration:

"Given an Army of 1,000,000 men what equipment would you require in guns of all natures — number of shells before you commenced a serious and sustained attack with a view to breaking through the German lines?"

This gives an idea of my views before the conference began.

Later on in the course of the proceedings this further question was posed:

"What weekly output of ammunitions should we aim at developing month by month in order to supply an army in France of 18 army corps of 54 divisions so as to allow it to develop its full power of offence?"

The following day we had two meetings and there were present, in addition to the British delegates, M. Albert Thomas, General Gossot of the French War Office, and a young French officer of the French Headquarters Staff by the name of Colonel Walch.

Before we came to the discussion of the guns there were some very important questions of coördination between the various Governments to be cleared up. The situation that had arisen abroad was illustrated in the lack of touch between the Allies on vital matters. Each of the Allied countries was running its own war on and behind the various fronts. I found that on munitions supply it was imperative there should be much more intimate contact between the respective Governments. At the beginning of the year the Allies were still competing in the American market and putting up prices against each other. We and the Russians were competing for T.N.T. whilst all the Allies were doing the same for other explosives and other materials. In one case the British Government withdrew from purchasing when it was discovered that it was being played off against the Russians. The price of picric acid was forced up by the demands of the French, and the whole metal and machinery market was deranged owing to the activity of certain people acting for Russia. Even amongst the Allies themselves there was no efficient system of controlling purchases and no co-ordination. France, for example, could not obtain export licences for coke from this country; and whilst demanding shell steel from us, suddenly stopped the export of ferrosilicon.

We then proceeded to consider the question of artillery. For hours we discussed the whole problem of the kind of guns which the experience of the war had proved to be most useful, especially since the war had resolved itself into a question of attacking and defending earthen fortresses. I soon discovered that the ideas of the French general were just as antiquated as our own. He had the same superstitious belief in the efficacy of the "*soixante-quinze*" for all purposes as our own generals had in the all-round potency of shrapnel. I had to contend not with a profession but with a priesthood, devoted to its own chosen idol. General Gossot had not much, if any, experience at the front in this war, and his ideas were purely historic. On the other hand, Colonel Walch had been a kind of artillery liaison officer, and in that capacity he had seen the French and German artillery in action from Switzerland up to the British lines, and he had observed with scientific care and accuracy the results produced by the different kinds of guns and shells. He was a young man not only of great intelligence but of reckless courage, for he threw over his commanding officer with some approach to contempt for his ignorance. That demands more fearlessness for an army officer than crossing no-man's land in the face of a machine gun. I found afterwards that he was an Alsatian Huguenot, and he was certainly imbued with a full measure of the spirit of Protestant revolt against authority. The Conference soon resolved itself into a dialogue between Colonel Walch and myself, neither Thomas, the French General nor General Du Cane taking much part. It was hardly a dialogue; it was rather a cross-examination on my part with a view to extracting from Colonel Walch all the information which he undoubtedly possessed and obtaining from him his definite opinion as to the kind of gun it would be most useful for us to manufacture for the service of our Army, having regard to the kind of warfare to which we were now committed.

The hotel was situated opposite the English Episcopal Church. A few yards lower down was the Scottish Presbyterian Church. After this talk had been going on for hours, I heard through the open windows a distant sound of hymns being sung in these churches and soon after saw the congregations pouring out from the two churches, carrying prayer and hymn books in their hands. It suddenly occurred to me that this was Sunday morning and that I had been discussing earnestly with these officers the problem which was repeatedly referred to by Colonel Walch as a question "which was the best gun for destroying material" and "which was the best gun for killing men." And this on a day consecrated to the worship of the Prince of Peace. The thought made me shudder. I pulled myself together only by reflecting that this was a war that had been forced upon us by the arrogance of brute force crushing down the weak, and that I had been driven by the relentless hand of Fate to choose between giving my individual assent to the shedding of blood and assenting to a surrender of international right and liberty in Europe.

By this time both General Du Cane and I had a very

clear idea as to the lines upon which our gun programme ought to proceed. I had the best evidence afterwards that, although he had taken no part in the proceedings, he had listened with great intentness and had not missed a word of the clear and emphatic statements of the young French artillerist.

By that time we had both come to the definite conclusion that our ideas as to the manufacture of artillery would have to be considerably enlarged, and that we should have to develop our gun construction on a very much larger scale than anything that had been hitherto contemplated, both as regards quantity and calibre. On leaving the hotel for the boat, General Du Cane expressed his satisfaction with what he regarded as the most fruitful Council of War he had ever attended, and then he said to me: "What I am about to say to you now will make you think much less of me." I asked him what it was and he replied: "After this conference I have completely changed my mind as to the requirements of the Army." I told him that his admission made me think far more highly of him and that it was creditable both to his intelligence and integrity. He promised that he would, after consultation with the Commander-in-Chief, prepare a revised estimate of the needs of the Army.

At that date the war had been going on for ten months. Guns and shells had been a subject of vexatious and fretful correspondence between the soldiers at the front and the War Office, and yet this was the first conference that had taken place on that subject between the artillerists of the French and British fronts with actual battle experience.

As a result of this conference, Sir John French sent to the War Office on June 25th, 1915, a revised estimate of his requirements of heavy guns. The War Office forwarded this letter to the Ministry of Munitions on June 30th, for observations, accompanied by a table showing the additional heavy guns which equipment on this scale would involve for a force of seventy divisions. After an exchange of correspondence, the Ministry submitted a programme of its expected monthly gun deliveries up to the following spring, and toward the end of July drew up a revised programme showing a faster rate of delivery of heavy guns.

I was not, however, satisfied with these programmes. In view of the information I had gathered at Boulogne, I was convinced that for the success of our operations, an overwhelming mass of guns of the heaviest calibres was essential — an opinion confirmed by the success of our advance at Hooge, after a thorough preliminary bombardment with heavy guns, in early August. After careful enquiry as to possible sources of supply in this country and abroad, I decided to put in hand a very greatly increased programme, which would provide guns on a scale ranging for some types up to 25 per cent. above the War Office allowance, and this not for seventy, but for one hundred divisions.

I felt that to break through the formidable entrenchments of the Germans would involve a battering by artillery far heavier than the War Office yet realised, and that there should also be a margin available to provide for contingencies. If the guns were not all required for the various fronts of the British Army, the surplus would be available to supply the urgent needs of the Russians, who were at that moment suffering severely from the superior artillery of Germany and Austria.

Sir H. Llewellyn Smith sent to the War Office, on behalf of the Ministry of Munitions, a statement showing my new programme, and explained in his covering letter:

> "I am therefore directed to state that orders have already been placed which will not only cover the additional numbers suggested in your letter of the 8th of September, but will also provide a very considerable margin for possible future needs.

The Minister has been influenced in providing such a margin by the important consideration that the ordering of these large quantities will make it worth while to have new machinery on a larger scale installed, both at home and abroad, which will hasten the dates at which considerable deliveries can take place in 1916. A larger number of heavy guns will by this plan be delivered during the critical first months of 1916 than would otherwise have been possible. . . ."

It might have been imagined that the War Office would be delighted to learn that its desires were thus being more than fulfilled. On the contrary, it was furious at the presumption shown by the Ministry in daring to increase or anticipate the programme laid down for it. The preliminary warning of a storm came in the shape of a letter from the War Office, dated October 1st, 1915, which stated that on learning that "the purchase of a large number of heavy howitzers over and above any demand made by the War Office was contemplated by your Ministry", Lord Kitchener had consulted with Sir John French to find out how many he wanted, and obtained his confirmation that the schedule submitted by him in June represented his requirements. The Army Council, therefore, had no wish for my extra guns, and suggested that the orders for them should be transferred to Russia's account.

I directed an impenitent answer to be sent to the War Office. The letter pointed out that the large orders were necessary to secure early delivery of even the War Office figure of requirements, while early delivery of the extra guns might well prove to have a decisive effect on the campaign. The letter continued:

"Should the Secretary of State differ from the above views, the Minister of Munitions is prepared at any time to discuss the matter with him, or if he should prefer, he might bring it before the attention of the Cabinet. The Minister is not, in any case, prepared to cancel the orders he has placed for the provision of heavy howitzers, unless the Government as a whole will take the responsibility of deciding that the proposed provision is excessive."

If in fact there proved to be a surplus, I said that it would still be possible to pass this on to the Allies. But I made no offer to adopt the suggestion that some of the guns should be manufactured to Russian patterns, as such an alteration of the orders I had placed would have upset the existing arrangements and caused considerable delay in gun production. This called forth the wrath of Lord Kitchener, who expressed his disapproval of the action of the Ministry of Munitions in a memorandum, entitled: "Supply of Heavy Guns to the Army", which he circulated to the Cabinet. In this memorandum he called on the Cabinet to judge between him and me. He recounted the history of the dispute, and pointed out that the additional programme which I had put in hand entailed a provision of the following heavy guns over and above the requirements of the War Office:

60-pdr.	120 guns,	equivalent to 15 Divisions.
6-in. howitzer ..	220 "	" " 27 "
8-in. " .. 9.2-in. " ..	259 "	" " 49 "
12-in. " .. 15-in. " ..	40 "	" " 45 "
	639	

After describing the latest exchange of correspondence with the Ministry on the matter he declared:

"The point I wish to emphasise is that, if these extra guns are ordered for the War Office the War Office will not be able to provide the personnel for the batteries required to place them in the field, for, even if the men were forthcoming, it would be quite impossible to find the artillery officers necessary for this service."

He urged, therefore, that these guns should be allotted to Russia, and should be manufactured to Russian calibres and patterns.

Thereupon the matter was thrashed out in the Cabinet. But I gave way neither in the issue of reducing my orders nor in that of making the guns to the Russian pattern, for if surplus guns should be available for the Russians it would be possible to furnish them with ammunition as well. I had for some time been urging that arrangements should be made to equip the Russians; but to change these orders to Russian calibres and patterns would have involved delays and complications in production. The Cabinet appointed a Committee under the chairmanship of Lord Crewe to deal with the matter. It sat once, at the Ministry of Munitions, and examined General von Donop, who repeated his objections to the enlarged programme. I did not state my case in reply. Here is an extract from Sir William Sutherland's notes, taken at the meeting:

". . . I was somewhat mystified as to what was the official finding of the meeting; the various speeches being severely critical as described, and Mr. Lloyd George, beyond outlining the position generally, not making the spirited and continuous fight so often showed by him in similar circumstances.

" 'I suppose, Sir,' said J. T. Davies when the meeting was over, 'that means the end of your programme.'

" 'No,' said Mr. Lloyd George. 'It means the end of the Committee,' and straightaway started his orders for the prodigious work."

In fact the Committee adjourned without coming to any decision, and never met again. The subject was dropped — but not the programme. I pushed that through. Before I ceased to be Minister of Munitions, it turned out that even more guns were needed by our Army than the large number I had ordered. I may here anticipate the course of events so far as to point out that when the Ministry of Munitions finally produced this "unhouselled and unannealed" surplusage of guns, the War Office resolutely refused to part with them to help Russia, on the ground that they were all needed by our own troops in France, and a good many more. It was with difficulty that I persuaded the Staff to dispense with a few of the lighter guns for Russia.

But at first there was a good deal of gibing and sniping about what was called my mad production of heavy guns, and I had evidence that the War Office meant to neutralise my extravagance by refusing to train artillerists to man this wasteful surplus. I decided to take the matter up with the Prime Minister, and if necessary with the War Committee, and in order to check the facts upon which I intended to base my case, I wrote on November 15th, 1915, to General Sir Ivor Philipps, who had been Military Secretary to the Ministry at the time the order was given, to ask him for his recollection of my instructions. He was at that time preparing to leave for France with the division he commanded. His reply was as follows:

"Headquarters,
38th (Welsh) Division,
Arlington Park Camp,
Winchester.

"My dear Minister,

"When the Big Gun Programme was under discussion you repeatedly urged on your staff that your main object in increasing the order for guns was to ensure the maximum possible delivery at the earliest possible date. This, you specially impressed on us, both verbally and in writing. The necessity for impressing early deliveries by giving larger orders to contractors was passed on by me to the departments concerned, and we did our utmost to see that your very clear orders on the subject were carried out.

"In many conversations with me you stated that your main objects in placing the Big Gun orders were:

1. To ensure earliest possible deliveries by giving large orders to firms to encourage them to increase their power of output.

2. To provide guns for 100 divisions, should necessity arise hereafter to put that number in the Field.

3. To provide a surplus of very heavy guns to meet the latest views of advanced French artillery experts that the teachings of the War tended to show that in future more and more of heavy guns would be required to secure victory.

4. That if these guns were in excess of our own requirements, they would be invaluable as a reserve to assist our Allies.

"It must be remembered that you laboured under great difficulties. You got no assistance from the War Office.

"After your Conference at Boulogne with M. Thomas and the French artillery experts, as a result of the information you then collected, the War Office at once put forward an increased and entirely revised programme.

"No suggestion of this increased programme had been mentioned by the War Office, while the ordering of guns was in their hands. When, however, the responsibility was on your shoulders, the demands of the War Office were at once increased.

"I do not think you need fear that you have ordered too many guns or shells. What you have to consider in the War Council is, whether you are preparing to man the guns or even half of them when delivered. I fear that the War Council is neglecting this point. You will remember that I prepared a note on the subject when at the Ministry. You have done your share of the work of providing guns and shells; the country will one day appreciate your great work in this respect.

Yours sincerely,
Ivor Philipps."

I have quoted this letter in full because it gives in compact form, and from the pen of a distinguished Army officer, a summary alike of my attitude to this issue, and of the War Office reluctance to admit the need for the guns I was providing. In contrast to their attitude then, I may add that a year later, Sir William Robertson, writing in November, 1916, said: "We must have a much greater amount of heavy artillery than we now possess, and be able to turn out an almost unlimited amount of ammunition."

At the same time Sir Douglas Haig wrote:

> "An ample supply of munitions is also an essential. The enormous quantities required have been furnished this year with unfailing regularity. But the great reserves required in readiness for next year can only be accumulated by reducing expenditure to an absolute minimum during the winter, and then only provided the output can be maintained at the full rates estimated."

The "Official History of the War" makes it clear that even the "extravagant" programme, for which I took responsibility, was insufficient for the purpose of bombarding the elaborate entrenchments constructed on the Somme plateau by the Germans. The official historian points out that we had a shortage of guns, more especially in the heavier calibres. These were the very calibres where I had exceeded the amended requisition of the War Office and thus drawn on myself Lord Kitchener's censure.

By November, 1916, a whole series of increased demands for big guns had been made by the War Office, and the Ministry of Munitions had been compelled to expand considerably the programme which I had been pressed so hard to curtail. Fortunately I had acquired machinery which was equal to the manufacture of this expanded requisition.

2. National Factories

Range of the Ministry's task — Growth of industrial control — Relations with the trade organisations — Developing new factories — Achievements of first seven months — Total by end of the war — Other munition works — The shell factories — Method of organisation — Projectile factories — Achievements of shell and projectile factories.

To increase the supply of shells was our most immediate aim; for it was the shell shortage which had chiefly impressed the popular imagination and brought about the crisis which gave birth to the Ministry. But along with shells I had undertaken the responsibility for all the rest of the wide range of military supplies — guns, rifles, machine guns, bombs, trench-warfare equipment, military transport, and optical instruments. Soon after the formation of the Ministry tanks were handed over by the Admiralty. Control of the output of the finished article led inevitably to control of the preliminary stages of manufacture, back to the raw materials involved.

The consequence was that the scope of control exercised by the Ministry widened steadily and ineluctably until before the end of the war it covered practically the whole industrial life of the nation. The form of control became increasingly stringent with the progressive shortage of materials, until by the end of the war no one could start a new business or enlarge an old one except for war purposes. Everyone was liable to have buildings, plant or machinery requisitioned for more urgent work. None of the industrial metals and few raw materials could be used by anyone without Government licence. The nation concentrated all its great strength and skill on victory.

The materials which the Ministry of Munitions brought under its control included nearly a hundred main categories, and extended not only to more obvious articles such as iron, steel, copper, chemicals, and machine tools, but to bricks, flaxseed, glassware, waste paper and yarn. Ultimately the Ministry assumed responsibility for all visible supplies of such materials, controlled all private importation and the distribution of materials to non-munition as well as to munition trades, thereby virtually bringing all the industries using materials which entered into production of munitions under the control of the department.

It was not an arbitrary bureaucracy; for the Ministry acted throughout in very close coöperation with the particular trade or industry controlled. Frequently, important members of the trade had official posts and executive authority in the Ministry; while in these and other cases an Advisory Committee representing the trade was constituted as a consultative body to advise the department or section of the Ministry concerned. Where a trade had already a representative association, we discussed matters with it; and if no such body already existed, we sought to promote its formation. By contributing to, or bearing the whole cost of, needed extensions and adaptations of factories on the one hand, and by arrangements for limitation of profits and the operation of the Excess Profits Duty on the other, our national industry was welded into a great public undertaking for the winning of the war.

Even after utilising every workshop and factory capable of turning out munitions, we found that the output would be inadequate unless we supplemented our resources by the setting up of emergency buildings. This was more particularly the case when we came to the larger calibre shells and facilities for shell-filling. I therefore took steps to press forward as soon as the Ministry of Munitions was set up the policy which I had already been promoting as Chairman of the Munitions of War Committee, of organising special national factories for the definite purpose of supplementing our existing resources for munition production; particularly for making shells and explosives, for shell-filling and completing ammunition.

The first few months of the Ministry's existence saw the establishment of an imposing group of these national factories. By the end of December, 1915, when the Ministry had been in existence only seven months, there were, in addition to the Royal Factories at Woolwich, Waltham Abbey, Enfield Lock and Farnborough — which had been transferred from the War Office in the course of the autumn — and certain factories for explosives, no less than seventy-three new national factories. Of these, thirty-six were national shell factories for turning out the lighter natures of shell; thirteen were national projectile factories, mainly concerned with heavier shell; thirteen were national filling factories. There were eight new factories for making explosives, a new factory for filling trench mortar bombs, and two gauge factories which I took over to ensure an adequate supply of gauges for the new concerns which were springing up everywhere to produce munitions. Progress had been hampered in every direction by the inadequate supply of gauges.

As time went on, this array of national factories was steadily increased, both in number and in the variety of the products for the manufacture of which they were erected or adapted. By the end of the war they numbered in all 218; and covered not only every kind of munition from cannon and aëroplanes to small-arms ammunition, but sawmills, factories for boxes, tools, optical instruments and ball bearings, and establishments for sorting and storing salvage.

The total of 218 included the four Royal Factories which were in existence before the war, the wood alcohol factory at Coleford set up by the Woods and Forests Department in 1913, and three or four explosives factories initiated by the War Office or by Lord Moulton's Committee on High Explosives between November, 1914, and May, 1915. Two of the national shell factories had already been begun under the Munitions of War Committee before the Ministry of Munitions was set up. Over nine-tenths of the remaining two hundred odd factories were constructed under the auspices of the Ministry, or with the aid of Government advances, leaving less than a score of establishments which were already engaged on production of necessary supplies such as gauges, ball bearings, cotton waste or acetone, before they were taken over and nationalised.

The total covers only concerns engaged in manufacture or repair. It excludes the large classes of inspection and storage depots, mines, quarries, and other similar undertakings which were controlled by the Ministry. It excludes also the State-owned plant within the works of contractors, even where operated by servants of the department. And, of course, it does not touch the vast array of private firms which, frequently with the aid of substantial Government subsidies, were busily engaged upon munition manufacture. The great nucleus of national factories stood at the heart of the munitions industry as a colossal supplement to the Royal Ordnance Factories and a guarantee, within the hand of the Government, that the supplies for our armies could be expanded to meet the rapidly increasing demands from the front.

The first group of these factories which I was responsible for setting up was the group of national shell factories. The pioneer of these was the factory at Leeds, started by the Local Munitions Committee in May, 1915. The Leeds engineering firms had been urged to arrange a scheme of coöperation for production of munitions, and like practical men, they went to Woolwich in April to study the processes involved. Thereupon they came to the conclusion that the best way for them to work was to take or erect premises where, with their joint assistance, tools, workmen, supervision and inspection could all be assembled and the work carried out on a non-profit basis by a committee of management.

By May 7th a draft scheme had secured general approval, and the next day the formal sanction of the Government was given and the work was put in hand forthwith. On May 31st a national shell factory was approved for Keighley, and when at the beginning of June I made my tour, as Minister of Munitions-elect, of the industrial districts, I was able to point to the Leeds effort as an example which could be widely applied. The idea was eagerly taken up, and as a result seventeen of these factories had been approved by me before the end of June, and ten more were added before the end of September.

These national shell factories were coöperative undertakings run by Boards of Management approved by the Ministry and provided by the local Munitions Committees. They represented in the main engineering talent which had not hitherto been engaged in any shell production, and at first they were chiefly concerned with the manufacture of the lighter types of shell. As time went on they were able to extend their range to include some of the heavier natures, and before the end of the war three factories at Leeds which had begun as shell factories were transferred to the ordnance factory class.

The national shell factories harnessed the ability of the engineering industry outside the existing armament firms. I was also concerned to make fuller use of the experience inside these firms, particularly for the production of heavy shell. In July, 1915, the actual output of this shell was far below the promises which had been made, and the demands of the army in the field for large high-explosive shell were rapidly growing. I was arranging a big increase in the programme of heavy artillery and I had to ensure an adequate supply of ammunition for these additional guns, as well as for those already in the field.

Accordingly, on July 13th, 1915, I held a conference with the representatives of nine leading armament firms to see what steps must be taken to ensure the completion not only of existing programmes, but of the new and much bigger programmes which would be required.

The method hitherto adopted by the War Office of relying upon the existing works, extended with the aid of the grants from the Exchequer which I had authorised in the previous autumn, had proved definitely inadequate. But the armament firms strongly disliked the idea of my proceeding to found new and independent national factories for the production of heavy shell. So we reached a compromise. The armament firms would themselves build and manage new factories, additional to their existing works, the Government providing all the capital, both for the building and the running. The new factories would be Government property and the armament firms would provide managers to run them as Government agents, and under the control of the Ministry. The firms setting up and managing these works for the Ministry would get a percentage commission on the output. I must add that Messrs. Cammell Laird refused to take any commission for erection or management of the factory they set up in Nottingham. These factories were known as national projectile factories, as distinct from the national shell factories which I have already described. Seven national projectile factories were started in the following month, August, 1915, and four in September; and by the end of 1915 the number had risen to thirteen. Before the war ended there were fifteen, and, in addition, five of the national shell factories were transferred to the Department of the Ministry managing the projectile factories on account of the nature of the work they were carrying out.

Some indication of the speed with which these national factories got into their stride, and of the service they were able to render, can be gathered from the following figures. Output from the national shell factories started, in the case of the first-established among them, in the summer of 1915, and from the earlier national projectile factories in the autumn of that year. In these closing months of 1915 their combined output was 200,400 empty shell, nearly all of the lighter natures. In 1916, their total output was 6,712,300, more than half of which was medium and heavy shell.

In just over three years, from mid-1915 to the close of hostilities in 1918, the combined total output of empty shell from the national shell and national projectile factories was 40,143,300.

Further, the cost of shell produced by these factories was decidedly lower than that of supplies from outside firms — so much so that in the case of the national projectile factories it amply compensated for the loss of value incurred through the difference between the original cost of their erection and equipment and the sums ultimately realised by them on disposal, while the lower costs achieved by the national shell factories not only made a large direct saving in expenditure on supplies, but enabled the charges of outside firms to be checked and reduced.

Like the national shell factories, the national projectile factories were used as time went on for a variety of other purposes in addition to shell production. In 1917, seven of them were busy on gun repair, one on making gun parts, and another on making guns. Yet another, Cathcart, turned over to aëroplane work from May, 1917. Grenade mortars, aëro-engines, and shells for the Italians were among the supplies turned out by these factories; and before the end of the war five of them had become classified as ordnance factories, and were mainly occupied in making and repairing cannon.

3. Filling the Shells

Supply of explosives — Lord Moulton's work — Explosives factories — Achievements of explosives factories — Military obstruction: Lord Moulton's protest — Waste of T.N.T. — Rivalry of the Services — Lord Lee of Fareham — The acetone problem — Work of Professor Weizmann — He solves the problem — Horse-chestnuts for acetone — Origin of the Balfour Declaration on Palestine — Filling confined to Woolwich — Breakdown of Woolwich filling capacity: transfer to M. of M. — "The Extract" — Appointment of Mr. Raven to Woolwich — Establishment of filling factories — Dangers of filling work — Courage of women workers: toxic jaundice — Hayes explosion — Progress of research in problem of shell filling — Work of Lord Chetwynd — Chilwell factory set up — Original methods at Chilwell — Tribute to work of Sir Eric Geddes.

The two groups of factories I have described, the shell and the projectile factories, ensured a provision of empty shell, but it was also necessary to provide explosives to fill and propel them, and works to carry out the filling and completion of rounds of ammunition. The story of the arrangements made for shell filling by the War Office is a sardonic comment on the attack directed against civilians for their presumptuous interference with the professional soldier in the discharge of his duties.

The need to secure outside sources of supply for high explosives had been realised early in the war by the War Office, for the excellent reason that the manufacture of high explosives had never been undertaken by the ordnance factories. There was practically no trade capacity for the manufacture of military tri-nitro-toluene, commonly known as T.N.T., a coal extract which eventually became an important ingredient in the bursting charge of high-explosive shell, and the stocks of the commercial explosive which were available needed treatment to bring them up to service standards.

The Defence of the Realm (Consolidation) Act, 1914, became law on November 27th, 1914. Under it the Government had power to take over factories engaged in the production of warlike stores, and the very next day the War Office descended on the Rainham Chemical Works, on the Thames opposite Woolwich, and commandeered them for the purification of crude T.N.T. At this time, however, the available supply was only about ten or twelve tons a week, provided by a single firm.

The Board of Trade, when approached by the War Office, recommended that a distinguished civilian, Lord Moulton, should be entrusted with the organisation of an adequate supply of explosives. He was the ablest scientific lawyer of his generation. He was appointed Chairman of a Committee of High Explosives. He insisted that a new State factory must be set up for T.N.T. production, and made an arrangement with a firm of acid manufacturers, Messrs. Chance and Hunt, in December, 1914, whereby they set to work in January, 1915, to erect at Oldbury a factory for the Explosives Supply Branch of the War Office. This was the first national factory for manufacturing T.N.T.

Lord Moulton further entered into an arrangement with the Admiralty to set up a big factory at Queen's Ferry for production of gun cotton. But the site could not be secured until May, 1915, and at the end of that month the Admiralty backed out of the arrangement. The new factory thus fell to the Ministry of Munitions, and was developed for the production of not only gun cotton, but T.N.T. On becoming Minister of Munitions I found that there had been no survey of the prospective demand for explosives in view of orders already given, and that the provision then made for the production of explosives was quite inadequate to supply prospective requirements. In July, 1915, four more national explosives factories were established by the Ministry, including the huge factory at Gretna for the production of cordite. The construction of this factory had been recommended in May by the Munitions of War Committee, of which I was Chairman, and was authorised by me as Minister of Munitions in the following month. It was also based on plans and proposals prepared, at the request of the Committee, by Lord Moulton.

The assistance rendered to the nation by Lord Moulton in this matter of explosives has never been sufficiently recognised.

By the end of the war there were no fewer than 32 H.M. explosives factories among the national factories controlled by the Ministry. We had been compelled to build these factories ourselves, because for some explosives, such as T.N.T., there was before the war an entire lack of industrial capacity, while for others, like cordite, there appeared to be no prospect of a large-scale demand after the war which would induce existing manufacturers to extend their works. In consequence of these arrangements in the case of explosives, the bulk of our home-produced war supplies came from these new national factories.

At the outbreak of the war, State production was limited to the Royal Gunpowder Factory at Waltham Abbey, which made about 75 short tons (*i.e.*, 150,000 lbs.) of cordite and gunpowder a week. By 1917, the national explosives factories were producing over ten times this quantity of cordite weekly, and of explosives of all kinds more than 2000 tons a week. In the course of the war, the grand total of their output of explosives was over 317½ thousand tons: being 236,251 tons of high explosive (mainly T.N.T.) and 81,341 tons of propellants (mainly cordite). The need for these factories is illustrated by figures given by Lord Moulton in a paper dated April 13th, 1915, which he prepared for the Munitions of War Committee. He showed that the total estimated amounts of high explosives required by the Navy and Army in the months of February and March, 1915, were 4,505,600 lbs. The actual supplies obtained and used were 1,038,802 lbs., or considerably less than a quarter of the requirements.

Like the national shell and projectile factories, these explosive factories proved of great value, apart from the essential importance of their output, in furnishing data for simplification of process and reduction of cost in the production of supplies by other firms. The system of cost and efficiency returns which was established in them gave rise to a general competition in economy, not only between different national factories, but between these and the trade manufacturers. They provided a very economical source of supply as compared with either American sources or British contractors, and enabled very considerable reductions to be made in 1917 in the contract price for explosives.

But our troubles over explosives were not confined to the difficulties and delays of construction and equipment of our factories in war time, when there was so much competition for labour and material. The most formidable obstruction I had to overcome came from the tardiness with which the War Office adapted itself to new conditions and fresh demands. It led to an emergency so critical that it very nearly wrecked the whole of our shell programme. This choice specimen of military rigidity in high quarters is best told in the words of Lord Moulton himself. Soon after I was nominated Minister of Munitions I received from him a letter which, apart from the fact that it is a startling exposure of military bureaucracy, is an interesting account of the kind and quantity of explosives fired in the war:

"Ministry of Munitions of War,
Explosives Department,
Institution of Mechanical Engineers,
Storey's Gate,
Westminster, S.W.
16th June, 1915.

"Dear Mr. Lloyd George,

"There is a matter of the greatest importance as to which

I must request your advice and help in your position as Minister of Munitions.

"From the time that I was first consulted on the question of the provision of high explosives I recognised that the lavish expenditure of these explosives which is characteristic of the present war made it absolutely impossible to proceed on the lines which up to that time had regulated our naval and military services. The adoption of T.N.T. as our principal high explosive was but two or three months old when the War began, and I doubt whether there was at that time a production of *20 tons per week* of this explosive in the whole of Great Britain, while the production of lyddite must almost have ceased by reason of the belief that it would be substantially superseded by T.N.T. Would-be suppliers were told by War Office officials that it would not be used. Of neither of these explosives was there any Government manufacture or even any industrial manufacture except such as I have mentioned. *When I add that in little more than two days the Germans fired off over 800 tons of such explosives* [my italics] you will see how absolutely impossible it was to rely on the sources of supply which then existed. . . . The only hope of obtaining an adequate supply of explosive lies in the proper production and utilisation of T.N.T.

"This produce has the property of animating explosives, of which it forms only a small part, the remainder being principally nitrate of ammonia, a substance which can be obtained in practically unlimited quantities. Schneiderite, which is at the moment the favourite explosive of the French, is of this type. Only one-tenth of it is T.N.T. . . .

"So soon as I had realised the position I put it before the naval and military authorities, and pointed out that it was absolutely necessary to widen the list of high explosives and not to be content with using T.N.T. or lyddite alone. I fear it produced little impression at the time. But two or three months after I had done so, the Research Department at Woolwich demonstrated that by mixing T.N.T. with nitrate of ammonia they produced an explosive which was much more powerful than T.N.T. and equally safe. They showed that this could be done to an extent of one to four without lessening its explosive force and that it could be done to an extent of nearly half and half without even interfering with the existing convenient method of filling shells by melting the T.N.T. and pouring it into the shells. Some two months ago the use of this mixture was approved and directions were given that it should be applied to the whole of the land service for six-inch shells downwards and experiments were directed to be made with regard to the larger shells. . . .

"To my great regret I find that those who have charge of the loading of shells have for the last two months completely disregarded the direction and now say that they do not propose to use the mixture for another month. I know of no reason except that they say that they have not got their warming cupboards for the nitrate of ammonia and it will take them some time to get them fitted up. I have no hesitation in saying that such a matter is quite trivial in comparison with the importance of so vital an improvement in our explosive supply at a critical period like this, and that to overcome such a difficulty should not have required more than a few days. . . .

"I am certain that the possibility of an adequate supply of high explosives for the needs of the Services depends on the cordial acceptance of the means of economising the T.N.T. such as I have indicated, by artillerists and more especially by those in charge of the loading of shells. *It is hopeless for me to struggle to meet the extraordinary demands created by the War if there is on their part a disregard of or a reluctance to accept the necessary modifications of our artillery methods which good sense and an appreciation of the magnitude of the problem before us dictate.*[1]

"You will excuse my speaking thus frankly, but I am satisfied that I have not said a word that I cannot support, and it is only by your coming to my help as Minister of Munitions that I can hope to obtain immediate and implicit acceptance of these all-important conditions of the supply to the Services.

Yours sincerely,

MOULTON."

[1] My italics, D. Ll. G.

I realised that unless I could persuade the War Office to accept some considerable modification in the character of the explosive used for filling it was no use pressing forward the manufacture of shells, for we should not possess a sufficient quantity of the necessary ingredients to complete them. But here I was up against the inveterate rivalry between soldier and sailor. The Admiralty would not forego their full quota of T.N.T. Why should the War Office be satisfied with a shell which was less perfect than that which the Admiralty insisted upon? This was not a question of factory supplies, but of departmental prestige. However, after a protracted struggle involving a loss of valuable time in the output of complete shell, a certain relaxation was achieved of the maximum requirements of the War Office. This enabled me to get along for a few weeks. But there was not enough T.N.T. to supply all the requirements of the shell programme, even in the reduced proportions which the War Office was prepared to allow. The delay was holding up the orders for machinery for the new filling factories, even the building of these factories. The character of the machine depended on whether the filling should be liquid or dry, and that again depended on the proportions of T.N.T. and ammonium nitrate, and the lay-out of the building depended on the kind of machinery which would be installed. The fight went on, and the consequent delays became more serious until the whole responsibility for design was wrenched from the War Office. We were turning out stacks of empty shell, but owing to these delays in deciding the mixture for the filling, the supply of complete shell was lagging seriously behind.

Two men in particular helped me to overcome this barrier erected by professional suspicion and procrastination. One was Sir Eric Geddes, of whom I have already spoken, the other was Colonel Arthur Lee (now Lord Lee of Fareham).

When Sir Ivor Philipps was appointed to the command of the Welsh Division in October, 1915, I invited Colonel Arthur Lee to become his successor. By training he was an artillery officer and thus possessed first-hand knowledge of some of our difficulties. I had known him for years as a Member of the House of Commons. He was an able critic of the policies in which I was concerned as a Minister. I recognised his efficiency and intelligence as an opponent. He had taken a leading part in the agitation for eight dreadnoughts in 1908, and I am not sure he was not the inventor of the very telling phrase, "We want eight and will not wait." I had on more than one occasion crossed swords with him in debate. He was a skilful swordsman who gave few openings because he had the gift of both mastering his case thoroughly and presenting it forcibly. Early in the year 1915, on his temporary leave from France, he had brought me some startling information as to the failure of our artillery to make any impression on the barbed-wire entanglements of the enemy. He was a man of untiring industry, great resource, and practical capacity. Although an officer in the Army and proud of his profession, he was one of the few whose judgment was not paralysed by an opinion expressed by a senior in rank. I found that in every crisis he had a cool head, a clear eye, and a stout heart. During the many ensuing years of almost crushing responsibility through which I was destined to pass I found his understanding, his loyalty, and his courage of immeasurable support. As soon as he joined me at the Ministry of Munitions he spent his first few days in scouting around to see what was — and what was not — going on. With unerring judgment he fastened on the shell-filling snag. He it was who also perceived that Mr. Eric Geddes was the best man in the Ministry to undertake the task of reorganising that essential part of our business.

Among the interesting developments to which the chemical side of warfare gave rise I must mention the story of acetone. Here again we nearly came to grief for lack of timely forethought. This chemical, which was an essential element in the process of manufacturing cordite, for cartridges great and small, was commonly produced by destructive distillation of wood.

Before the war there was a small factory in the Forest of Dean set up by the Office of Woods and Forests to utilise waste cordwood. In May, 1915, this Office set up two fresh factories at Bideford and Dundee, which were transferred, together with the Coleford factory, to the Ministry in October. Messrs. Kynoch's also set up a factory in the New Forest, which was nationalised in 1917. But this country is not one of the great timber-growing lands, and it takes a great deal of wood to produce a ton of acetone, so in practice we were dependent for the great bulk of our supply on imports from America.

But by the spring of 1915 the position in the American acetone market had become extremely delicate. British cordite firms were competing with each other and with the agents for the Allies. Prices were being forced up. American contractors were selling their output twice over and defaulting on their contracts. They even went to the length of insisting upon an advance in price upon their existing contracts with the British Government, and in the case of their default it proved impossible to recover damages from them.

Prompt steps were taken over here to eliminate the competition between British cordite makers for American acetone. But when this had been done and arrangements had been made for the purchase of all overseas supplies immediately available, I was confronted by a much more serious crisis. In the survey we made of all the various prospective requirements it soon became clear that the supplies of wood alcohol for the manufacture of acetone would prove quite insufficient to meet the increasing demands, particularly in 1916. The matter was urgent, for without the acetone there would be no cordite for our cartridges, for either rifles or big guns.

As Chairman of the Munitions of War Committee I took this matter greatly to heart. While I was casting about for some solution of the difficulty, I ran against the late C. P. Scott, Editor of the *Manchester Guardian.* He was a friend in whose wisdom I had implicit faith. I told him of my problem and that I was on the lookout for a resourceful chemist who would help me to solve it. He said: "There is a very remarkable professor of chemistry in the University of Manchester willing to place his services at the disposal of the State. I must tell you, however, that he was born somewhere near the Vistula, and I am not sure on which side. His name is Weizmann." Scott could guarantee that whatever the country of origin, Weizmann was thoroughly devoted to the cause of the Allies, that the one thing he really cared about was Zionism, and that he was convinced that in the victory of the Allies alone was there any hope for his people. I knew Mr. Scott to be one of the shrewdest judges of men I had ever met. The world renown of his great paper had been built up on the soundness of his judgment — of men as well as of affairs. But I also trusted his patriotism implicitly. Pacifist as he was, he believed in the essential justice of our intervention in this war. I took his word about Professor Weizmann and invited him to London to see me. I took to him at once. He is now a man of international fame. He was then quite unknown to the general public, but as soon as I met him I realised that he was a very remarkable personality. His brow gave assurance of a fine intellect and his open countenance gave confidence in his complete sincerity. I told him that we were in a chemical dilemma and asked him to assist us. I explained the shortage in wood alcohol and what it meant in munitionment. Could he help? Dr. Weizmann said he did not know, but he would try. He could produce acetone by a fermentation process on a laboratory scale, but it would require some time before he could guarantee successful production on a manufacturing scale.

"How long can you give me?" he asked. I said: "I cannot give you very long. It is pressing." Weizmann replied: "I will go at it night and day."

In a few weeks' time he came to me and said: "The problem is solved." After a prolonged study of the microflora existing on maize and other cereals, also of those occurring in the soil, he had succeeded in isolating an organism capable of transforming the starch of cereals, particularly that of maize, into a mixture of acetone butyl alcohol. The generations of these organisms die very quickly; and in quite a short time, working night and day as he had promised, he had secured a culture which would enable us to get our acetone from maize.

Now maize contains about two-thirds its weight of starch, and our sources of supply were very wide; so that this discovery enabled us to produce very considerable quantities of the vital chemical. To-day this discovery is the centre of an important industry.

In King's Lynn there was an oil-cake factory which had been converted in 1912 to make acetone from the starch content of potatoes. It had come into the field with promises of supply, but the quality of its output was not satisfactory, and financially the company was unsteady. So in March, 1916, it was nationalised, and by June it was making acetone from maize by the Weizmann process with highly successful and valuable results. The shipping shortage in 1917, which forced us to restrict all unnecessary imports, induced yet another experiment. In the autumn of that year, horse-chestnuts were plentiful, and a national collection of them was organised for the purpose of using their starch content as a substitute for maize. The King's Lynn factory carried out the manufacture, and though at first the poor quality of the material hampered output, these difficulties were overcome and the Weizmann process was turning out acetone from horse-chestnuts by the time the factory was closed in 1918.

When our difficulties were solved through Dr. Weizmann's genius I said to him: "You have rendered great service to the State, and I should like to ask the Prime Minister to recommend you to His Majesty for some honour." He said: "There is nothing I want for myself." "But is there nothing we can do as a recognition of your valuable assistance to the country?" I asked. He replied: "Yes, I would like you to do something for my people." He then explained his aspirations as to the repatriation of the Jews to the sacred land they had made famous. That was the fount and origin of the famous declaration about the National Home for Jews in Palestine.

As soon as I became Prime Minister I talked the whole matter over with Mr. Balfour, who was then Foreign Secretary. As a scientist he was immensely interested when I told him of Dr. Weizmann's achievement. We were anxious at that time to gather Jewish support in neutral countries. Dr. Weizmann was brought into direct contact with the Foreign Secretary. This was the beginning of an association, the outcome of which, after long examination, was the famous Balfour Declaration, which became the charter of the Zionist movement. So that Dr. Weizmann with his discovery not only helped us to win the war, but made a permanent mark upon the map of the world.

Dr. Weizmann is still the same busy, devoted, self-forgetful enthusiast. When I saw him recently he had just returned from a collecting trip abroad for the Zionist cause, in which he raised £70,000. He has collected something like fifteen or sixteen million pounds sterling for the rebuilding of Zion. It is the only reward he seeks, and his name will rank with that of Nehemiah in the fascinating and inspiring story of the children of Israel.

I have paused to tell of Professor Weizmann and his work, because it illustrates the multiplicity of different personalities and interests which were blended into the munition effort of this country. It is, too, a page of world history, the opening sentences of which were written in the Ministry of Munitions.

The story of our successful efforts to produce explosives brings me to the tale of our national filling factories. They really represented the most worrying aspect of the shell problem, for even more serious than the failure of the War Office arrangements for making shells was their neglect to realise practically that ere shells were fired they must first of all be filled and fused.

At the outbreak of the war, practically the whole of the gun ammunition used by both the Army and the Navy was filled or assembled at Woolwich. There were five firms in the country which could fill shells. One of them had filled lyddite in the South African war. The other four had done some shell filling for foreign countries. But throughout the opening months of the war Woolwich was and remained substantially the only place where shell was filled.

In May and June, 1915, the national shell factories had started. In July I arranged, at the conference of armament firms of which I have already told, for the erection of national projectile factories. But the provision for shell filling in the country was at that time quite inadequate to deal with the growing supplies of empty shell coming from these factories, from the trade, and from American and Canadian orders. Woolwich was getting choked with stacks of empty shell, while our Army was without ammunition. It was therefore essential to my task that Woolwich should be under the control of the Ministry. Without it I could only manufacture shell carcases. At first the War Office refused to surrender the famous Ordnance Factory to the Ministry. They were supported in this refusal by the Admiralty. It soon became evident that I could not provide complete shells unless the means of filling these were transferred to my control. We were short of shells for the great battle which was being fought in France in September. We had a large stock of empties, but we were short of the completed article. The only practical result of Loos was to transfer Woolwich to the Ministry of Munitions. It was the first War Office institution of whose working I had any experience.

Soon after I entered its mysterious portals I came up against a ghostly potentate known as "The Extract." What was "The Extract"? I received account of it in a carefully prepared report that was presented to me as soon as I took over Woolwich.

In order to understand the procedure which governs the productive power of Woolwich and similarly of Enfield and Waltham Abbey with slight modifications, one must realise that the mainspring of the whole fabric, from a procedure point of view, is this document — "The Extract." "The Extract" is a term with an historical origin, which I need not enter into here, save to say that it was an extract from the proceedings of a Board of Ordnance which met at the Tower, and that this "Extract" was passed from official to official of equal rank who were not in a position to give orders to each other. An "Extract", however, is merely an order to do certain work. This phantom of "The Extract" was backed up by a frightening array of capital letters, M.G.O., D.D.O.S., S.O.S., D.E.O.S., I.R.E.S., C.S.O.F., etc., with a host of other alphabetical combinations glowering in the background. They were entrenched in well-worn professional traditions behind entanglements of red tape, and all ready from "Alpha to Omega" to die in their ditch rather than surrender the fortress held by them and their official forefathers to the barbarians who threatened their empire from the dark forest of politics.

When I took over Woolwich I soon found why, in the words of M. Albert Thomas, it was *"une vieille boîte."* It was due to the working of "The Extract" by the Capital Letters. They jostled each other, they were in each other's way, hindering but never hustling, and only acting together when there was any resistance to be offered to the political Hun. They were an alphabetical nightmare. My first duty was not exactly to lay these ghosts but to put them in their proper places; to see that each of them pushed his own trolley without running into anybody else's. I saw why we had been delayed in divers ways. The men or Ministry that ordered "The Extract" controlled the output, and until Woolwich was transferred to the Ministry of Munitions and at least a few Capital Letters were on my side, I could not really get along with shell filling and its components.

The first step taken by me in the reorganisation of Woolwich was the promotion of Sir Frederick Donaldson, the head of the Arsenal, to an important post I created for him outside Woolwich. He was a man of high intelligence and great knowledge of the technique of his job. To this he added undoubted charm. But years of routine in tranquil days when time did not count, when shells were manufactured to fire at safe targets, when all that mattered was that you should keep the Admiralty and the War Office sections at Woolwich from interfering with each other, and, above all, ensure that the last penny provided by the estimates should be judiciously expended within the financial year, disqualified him for an emergency where hours were precious to the safety of the State and improvisations had to supersede routine and regulation. I appointed in his place Mr. Vincent Raven of the London and Northeastern Railway, and his quickening influence was soon felt throughout the Arsenal and resulted in an increased production of completed shell.

Woolwich, with the best management, could not provide anything like the facilities for shell-filling demanded by the number of shells already ordered or about to be manufactured. I decided, therefore, to extend the range of national factories by setting up a number of national filling factories. Two were arranged for in July — one at Aintree, and one at Coventry. Four more were begun in August, six more in September. Before the end of the war there were eighteen national filling factories engaged in filling shell. Some of them were directly controlled by the Ministry; some by agents, like the national projectile factories; some by Local Boards of Management, like the shell factories, the members serving without fee or reward.

The chief technical difficulties in connection with the carrying through of successful filling operations were not those of skilled labour. The actual filling was a simple process, and the great bulk of the labour in the filling factories was that of unskilled women workers. Such labour difficulties as arose were associated rather with the danger of the work, such as the scare of T.N.T. poisoning which towards the end of 1916 temporarily depleted the staffs; the difficulty of getting workers to observe the regulations for minimising risk of explosions; the repellent character of some of the precautions which had to be adopted, such as the wearing of respirators when handling fulminate of mercury compounds, or the smearing of the face with special grease if engaged with work on tetryl.

The courage of the girls and women engaged in these

factories has never been sufficiently recognised. They had to work under conditions of very real danger to life and limb; and what some of them probably dreaded still more, of grotesque disfigurement — for one of the perils which was associated with the shell-filling factories was toxic jaundice, resulting from T.N.T. poisoning. This ailment turned their faces a bright and repulsive yellow. The poor girls for this reason were nicknamed by their associates outside as "canaries." They were quite proud of this designation for they had earned it in the path of duty.

Plutarch relates that at the Battle of Pharsalus, Julius Cæsar told his legionaries to thrust their spears at the faces of Pompey's cavalry — patrician exquisites of Rome; and that these young gallants, who would have been brave enough in facing bodily wounds and death, were so terrified of facial disfigurement that they turned in horror and galloped away, holding their hands before their eyes. For girls and women, whose natural instinct it was to prize their looks and complexion, the blotching ugliness of T.N.T. poisoning was perhaps a peril which tested their courage even more than the risk of explosion. In 1916 there were 181 cases of this toxic jaundice, of which 52 ended fatally, and in 1917 there were 189 cases, with 44 deaths. But in the course of that year the methods of preventing it were being rigidly perfected, and by 1918 the figures were brought down to 34 cases, of which 10 ended fatally. Despite the number so stricken, and the scare which found expression in the Press, there was no labour shortage at the filling factories.

Another fine story of courage comes from the factory at Hayes, where girls and women were employed to fill gaines. A gaine, it should be explained, is a tube filled with explosive, attached under the nose-cap of a high-explosive shell, and sticking down into the T.N.T. filling. Its purpose is to ensure that the detonation of the fuse in the nose-cap shall effectively detonate the contents of the shell.

In 1915 the frequency of prematures and blinds led to the discovery that a large stock of gaines sent from America had a left-hand instead of a right-hand screw, and tended to come unscrewed in the shell as it rotated in flight. To prevent this, the screwed-in gaines had to be stabbed in two places with cold chisel and hammer to break the thread so that they could not unscrew.

Women workers in the factory at Hayes undertook a large part of this work — risky work, for if a trace of the fulminate were ignited by the blow, the gaine would explode and disembowel them. One morning, news came that there had been a terrible explosion at Hayes, in which several women had been killed. My representative went down to visit the scene. Work was being done in a number of little huts, separated off from each other. One of them was badly shattered. At its entrance Lord Lee ran against a busy little woman, about five feet high, white-faced but resolute. "Is this where the explosion took place?" he asked. "Yes," she answered. She was in charge of the hut, and when he entered it he saw bloodstains on the floor, and the survivors carrying on at full speed, with hammer and cold chisel, stabbing gaines.

Lord Lee spoke with the little forewoman. She had at one time been a lady's maid. Now she was doing her bit for the country in the munition factory, and when the explosion had occurred that morning she had calmed and steadied her girls and headed them back to their grim and dangerous task. All she would say was: "I am not going to run away, especially when I think of those poor boys in France who are facing more dangers than we are here."

Before long a safety device was produced to guard workers against the dangers of explosion when stabbing gaines; and later on the introduction of an improved pattern made such stabbing unnecessary. But till that time the girls and women carried on their risky work in the pluckiest fashion, and if one of them was blown to horrible destruction the others would keep up their spirits by singing at their work — singing songs with words of their own composition, which had little perhaps of literary grace, but plenty of crude vigour and unfaltering courage.

That was the kind of spirit shown by our women munition workers. Granted efficient direction, there was nothing it could not accomplish.

The experiences I have narrated in regard to our dealings with Woolwich Arsenal, and the facts set out in Lord Moulton's letter, gave some slight hint of the official obstacles which continually interfered with our progress. It has to be borne in mind that we were not carrying on a smooth-running concern, but building from the ground up a vast new range of industries for the production of articles — many of them never before manufactured in this country. We had to find out how to make the best use of whatever materials were available, and this meant that it was impossible to rest content with standard specifications for ingredients, and standard processes of manufacture, however ideal these might be for the leisurely and limited munition production of peace time.

At the beginning of the war, for example, lyddite was our only high explosive for shell filling. That was all very well when a few tons would satisfy our needs for months, but not when we wanted to fire off hundreds of tons a day; for besides being expensive, lyddite was a substance for the manufacture of which imported materials were needed. Hence the adoption of T.N.T. But again, T.N.T. was costly and limited in amount, and as the demand for high-explosive shells grew, it became obvious that the supply of pure T.N.T. would be nothing like adequate. Hence the development of the amatol mixtures of T.N.T. and ammonium nitrate. But the approved method of filling a shell with T.N.T. was to melt the explosive and pour it in through the opening at the nose where the fuse would eventually be screwed on. When ammonium nitrate was mixed with the hot melted T.N.T. — like sand mixed into treacle — the mixture poured more and more stiffly, and with more than 40 per cent. of the nitrate it would not pour at all. So some way had to be found of mixing the two ingredients dry, and filling shells with the powder, if the maximum economy in the use of T.N.T. was to be observed.

For solving this problem fertile and original minds were needed. Britain is rich in such, and one of my most interesting tasks at the Ministry of Munitions was to get hold of men of real inventive and administrative ability and harness their capacities to the service of our immense task. Often they were men with a holy terror of red tape and official formalities, who would not readily submit to dictation, but if given their head would do work of the very greatest value. They had to be chosen with discrimination so as to separate the men of practical, if somewhat intractable, genius from the mere inventing cranks.

To help us with the problem of shell filling, I had the good fortune to secure the services of Lord Chetwynd, who was recommended to me by Mr. Ellis as the best man to help us in our difficulty. He had, as far as I remember, no practical experience in dealing with explosives, but he had a tremendous store of resource and ingenuity. I was, however, warned that he was very sensitive to any attempt to control him by a bridle of red tape.

We told him he was wanted to build and run a factory that would fill a thousand tons of high-explosive shells a week. He stipulated for and got a very free hand, without

Photo. reproduced by courtesy of Viscount Chetwynd

SHELL FACTORY AT CHILWELL

The picture shows H. M. The King and Viscount Chetwynd during the visit paid on the 15th of December, 1916, and also a portion of the 335,956 filled shells which were on the floor that day. The factory had only been constructed a bare year previously, and had already sent to France 2,468,041 filled shells

control by the departmental managers of the Ministry, and a contract valid till after the cessation of hostilities.

Thus equipped, he went straight ahead in glorious independence. He found a site at Chilwell, near Nottingham, and designed and built his own factory there. While it was being erected he went over to France in October, 1915, as one of a deputation I sent to study the French methods of shell-filling, and satisfied himself that the French practice of filling powdered explosive, by pressing it in through the nose of the shell, could be adapted for amatol. This was important, for to make our supplies of T.N.T. go as far as possible it was desirable to use it with 80 per cent. of ammonium nitrate, which involved filling dry, as such mixture could not be poured. At Woolwich they had designed a process for filling with this "80:20" amatol by compressing the powder into cakes and insetting these in the shell. But that meant either having a detachable bottom for the shell or a detachable tapered end, and both these devices proved in practice not only an additional complication and delay, but unsatisfactory and a cause of premature explosion.

Lord Chetwynd went back to Chilwell and determined to fill 80:20 powder by pressing through the nose. He hastily designed and ran up a small experimental plant to show it could be done, and when there was a talk of abandoning the 80:20 amatol on account of the unsatisfactory results achieved by the Woolwich shells, he challenged a test of those filled by him by pressing through the nose — a test from which they emerged triumphantly. His initiative in this matter was of incalculable benefit to the country, and made possible an immense increase in both the speed and the volume of shell-filling. The Chilwell factory was an amazing place, where powerful explosives were milled and mixed like so much flour. Lord Chetwynd designed his own plant and processes, aiming always at speed, simplicity, and the fullest use of machinery on mass-production lines. He passed his raw material through machines originally used for coal-crushing, stone-pulverising, sugar-drying, paint-making, sugar-sifting. The T.N.T. he ground between the porcelain rollers of a flour mill. A bread-making plant did the mixing. He bought up derelict works that had been producing lace-making machinery and used them to manufacture the appliances he designed for filling shells. People objected that it must be highly dangerous to treat high explosives so unceremoniously. Lord Chetwynd's retort was to move to a house at the end of his press houses. "If anyone is to be blown up, I'll be the first!" he remarked; and his action greatly encouraged his workers. A Zeppelin hunted up and down the Trent all through a January night in 1916, trying to locate and bomb the factory, but without success. A rumour spread next day in true war-time fashion that Lord Chetwynd had caught three German spies trying to signal the Zeppelin with lights, and had shot them out of hand. He was prompt to turn it to account, so he set a policeman as sentry all day over an empty room, and at night made a labourer dig three graves on the hillside. Into these he put stones and filled them in, with a black post at the head of each. That turned the rumour into unquestioned history, and discouraged would-be spies and the unwanted curious from prying round the place.

I have given these notes about Chilwell because they will convey some idea of the difficulties with which we were faced in our task of producing filled shell; and some idea, too, of the men who came to our aid. Besides, Chilwell was the largest of our national filling factories, and was our principal source of supply for the heavier natures of filled shell. Of the high-explosive shell filled during the war in the national factories, of sizes from 60-pounder to 15-inch, over 50 per cent. were filled at Chilwell, which turned out 19¼ million of these heavy shells, in addition to a considerable number of lighter shells, aërial bombs, etc.

Chilwell started shell-filling in January, 1916. Some of the national filling factories had begun filling of components — gaines, fuses, etc. — even before this. I had placed Geddes in charge of the whole filling section at the end of 1915, and such were his energy and resource that by the middle of 1916 the new filling factories had got into their stride and were furnishing the Army with complete ammunition on a scale which made possible the terrific bombardments of the Somme offensive.

4. Machine Guns

Machine-gun supply in first year of war — General Baker-Carr's account of military indifference — Supplies for the French — Maxim superseded — Rifles or machine guns: Geddes sees Lord Kitchener — A chit signed — My revision of Kitchener's estimate — Planning the new programme — Fresh orders for Lewis guns — Development of the Hotchkiss gun — Reductions in the cost — Summary of achievements.

During 1914 and the first half of 1915, responsibility for the design and supply of machine guns rested with the Master-General of Ordnance at the War Office. How completely the military direction failed to appreciate the important part this arm would play in the war is shown by the fact that between August, 1914, and June, 1915, four contracts only were placed by them with Messrs. Vickers for a total of 1792 machine guns. This would work out at two machine guns per battalion with none left for training at home as provision for machine-gun companies and no margin for losses or breakages.[1] The first order was dated August 11, 1914, and was for 192 guns. The second, on September 10, was for 100. The third, dated September 19, was for 1000, and the fourth, a few days later, for an-

[1] In 1918 our equipment of machine guns was 36 Lewis guns per infantry battalion and 64 Vickers guns per machine-gun battalion. Deficiencies were replaced immediately from reserves at home.

other 500. A provision in the third contract laid it down that the rate of delivery should be 50 guns per week. Only 10 to 12 had been the rate specified under the first order. The whole 1792 guns were to be delivered by June, 1915. In fact, however, only 1022 had been received by that date.

At the outbreak of the war the allotment of machine guns to each battalion was only two. This was the equipment of our first Expeditionary Force. An explanation of the failure of the military authorities to realise the importance of this weapon is to be sought in the fact that as one distinguished officer wrote: "The machine gun was regarded by British authorities as a weapon of opportunity rather than an essential munition of war."

It took our generals many months of terrible loss to realise the worth of the machine gun. They were converted by representations from officers who had witnessed its deadly effect in action. The farther they were from the fighting line the less impressed were military commanders with the power and peril of the machine gun. Brigadier-General Baker-Carr, the founder of the Machine-Gun Training Corps, has given in his recent book [1] a piquant account of the difficulties he experienced in establishing his training school and in convincing the higher command of the importance of the machine gun. As it bears upon the attitude of the War Office in reference to the manufacture of this devastating weapon, I may be permitted to quote one or two passages.

This is the attitude before the war:

"At that time, the sole mention of machine guns was confined to a dozen lines in the *Infantry Training Manual.* Nobody in authority concerned himself with this weapon of enormous potential importance, and battalion commanders before the War frankly and cordially disliked it.

[1] "From Chauffeur to Brigadier."

" 'What shall I do with the machine guns to-day, Sir?' would be a question frequently asked by the officer in charge on a field day.

" 'Take the damned things to a flank and hide 'em!' was the usual reply."

In 1915 he was urging an increase in the number of machine guns:

"The fighting line, at any rate, had awakened to the realisation of the automatic weapon and many commanders were showing themselves eager to learn anything they could, which would help to strengthen their front without increasing the number of men.

"Already I was urging the advisability of doubling the number of machine guns per battalion, *i.e.*, raising it from two to four. I had put forward the suggestion very tentatively to G.H.Q. and had been promptly told to mind my own business. The commanders of larger units, such as armies and army corps, did not at that time appreciate the vast saving of man-power that could be effected by the substitution of machinery for brawn, and it was only when we got within the danger zone that the proposals drew forth a cordial response."

He states that after having met with very little encouragement he set up his machine-gun school behind the lines:

"Not one single member of the Staff of G.H.Q. ever took the trouble to pay a visit to the School during the six months that it was quartered in the Artillery Barracks, a quarter of a mile distant from the General Staff Office."

He talks about the enormous fire power of the German machine gun and the faith of the German Army in its potency both in attack and defence, and he adds:

"Although this fact was flagrantly and terribly patent to the soldier in the front line, who was called upon to face the enemy machine guns, the High Command was unable to realise the crucial importance of it, even after the Battle of the Somme, and it was only in the following year, during the ghastly and bloody fiasco known as the Third Battle of Ypres, that the full truth was forced upon them."

At last, after great pressure from the fighting line, sanction was given to increase the number of machine guns per battalion from two to four. This was in the summer of 1915. He then says:

"Within twenty-four hours of hearing the news I put forward a proposal to double this amended establishment. G.H.Q. was horrified.

" 'Look here, Baker,' I was told indignantly. 'We've given you two extra guns per battalion. You ought to be satisfied.'

"Vainly I pointed out that the additional guns were not a personal present to me, but a badly needed increase in the arrangement of the fighting troops. But it was useless to argue."

It is an incredible story for anyone who had no actual experience of the fanatical hostility displayed by the Higher Commands to any new ideas.

Despite the meagre output for our own Army, a plant was laid down in this country in October, 1914, to provide fifty guns a week for the French Government, subject to the proviso that the output for the British Forces should not thereby be delayed. When the Ministry of Munitions was established, it was discovered that negotiations were actually taking place for the payment of £50 premium upon each gun delivered in excess of an average of fifty per week up to the end of December, 1915.

The Vickers gun had been adopted to replace the Maxim, which was obsolescent at the outbreak of the war. Maxims already in service were retained; but the total output of these guns from the Royal Small Arms Factory, Enfield, during the first two or three years of the war amounted to only 666 guns, and production of them ceased entirely in March, 1917, in accordance with the policy, already settled before the war, of abandoning this weapon for land service.

The growing importance of machine guns became more and more manifest as reports came in from battle after battle describing the appalling casualties inflicted upon our men by this deadly little mechanism. The Germans were the only nation which had realised before the war the potentialities of the machine gun, and they were arming their troops with sixteen per battalion.

But this estimate of the value of the machine gun was not shared in the War Office. The echo of its devastating racket had not yet penetrated that tranquil sanctuary of the God of War.

The manufacture of machine guns raised the very important issue of priority as between rifles and machine guns, of both of which there was a serious immediate shortage; for the manufacture of both these weapons called for the same raw materials, the same machinery, and the same class of workmen. Mr. Geddes, whom I had placed in charge of the output of both machine guns and rifles, found it impossible to get from the War Office any satisfactory estimate either of the numbers of each that would be required, or of the relative priority to be given to their production. Eventually he went, with Sir Percy Girouard, his immediate superior, to lay the matter before the Secretary for War himself, so as to obtain a ruling for the guidance of manufacture during the next nine months. The report of that interview is perhaps best told in Geddes's own words:

"I told Kitchener that rifles and machine guns were the same as shillings and pounds: that nine rifles were equal to a Lewis automatic gun and thirteen rifles to a Vickers machine gun in the productive effort required for their manufacture. I wanted to know the proportions of each wanted for nine months ahead so that I could make my plans. His reply was, 'Do you think I am God Almighty that I can tell you what is wanted nine months ahead?' I replied, 'No, Sir! And I do not think that I am either. But we have to work it out between us and try to get it right.' Then he gave me the old War Office answer, 'I want as much of both as you can produce.'

"My patience was wearing thin, and I think I spoke fairly definitely. I told him of the weeks I had spent trying to get these very elementary facts out of his subordinates. Eventually he said that the proportion was to be two machine guns per battalion as a minimum, four as a maximum, and anything above four was a luxury. That was the opinion of the Secretary for War, who was looked upon generally as our greatest soldier on July 26, 1915.

"I sat down in the War Office and wrote this down. So elated was I at my success in having at last got something upon which I could work that I spelt 'luxury' wrong. I asked Kitchener to sign it. He always had a reluctance to sign documents and said that he gave orders and expected them to be obeyed. I replied that doubtless was the military way, but I had been brought up to accept a signature as an authority for money I spent, and unless he would sign it, the document was no good to me. He walked out of the room. Girouard caught him in the doorway and said, 'Geddes is like that: he won't act unless you sign a paper.' So Kitchener came back and initialled the document."

Elated at his success in getting this documentary statement from the War Secretary, Geddes brought it to me. As Minister of Munitions I was officially expected only to fulfil the requirements of the War Office, and was not authorised to go beyond them. But I had made enquiries of my own amongst the fighting soldiers who had been in action and they were all in agreement as to the need for more and more machine guns, so that, when I read this miserable estimate, I was so indignant that I should have torn it up if Geddes had not rescued it from me. He treasures it still.

Memo of Meeting with Lord Kitchener on machine guns.

Essential 2 per Battalion

If possible run to 4 per Battalion

And above it may be counted as a luxury

K

26/6/15

FACSIMILE OF A MEMORANDUM, DRAFTED BY SIR ERIC GEDDES AND INITIALLED BY LORD KITCHENER, DEALING WITH THE SUPPLY OF MACHINE GUNS TO THE ARMIES

Geddes reports that I said to him: "Take Kitchener's maximum; (four per battalion); square it, multiply that result by two; and when you are in sight of that, double it again for good luck."

This calculation gave thirty-two machine guns per battalion with another thirty-two for a margin. That of course meant not that each battalion should take sixty-four machine guns into action, but that manufacture should be on that scale to provide for all contingencies. As a matter of fact, in November, 1915, the War Office raised their establishment requirements to sixteen machine guns per battalion and this was progressively raised by successive stages until before the end of the war the total number of these guns issued to the fighting forces was not far short of a figure equivalent to an average of sixty-four per battalion. These included the guns issued to the Machine Gun Corps and the Air Force, and we had also an ample margin for losses, which were very heavy. The numbers we had in France at the date of the Armistice were the equivalent of over eighty per battalion. In addition there was ample supply in England to replace inevitable losses and breakages.

As a matter of history, what with the demands from our own forces and the assistance we gave to our Allies, I do not think we ever had too many machine guns up to the end of the war. On the contrary, the proved utility of this weapon was so great that on February 23rd, 1918, I find that the programme we authorised for that year was an output of 138,349 further machine guns, and another 192,000 in 1919; this, in comparison with a total stock of 1330 of this arm, old or new, in the hands of our troops on June 1st, 1915.

Nor do I think that the Army ever had cause to regret that the supply proposed by Lord Kitchener in July, 1915, was increased sixteenfold. Photographs taken of dead Highlanders lying in swaths in front of a single German machine gun on the battlefield of Loos, which I saw some weeks later, taken by Colonel Arthur Lee and brought to me, finally disposed of any qualms I may have had at having taken upon myself the responsibility for overriding military opinion.

The realisation of this expanded programme naturally involved very careful planning on the part of the Ministry. A long view was needed for machine-gun contracts, and as Geddes pointed out at the time, to create a new output of this class of weapon one must formulate a definite concrete plan nine to twelve months in advance.

The Ministry began by placing a contract with Messrs. Vickers on July 19th, 1915, for 12,000 Vickers machine guns. Financial assistance was given to enable the firm to extend their plant at Erith and Crayford. The productive capacity of these factories ultimately reached 5000 machine guns a month.

We also turned our attention to the Lewis gun. This weapon had been rejected for land service by the military authorities in 1912, on the ground that it was undesirable to multiply types of arms. At the outbreak of the war, they were still emphatic in their preference for the Vickers rather than the Lewis gun. The latter was a much lighter weapon than the Vickers gun and could therefore be moved about by the soldiers with greater ease. It was indispensable for an advance and for aëroplanes.

But during August, 1914, forty-five Lewis guns had been ordered for the Air Service, and in the first week of September contracts were placed for two hundred more for general service to be delivered at the rate of twenty-five per week. The orders were subsequently increased by the War Office, but no effective steps were taken to increase facilities for manufacture and to expedite delivery, so that despite increased requisitions during the nine weeks ended

June 12th, deliveries to the War Office averaged only thirty-six per week.

When the Ministry assumed control I had the position investigated, and found that any effective increase in output was dependent upon the placing of larger orders, which would justify the Birmingham Small Arms Company and the manufacturers in making a considerable extension of their plant. It also depended on arrangements being made to increase the output of the necessary machine tools and gauges for manufacture. Hitherto the War Office and the Admiralty between them had given contracts for under 2000 Lewis guns — just enough to keep the firm from accepting foreign orders. So an order was placed with them for 10,000 machine guns to be delivered before the end of May, 1916, and while this contract was running I negotiated a further agreement with them whereby the output was to be extended to 750 guns weekly, with a running contract for this number for the duration of the war. In May, 1917, arrangements were made for this to be increased to 1800 a week.

In February, 1915, plant and skilled workmen had been brought over to Coventry from France for the manufacture of Hotchkiss guns, and a factory started, from which the Admiralty ordered a thousand of these machine guns. The anticipated output of the factory was twenty-five to fifty guns a week.

On August 13th, 1915, I decided to sanction a scheme for doubling the output of this factory, although the British military authorities did not then accept this type of gun for service use. Accordingly, in September, 1915, the Ministry placed an order for 3000 machine guns, and by the beginning of June, 1916, the factory had delivered 1013. Its output rose to 690 guns a month by the end of October, 1916. The ultimate importance of this weapon, especially for the armament of the tanks, is of course familiar history.

It would be a mistake to suppose that these immense expansions of the supply of machine guns were carried through with a reckless disregard for expense. Output was of course the chief concern, since the lives of our soldiers were in the balance. But cost was carefully studied. For example, the orders placed by the War Office with Messrs. Vickers in August and September, 1914, ranged from £167 to £162 per gun. The price fixed by the Ministry of Munitions in July, 1915, was £125 per gun. In 1916, it was reduced to £100. In 1918 it was still further brought down to £74.

Our progress in the task of supplying our forces with machine guns may be summarised as follows:

At the outbreak of the war, if we ignore the obsolescent Maxim, of which a few were still being turned out at the Royal Small Arms Factory at Enfield (which produced just over eighty of them during the first eighteen months of the war), the only supply of machine guns was the ten to twelve a week which were the maximum that Vickers could then turn out.

By the end of May, 1915, the total machine guns delivered to the War Office since August, 1914, were 1039 — 775 Vickers and 264 Lewis; and the total number in service, including Maxims, was 1330. Guns so far ordered numbered 2305.

How the output of machine guns rose thereafter is shown by the following little table:

Year	*Total output*
1914	287
1915	6,102
1916	33,507
1917	79,746
1918	120,864
Total	240,506

Out of this total of 240,506 machine guns which were manufactured in this country during the war we supplied 26,900 to our Allies, or twenty times as many as our whole stock at the time the Ministry of Munitions was formed.

5. Machine Gun Corps

The corps authorised — War Office neglects to develop the corps — My memorandum of 13/11/15 — Support of General Sir Archibald Murray — Value of the new force.

It was my duty as Minister of Munitions to furnish the machine guns required by the Army — and, as I have related, I went at one time considerably in advance of their official requirements in the direction of an intelligent anticipation of the number of guns they would presently find it necessary to apply for.

Officially, it was perhaps hardly a part of my duty to ensure that the best use was being made of the large supply of machine guns, but obviously this was a matter in which I could not fail to be keenly interested. In October, some three months after the question of the number of guns to be provided had been settled by me, and when their production was getting into its stride, the project of forming a special Machine Gun Corps received the Royal Assent.[1] This was a plan which I strongly supported. I had been informed of the very effective methods employed by the enemy to get the best results from this weapon — methods involving the use of special machine-gun companies, not permanently attached or allotted to any battalion or division.

But I was greatly alarmed to hear, shortly afterwards, that although this Machine Gun Corps had been authorised, little was being done to make it a reality, and hardly any men were being brought into training for it, out of the millions of men that had been recruited. Orders had, in fact,

[1] Royal Warrant. Army Order No. 416 of October 22nd, 1915.

been issued that no man should be recruited for it or transferred to it from other units. By this date my capacity for amazement at professional repugnance to new ideas or formations had reached saturation point. The estimated deliveries of machine guns would by March, 1916, reach a cumulative total of more than 10,000, and by midsummer of over 20,000. No doubt there were many other demands for men being made upon the War Office, but the machine gun was obviously such a formidable factor in defence and attack that only some curious form of unbelief and opposition could be responsible for this, to my mind, otherwise inexplicable and unintelligent failure to train men especially to make the best use of it. I determined, therefore, at the risk of once again interfering in something which was not departmentally my concern to ascertain the exact position.

In the War Committee of November 13th, 1915, I took up this matter. I laid before the Committee a memorandum setting out the estimated deliveries of machine guns, and urging adequate preparation for the effective use of this weapon. The memorandum continued:

"I believe that one machine gun, with its detachment of ten men, is at a very low estimate equivalent in destructive power to fifty riflemen, especially on the defensive. If that is a correct basis of comparison we could make up for our shortage in men and obtain equivalent fighting value by training 200 machine gunners instead of 1000 riflemen. In other words, with 50,000 machine gunners we could do the work of 250,000 infantry. We could also save in rifles, in which, so far as I can see, the Allies are never going to obtain the numerical superiority over the Germans necessary for a decisive victory.

"It seems also, that if our machine guns are employed on a large scale, on a comprehensive plan, they will, in conjunction with barbed wire and fortification, give us the strategic power *so far enjoyed by the Germans alone* of taking large numbers of troops away from one front, where no offensive is in contemplation, and transferring them to a quarter where active operations are intended.

"This is what the Germans have done on the Western Front, to release men for the thrust against Russia, and what they are doing on their Eastern Front, to set free men for attacking Serbia, and for action on the Western Front. This power to replace men, which amounts to strategic elasticity, applied especially, I think, to our present intentions on the Western Front."

General Sir Archibald Murray, who was then acting as Chief of the Imperial Staff, under Lord Kitchener (at the time away in the Mediterranean), was present at the War Committee, and supported my view. He said that the General Staff had actually started a machine-gun school at Grantham, intended to train a corps of men in machine-gun handling and tactics; but the Adjutant-General would not supply them with any men. They wished to train 10,000 men at a time, taking in a fresh supply every two months, but so far had only had 3000 men. He confirmed my estimate that one machine gun was equal to fifty rifles, and contradicted Mr. M'Kenna's suggestion that mobility was lost with machine guns.

As a result of my pressure, the War Council decided to ask the Army Council to provide for 10,000 men to be put continuously under instruction. Actually some considerable delay occurred before this instruction was carried out, but eventually a number of men were drafted from various units to the Corps Training Centre, and even then they were not especially picked men like the German machine gunners, whom Sir Douglas Haig has described as a *"corps d'élite."* None the less, they added immensely to the efficiency of our Army. Four years later, in November, 1918, the strength of this new branch of the Army which had been initiated under such difficulties amounted to 6427 officers and 123,835 other ranks.

When one recalls the devastating use made by the Germans of their picked machine gunners both in attack and defence, and how they saved their own infantry by that process, one is astounded at the tardiness with which our military leaders came to any realisation of the power of the most lethal weapon of the war.

6. Design and Invention

Decisive importance of mechanical warfare — Machines more valuable than man-power — Our unpreparedness at the outbreak of war — War Office reluctance to adopt new weapons — Woolwich drawing office gets choked up — The Royal Society appoints an investigation committee — Divided responsibility between War Office and Ministry — Action of G.H.Q. and Admiralty to promote design — The Stokes gun — Growing need for examination of inventions by Ministry — Tank research taken over from Admiralty — Inventions Department set up by Ministry: Mr. Moir's appointment — My speech in the House, 28/7/15 — Duel with War Office: arrangement with Kitchener — Mr. Moir's complaint — War Office removes military experts from Ministry — Further letter: Colonel Goold-Adams removed — Delays caused by War Office control of design — General Du Cane's letter — War Office not protecting the troops — My letter to Mr. Asquith — Transfer of design to Ministry — Ordnance Board dissolved — War Office makes a last fight — General Du Cane's memorandum — War Office refusal to carry out instructions — War Office letter: still trying to retain control — Final decision of Cabinet War Committee.

In this war the engineer and the chemist dominated the battlefield. When war broke out the Central Powers were much better prepared than the Allies on the mechanical and chemical side in this respect. The great howitzers of the Germans played a decisive part in the opening conflicts of the war. Even in 1916 the French artillery was inferior in this type of weapon. We had practically nothing that counted in trench warfare until late in 1915. The Teutonic heavy guns (German and Austrian) smashed the concrete fortifications of Liége, compelling in a few hours the surrender of defences which we reckoned would hold out for days if not weeks. The Germans who captured Antwerp were in numbers but a third of the garrison, and in quality they were the second-best of the German troops. Big guns did the work for them. The German 5.9 shell with its terrifying explosion stopped the French advance, and hurled their armies back towards Paris. Whilst the German engineers in their workshops gave their comrades superior weapons for attack, their field engineers constructed for them the best defences. Deep and skilfully constructed entrenchments protected by wire and defended with machine guns, *Minenwerfer,* and grenades defied the repeated efforts of the Allies to push the German invaders back out of France and Belgium. Their use of poison gas broke the French and British fronts at Ypres in 1915, and helped to scatter the Russians in Poland.

On their Eastern Front the Germans could defeat and hurl back Russian armies thrice as strong numerically, but destitute of the guns, shells, mortars, and gases which the Central Powers possessed. Human valour is no shield against high explosives or machine-gun bullets. As deadlock gripped the battle front, it became increasingly clear that if Allied strategy declined to seek a back door, the only hope of gaining a decisive victory was to produce some new contrivance or improvement in our weapons which might turn the balance. And even a back door, if barred, needs smashing in.

It soon became evident to clear eyes and gradually to the most obtuse vision that the war would be fought and ultimately decided in the workshop and the laboratory.

Unhappily, at the outbreak of the war and all through its opening months we were definitely behindhand in the field of munition design. Our artillery had not been tested in a great war. Our little stage manœuvres taught us nothing as to what real war would be like. Our heavy artillery was a joke to our foes. We had no trench mortars or grenades. We had vested our confidence so much in shrapnel that we had not worked out a safe high-explosive shell. When we started manufacturing high-explosive shells we had not thought out the problem of how we were to produce a sufficient quantity of explosive for so stupendous a demand, nor had we invented a competent fuse to explode such shells as we were able to fill. Our only modern big gun was the solitary experimental 9.2 in., which was sent out to the front in September, 1914, and which was nicknamed "Mother" by the troops. Our machine guns were few in number, and many of them were obsolescent in design. The War Office had refused to consider the Lewis Gun for land service. We had no trench mortars and no reliable hand grenades. The enemy had both.

Research and design for munitions of war were under the control of the Master-General of Ordnance. During the opening months of the war he held that, as it would soon be over, it would be foolish to divert to the lengthy and tedious process of working out and approving designs for new weapons the energy which could be better used for producing existing standard types. Thus, when early in the war a request came from the front that specimens of captured German *Minenwerfer* should be examined with a view to providing the Army with trench mortars, the proposal was postponed on the ground that other demands on the capacity of the Ordnance Factory and armament firms were more immediate.

But as the war progressed the military authorities were compelled to face ever-multiplying problems of new designs and types of munition which were required by the army in field. They had also to arrange for the immense growth of output of all supplies, new or old, and this threw a great deal of extra work on the drawing office at Woolwich. It was inevitable that it should become thoroughly congested and hopelessly in arrears. The Admiralty, which also relied on Woolwich for the same class of work, became so impatient that in May, 1915, it established its own drawing office at headquarters, and gradually developed it to include simple designing.

Britain is very rich in scientific and inventive ability, and in November, 1914, the General War Committee of the Royal Society was appointed to "organise assistance to the Government in conducting or suggesting scientific investigation in relation to the War, the Committee to have power to add to their number and to appoint Sub-Committees not necessarily restricted to Fellows of the Society." By this step the Government mobilised the most distinguished body of scientists in the world to assist the nation. The Admiralty made considerable use of this body, and referred to it such inventions and suggestions sent in as seemed to hold out some promise of being useful. But the procedure of the War Department remained practically unaltered. Apart from some slight coöperation with the Chemical Sub-Committee which had been set up by the Royal Society, little use was made of the War Committee of the Society for military purposes.

When the Ministry of Munitions was first set up, the Army Council retained responsibility for the kind and quality of the stores we were to supply. The fixing of designs and specifications and the tests to be applied, the research and experimental work in connection with munitions, were still under the War Office, and though the Ministry of Munitions was responsible for providing guns, ammunition, rifles, and other munitions, it was entirely dependent upon the War Office authorities for decision and investigation in respect of the patterns, ingredients, and specifications of these stores.

I soon discovered that the separation of design and manufacture was a serious mistake and led to blunders and delays. It was not improved by the reactionary attitude of the War Office. Our soldiers in the battle line were more progressive.

Sir John French set up, early in June, 1915, an Experimental Committee at G.H.Q. to deal with inventions and the application of modern science to the needs of war. At home there was a popular demand for a similar organisation to serve the needs of both the Army and the Navy, and on June 22nd, 1915, Mr. Balfour, who was then First Lord of the Admiralty, definitely formulated a scheme for this purpose. The War Office held aloof, and in July the Admiralty set up an Admiralty Board of Inventions and Research to serve the needs of the Senior Service alone. A similar organisation was shortly afterwards established by me for the Ministry of Munitions.

A very short experience convinced me that the unnatural divorce of design and production was quite unworkable. In particular, I felt it important that the Ministry of Munitions should be able to examine new suggestions and inventions of possible value — a view confirmed by the history of the Stokes gun — and I proceeded to press for the transfer to the Ministry of at least the authority to deal with such new ideas and designs.

The history of the Stokes gun affords an illustration of the impracticability of the dual system. The army were clamouring for a mortar that would enable them to reply to the bombing appliances with which the Germans harried our trenches. As early as January, 1915, Mr. Wilfred Stokes, an East of England manufacturer of agricultural machinery, had submitted to the War Office a design for a trench mortar of extreme simplicity — a plain steel tube, into which a bomb could be dropped with a cartridge fitted to its base, which would explode on hitting a striker at the base of the tube, and propel the bomb into the enemy trench. You could fire the gun as rapidly as you could drop bombs into it.

The War Office did not approve the type of fuse fitted

to the bomb, and turned down the invention. It was brought forward again in March, and again rejected.

Hearing favourable reports of this gun, I arranged to see it for myself, and on June 30th I witnessed it in action in a demonstration at Wormwood Scrubs. I was accompanied by Major-General Ivor Philipps, the Military Secretary to the new Ministry. Both of us were very impressed with its performance. It struck me as having great possibilities.

Officially I was limited at this time in the Ministry to the manufacture of those stores which the War Office approved. It was impossible to pretend that it had passed the design for the Stokes gun — on the contrary, it had twice over rejected it.

Happily I had received just before this a donation of £20,000 from one of the Indian Maharajahs, to be expended by me on whatever war purpose seemed most useful for the Empire. On the strength of this fund, and in spite of my knowledge that the War Office was opposed to using the Stokes gun, I gave instructions for 1000 of them to be made forthwith, together with 100,000 bombs — these last not to be completed till a satisfactory fuse had been prepared for them. Meantime I set about reopening the issue with the War Office.

By the second week of August they had been brought to the point of carrying out a further test of the mortar at Shoeburyness. By this time a fuse had been fitted to the bombs, similar to that used on the Mills hand grenade. The Ordnance Board now reported that the gun was better than a 3.7-inch trench mortar which the War Office had been manufacturing, and it was formally approved on August 28th. This was just as well, for already on August 22nd General Headquarters in France had telegraphed the War Office for as many Stokes mortars as could possibly be supplied by September 1st, and had sent over an officer to consult with the Trench Warfare Department about the smoke bombs it was desired to use in them for a smoke screen in the coming Battle of Loos. Thirty were hastily improvised and sent out.

During the remainder of the war, the Stokes gun became and remained the trench mortar in highest favour and most constant demand. Out of 19,000 trench mortars and trench howitzers issued during the war to our troops, 11,500 were Stokes guns. Throughout 1917 and 1918 the 3-inch Stokes gun was the only form of light trench mortar manufactured, as by this time it had clearly proved its superiority to all rival patterns. And this was the weapon which the Ordnance Department of the War Office had done its best to fling aside as worthless.

Naturally after this experience I was more than ever anxious to bring the supervision of new inventions and improvements in design under the control of a progressively minded body, which would not suffer from an ingrained habit of rejecting every fresh idea on principle. The fact that we were at that time being held up by the delay in settling the ingredients of shell filling and the design of fresh fuses and gaines made me still more desirous of having complete control in those vital matters. The Admiralty, as I have said, was showing itself far more alert in this respect than the War Office, and in face of the failure of the Ordnance Department to do anything in the matter, was even studying new ideas for land warfare. On the plea that they would be of value to the Royal Naval Air Service, Mr. Churchill had as early as January, 1915, begun investigations into the possibilities of armoured cars, and had set up in February the Admiralty Landships Committee, which carried out work of immense value for the evolution of the tank.

I was, naturally, being deluged at the Ministry of Munitions with letters and calls from people who had some new invention or improvement to propose. The great majority of these ideas were, of course, useless, and many of them came from cranks and lunatics. But it was clear, as in the case of Mr. Stokes, that some of them might prove of value, and it was also evident from the result of the Admiralty researches into land warfare and the rejection of Lord Moulton's recommendations about explosives, that the War Office was failing to carry out the work urgently required in this field. Early in June, I arranged with Mr. Balfour to take over all the work of the Admiralty in reference to expedients and inventions for land warfare. This meant, amongst other things, that the manufacture of tanks was handed over to the Ministry.

In reply to a request I made to him, Lord Kitchener sent a message through Sir Reginald Brade that he was agreeable to my taking over the inventions work relating to munitions, for the supply of which my Department was responsible.

Accordingly, on July 13th a meeting was held at which a new Department of the Ministry was set up for dealing with inventions having relation to Munitions of War.

To carry out the duties of this Department I appointed Mr. Ernest Moir. This development was described by me as follows, in the course of a speech which I made in the House of Commons on July 28th on the work of the Ministry:

"I should like to say one word as to what we are doing with regard to inventions. It is essential for the conduct of the war that the fullest use should be made of the best brains of inventors and scientific men. Perhaps hitherto there has been a want of coördination among the various methods of dealing with the projects of inventors. So far as naval inventions are concerned, the First Lord of the Admiralty has set up an Inventions Board under the distinguished presidency of Lord Fisher.

"I have just concluded arrangements to constitute an inventions Branch of the Ministry of Munitions, and I hope it will do for inventions for land warfare what Lord Fisher's Committee will do for sea warfare.

"The War Office is handing over the whole question of inventions to us, and careful arrangements have been made to secure that the new branch shall keep in close touch with Lord Fisher's Board to avoid duplication and overlapping, and also with the War Office experts and Army authorities who must have the ultimate voice in deciding whether any particular invention is of service in actual warfare.

"I have appointed Mr. E. W. Moir, a distinguished engineer who has already given valuable assistance to my department on a voluntary basis, to take charge of the new branch, and he will not only have an expert staff, but also a panel of scientific consultants on technical and scientific points. It ought to be clearly understood that only a very small minority of inventors' projects are of practical value [laughter]. Many projects fail from technical defects, and many others, though technically perfect, are unsuited to the practical conditions of warfare.

"The new branch will have justified its existence if one project in a hundred, or even in one thousand, turns out to be of practical utility in the present emergency.

"We have got a good many which we are experimenting upon very hopefully."

Despite the optimism of that speech, it turned out that the setting up of this Inventions Department was only the beginning of our troubles. Although their political heads had given consent to the transfer, the officials of the War Office were most reluctant to part with any vestige of their authority, and a duel began between them and my own officials.

By the beginning of September very little progress had been made. I accordingly saw Lord Kitchener, and secured his consent to an arrangement whereby Colonel Hickman of the War Office and Mr. Moir should keep in touch with each other so that new ideas and suggestions received by the War Office should be passed along to the Ministry.

But despite this friendly effort to come to a satisfactory arrangement, and the accommodating spirit displayed by the Secretary for War, the trouble with the War Office went on unabated. At the end of September the Ordnance Board set up rival bodies analogous to the Advisory Panel of the Ministry of Munitions. On October 16th I received a letter from Moir which I will transcribe, as it gives a vivid picture of the campaign of obstruction which was at that time being waged by the War Office against the Ministry on this and other issues.

"Ministry of Munitions,
Princes Street,
Westminster, S.W.,
16th October, 1915.

"The Rt. Hon. David Lloyd George, M.P.,
6, Whitehall Gardens, S.W.

"Dear Mr. Lloyd George,

"Having been asked by General von Donop to call on him on Thursday the General informed me that he saw some difficulty in transferring to the Inventions Branch of the Ministry of Munitions the powers granted to the Secretary of State for War by Clause 30, Sub-Section 12, of the Patents Act, 1907. This Sub-Section provides that the submission of an invention to the War Office or the Admiralty shall not act as publication, and on the 2nd October application was made through Sir Herbert Llewellyn Smith for a transfer of that provision to the Ministry of Munitions.

"General von Donop's point was that in sending on from the War Office to the Munitions Inventions Department such inventions as the War Office thought were of no use (for these are admittedly the only suggestions that they are sending us at the present time) they might be running some risk of complaint by the inventor should such ideas leak out through their submission to our Panel of Experts. In such cases the War Office might be blamed. My answer to this was that up to the present as they had only sent to this Department things that, according to their lights, were of no use, I naturally had not insulted our Panel by putting these before them, and had dealt with them myself.

"Incidentally, I went on to say that I hoped there would soon be some arrangement made by which this Department would not only see the worthless but also the possible ideas that were useful from the War Office point of view.

"I also enlarged on the fact that this Department could get no military assistance, and that the assistance which we already had in the shape of Colonel Goold-Adams and Colonel Heffernan was going to be withdrawn from our Panel for, so far as I could ascertain, no sufficient reason. These two experts on artillery, I told General von Donop, were of immense value to us, and far from wanting to reduce the military members of the Panel we wanted to increase them. The reason for suggesting their removal General von Donop said, was because the balance of the Ordnance Board was overworked and consequently Colonel Goold-Adams and Colonel Heffernan must return to Woolwich. I asked him if he could get someone to take these two gentlemen's places temporarily on the Ordnance Board. *He said that if they did not return he would have them removed from the Board and would not allow them to return even after the War.*

"During the course of conversation I pointed out that although this Department had been informed that we could not be given any military assistance the War Office had been able to get together an Inventions Board numbering 14, and including seven Generals, three Colonels, and three Majors. I also told him that my view of the matter was that our Inventions Department had probably relieved the War Office of a good deal of work.

"The whole matter seems to me to be a further indication, if any were necessary, of the spirit of objection to civil assistance by the military authorities, and I think that a good deal of the resistance comes from the gentleman with whom I had the interview.

"I have not seen Colonel Goold-Adams, but Colonel Heffernan, with some trepidation, admitted to me recently that he enjoyed his work with us very much, and that he did not want to give it up. He would be quite willing to carry it on on Saturdays or Sundays if he could not do so in any other way. Unfortunately an engagement of this sort would be a very difficult one to carry out except so far as concerns the attending of experiments or visiting work which is going on.

"Both Colonel Goold-Adams and Colonel Heffernan are highly intelligent men, and I consider that they should not be removed from your department either in connection with inventions or anything else. The other six members who are left behind on the Ordnance Board should, I imagine, under stress of war conditions, either be reinforced or could probably find it possible to do the work among themselves.

"Of course, we can get on without anybody, but there is, I think, an obvious effort to defeat the objects that you have set yourself out to attain, at least in some of their departments, on the part of the Military Authorities.

Yours faithfully,

E. Moir."

The two officers mentioned in this letter were members of the Inventions section of the Ordnance Board, who had been seconded for work with the Ministry's Inventions Board as a means of keeping liaison with the military authorities. This was part of the arrangement I had come to with Lord Kitchener at the time when it was agreed that inventions should be transferred to the Ministry of Munitions for research and investigation.

A fortnight later, Mr. Moir wrote me the news that Colonel Goold-Adams had been recalled by the War Office. He enclosed the colonel's letter, which was in the following terms:

"Ordnance Board Office,
Royal Arsenal,
Woolwich.
29th October, 1915.

"Dear Mr. Moir,

". . . I regret to say that I have been officially informed to-day that I am to sever my connections with the Ministry of Munitions, and no reason is given.

"I am more than sorry to have to do so, but it cannot be helped.

"When you have had an opportunity I hope you will express my regret to Mr. Lloyd George.

Sincerely yours,
H. GOOLD-ADAMS.

"P.S. — I need hardly say that if my services or advice are wanted officially at any future date I shall only be too glad to be of assistance.

H. G. A."

The whole position was unsatisfactory. Had the Design Department of the War Office been not only efficient and energetic, with an appreciation of the value of time in war, and had it also worked harmoniously and with good will with the new Manufacturing Department, then no serious mishaps or delays would have ensued. But that was not the case. The process of manufacture in every direction was being held up by mistakes here and procrastination there.

It must be remembered that up to this stage, the Ministry of Munitions had merely been accorded power to make researches and investigations with regard to new inventions and improvements. It had no control over the design of either new or old patterns of munitions. That was still in the hands of the War Office, which retained its Inventions Board with overriding authority over the Ministry's researches.

Moreover, in connection with the expansion of manufacture there constantly arose questions of the possibility of modifying or adapting specifications to suit the exigencies of production; and in these questions the Ministry, which was responsible for production, was powerless until a lengthy process of consultation with the War Office and experimentation by these officials produced ultimate sanction. Such questions arose daily, for the practical experience of war was making matchwood of old theories and traditional patterns of munitions. The standard fuses proved unreliable and caused prematures and "duds", the guns and gun carriages were seen to be capable of improvement, and the new forms of warfare which developed were calling constantly for new types of weapons, or modifications of existing types. The difficulties with regard to the composition of shell explosive and the ingredients of cordite were causing grave anxiety and delay, and the fuses were thoroughly unsatisfactory. The Ministry, responsible for meeting all these changing demands, was unable to move because of the division of authority with the Ordnance Board. While the Board had been responsible for design and production, it had been able to coördinate the two, if it so willed, without delay. Obviously, it was desirable, since the Ministry had taken over production, that it should also have the responsibility for design. This divided authority, with the consequent delays on the part of the War Office in coming to vital decisions on fuses and explosives, seriously impeded the work of production of completed shells. Shell cases multiplied at a great rate, but the same pace could not be kept in the matter of the completion until the design of the fuses and the ingredients of the explosives were finally settled.

As I have pointed out, the position with regard to explosives was critical and threatened us with a disastrous shortage of shells for the front. The delays of the War Office in coming to a decision were seriously impeding production.

A letter written by General Du Cane on the 22nd of October, 1915, to Colonel Arthur Lee, who had just taken over Sir Ivor Philipps's position as Military Undersecretary to the Ministry of Munitions, revealed other directions in which the handling of design by the War Office was proving a source of danger as well as of delay. General Du Cane presided over the Experiments Committee at G.H.Q. in France. The gaines which detonate the shells were so ill-designed that they caused premature explosions which burst our guns at an alarming rate. The total number of our guns at that date was not high.

Here is an extract from General Du Cane's letter:

". . . I feel pretty confident that you will never get your show running smoothly until you get full responsibility for pattern and experiments. I am pretty sure that you will find that the system by which the War Office and Ordnance Board retain the responsibility for these matters is your great stumbling-block. The M.G.O.'s people seem to me to be mentally exhausted and the Ordnance Board and Experimental Department at Shoebury to be hopelessly congested.

"K's great argument for keeping control was that he must be responsible for the safety of the troops, because being voluntary soldiers they would all run away or desert if we burst guns like the French. He has failed hopelessly as regards safety, and the result of his control now is to prevent the causes of the trouble being definitely ascertained.

"At present our H.E. for 13 and 18 pounders is so unreliable that we cannot use it in large quantities. We have lost 36 guns since the 21st September for an average of one accident to something between 4000 and 5000 rounds. That is worse than the French ever were.

"During the recent operations the French accidents were one to 120,000 rounds. We have a long way to go yet. I suggested to L. G. that he shall ask the French for 200,000 of their fuses so that we could use them while we are getting our own right. . . .

"The loss of 36 guns in a month by prematures represents the highest percentage of bursts ever suffered by any artillery on either side in this war."

Accordingly in mid-November I wrote the following letter to the Prime Minister:

"6, Whitehall Gardens,
Whitehall, S.W.

"My dear P.M.,

"I hope it will now be possible to come to a decision as to the future of the Ordnance Board.

"Important munitions are being held up or retarded, and I am receiving serious complaints from the Department as to the position of matters. The present situation is an impossible one. M. Thomas has complete control of design as well as manufacture, but I am helpless.

Yours sincerely,
D. Lloyd George."

Mr. Asquith was at that time temporarily acting as Secretary for War, in the absence of Lord Kitchener, who had gone to the Mediterranean, and he supported my attitude. Strong protests were raised by the officials at the War Office. General von Donop foresaw a general relaxation of strictness of design which would endanger the safety of the Army. Sir Charles Harris, the Assistant Financial Secretary, protested against the breach with precedent and the overthrowing of the remarkable instrument of efficiency existing in the Ordnance Board. Manufacturing questions were, according to him, a part only, and that not the most important part, of the Board's work. "To make a civilian department responsible for the design of munitions as well as for their supply would be to head straight back to the inefficiency that had been experienced in the Egyptian campaign of 1880. The Ordnance Board ought to be strengthened, not abolished."

But in November, 1915, people were more impressed with the hindrances to action before their eyes than with what a Treasury clerk witnessed in 1880, and despite these protests the Prime Minister decided to transfer design of munitions to the Ministry, and to abandon the Ordnance Board control. This decision was embodied in the following memorandum, noted by Sir Reginald Brade:

"The transfer to the Ministry of Munitions of the responsibility for designs, patterns, and specifications for testing of arms and ammunition, and for the examination of inventions bearing on such munitions, leaves to the War Office the following functions only in regard to munitions of war, *viz.:*

"1. — The duty of fixing the requirements of the Army both as regards the general nature and amount of the munitions required, together with the duty of allocating all such material.

"2. — The duty of receipt, custody, and actual distribution of all such supplies.

"These functions fall to the general staff and the Quartermaster-General's department respectively. This is the system in force with the Army in the field, and, in altered conditions, should be followed in the War Office during the War.

"As regards the staffs hitherto employed in this work, such officers and others as are necessary for the performance of the limited functions remaining to the War Office should be retained; the balance being placed at the disposal of the Ministry of Munitions. The exact details must be worked out in conference between representatives of the two offices.

"The above was dictated to me by the Prime Minister with instructions to notify it as his decision arrived at after consideration of the relative positions of the War Office and the Ministry of Munitions in which each stands, now that the transfer of duties . . . has been approved."

Following this decision, on November 29th, 1915, the new duties in regard to design were formally undertaken by the Ministry, and the control of experimental and research bodies, such as the Research Department, Woolwich, was also transferred from the War Office. The Department of Munitions Design, formed within the Ministry, was placed under the control of General Du Cane. The Ordnance Board was dissolved on December 4th, 1915, and reconstituted as the Ordnance Committee and advisory body to both the Ministry of Munitions and the Admiralty.

I quote an extract from a letter I wrote at this date, November 30th, 1915:

"Lord Kitchener comes home to-day. They have not been able to keep him away. However, in his absence the Prime Minister has handed over the Ordnance Board to me. I have been fighting for this for months, but the War Office have dodged me, and by keeping the Ordnance Board have been able to limit very considerably the energies of all this department. Moreover, when anything *was* accomplished it was only after hard fighting and much unpleasantness."

One last fight remained. Whatever else the War Office failed to do, it at least lived up to the old tradition of the British Army of never knowing when it was beaten. Not only inventions, but design and inspection had now, in set terms, been transferred to the Ministry of Munitions. "Very well," said the War Office in effect, "go ahead, and design and inspect your munitions. But before we issue them to the Army, *we* reserve the right to submit them to our own tests and inspection, and to send out only those designs of which we also approve."

Accordingly, the War Office refused to transfer their testing and experimental staff at the school of musketry at Hythe, maintained the department of the Director of Artillery at the War Office as an overriding authority superior to the Ministry of Munitions, and generally set themselves to nullify wherever possible the change which had been decided on.

General Du Cane, fresh from the battle zone, found himself pitchforked into this internecine conflict. On December 14th, he submitted the following memorandum upon the position:

RELATIONS WITH THE WAR OFFICE

When the Prime Minister and Mr. Lloyd George first discussed with me the formation of a Military Department in the Ministry, to be responsible for the design of munitions, I pointed out to them that this proposal would depend for success on two conditions being fulfilled, *viz.:*

1. — The necessary officers being placed at the disposal of the Ministry.

2. — The removal of possible causes of friction that might result from the maintenance of a rival technical department in the War Office.

The first of these conditions has been fulfilled, but the second has not.

Before I was appointed to my present position I had an interview with the Prime Minister at the War Office, at which he said that he fully recognised the difficulties that must result from my having personal relations with the M.G.O. and the officers of the D. of A.'s directorate in the circumstances that must result from the contemplated measure of reorganisation, and instructions were issued by him that the General Staff would deal with the "requirements and allocation," and the Q.M.G. with "distribution."

These instructions have not been carried out, and the D. of A.'s directorate still exists at the War Office and deals with these subjects. It is true that arrangements have been made for references from the Ministry on the subject of "requirements", to be sent to the Director of Staff Duties, but this officer refers them again to the D. of A. and merely passes on his replies.

The difficult situation that it was hoped to avert, therefore, actually exists. There is still a rival technical department at the War Office, tenacious of its position. The officers of this department feel deep resentment at being deprived of their most important functions, and while they are the officers that should be in the closest possible touch with my department, working harmoniously with my officers, the relations are so strained that they result in their avoiding one another as much as possible. The bad effects of this situation are already beginning to be felt, and if it is allowed to continue it will inevitably result in acute friction and loss of efficiency.

I submit that it is essential that effect should be given at once to the Prime Minister's decision, that a proper channel of communication should be established with the War Office, and that cordial and harmonious relations should be established without any further delay. If this cannot be brought about, I must confess my inability to look forward to the task before me with confidence.

J. P. Du Cane,
D.G.M.G., M.G.

14/12/15.

This was plain speaking, and not by a civilian, but by a highly placed staff officer of acknowledged ability and of long military experience. But the War Office still fought on, and on January 5th, 1916, a letter was received at the Ministry, in the following terms:

"War Office, London,
January 5th, 1916.

"Sir,

"With reference to your letter No. D.G.M.D./General/8, dated the 13th December, 1915, I am commanded by the Army Council to inform you that they observe that it is proposed in the letter under reply that the final approval to new designs, or amendments to existing designs, should be given by the Director-General Munitions Design. The Army Council, however, consider it most desirable that the approval should not be given until they have expressed their concurrence as to its suitability for adoption as meeting the requirements of the Service. I am to add that the Army Council are strongly of opinion, confirmed by experience, that in most cases before final approval is given to inventions or designs, practical trials on conditions formulated by the Army Council, carried out by troops under the orders and observation of responsible military commanders selected by the Council, are essential. Any special conditions which the Ministry of Munitions desired would be added to those formulated by the Army Council.

"In accordance with the views expressed above, the Council desire to retain at their own disposal an experimental staff at Hythe, but they will be glad to arrange for the Director-General Munitions Design to obtain from this staff and that of the Machine-Gun School any assistance that he may desire, and, so far as is possible, they will endeavour to meet the wishes of the Ministry of Munitions as regards the transfer, or loan to that Department, of individual officers now serving at Hythe.

I am, etc.,
R. H. BRADE."

I do not need to point out that this letter, was in effect, a flat refusal on the part of the Army Council to acquiesce in and carry out loyally the decisions already made as to the transfer of design and inspection to the Ministry. I had no option but to bring the matter before the Cabinet War Committee — somewhat, I think, to the Prime Minister's bewilderment, for he had assumed that this was all settled and done with. It was thrashed out in two meetings, on January 26th and February 3rd, 1916, and a formula ultimately agreed which laid it down that:

"(*a*) The responsibility for designs, patterns, and specifications and for testing arms and ammunition rests with the Ministry of Munitions.

"(*b*) The Army Council is responsible for the general nature and amount of the weapons and equipments required, but there shall be no court of appeal set up in the War Office from the decisions of the Ministry of Munitions under (*a*).

"(*c*) When it is necessary that new weapons, stores or articles of equipment should undergo practical trials by troops, either at home or in the field, the coöperation of the Army Council should be sought by the Ministry.

"(*d*) The Army Council should be represented on Advisory Committees or bodies under the Ministry of Munitions to the extent that the Army Council think desirable."

By this time the War Office had shot their last bolt, and the decisions embodied in the above clauses formed the basis upon which the work of munition design was carried forward thereafter by the Ministry with ever-increasing smoothness and efficiency. But after what expenditure of time, mental concentration and energy! Meanwhile we had to put up with unsatisfactory gaines and fuses which often caused more trouble to our troops than to the enemy. In February, 1916, a decision was arrived at which ought to have been reached in June, 1915. It naturally took the new department some time to perfect their designs. Manufacturers proceeded with the mechanisms already settled and sanctioned, and when the great battle was fought later on in the year, we suffered in the quality of our shells from the delay.

7. Tanks

Value of the new weapon — My connection with its development — Early experiments — Initiative shown by Mr. Churchill — Colonel Swinton's suggestions — Ministry of Munitions undertakes supply — Trial of the "Mother" tank at Hatfield — Lord Kitchener's view of the tank — A partridge's nest spared — Manufacture and first use of tanks — A well-kept secret — Premature use a blunder — Irresolution of Army Council — Ultimate triumph of the new weapon.

British in conception, design and manufacture, the Tank was the one outstanding and dramatic innovation brought forth by the war in the sphere of mechanical aids to warfare. It was the ultimate British reply to the machine guns and heavily fortified trench systems of the German Army, and there is no doubt whatever that it played a very important part in helping the Allies to victory. It might have played a still greater part if it had been developed more promptly through a livelier display of sympathy and encouragement on the part of the War Office; and if its use in the field had been more intelligently exploited. Even in spite of blunders in these respects, the Tank saved an immense number of British lives, and gave invaluable stimulus to the morale of our troops, while spreading terror and alarm among those of the enemy.

I am not concerned here to enter upon the controversial question of the origin of the Tank. The idea of a mechanically propelled, travelling fortress was one which had occurred to a number of inventive minds, even before the war. My own connection with its development only started after I had entered on my duties as Minister of Munitions. In that office, and subsequently as Secretary of State for War and as Prime Minister, I had a good deal to do with the later stages in the evolution and manufacture of this new weapon. The first tentative experiments, mainly carried out by the Air Department of the Admiralty, and backed by the enthusiasm of Mr. Winston Churchill, had already been undertaken when I came on the scene.

My first encounter with the early attempts to produce a self-propelled machine, capable of crossing trenches and forcing its way through entanglements, was when on June 30th, 1915, I was invited with Mr. Winston Churchill to witness an exhibition by R.N.A.S. officers at Wormwood Scrubbs of experiments with a wire cutter affixed to a caterpillar tractor. This was not a Tank, nor indeed anything like it; but it was one of the early experimental models, tested and later abandoned in the search for a device which would accomplish what the Tank ultimately achieved.

I was surprised to find that these experiments were being conducted by naval men, mostly temporary officers and ratings of the Armoured Car Division of the Royal Naval Air Force. On enquiry I found that the Admiralty had till then been, and still were, responsible for the experimental work of developing this machine for land warfare, and were carrying out their work with funds voted for the Navy and with naval personnel! This was sufficiently astonishing. But my astonishment was succeeded by admiration of Mr. Churchill's enterprise when I discovered that he alone of those in authority before whom the idea of a mobile armoured shelter was placed, had had the vision to appreciate its potential value, and the pluck to back, practically and financially, the experiments for its development.

Later I discovered that the project for a machine-gun destroyer propelled on the caterpillar principle, had in fact been put forward in October, 1914, by a soldier, Colonel Swinton, who realised how deadly the German machine guns were proving to our infantry, and laid his idea before the Secretary of the Committee of Imperial Defence, Colonel Hankey, who quickly appreciated its value and importance. Colonel Swinton had followed this up at the beginning of January, 1915, by pressing the matter personally on the War Office. Colonel Hankey had put forward the suggestion, along with other new ideas, in a memorandum dated December 28th, 1914, to the Committee of Imperial Defence. Mr. Churchill wrote to the Prime Minister on January 5th, 1915, supporting the proposal, and fortunately he also proceeded to initiate independent measures for investigation and experiment, financed from the Navy vote. "Fortunately," because though the War Office set up a Committee to investigate Colonel Swinton's suggestion, it dropped the project after a few experiments and decided to take no further action. As Mr. Churchill, when Secretary of

State for War, said four-and-a-half years later in his evidence before the Royal Commission on Awards to Inventors, with reference to the part played by the War Office: "Certain investigations and experiments were made, but the matter came to a dead end. . . . I formed the opinion that no real progress was being made and that the military authorities were quite unconvinced either of the practicability of making such engines or of their value when made."

After seeing the experiments at Wormwood Scrubbs, I arranged with Mr. Balfour, the new First Lord of the Admiralty, that the Ministry of Munitions should undertake responsibility for the manufacture of Tanks, while the Admiralty Committee continued experiments. Major Albert Stern, as chairman of the Ministry's Tank Committee threw great energy into their production.

The first fruits of this arrangement appeared when, at the beginning of February, 1916, I went with other Ministers, including Lord Kitchener and various naval and military officers and some representatives from G.H.Q., France, to witness the official trial of the first machine — later known as the "Mother" Tank — at Hatfield Park. The experiment was a complete success, the Tank achieving even more than it was asked to accomplish. And I can recall the feeling of delighted amazement with which I saw for the first time the ungainly monster, bearing the inscription "H.M.S. Centipede" on its breast, plough through thick entanglements, wallow through deep mud, and heave its huge bulk over parapets and across trenches. At last, I thought, we have the answer to the German machine guns and wire. Mr. Balfour's delight was as great as my own, and it was only with difficulty that some of us persuaded him to disembark from H.M. Landship whilst she crossed the last test, a trench several feet wide.

Sir William Robertson was also very favourably impressed, but Lord Kitchener scoffed as the huge, clumsy creature lumbered and tumbled about, though always moving forward, and expressed the opinion that it would be very quickly knocked out by artillery. He certainly gave me the impression at the time that he thought little of the invention; but a different light is shed upon his attitude by a letter I have quite recently received from General Sir Robert Whigham, who in 1916 was a member of the Army Council, and accompanied Lord Kitchener to the Hatfield trial. He writes:

> ". . . Lord Kitchener was so much impressed that he remarked to Sir William Robertson that it was far too valuable a weapon for so much publicity. He then left the trial ground before the trials were concluded, with the deliberate intention of creating the impression that he did not think there was anything to be gained from them. Sir William Robertson followed him straight away, taking me with him, to my great disappointment as I was just going to have a ride in the tank! During the drive back to London Sir William explained to me the reason of Lord Kitchener's and his own early departure, and impressed on me the necessity for maintaining absolute secrecy about the tank, explaining that Lord Kitchener was rather disturbed at so many people being present at the trials as he feared they would get talked about and the Germans would get to hear of them. It is a matter of history that after these trials fifty tanks were ordered and that Lord Kitchener went to his death before they were ready for the field. I do know, however, that he had great expectations of them, for he used to send for me pretty frequently while he was S. of S. and I was D.C.I.G.S. and he referred to them more than once in the course of conversation. His one fear was that the Germans would get to hear of them before they were ready."

Out of fairness to Lord Kitchener's memory I insert this letter here.

If this is the correct interpretation of Lord Kitchener's view, I can only express regret that he did not see fit to inform me of it at the time, in view of the fact that I was responsible as Minister of Munitions for the manufacture of these weapons.

The mention of this tank test recalls to my mind an incident which amused us all at the time, on the occasion of another similar test which took place on Lord Iveagh's estate. The elephantine monstrosity crashed through shrubberies, smashing young trees and bushes into the earth, and leaving behind it a wide trail of destruction. I went to inspect this mashed and mutilated track, and there in the middle of it I found a partridge's nest full of eggs — and, incredible to relate, not a single egg had been broken!

The work of production and supply naturally fell to the Ministry of Munitions, and on February 12th, 1916, a few days after the trials at Hatfield, the War Office formally placed an order for one hundred Tanks. Soon after manufacture had started, the number of Tanks asked for was increased to one hundred and fifty, and work was pressed on at full speed, since the necessity was urgent; but production presented special difficulties, because the type was entirely new and parts had still to be improvised. Shortly after the commencement of the Somme battle, the military authorities decided to make use of a number of the machines as soon as they could be produced, to help on our renewed offensive before the winter months, and in August, 1916, upwards of fifty were shipped over to France. On September 15th, just seven months after the signature of the "charter" authorising their construction, some forty-nine of these were thrown into the battle.

Not the least remarkable thing about the introduction of these new weapons is the fact that although thousands of persons of all grades necessarily knew all about them, the secret of the Tanks was so well kept that their first appearance came as a real surprise to the enemy. The very name "Tank" reflects the fact that during construction they were camouflaged even in name by being described as tanks and water carriers. Hence the tests at Hatfield were described on the programme as a "Tank Trial."

But the decision of the Army Chiefs to launch the first handful of these machines on a comparatively local operation in September, 1916, instead of waiting until a much larger number was available to carry out a great drive, has always appeared to me to have been a foolish blunder. It was contrary to the views of those who had first realised the need for such a weapon, had conceived it, fought for its adoption, designed it, produced it, and carried out the training of those who were to man it in the field. We made the same error as the Germans committed in April, 1915, when by their initial use of poison gas on a small sector alone they gave away the secret of a new and deadly form of attack, which, had it been used for the first time on a grand scale, might have produced results of a decisive character.

Mr. Montagu, who succeeded me as Minister of Munitions, supported the "tankers" in their earnest endeavours to keep the Tanks from being thrown into action until several hundred had been manufactured and manned by trained crews. I saw the Prime Minister, and begged him to intervene authoritatively. He did not disagree, but referred me to Sir William Robertson. I urged the C.I.G.S. to exert his influence with the Commander-in-Chief. He answered in his most laconic style, "Haig wants them." So the great secret was sold for the battered ruin of a little hamlet on the Somme, which was not worth capturing.

In spite, however, of this decision by the Commander-in-Chief in the field, and of the remarkable moral effect produced by the Tanks when they went into action, an atmosphere of doubt and prejudice lingered for some time at the War Office. On September 26th, 1916, the Army Council asked for an additional 1000 Tanks; but after the orders for these machines, and for the vast number of component parts required had been placed, and the complicated machinery for the production of this mass of materials had been set in action, I discovered that the demand had without my knowledge been cancelled by the Army Council. I at once countermanded this cancellation, and took steps to ensure that production should continue.

I retained my belief in the Tanks, and my interest in their development and use, throughout the war. Even when I had ceased to be directly concerned in their production or employment, the subject not infrequently came under my notice as Chairman of the War Cabinet to which questions were referred, owing to the disagreement of some of those responsible for the origin of the Tanks with the methods and tactics employed in their use. Questions of delay in production and supply, sometimes due to lack of continuity in the policy of G.H.Q., sometimes due to difficulties of manufacture, also came up. Indeed, there were moments when I regretted that in the case of the Tanks I had not taken the same course as I had adopted in regard to heavy artillery and machine guns, and organised at the outset for a larger supply than the War Office demanded.

I do not consider that the Tanks were correctly used until the Battle of Cambrai in November, 1917. This action, though indecisive, if not sterile of result — through no fault of the new arm — will, I think, go down to history as one of the epoch-making events of the war, marking the beginning of a new era in mechanical warfare. Nevertheless, even after the remarkable success of the machines, there was a slowness to realise and a reluctance to admit their potentialities, alike as savers of life and as begetters of victory. But by the summer of 1918 their value was definitely established. Joint arrangements were made by the British, French and Americans for their production on a great scale, and the plans for the continuation of operations during 1919 contemplated their employment, as well as that of cross-country tractors, in immense numbers. In fact, had the advance of the Allies in 1919 taken place, it would have been a devastating march of hordes of mechanical caterpillars.

8. Summary of Achievements of the Ministry

Complex problem of munition manufacture — Increase in shell production during first year — Supply of shells in Somme battle — Gun production — Evidence from the German side — Preparation for expanded output — Early criticism of the Ministry — Principles on which the Ministry was organised.

I will not weary my readers by further details of the complex problems which the Ministry of Munitions had to tackle. Some indications of their variety may be gleaned from the fact that the preparation of a single product such as a complete round of 18-pounder high-explosive shell involved the manufacture and assembly of seventy-eight accurately gauged components — fifteen for the cartridge, eleven for the shell, and fifty-two for the fuse, gaine, etc. And the main types of shell ran to some twenty-six different sizes and kinds.

By September, 1915, three months after I had taken over the Ministry of Munitions, we were producing 120,000 filled shells of all kinds weekly, as against 70,000 a week when I took over the job of munitions. In January, 1916, the figure had risen to 238,000 per week; and in mid-July, just after I had left the Ministry of Munitions to go to the War Office, the total weekly output of filled shell rose to 1,025,659.[1] These figures exclude our purchases from abroad. In commemoration of the passing of the million mark, Sir Eric

[1] These figures do not represent the full scale and weight of the increase. The most valuable results were in the increased production of heavy shells.

Geddes supplied me with a table, signed by himself, showing this remarkable progress, which I reproduce here.

To show the progress which was achieved by the methods we instituted in the Ministry of Munitions, I also give the following table, which sets out the total supplies of filled shell which were forthcoming from all sources during the ten months from August 1st, 1914, to June 30th, 1915, and in the twelve months, July, 1915, to June, 1916:

Total output of filled shell or complete rounds:

	Aug. 1914, to June, 1915.	July, 1915, to June, 1916.
Light	1,877,300	14,748,800
Medium	389,000	3,895,800
Heavy	26,500	566,500
Very Heavy	14,000	288,300
Total	2,306,800	19,499,400

On the 6th of July, 1916, the day on which I left the Ministry of Munitions to become Secretary of State for War, I was furnished with a report signed by Sir Walter Layton, which stated that:

"A year's output at the rate prevalent in 1914–1915 can now be obtained in the following periods:

Shell.	18-pdr. Ammunition	Three weeks
	Field Howitzer ditto	Two weeks
	Medium Gun and Howitzer ditto	Eleven days
	Heavy Howitzer ditto	Four days

"The present weekly output in the first three classes is practically equivalent to the whole stock in existence before the War. There was no stock of heavy howitzer ammunition before the War.

"A statement could be made on similar lines for other munitions."

Comparison of Shell Filling.

Weeks Ending Sept. 25th 1915, Jan.y 8th 1916 and July 15th 1916.

Nature.	Week Ending Sept 25th 1915.	Week Ending Jan.y 8th 1916	Week Ending July 15th 1916	Nature.	Week Ending Sept 25th 1915	Week Ending Jan.y 8th 1916	Week Ending July 15th 1916.
H.E.				Brought Forward.	33 111	86,937	593,396
				Shrapnel.			
18 Pr.	—	18,492	264,207	18 Pr. Home.	50,964	125,084	338 554
13 Pr	—	2,000	7,144	18 Pr. Abroad.	—	43,300	153,362
4.5"	20,989	36,985	180,411	15 Pr.	6,924	—	—
4.7"	626	7,284	8,538	13 Pr	14,740	1420	20,252
4.7" Chemical	—	—	3,512	4.5"	10,858	11,803	—
5"	—	3,770	3,071	4.5" Incendiary	—	—	790
60 Pr	3,153	7,912	30,288	10 Pr.	—	4,297	—
6"	5,451	5,025	39,181	2.75"	—	499	1,971
8"	1,585	4,019	30,469	4.7"	—	—	5,900
9.2" How.r	1,227	529	23,322	5"	442	127	131
9.2" Gun.	—	638	544	60 Pr.	2,862	7890	20,861
12"	80	283	2,491	6"	—	—	355
15"	—	—	218	Anti Aircraft Special	—	256	43,449
				Home	119,901	238,313	1,025,659
Forward	33,111	86,937	593,396	Total Abroad		43,300	153,362

	Total Rounds	Total Round 4.7" & Above	Tons of H.E.	Tons of Propellant
Week ending Sept 25th 1915	119,901	15,426	123	110
Week ending Jan.y 8th 1916	281,613	37,477	239	217
Week ending July 15th 1916	1,179,021	168,881	1,651	1,111
% age increase July 1916 over Sept 1915	883	995	1,242	910

With Sir Eric Geddes Compliments to Mr Lloyd George 15 July 1916

FACSIMILE OF TABLE SUPPLIED BY SIR ERIC GEDDES TO MR. LLOYD GEORGE, SHOWING THE REMARKABLE INCREASE IN SHELL PRODUCTION DURING THE FIRST YEAR OF THE MINISTRY OF MUNITIONS, SEPTEMBER, 1915, TO JULY, 1916

I have already shown how, when I took over the Ministry of Munitions in June, 1915, the allowance of shells per battery was 8 rounds per day (2 rounds per gun). Contrast this with the following extract from the diary of an artillery officer (taken from the Royal Artillery Commemoration Book):

"August 18th, 1916.

"The men are very tired, and the layers are nearly exhausted, although we have changed them as often as possible.

"My guns have already fired nearly 1000 rounds each and are almost too hot to touch. . . . At three in the morning I got a telephone message to say that the remainder of the programme was cancelled, and that I was to drop back to my normal 400 rounds a day."

The same officer, under the date August 1st, 1916, writes: "There are 15 batteries altogether . . . on a piece of ground four hundred yards long by two hundred wide."

Similar progress can be recorded with respect to artillery. At the outbreak of the war the total number of guns available was 1902, of which 1573 were light, and 329 were ranked as heavies at that date (*i.e.*, 4.7-inch guns and upwards). In the following ten months to June 30th, 1915, there were manufactured 1105 fresh guns, 1011 light, and 94 heavy. Between July 1st, 1915, and June 30th, 1916, the number of guns manufactured was 5006 — 4112 light and 894 heavy. The number of guns of 6-inch calibre and upwards was multiplied nearly fivefold.

I have given elsewhere the figures for the notable growth in our machine-gun supply in this period. Of grenades our output during the year July, 1915–June, 1916, was 27,000,000 as compared with 68,000 produced from August, 1914, to June, 1915. We similarly produced 4279 trench mortars as compared with the War Office 312.

The effect of this artillery can perhaps best be understood

by the evidence of some German records which I will quote. The history of the 27th (Württemberg) Division, one of the best divisions which fought at the Somme, states:

". . . A culminating point was reached which was never again approached. What we experienced surpassed all previous conception. The enemy's fire never ceased for an hour. It fell night and day on the front line and tore fearful gaps in the ranks of the defenders. It fell on the approaches to the front line, and made all movement towards the front hell. It fell on the rearward trenches and the battery positions and smashed men and material in a manner never seen before or since. It repeatedly reached even the resting battalions behind the front, and occasioned there terrible losses. *Our artillery was powerless against it.* . . . In the Somme fighting of 1916 there was a spirit of heroism which was never again found in the division, however conspicuous its fighting power remained until the end of the war."

The history continues that the men of 1918 had not the "temper, the steadfastness and the spirit of sacrifice of their predecessors. . . ."

Captain von Hentig, of the General Staff of the Guards Reserve Division, writes:

"The Somme was the muddy grave of the German field army, and of the faith in the infallibility of the German leadership, dug by British Industry and its shells. . . ."

Captain Hierl, an acute critic of the war, says of the Somme:

"The immense material superiority of the enemy did not fail to have its psychological effect on the German combatants. The enemy commanders may put this down to the credit side of their account as the profit of their attrition procedure. . . . The great enemy superiority in war apparatus and men was thus made to pull its weight, whilst the superiority of the German leadership and training did not get its proper return. . . ."

This evidence from the other side of the battle front demonstrates beyond challenge the importance of the success achieved by the Ministry of Munitions in equipping our forces for battle.

The figures I have given for the increase of output in 1915–16 represent only the first fruits of the hard work put into the organization of the Ministry of Munitions. But its greatest claim to recognition is due to the fact that it was organized with a view to expansion if the necessity arose. The business was planned from the commencement not to furnish adequate supplies for one final battle in 1916, but on the assumption the war might last for years, that there might be a succession of prolonged fights on a great scale, and that the demand for munitions of every kind would probably increase and not diminish. That is why up to the end of the war manufacture kept pace with the growing need for more guns, more trench mortars, more machine guns, more rifles, more ammunition, more explosives, more tanks, and more lorries.

When we organised our factories and ordered our machinery it was on the basis of a demand far beyond that which was contemplated by the Military Staffs in 1915. I was then accused of megalomania because I took this view of the undertaking which was entrusted to me. But in 1916, 1917, and 1918, the generals were very pleased that the swollen-headed plans of 1915 had all materialised and that the stocks in hand were ready to answer to every call made upon them by the soldiers at the front.

It was a much criticised Ministry. When we had hardly begun to pull things together, and to restore order out of chaos, all the confusion was attributed to the new Ministry. "The house that is building is never like the house that is built" and we were blamed for all the untidiness, for the mortar and material scattered about, for the girder skeleton, the unfilled framework, and the unfinished state of the structure.

When I first went to the Ministry of Munitions there was no organisation — when I left it there was no better organised Department in Whitehall, and I should like any of its critics to name one of the old, established Departments which was superior to it in all-round efficiency. The organisation of a big business from the foundation is not an easy task when all the circumstances are favourable. It is none the easier when the ground is cumbered with ill-designed, badly constructed and ramshackle buildings thrown about at random. It is especially difficult if the old directors from whom this part of the business has been wrenched, and who are thoroughly unfriendly to the new management, still retain an overriding jurisdiction in vital details.

That we should have succeeded in spite of these difficulties was a triumph for the capable men who threw the whole of their energies into the performance of their arduous duties. Without their ceaseless toil, and their great resourcefulness, achievement would have been quite unattainable in the time and under the conditions.

My view of the functions of the head of such a concern was that its success would depend upon his having a clear idea in his own mind as to the objectives which he should strive to attain, and a definite plan as to the best way of reaching them. After that success would depend upon his gift of choosing the right persons to direct every branch of the business, upon his power of drawing the best service out of them by encouragement, stimulation and support; upon the exercise of such a close and constant supervision over every detail (without getting lost in a jungle of details) as would enable him to discover where things were going wrong, and upon his taking the right steps to remedy deficiencies when he found them, and taking them in time.

I claim for my competent staff and for myself, that when at a critical moment in our history this crucial task devolved upon us, we did not fail our country.

CHAPTER III

ALLIED RELATIONS WITH AMERICA

A source of munitions supply — Problems of neutral countries in war time — Pre-war attitudes of the U.S.A. to Europe — Colonel House's interest in preservation of peace — Opinion in America during the early months of the war — Remoteness from the conflict — Ambiguity of the moral issue to American eyes — Hostility to Russia and Britain — America's interest in neutrality — Trouble caused by the British blockade — Allied perplexity as to President Wilson's attitude — The copper dispute — Success of British action — German treatment of neutral shipping — Decline of American interest in the war — Views in the Middle West — The *Dacia* incident — Germany's submarine blockade — The British retort: food and raw materials cut off — *Lusitania* sunk: Colonel House advises war — President Wilson's notes to Germany — Lord Robert Cecil's work in organising blockade — Roosevelt's demand for war — The sinking of the *Arabic* — German plots against U.S.A. factories — Success of American loan for the Allies.

DURING the first part of the war, I was not departmentally concerned in our diplomatic relations with the Neutral Powers. I had, however, a very definite interest in the attitude adopted by the United States of America towards the Allies, inasmuch as that great country represented the one important outside source of supply for munitions of war — a matter with which, as I have already related, I very early concerned myself. As a member of the first Cabinet Committee on Munitions Supply, I was already in October, 1914, promoting arrangements for large orders of munitions from the States, and as Chairman of the Munitions of War Committee, and later as Minister of Munitions, I was responsible for a steadily growing stream of supplies from across the Atlantic, which swelled by degrees to considerable dimensions, up to the point when we perfected arrangements for manufacture at home.

During this period, therefore, I had a very special incentive to watch the course of our relations with America. The maintenance of a good understanding with her was not only a necessary condition if our munition supplies were to continue uninterrupted, but a factor of vital importance in ensuring a just and satisfactory settlement of the struggle, whenever the hour of peace should strike.

When a war is in progress, neutral countries are often placed in an embarrassing position. Themselves at peace with all the world, they naturally seek to maintain their normal commercial relations with both the belligerent parties. In addition, they endeavour if possible to improve the shining hour by doing an increased and more profitable business, by supplying the additional demands created by the war at the inflated prices made possible by war's restriction of supplies. But while they thus earn greater profits, they are subject to greater hazards and less consideration. Nations fighting for their lives cannot always pause to observe punctilios. Their every action is an act of war, and their attitude to neutrals is governed, not by the conventions of peace, but by the exigencies of a deadly strife.

The country which is determined at all costs to remain neutral must therefore be prepared to pocket its pride and put up with repeated irritations and infringements of its interests by the belligerents on both sides; compensating itself for these annoyances by the enhanced profits of its war-time trade. Should the difficulties of neutrality prove too great, it is left with the choice either of treating the violation of its rights by one of the belligerent parties as a *casus belli,* or of taking sides, not on the strength of war-time incidents, but rather on its view of the rights and wrongs of the principal conflict. Such, briefly stated, was the problem which confronted the United States of America during the course of the World War. Prior to Armageddon, the firm tradition of the States was to hold utterly aloof from all concern with the tangled relations of the Old World — a tradition enshrined in its Doctrine of America for Americans, and let Europe keep its greedy hand off our continent. In turn, America would leave the rest of the world to Europe alone. Up to the date of the Great War, Americans maintained with ostentatious stiffness this traditional attitude. They sought to return to it with a snap when they let go their end of the Treaty of Versailles. Gradually in Europe, Asia and Polynesia alike American statesmen have been driven out of this position by inexorable facts.

It is true that Colonel House, President Wilson's "*alter ego*", was keenly interested in international affairs, and visited Europe in the summer of 1914 in the rôle of disinterested and benevolent adviser, to urge a better understanding between everybody and everybody else. It is to his credit and that of Mr. Theodore Roosevelt that they both understood that the theoretical aloofness of America no longer had any basis in realities, and that she would be intimately affected by any European upheaval, whether she professed to ignore it or not. The affable Colonel's visit to Europe was, through no fault of his own, fruitless. Wisdom expressed in gentle tones could not be heard above the roar of the nearing cataract. He found hearty sympathy for his ideas in England, a trumpeting militarism in Germany, and political chaos in France. The mass of the American public was as remote in its thoughts and interests from these things as though they were happenings on another planet.

During the opening stages of the war, opinion in the United States was quite as overwhelmingly in favour of maintaining firm neutrality towards the European struggle as opinion was in Britain three days before the declaration of war. With regard to the merits of the respective belligerents, the predominant opinion in America was supposed by this country and France to be pro-Ally, though there was a strong pro-German section among the large German-American population of the Middle West, and a chronic hostility to England amongst the Irish-Americans. The intellectuals were believed to be pro-Ally. A careful sounding of opinion among American universities and colleges carried out by Sir Gilbert Parker, the distinguished Canadian novelist, in October, 1914, showed an overwhelming sympathy for the Allies. But despite this general tendency, it would be true to say that on the whole, opinion in the States was neither pro-Ally nor pro-German, but simply and solely pro-American. In war, sympathy is a long way off support. President Wilson was universally acclaimed when in mid-August he made a speech calling on the citizens of the United States to observe strict neutrality in act and speech, and at that date even Mr. Theodore Roosevelt rejoiced that his country was geographically able to keep out of the fight. An analysis of the American Press made by Sir Gilbert Parker, at the end of September, 1914, showed that while far more of the leading papers were friendly to the Allies than to Germany, the majority were definitely neutral, and viewed the merits on both sides with a detached impartiality.

Belgium was thousands of miles away from Illinois. German destroyers and submarines at Ostend were not within a few steam hours of New York. German guns at Calais could not block the principal highway to America's powerful ports. German Zeppelins could not bomb Washington and kill women and children in their homes. These things were very remote. We cannot impute this indifference to callousness. An earthquake in Japan with a loss of tens of thousands of lives does not occupy as many columns of a British newspaper as does a railway accident near Carlisle with the loss of a score of lives.

Apart from this, the moral issues were not so free from ambiguity to the American conscience. Many people in this country were unreasonably astonished at this attitude on the part of America. Filled with anger at Germany's wanton aggression in Belgium, and with fear at the threatening monster of Prussian militarism, they could not understand how the great Democracy of the New World should hesitate for an instant about the merits of the issue upon which we had drawn our sword, or should fail to ally itself with us in defence of liberty and justice.

But to the onlookers in America, the issue was not so simple. On August 22nd, 1914, Colonel House wrote to President Wilson:

> "The saddest feature of the situation to me is that there is no good outcome to look forward to. If the Allies win, it means largely the domination of Russia on the Continent of Europe; and if Germany wins, it means the unspeakable tyranny of militarism for generations to come."

Britain and France never quite realised the handicap to their propaganda in neutral countries which was involved in the alliance with the Czarist régime. America shuddered at the idea of any close association with the Government of Russia — brutal, tyrannical, and corrupt, in fact, rotten to the core — and that went far to neutralise the horror felt at the Belgian tragedy. America also had a large and politically important Irish-American population, trained to hatred of England as to a religion. Let us be fair. Britain had for centuries given cruel cause for this rooted animosity, and we had not yet repaired the wrong we had burnt into the sensitive and retentive Irish soul. Add to this the fact that Americans were by long tradition accustomed to think of Britain as the despotic monarchy from whose greedy clutch the States had wrested themselves free in the heroic struggles of the War of Independence. There were other considerations which compelled neutrality. The German population in America were a highly respected, diligent, and peaceable element of the community, with characteristics that furnished little evidence in support of the legend of Prussian ferocity. Moreover, they commanded millions of useful votes, which might determine the issue of crucial elections. In these circumstances it will be clear that the general sympathy of America with the Allied cause was bound to be considerably qualified. Americans might strongly desire to see the Allies victorious, but not strongly enough to be prepared to endure with patience losses or inconvenience to themselves, or risks to their respective political parties, as the price of Allied victory.

In short, America was not bound by treaty commitments to enter the war on either side. While the predominant opinion (whenever an opinion was formed) was that, on balance, the Allies were in the right, that verdict was too qualified to impose an obligation of honour to march with them to and through the gates of hell. Failing such obligation, the issue of neutrality or participation in the war became one purely of relative expediency for America. It was her interest to maintain her trade, her prestige, the security of her citizens, and to keep her young men out of the shambles. She would only be forced to fight if fighting was better calculated than neutrality to defend these interests.

It so fell out that while American intellectual sympathies were in the main with the Allies, American commercial interests were open to more frequent and obvious interference by them. Germany's chief power was on land, Britain's on the sea. Germany's invasion of Belgium, her devastation of France, might rouse disinterested wrath in America. But it did not touch American pockets. On the other hand, Britain's firm measures to prevent contraband of war from reaching Germany, and her wide and constantly widening interpretation of contraband, caused serious inconvenience to American shipping, and direct interference with Amercan business. Time and time again, the friction created by this interference generated between the two countries a perilous heat, which seemed to be within an ace of producing a rupture of diplomatic relations. Once or twice the language of protest bordered on the minatory. These protests undoubtedly introduced a certain element of timidity into our blockade, and Germany profited by the relaxation. Later on, Lord Robert Cecil tightened up our clutch.

To be weighed against these annoyances was the fact that Britain was far and away the wealthiest of the belligerents and was able to place in the United States — and pay cash for — orders for colossal war supplies for herself and her Allies. If we were interfering with America's potential trade with our enemies, at least we were providing her with a magnificent market in Britain, France, and Russia, which stimulated her industries to an unprecedented level of activity. This fact had its influence in holding back the hand of the American Government whenever, excited to intense irritation by some new incident of the blockade, it contemplated retaliatory measures.

Throughout 1914 and 1915, until the prospect of the presidential election of 1916 began to loom high above the horizon and import a new complication of the issues, the story of the relations between America and the belligerents is that of a country driven backwards and forwards between the two sides by an alternation of incidents, any one of which might easily have tipped the scales for war, had it not been counterpoised by new troubles on the other side; and had it not also been for the stubborn determination of President

Wilson to keep his country out of the fight if he possibly could.

The opening weeks of the war found American opinion as I have said, strongly on the Allied side. We never quite knew where President Wilson's real sympathies lay. We felt that in the tremendous struggle which was constantly before his eyes, he would have been more than human had his heart not been engaged on one side or the other, whatever his hand might do or his tongue might speak. But his deportment was so studiously unpleasant to both sides that they each suspected him of being antipathetic to their own side. We only knew for a fact that the President was severe in his judgment of Allied actions, and we did not realise that this was due to the fear lest his private sympathies should pervert the strict impartiality of attitude which he was imposing on himself.

Very shortly, the use which Britain made of her sea power to prevent supplies reaching the Central Powers, even through neutral countries, provoked an outcry in America, particularly from the powerful Copper Trust. Copper was a vital necessity for munitions, and we did our best to stop any supplies of it from reaching Germany. Had Germany been confined to the use of her own ports, this would have been quite a simple matter. But she was bordered by neutral States — Holland, Scandinavia, and at first Italy — and consignments, ostensibly destined for these countries, were really being sent for her benefit. And the United States were very large producers of copper.

On October 5th, 1914, Sir Cecil Spring-Rice, our Ambassador in Washington, wrote: "The copper interests here are very powerful. . . . We shall have to find some means of crippling Krupp without ruining the mining States here, who possess the ear of the Secretary of State and have a commanding influence in the Senate."

On November 3rd, he wrote: "We have command of the seas and this is a reason why we are likely to fall foul of all the neutrals. The American conscience is on our side, but the American pocket is being touched. Copper and oil are dear to the American heart and the export is a matter of great importance. We are stopping the export and the consequence is a howl which is increasing in volume. We should probably do the same. But the howl may become very furious soon. . . ."

Early in November, 1914, in accordance with a plan prepared by Mr. Leverton Harris, an agent was sent to New York from this country to attempt to solve this problem by buying up as much as possible of the American stock of copper on condition that the producers should undertake to sell only to purchasers approved by us. But this business proposition was not successful, for pro-German influences were exerted to defeat it. We then proceeded, at Gilbraltar and elsewhere, to hold up all copper consignments to neutral countries until we were satisfied as to the *bona fides* of the consignees. The Governments of the neutral countries in Europe came to the aid of their manufacturers by prohibiting the export of copper, which simplified our release of cargoes to meet their *bona fide* requirements. We then told the American copper producers that if they continued to sell copper to Germany, we should buy none from them ourselves, but should hold up all their European consignments. Two of the largest American refining companies promptly entered into an agreement with us, and before long most of the others were glad to come into line. One of the last to come in was the great Guggenheim group. Its hand was forced by an announcement made, in reply to a question in Parliament, that the firms whose consignments were safeguarded by agreements with us were welcome to announce the fact, so that orders might be placed with them. Thereupon Guggenheim cabled their representative in London to sign an agreement with the Admiralty.

By the beginning of March, 1915, we had secured control of 95 per cent. of the exportable copper of the United States, and the powerful influence of the Copper Trust was no longer a menace to good relations between us and the States.

Fortunately for the Allies, American annoyance at any action on our part which hampered their trade would ere long be counterbalanced by anger at some more exasperating deed by the Germans. If, in the autumn of 1914, we were holding up neutral vessels and requiring certificates of ultimate destination before we would release their cargoes, the Germans were sowing mines all round the narrow seas, which sank neutral shipping without warning, and were brutally bombarding the unprotected watering places of Scarborough and Whitby. In January, 1915, the Germans took the further step of bombing with Zeppelins the towns of King's Lynn and Yarmouth, and at the end of that month their submarines began a form of attack which was in the end to bring the United States into the war, by sinking unarmed merchant vessels in the open sea.

While these acts increased the moral condemnation of Germany by American opinion, it remained the case that our actions regarding contraband were a more frequent irritation. From a well-informed source we learnt in January, 1915, that the United States was growing less interested in the war as a main item of news. "The air-raid has been commented on in the strongest terms in every paper I have seen, but these things no longer excite surprise. I think I told you that I had seen signs of the public being bored with the war. The proof came last week when the earthquake was reported and the war went to the second or third page." And from another source we were told: "There is a lack of proportion in the information we have concerning the British Navy. We scarcely ever hear of it except when some British ship is blown up by a German torpedo, or when a British ship holds up an American cargo. You can readily see the dangerous psychological effect of this . . . 'War news' no longer sells. But 'interference with American trade' does sell. It sells, and it has a certain unfortunate effect upon what I call the 'headline mind'."

As to the general sentiment in the Middle West, we were told: "The German Army wins admiration for its efficiency and courageous performance, but sympathy with its purposes or ideals was lost the day it stepped into Belgium. The war is deplored as unnecessary and preventable, and no one desires anything more than a speedy and conclusive peace. But it must be conclusive. Peace without definite victory would satisfy no one. 'This thing has got started,' they say, 'so let's have it finished once for all.' Meanwhile everyone out here is very busy with his own affairs."

Towards the end of January, 1915, an adroit attempt was made to embroil us with America. The *Dacia,* a German merchantman, laid up in America since July, 1914, was bought by a German-American, registered as an American vessel and sent with a cargo of cotton for Bremen, via Rotterdam. We made it known that we refused to recognise the transfer of flag, and Germans waited hopefully for us to seize an American ship and thus produce a storm in the States. The *Dacia* was duly seized, but by the French Navy, and the plot miscarried. The French cause was popular in the States, and hitherto they had played a minor part in the capture of contraband. President Wilson could of course protest to France, and did so without avail. But his protest did not mark a culmination — perhaps critical — of a series of protests, as it would have done had Britain been the culprit.

Germany thereupon proceeded to announce a submarine blockade of Britain, and declared she would sink every merchant vessel in the seas surrounding these islands after February 18th, 1915, and would not guarantee safety to passengers or crews, even of neutral shipping, since British vessels might be hoisting neutral flags in these dangerous waters, and her submarines would therefore ignore the nationality of flags. This called forth a very strong note from President Wilson, to which Germany only replied that if he would stop all exports of munitions to the Allies, and take steps to ensure supplies of raw materials and food to Germany, they would reconsider their attitude.

Britain replied to the submarine campaign by an Order in Council virtually blockading Germany. We did not actually use the technical term "Blockade", as what we announced was not merely or mainly a close investment of German ports, but a cutting off of supplies for Germany by detaining all vessels carrying goods of presumed enemy destination, ownership, or origin. This was of course a novel though obvious variation of the principle of blockade, made necessary by modern progress in transport, which turned every neutral harbour on the Continent into a potential German port. Naturally the flutter of notes back and forth across the Atlantic grew denser and intenser.

During these months, Colonel House was visiting the belligerent countries of Europe as the President's emissary, to take soundings as to the possible terms of peace. His presence, and the understanding he achieved of the practical realities of the situation, doubtless helped to ease friction between us and America. But his peace efforts were doomed to frustration. At that stage of the war, he found in Britain a readiness to consider a peace based on restoration and indemnity for Belgium, but Germany refused to promise restoration, and would not hear of indemnity.

On May 7th, 1915, while Colonel House was in London, news came of the sinking of the *Lusitania*. That put a sharp end to all possibility of promoting peace talk between England and Germany. The question of the moment became rather whether the United States themselves could any longer maintain their neutrality. The Colonel himself held that they could not and should not hold back any longer. He wrote on May 9th, to President Wilson:

". . . Our intervention will save, rather than increase the loss of life.

"America has come to the parting of the ways, when she must decide whether she stands for civilised or uncivilised warfare. We can no longer remain neutral spectators. Our action in this crisis will determine the part we will play when peace is made, and how far we may influence a settlement for the lasting good of humanity. We are being weighed in the balance, and our position amongst the nations is being assessed by mankind." [1]

President Wilson sent a strong note to Germany: but it was a protest, not an ultimatum. The Austrian Ambassador at Washington sounded Bryan, the Secretary of State, and got the assurance that America did not mean to fight. He promptly advised Berlin, which was encouraged to be unaccommodating to Wilson. The click of the President's typewriter had no deadlier rattle behind it. House, meantime, was trying to arrange that Germany would abandon her submarine warfare if England ceased to stop food supplies for Germany. Sir Edward Grey was prepared to consider this.[2] But he never consulted the Cabinet as to this proposal. Had he done so they would have turned it down emphatically. Whether he consulted the Prime Minister before expressing his readiness to enter into an arrangement on this basis I am not prepared to say. Germany, however,

[1] "Intimate Papers" of Colonel House, Vol. I, page 434.
[2] *Ibid.*, page 443.

stiffened by the reassurance that America would in no circumstances fight, refused the proposal, and said that she had plenty of food. What she wanted was raw materials. Naturally there could be no thought of letting these in for her munition manufacturers, and the proposal fell through. Had Germany accepted Colonel House's suggestion, the whole course of the war might have been changed. There certainly would have been no starving population in Germany in 1918. That means there would have been no revolution in November, 1918, and the war would have been prolonged for another year. But apart from that, Germany might not have declared that indiscriminate sinking of all ships which brought America into the war. Once more German military arrogance had blundered and by doing so had saved us from one of our worst blunders.

In connection with our blockade policy I should like to pay tribute here to the services rendered by Lord Robert Cecil in pressing forward the firm maintenance and full development of our activities in this field. When he became Undersecretary of State for Foreign Affairs on May 31st, 1915, the Reprisals Order was already in force. Nevertheless, there was hesitation in high places about maintaining its provisions, as exemplified by Sir Edward Grey's readiness to consider abandoning an essential part of it on Colonel House's suggestion. Such hesitation was not shared by Lord Robert Cecil. In Council and in public he urged its strict observance. His advice was consistently in favour of bold measures. His activities in the Foreign Office were directed to the same end. Ultimately, in February, 1916, it was decided to appoint a Minister of Blockade, with Cabinet rank, to coördinate the work of all the various Committees and Departments dealing with this matter in its various aspects. Lord Robert Cecil was the obvious choice for this post, and he agreed to undertake it — without salary — in addition to his work as Undersecretary to the Foreign Office. He was appointed on February 23rd, 1916, and it was largely due to him that the great national and international organization of the blockade weapon was tightened so that it became one of the decisive factors in our ultimate victory.

Notes continued to pass between the United States and Germany throughout 1915 about the *Lusitania.* That a thousand noncombatant passengers — men, women, and children — including over a hundred American citizens, should have been thus massacred in cold blood was a severe strain on the President's pacifism. He stood it, although Germany repeatedly refused his request that she should at least disavow the action of her submarine commander. Gerard, the American Ambassador in Berlin, wrote to Colonel House on June 1st, that: "It is the German hope to keep the *Lusitania* matter 'jollied along' until the American people get excited about baseball or a new scandal and forget." President Wilson put the best face he could upon the matter by making a speech in which he suggested that the American people were "too proud to fight." He shrank from taking the action urged upon him by his principal adviser. Mr. Theodore Roosevelt launched a characteristic attack on the President's inaction:

"Unless we act with immediate decision and vigour we shall have failed in the duty demanded by humanity at large, and demanded even more clearly by the self-respect of the American Republic. . . . For many months our Government has preserved between right and wrong a neutrality which would have excited the emulous admiration of Pontius Pilate, the arch-typical neutral of all time.". . .[1]

The situation was complicated by the fact that while

[1] "Fear God and Take Your Own Part", page 353.

notes were passing about the *Lusitania,* another liner, the *Arabic,* was also torpedoed and sunk. Colonel House now wanted the President to proceed to war without further notes, and for a time the situation was exceedingly strained. But the German Government promised to instruct their submarine commanders not to sink further liners without warning, and after very strong pressure even went so far as to proffer a tentative disavowal of the action of the submarine commander who sank the *Arabic.* This belated action just — only just — enabled the "will to peace" of the President to survive the presidential election.

The situation was not eased by information coming to light just at this time, through an indiscretion of the Austrian Ambassador, that the Austrian Embassy, aided by Von Papen, the German military attaché, was planning to cripple American munition plants, so as to interfere with supplies for the Allies. Von Papen and Boy-Ed, the German attachés, and Dumba, the Austrian Ambassador, were sent home, but President Wilson still kept his temper. The presidential election was drawing nigh, and Wilson was determined to stand for reëlection as the man who kept America out of the war.

Probably there was no very powerful desire among the American people at this stage to join in the fight. On September 17th, 1916, Spring-Rice wrote: "The majority want to make money and not to make war." In November he reported that anti-German feeling was growing stronger, together with the view that a victory of the Central Powers would be an immense calamity to the States. But in practice this sympathy showed itself rather in a greater eagerness to do business with the Allies than to make war on Germany. At the beginning of October we raised a loan on the American market to finance purchases of supplies. The loan was for $500,000,000, secured on the joint credit of France and Britain, in the form of 5 per cent. five-year bonds. In two days it was over-subscribed by about $200,000,000. As a proof of good will to the Allied cause, this was very gratifying. But Sir Cecil Spring-Rice, writing on October 7th, 1916, of the success of the loan, declared again: "It cannot be too often repeated that the American people are determined to hold aloof if they possibly can, and that the Government cannot take any action of which the great mass of the people do not approve."

Such, in brief outline, was the course and temper of American neutrality prior to the winter of 1916, when the reëlected President made his public bid for peace, to which I shall have later on to refer.

But in the course of these first two years of war, President Wilson was continually on the alert for an opportunity to intervene and shorten or end the conflict. One effort in particular which he made, in the winter and early spring of 1915–16, was of special interest. As I was called into the discussion that followed, it is an essential part of my War Memoirs.

CHAPTER IV

PRESIDENT WILSON'S PEACE MOVES

Wilson's letter to the belligerents — The nations committed to war -- Mr. Thomas Nelson Page's letter from Rome — Peace whispers at end of 1915 — President Wilson's anxiety for peace — Colonel House's peace mission — Attitude of Germany — House's proposals to Paris and London: conditional American intervention — French attitude — Divided views in Britain — Sir John Bradbury's doubts — Pessimism of Mr. John M. Keynes — An acrobatic economist — Scepticism of the Keynes theory — Mr. Keynes as the prophet Baxter — Dinner with Colonel House — My views as to the right procedure — Colonel House accepts the conditions — Why no conference was summoned — President Wilson's "Probably" — America's entry would have shortened the war — Germany's peace terms — Wilson's resolute pacifism — Colonel Roosevelt's letter — America opposed to a bold policy.

SEVERAL tentative movements were made in neutral countries for mediation during the first few weeks of the war, but they came to nothing. Whether President Wilson could have succeeded in arresting the mad plunge of Europe into war, had he intervened authoritatively and in time, will always remain a matter of conjecture. He made no effort. The suddenness with which the negotiations flared up and exploded the powder magazine probably took him by surprise. In that respect he was not alone.

When the war broke out, President Wilson made a well-intentioned but quite ineffectual gesture. He wrote on August 5, 1914, to each of the belligerent monarchs a letter in the following terms:

"Sir, — As official head of one of the Powers signatory to the Hague Convention, I feel it to be my privilege and my duty under Article 3 of the Convention to say to your Majesty in a spirit of most earnest friendship, that I should welcome an opportunity to act in the interest of European peace, either now or at any time that might be thought more suitable as an occasion to serve your Majesty and all concerned in a way that would afford me lasting cause for gratitude and happiness. — WOODROW WILSON."

While that letter was crossing the Atlantic, the Austrians were pressing down on their coveted prey, Serbia; French troops were singing as they swept over the frontier into the lost provinces of Alsace and Lorraine; the German General Staff was at last putting into effect its darling plan, minutely elaborated for years past, of an advance through Belgium that would encircle and destroy the army of France, and bring decisive victory in six weeks. To attempt to hold back the momentum of these vast forces with an offer of mediation was at that stage as futile as to think of arresting the descending blade of the guillotine with an appeal for mercy. Where Sir Edward Grey's proposal for a conference, made before war was declared, was scarcely heard (it certainly was not heeded) in the confusion, the polite and formal plea of a comparatively unweaponed America for pause and reflection, coming as it did when armies were on foreign soil, could serve only to place on record her good will to all parties alike.

The replies were not hurried, and when they came they were universally discouraging. Having started, however reluctantly, the combatant nations all meant to fight it out to the bitter end. Germany was on the whole winning, so her rulers were in no mood for peace. France was pulling herself together after an inglorious beginning. Britain had barely started, but her stubborn spirit had caught a fire which could not easily be put out. Austria, in the act of inflicting what she thought would be an easy castigation on Serbia, had the whip wrenched out of her hand by the gallant army of the Serbs, and her flesh stung with the shame of a scourging inflicted upon her by the people she had despised. She was in a mood to revenge the humiliation by overwhelming force. The Russian tradition had always been to make a clumsy start. The defeat of Tannenberg did not, therefore, dismay this loose-limbed but stout-hearted giant. No one wanted peace. Every nation engaged in the struggle resented the idea of stopping the fight once it had begun. There were far fewer pacifists amongst them on January 1st, 1915, than on August 1st, 1914. There was a deep instinct in the minds of men that this conflict had been coming for a long time, and once it had begun it was better to get it over and done with. The voice of the mediator, was, therefore, not heard in any land, and his rôle was everywhere an unpopular one. President Wilson's time for intervention had already passed, and it could not be resumed until the nations were beginning to feel the strain.

The message sent in November, 1914, by Mr. Thomas Nelson Page, the American Ambassador in Rome, to Mr. W. J. Bryan is remarkable, not only for its picture of the belligerent frame of mind but also for the prophetic vision of post-war troubles:

"American Embassy, Rome,
November 19, 1914
[received December 7.]

". . . I am conscious here of a strong undercurrent of conviction that when one side or the other in the present war prevails, America will become the next objective of attack, either on the part of Germany or of Japan, as the case may be. It seems to be considered that the War will not end until one or the other party is absolutely discouraged and that no tenders of friendly offices will avail before that crisis. Also there is frequent expression of the thought that even should the War be ended in its present status, it would only be a truce until the belligerents, more especially Germany, had recuperated sufficiently to attack again with better success, and that permanency of peace will depend on a condition in which absolute disarmament can be insisted upon. . . .

THOMAS NELSON PAGE."

At the close of 1915 there was some peace talk whispered about. The losses on all sides had been beyond anything the students of war had ever contemplated. The advantage was still with the Central Powers, but it was becoming increasingly clear to them that they could not cash their gains without incurring further sacrifices even more appalling than those which they had already sustained. The great new army of the British Empire, well drilled and fully equipped, would come into action in its full strength for the first time in the impending campaign of 1916. Neutral spectators had, therefore, some hope that the hour was propitious for taking definite steps towards mediation.

President Wilson was anxious for peace. Apart from the fact that his humane instincts were horrified with the slaughter and barbarity of the war on land and sea, his embarrassments as a neutral were increasing and intensifying each successive month. As I have already related, the British were searching his ships and the Germans were threatening to sink them. The British blockade was interfering daily with American commerce. That roused angry resentment in the American breast. On the other hand, the German counter-measures were an outrage on humanity. The reverberations of the war in the American electorate were complicating American politics, and the presidential election was not so far off. There was a powerful German-American vote which resented the tolerance extended by the Administration to the manufacture of munitions of war for the Allies. There was a still more powerful Irish-American vote which hated Britain. Apart from these groups, American sentiment was on the whole on the side of the Allies. The wanton trampling down of Belgium by the German legions was largely responsible for the creation of that opinion. War against the Allies was impossible. No Government could have carried the American public into such a war. Intervention on the other side would also mean a divided nation. The poor President was, therefore, harassed and perplexed by a terrible dilemma. What would suit him best would be the part of peacemaker. It fitted in with his temperament as well as with his political difficulties. He therefore sent Colonel House from the ark as a dove of peace to spy out the waters of the deluge in Europe and to report to his chief whether there was a sign of subsidence and any peak visible on which the harbinger of peace could plant her feet.

In this capacity Colonel House visited France, Germany, and Britain with a view to taking soundings about the possibility of bringing the war to an end, and as to the response which would be accorded to any proposal made by President Wilson in that direction. He flew from capital to capital. In Germany he found no prospect of any readiness to consider a peace which would conform to the President's ideals, let alone to the aims of the Allies. The farthest he got with Von Bethmann-Hollweg was that Germany might consent to relinquish her conquests of Belgian and French territory in return for a sufficient indemnity. In his highly interesting "Intimate Papers" he gives a graphic account of the American Ambassador's interview with the German Emperor:

> "The Kaiser talked of peace and how it should be made and by whom, declaring that 'I and my cousins, George and Nicholas, will make peace when the time comes.' Gerard says to hear him talk one would think that the German, English, and Russian peoples were so many pawns upon a chess board. He made it clear that mere democracies like France and the United States could never take part in such a conference. His whole attitude was that war was a royal sport, to be indulged in by hereditary monarchs and concluded at their will. . . ."[1]

Colonel House reached Paris with an intensified conviction that the German Government would not agree to

[1] "Intimate Papers", Vol. II, page 139.

peace terms which even the most moderate of Allied statesmen could accept. Thereafter he developed the line that any American intervention must take the form of a threat to Germany, followed if necessary by open hostilities, with a view to shortening the war; and, moreover, that such intervention was necessary not only to shorten the duration of the conflict, but to ensure that the peace ultimately made should be one of justice embodying the ideals of the President, rather than one of victorious Allies carving up their defeated foe.

To this end, Colonel House urged both in Paris and in London that at a suitable moment the Allies should accept an offer from the President to call a conference of all the belligerents to discuss terms on which the war might be ended; it being understood that if terms acceptable to Wilson were agreed to by the Allies but rejected by Germany, the United States should come in on the side of the Allies to compel Germany's agreement.

It is difficult to come to any clear conclusion as to the reception accorded to the House mission in Paris. He himself clearly formed a favourable impression of the attitude of M. Briand, who was then Prime Minister of France, towards his pacific efforts. But M. Briand was one of those pleasant men who take a long time to understand, and after a prolonged acquaintance you were never quite sure that you knew him sufficiently well even then. He was an enigma even to his closest friends, and no one ever knew what his innermost thoughts were on any subject. However, by disposition he was a conciliator. He had a greater personal delight in reconciliation than in strife. But although inscrutable where his own individual opinions were concerned, there could be no doubt as to his sensitiveness to parliamentary opinion. And any suspicion of leanings towards pacifism was a crime in Paris. M. Clemenceau was a typical representative of the general attitude of the governing classes in the French metropolis. As for the French peasantry, they had resigned themselves to the leadership of Paris, and they were prepared to go through right to the end if those who were in supreme charge of the interests of their country felt it was necessary for the honour and safety of France to fight on. M. Briand could hardly have dragged France into a Peace Conference at that date unless he had had the most complete assurance that the terms offered would be favourable to France and would contain a guarantee for her future safety. Any rumour of a disposition on his part to countenance such a parley would have ensured his immediate downfall. British Ministers, therefore, felt that Colonel House's sanguine disposition had misled him into taking too hopeful a view of the coöperation of France in an endeavour to initiate *pourparlers* with an enemy whose arms, taking the terrain of the war as a whole, were triumphant in the East and the West.

In Britain, the British Cabinet was divided between two points of view. It was not so much that there were some Members of the Cabinet in favour of peace and others opposed, as that the majority were still convinced of the certainty of ultimate victory, while a formidable minority entertained doubts of the possibility of success, if the war were prolonged beyond this year. The leading members of this defeatist junta were the Chancellor of the Exchequer, and the President of the Board of Trade. Their pessimism had deepened Sir Edward Grey's natural gloom. Mr. Runciman was anxious as to the effect of the submarine campaign upon our sea transport. In his opinion our shipping capacity had already been strained to the utmost by the demands made upon it for the feeding of our population and of our armies, and the carriage of essential raw material for ourselves and our Allies. A few more thousands of our tonnage sunk by the German swordfish that swarmed around the approaches to our harbours and we could not carry on. Mr. M'Kenna had also serious misgivings as to the financial position. He doubted whether it would be possible much longer for us to raise the funds necessary to enable us to finance essential purchases for ourselves and the Allies in countries across the sea, at the rate we were then expending our reserves on the war. He circulated to the Cabinet in September, 1915, two dismal papers from Sir John Bradbury and Mr. J. M. Keynes respectively. Sir John Bradbury was an exceptionally able man, with exceptionally orthodox ideas about finance and the gold standard. He ends an elaborate and discouraging review of the financial possibilities with the conclusion:

"It seems clear . . . that unless there is either an early and very large reduction of civil and military consumption, an increase of production by the withdrawal of a part of our forces in the field and their return to civil employment or a drastic curtailment of credits to Allies, further borrowing here will only be possible at the price of such an inflation of credit in relation to available commodities as will finally upset the balance of exchange and seriously impair our power to purchase either munitions or foodstuffs in America."

Mr. Keynes was more alarming and much more jargonish in his formidable paper. With the help of what he hints is an over-sanguine estimate of our borrowing possibilities in America, we would get through to the end of the financial year, *i.e.*, the 31st of March, 1916, provided our liabilities were not increased by fresh orders — he does not specifically mention our orders at the Ministry of Munitions for machine tools and rifles — but after that, the Deluge — unless peace intervenes. As to our existing commitments:

" . . . *We ought to be able to do this without producing a catastrophe in the current financial year,* [i.e., up to 31st March,

1916] *provided peace puts us in a position to cancel the inflationism immediately afterwards. Otherwise the expenditure of the succeeding months will rapidly render our difficulties insupportable. This leads us to the meaning of 'inflationism' and the consequences of depending upon it.*"

Then comes a professional exposition on the character and inevitability of "the catastrophe", and he concludes:

"The alternatives presented to us are, therefore, alternatives of degree. If by flinging out our resources lavishly we could be sure of finishing the war early next spring, I estimate that they might be about equal to our needs. If, on the other hand, it would be over-sanguine to anticipate this, it must be considered whether it is more desirable to average our expenditure, or alternatively, to be lavish until about next January, to appreciate the prospects in front of us somewhat suddenly at about that date, and then, having regard to the near future, to curtail rigorously, and tell our Allies that for the future they must look to themselves.

"It is certain that our present scale of expenditure is only possible as a violent temporary spurt to be followed by a strong reaction; that the limitations of our resources are in sight; and that, in the case of any expenditure, we must consider not only as heretofore, whether it would be useful, but also whether we can afford it."

Mr. Winston Churchill, in one of his amusing outbursts, once said that this country was governed by the 31st of March. Put the British Empire at one end of the scale and the 31st of March at the other, and the latter would win every time. That was Mr. M'Kenna's view.

The Chancellor and President of the Board of Trade more than hinted at the possibility of starvation for our sea-fed island. Mr. M'Kenna's nerve was shaken by these vaticinations of his chief adviser, Mr. J. M. Keynes. The latter was much too mercurial and impulsive a counsellor for a great emergency. He dashed at conclusions with acrobatic ease. It made things no better that he rushed into opposite conclusions with the same agility. He is an entertaining economist whose bright but shallow dissertations on finance and political economy, when not taken seriously, always provide a source of innocent merriment to his readers. But the Chancellor of the Exchequer, not being specially gifted with a sense of humour, sought not amusement but guidance in this rather whimsical edition of Walter Bagehot, and thus he was led astray at a critical moment. Mr. Keynes was for the first time lifted by the Chancellor of the Exchequer into the rocking-chair of a pundit, and it was thought that his very signature appended to a financial document would carry weight. It seems rather absurd when now not even his friends — least of all his friends — have any longer the slightest faith in his judgments on finance.

Luckily Mr. Bonar Law and I knew well what value to attach to any counsel which came from the source of the Chancellor's inspiration and, therefore, we both treated the fantastic prediction of British bankruptcy "in the spring" with the measure of respect which was due to the volatile soothsayer who was responsible for this presage of misfortune. I was still less impressed by these prophecies of evil because I knew it was part of the campaign which the Treasury were waging against my great gun programme. They had succeeded in scaring Lord Kitchener. I knew more about the resources of credit of this country. Mr. Bonar Law urged that American (North and South) securities held in this country should be mobilised and sold or pledged to pay for purchases overseas. This practical suggestion was subsequently adopted and all went well.

When the hour of indicated doom struck and we still bought greater quantities than ever of food, raw material and munitions from abroad and were paying for them and our credit was still high, the date of impending collapse was postponed until the autumn. The fall of the year and the fall of the British Empire would arrive on the scene arm in arm. In his forecasts Mr. Keynes made the same mistake which had brought the late Mr. Baxter's prophecies into disrepute. He had been too definite in the dates for the end of the world. Some of these had already passed. When the fateful days arrived without any indication of the heavens above us being rolled together as a scroll, a fresh date farther on was chosen. You may do that kind of thing once and perhaps twice, but repeated failures discredit the prophet. The Cabinet as a whole were not, therefore, at this time unduly depressed by Mr. M'Kenna's pictures of approaching famine because they had ceased to believe in the impish Baxter who at the Chancellor's invitation had wandered into the Treasury.

After Colonel House had put his views before Sir Edward Grey and the Prime Minister, the latter decided that it would be desirable that other Ministers should be brought into consultation. It was therefore arranged that on February 14th, 1916, Mr. Asquith, Sir Edward Grey, Mr. Balfour and myself should be invited to meet Colonel House at dinner at Lord Reading's house. He there placed before us his ideas as to the summoning by President Wilson of a conference of all the belligerents to discuss peace terms. Colonel House has given some account of this important talk in his "Intimate Papers", but that account is by no means complete, and unless the whole purport of the conversations is given, the public cannot judge the reasons for the failure of this peace move. He states in his book that at the Reading dinner the terms of an acceptable peace were outlined by me, who, "somewhat to his surprise and apparently also of Sir Edward Grey", was ready to agree to intervention by the President. As the sequel was determined by these terms, I propose to set out exactly what my proposal was: I was opposed to the summoning of a conference without some preliminary understanding with the President as to the minimum terms which the Allies were to insist upon with his sanction and support. A conference without such an agreement would have been productive of the most serious consequences to the morale of the Allied countries, in the event of its failure. Having regard to the unpropitious military situation, such a fiasco was quite within the realms of probability. In my opinion, therefore, it was undesirable to take such a risk unless we were practically assured beforehand that if Germany proved intractable on these terms the U. S. A. would throw in her lot with us.

These terms were acceptable to the Prime Minister, Sir Edward Grey, Mr. Balfour, Lord Reading, and also to Colonel House. The latter, who knew President Wilson's mind better than any living man, was convinced that the terms would also meet the President's view of the justice of the case. It is interesting to recall these terms in order to show the conditions of peace which would have satisfied the British leaders at that date. They included the restoration of the independence of Belgium and Serbia, and the surrender of Alsace and Lorraine to France, provided that the loss of territory thus incurred by Germany would be compensated by concessions to her in other places outside Europe. There were to be adjustments of the frontiers between Italy and Austria so as to liberate Italian communities still under the Austrian yoke. Russia was to be given an outlet to the sea. There were also to be guarantees against any future recurrence of such a catastrophe as this World War.

Colonel House promised to cable to President Wilson a full report of the proceedings and to obtain his assent to the conclusions arrived at before the British Government notified their acceptance of President Wilson's proposal. Sir Edward Grey insisted that before any final decision was taken the Allies should be consulted.

Why was this conference never summoned? Who was responsible? Had it come off either Germany would have accepted the terms as soon as she realised that President Wilson was committed to their enforcement, or, in the event of their rejection, America would have come into the war in the spring of 1916, instead of twelve months later. The world would have been saved a whole year of ruin, havoc and devastation. What a difference it would have made! Was the fiasco due to Sir Edward Grey's reluctance to press the idea upon our French Allies, or was it attributable to the insertion by President Wilson of one fatal word in the gentlemen's agreement suggested by Colonel House? The document as cabled by Colonel House definitely committed the President to war (subject of course to the assent of Congress) in the event of rejection by Germany of a conference into which he was prepared to enter with a pledge to the Allies of support for minimum terms. The President in his reply inserted the word "Probably" in front of the undertaking. Sir Edward Grey's view was that this completely changed the character of the proposal, and, therefore, he did not think it worth while to communicate the purport of the negotiations to the Allies. As far as I can recollect, he made no effort with President Wilson through Colonel House or any other intermediary to restore the position as it was left by the Reading dinner conversations. The real explanation probably is that President Wilson was afraid of public opinion in the U.S.A. and Sir Edward Grey was frightened of our Allies. The world was once more sacrificed to the timidity of statesmanship. This great and at one time promising plan thus fell through. The bloody campaigns of 1916 were fought without any decision. Hundreds of thousands of brave young men fell on the scarred heights of Verdun — on the muddy plateau above the Somme, in the foothills of the Istrian and Tyrolese Alps, in the forests and swamps of Russia, on the slopes of the Carpathians, and in the torrid regions of Mesopotamia and Central Africa. Every military staff in all the armies at every stage of the sanguinary road was convinced that victory was awaiting their strategy just round the next corner. Politicians must not be allowed to snatch triumph out of their grasp just as it was all but within reach. Peace discussions were therefore postponed until the deafening sound of the great guns abated.

Looking back on this period in the light of the information which came later to hand, it is clear that if Colonel House's plan had been acted upon, the most that could have been hoped from such a conference as President Wilson could then have assembled would have been the earlier entry of the United States into the struggle, and the shortening of the war which that event would have brought about. Nothing is more certain than that Germany in 1916 would have insisted on terms which would have been entirely incompatible with those that the President's vicar-general in the outside world, Colonel House, had agreed upon with us. A secret despatch from Washington in the spring of 1917 advised us that when Bernstorff handed to the State Department of the U.S.A. the note informing them of Germany's intention to embark upon unrestricted submarine warfare, he made simultaneously a confidential communication to Colonel House, putting in writing Germany's peace terms. These were:

(1). The practical occupation of Belgium;

(2). The straightening out of their French frontier in order to include the French iron fields;

(3). Indemnity from France;
(4). Full compensation for all commercial losses.

It will be seen that these terms were not only entirely at variance with those which had been suggested by America, but were obviously utterly unacceptable to the Allies. They were in fact terms which assumed Germany to be victorious, and no peace could possibly have been based on them.

Whether the declaration of these terms by Germany at a conference would have brought President Wilson into the war on the Allied side in 1916 is perhaps slightly less certain. The President was at that time resolutely pacifist, and it is possible that Colonel House credited him with a greater readiness to participate in the struggle than he would actually have shown when it came to the test. While he could not have accepted the German terms, he might at that stage have contented himself with trying to balance them against the proposals of the Allies, and urge the *via media* of an unacceptable and inconclusive peace. Count Bernstorff noted in the course of a report on September 6th, 1916, that: "Wilson regards it as in the interest of America that neither of the combatants should gain a decisive victory." President Wilson fought his election in the late autumn on his policy of keeping America out of the war. On this he won.

In this connection I am tempted to quote an interesting letter which Theodore Roosevelt wrote after the American presidential election in November, 1916, to Lord Lee of Fareham. At that time Roosevelt was an energetic supporter of the Allied cause, and Lee had suggested that he should visit England and lecture on the issues of the war. Writing to decline the invitation, he hints — what was in fact the case — that his uncompromising support of the Allied cause had lost him the sympathy of both the political parties in the States to such an extent that no one, least of all Wilson, would dare to associate himself with a policy publicly advocated by him. His letter was in the following terms:

"Sagamore Hill,
November 10th, 1916.

"Dear Arthur,

"I have carefully considered your letter (no letter from Grey has come). My dear fellow, I hate not to do anything you ask. But my judgment is most strongly and unqualifiedly that it would be a grave error for me to do so in this case. I have consulted Whitridge and Bacon, both of whom are at this moment more interested in the success of the Allies than in any internal American questions, and they agree with me — Whitridge feeling at least as strongly as I do in the matter. Wilson has probably been elected, and if Hughes were elected it would only slightly alter the case so far as this particular proposal is concerned. For a number of months to come the American public would positively resent any conduct on my part which could be construed as indicating my presuming to give advice about, or an expression of, American opinion. Wilson would certainly endeavour to do exactly the opposite to what he thought I had indicated; even Hughes, if elected, would resent any seeming desire of the British and French to consult me; and my coming over would give every greedy sensation-monger in the Yellow Press, and even in the Pale Saffron Press, the cue to advertise the fact, with statements and inferences grotesquely false but very mischievous. Moreover, those whom I spoke to on your side of the war could not but feel that my words carry weight, and to this extent I cannot be guilty of deception towards them, for my words carry no weight, and it would be unwise to pay any heed to what I said as representing the American people. At the moment I am as completely out of sympathy with the American people as I would have been out of sympathy with the English people in 1910 or the French people in 1904. The Wilson 'policies' are those of the Democrats, who have just polled a bare plurality of the popular vote. Mr. Wilson would like to antagonise every proposition I make. The

Republicans by an overwhelming majority nominated Hughes precisely because he did *not* represent my views; they thought it wise to dodge the issues I thought it vital to raise. No other man of national importance (for Root really exerted not the slightest weight in the campaign and only spoke once to a half-empty hall) took the stand I took — which I took in every speech. I was the only man who raised my voice about Wilson's iniquity in suffering the German submarines to do as they did on our coast.

"If I went abroad I could give you no advice of even the slightest worth. I would diminish my already almost imperceptible influence here at home. I would expose myself to bitter malefications — no matter how much one condemns one's own country, one cannot stand condemnation of it by promiscuous outsiders (*you* may say *anything* and I will say ditto to it). I would like to visit the front at the head of an American division of 12 regiments like my Rough Riders — but not otherwise.

Always yours,

THEODORE ROOSEVELT.

"P.S. The amiable Bryce steadily exerts what influence he has here on behalf of the Pacifist crowd, who are really the tepid enemies of the Allies."

This rather bitter and disillusioned letter shows the doubts and uncertainties with which the strongest American leader of his time viewed the prospect of his country taking a really bold and decided course in its dealings with the combatant nations of Europe. Later on, history was to afford another proof that the bold course is the best one.

CHAPTER V

THE IRISH REBELLION

Part played by Irish problem in World War — Threats of Irish war in summer of 1914 — Home Rule Act suspended for the war — War Office tactlessness — Growth of sedition — Difficulties for Liberal statesmanship — The Easter rebellion — Mr. Asquith visits Ireland — I am asked to negotiate a settlement — My plan for Russian visit upset — Mr. Asquith's letter that saved my life — The negotiations begun — Personalities among the Irish leaders — Summary of my proposals — The settlement accepted — And smashed — Memorandum by Tory minister — Manifesto of the five peers — Lord Lansdowne's letter — Lord Lansdowne's speech — Carlton Club meeting — The agreement wrecked — Return to *status quo*.

THE long-drawn-out and wearisome tragedy of the relations between Great Britain and Ireland played an important part in the World War. There can be little doubt that the expectation on the Continent that Britain had for the moment sunk so deep in the quagmires of the Irish bog as to be unable to extricate her feet in time to march eastward, was one of the considerations which encouraged Germany to guarantee Austria her unconditional support in her Serbian adventure. The continued unrest in Ireland, and the political differences between statesmen here as to the proper method of dealing with them, imported an undercurrent of divided counsel and party feeling into our deliberations about our principal task. And ultimately, the rebellion of Easter, 1916, quickly though it was suppressed, interposed a deplorable distraction and left an aftermath of bitterness and danger which hampered us throughout the remainder of the war and for years afterwards.

Nor can it be forgotten that the Irish situation formed

an abiding ground of antagonism to Great Britain amongst the large and politically powerful Irish-American section in the United States. Had there been no Irish grievance, it is by no means improbable that America would have come much earlier into the war, and by so much shortened its duration.

I do not propose to enter on a discussion of the Irish question. But in considering the events of 1916, and the part I was called on to play in bringing about some alleviation of the trouble, it is important to bear in mind the background against which those events were set.

In the early summer of 1914, in view of the fact that the Liberal Government had succeeded after a three years' fight in carrying through a measure of Home Rule, the Protestant North had reached a state of incipient rebellion, and was arming and drilling for resistance to the decision of the Imperial Parliament. The Catholic South had begun to copy these tactics, and raise National Volunteers to match the Ulster Volunteers of the North. There was a gun-running at Larne to supply Ulster with guns from Germany; and then one at Howth to supply Southern Ireland. The paradox of the situation was that Ulster's rebellion was acclaimed by a powerful section of British opinion as loyalty, while Southern Ireland's preparations to defend the decision of the Imperial Parliament were denounced as sedition.

At the outbreak of the Great War, the Home Rule Act was suspended in order to allay the threatened rebellion of Ulster, backed by the Unionist Party in Great Britain, and to procure a measure of unity, in face of the common danger. For the moment this action achieved its purpose, but it may be doubted whether in the long run it proved profitable. For Southern Ireland, seeing its hopes dashed at the moment when they were about to be realised, at first sulked in resentment and soon became a mass of seething disaffection; and after an interlude of strife and suffering of a deplorable character, it had to be pacified by concessions far more extensive than would have satisfied it in 1914.

The irritation of Southern Ireland was exacerbated by a number of needless follies. When the World War broke out, its spokesman, Mr. Redmond, pledged its full support to Britain in the conflict, and heartily encouraged the efforts to recruit its young men for the army. But with extraordinary tactlessness, old officers were let loose on Munster, Connaught and Leinster to lure men to the Colours to the strains of "God Save the King." Both the tune and the tone were anathema in those parts, and roused every instinct of sedition. I have already related, in my sketch of Lord Kitchener, how he approved the embroidery of the Red Hand of Ulster, on the banner of the Northern Division, but banned the South Irish Harp on the Southern. The slap in the face which this curious procedure administered to Southern Ireland stamped out every spark of kindling enthusiasm there, and caused a serious setback to recruiting.

Throughout 1915 and early 1916, seditious movements grew in strength. The Irish Volunteers, a body openly formed to enforce the Sinn Fein policy of complete independence for Ireland, drilled publicly and rapidly recruited their numbers. Funds came to them from America, with leaflets designed to increase disaffection. In Dublin especially the note of rebellion was everywhere to be heard. Full information of these developments was supplied to the Irish Secretary, Mr. Augustine Birrell, but he, wisely or unwisely, refused to sanction any drastic action to suppress the movement. He was content to hope and pray that matters would not come to a head till the war was over — after which the coming into force of the postponed Home Rule Act would solve the difficulty.

Admittedly the problem was an awkward one for statesmanship. How could action be taken against the Irish Volunteers unless corresponding action were also taken against the Ulster Volunteers, who were also armed to resist the Government and to oppose an Act now on the Statute Book? How could we defend the rights of Belgium and in the same breath coerce Ireland for arming to secure for itself a measure of independence which the majority of the House of Commons had admitted to be just? How could we resort to coercion in Ireland — unless events made it inevitable — and maintain with America the friendly relations which were essential to our success in the war? There seemed plenty of excellent reasons for doing nothing. There always are. So nothing was done.

In April, 1916, the inevitable happened. Encouraged by Germany and the Irish-Americans, the Sinn Fein leaders in Dublin decided to bring matters to a head by an open rebellion. A ship was to come over from Germany to Ireland, bringing the Irish revolutionary leader, Sir Roger Casement, and an outbreak was timed to take effect on Easter Day, April 23rd, two days following his arrival.

Sir Roger Casement failed to turn up in Ireland on the 21st, and on the following day the news appeared that he and the ship which bore him had been captured by the British. Notices were hastily sent out by the Irish Volunteer headquarters to postpone the Sunday arrangements. But on Easter Monday, April 24th, a rising occurred in Dublin and some parts of the country.

The provincial disturbances were small and easily suppressed. The Dublin outbreak was far more serious, and for a time the Irish capital was held by the forces of revolt. Troops were hastily summoned, martial law proclaimed, and in a couple of days the rising had been quelled, not without bloodshed. Several of the rebellious leaders were tried by court-martial and shot.

Obviously matters could not be allowed to rest there, and after going into the matter carefully, Mr. Asquith went over to Dublin to examine the situation on the spot. Martial law was still in force, and the three principal officers of the Crown: The Lord Lieutenant, Lord Winborne; the Chief Secretary for Ireland, Mr. Birrell; and his Under-secretary, Sir Matthew Nathan, had all resigned their posts.

On his return, Mr. Asquith approached me with the suggestion that I should take up the task of trying to negotiate a settlement with the Irish revolutionary leaders. My sympathy with their cause was known. On the other hand, I had been recently very much detached from the Irish developments, as I had been fully immersed in my task of equipping our armies with munitions, especially in view of the coming campaign on the Somme.

The request came at an awkward moment. For some time I had been urging on our leaders a measure of closer coördination with our Russian Ally, and had at last got them to agree to a practical step in this direction. Lord Kitchener was to proceed to Russia via Archangel to consult with the military authorities there about closer coöperation in the field, and it had been arranged that I should go with him to find out for myself the truth about the appalling shortage of equipment of which we had heard, and see in what way the Ministry of Munitions could best help to remedy it. These were matters in which I was for the moment far more closely interested than I was in the pitiable and rather squalid tragedy which had overtaken our lack of policy in Ireland.

But my plans were upset by Mr. Asquith's proposal. It was conveyed to me in a letter which I reproduce in facsimile, the terms of which were as follows:

10, Downing Street,
Whitehall, S.W.

Secret 22 May 16

My dear Lloyd George,

I hope you may see your way to take up Ireland: at any rate for a short time. It is a unique opportunity, and there is no one else who could do so much to bring about a permanent solution.

Yrs very sincerely
H. H. Asquith

FACSIMILE OF THE LETTER WRITTEN BY MR. ASQUITH WHICH INDUCED MR. LLOYD GEORGE TO ABANDON HIS PROPOSED VISIT TO RUSSIA WITH LORD KITCHENER

"*Secret.*

"10, Downing Street,
Whitehall, S. W.
22nd May, 1916.

"My dear Lloyd George,

"I hope you may see your way to take up Ireland; at any rate for a short time. It is a *unique* opportunity and there is no one else who could do so much to bring about a permanent solution.

Yours very sincerely,
H. H. ASQUITH."

For me at least this letter has a peculiar interest, for it saved my life! Much against my own inclination, I decided that I could not refuse Mr. Asquith's request, so I had to tell Lord Kitchener that I could not accompany him on his voyage, and I asked him to do his best to find out for me the munition position there and the way in which he thought the British Munitions Ministry could render any help in the equipment of the Russian Armies. Even while Mr. Asquith was penning his letter, an obscure German vessel was steaming across the North Sea towards the cold northern waters around the Orkneys, bearing a mine which it was presently to loose at a venture off the Scottish coast in the hope of sinking some vessel from the Grand Fleet cruising around these wind-swept Scottish islands. A fortnight later that mine struck the *Hampshire* with the renowned and almost legendary figure of our British Minister of War aboard. But for this letter, I should have been with him and have shared his fate. This escape, at least, I owe to Ireland.

On May 25th, Mr. Asquith announced in the House of Commons that I had undertaken to devote my time and energies to seeking a solution of the Irish situation, and he explained that my decision was the outcome of the unanimous request of all my colleagues in the Government. I had already begun to consult with the political leaders of both the Irish Nationalist and the Ulster Unionist parties. The negotiations were conducted at the Ministry of Munitions. The Nationalists were represented by Mr. John Redmond, Mr. John Dillon, Mr. T. P. O'Connor and Mr. Devlin. Ulster was represented by Sir Edward Carson and Mr. James Craig.

Redmond was not only a great orator but possessed elements of statesmanship of a high order. The fact that he was given no chance to apply his qualities in the rebuilding of his native land is one of the myriad tragedies of Irish history. Devlin had all the charm, wit and eloquence of Irishmen at their best. To these graces and powers he added fundamental shrewdness and sagacity. Of Carson — one of the most remarkable products of Irish soil — I speak later on. Craig (now Lord Craigavon, the Irish Premier) possesses all the gifts of an American political boss of the nineteenth century. T. P. O'Connor had a much wider experience of the world than his colleagues and that made him more tolerant and accommodating as a negotiator. Redmond, O'Connor, Devlin, Carson and Craig displayed a genuine anxiety to reach a settlement. Dillon was difficult. He had the temperament and mental equipment of the fanatic. He always found it hard to accommodate his ideas to the tyranny of facts. In private he was genial, pleasant and gentle of speech. In public he was a scold. In negotiation he was inclined to be truculent and unyielding. His stubbornness over comparatively trivial details helped to wreck the Buckingham Palace negotiations just before the war. When he ultimately gave assent to the terms reached in these negotiations he did so with a mental reservation, and his rigid and niggling interpretation of the arrangement arrived at proved to be fatal later on, for it made it impossible for Redmond and Devlin to meet Unionist misgiving by even the slightest appearance of concession.

After a discussion I laid before them a series of proposals. These proposals were:

1. To bring the Home Rule Act into immediate operation.
2. To introduce at once an Amending Bill, as a strictly War Emergency Act to cover only the period of the war and a short specified interval after it.
3. During that period the Irish members to remain at Westminster in their full numbers.
4. During this war emergency period six Ulster counties to be left as at present under the Imperial Government.
5. Immediately after the war an Imperial Conference of representatives from all the Dominions of the Empire to be held to consider the future government of the Empire, including the question of the Government of Ireland.
6. Immediately after this Conference, and during the interval provided for by the War Emergency Act, the permanent settlement of all the great outstanding problems, such as the permanent position of the exempted counties, the question of finance, and other problems, which cannot be dealt with during the War, would be proceeded with.

The above is an abbreviated summary of my proposals, which in their full form extended to fourteen clauses. Sir Edward Carson and Mr. Redmond promptly went over to Ireland to consult with their respective followers about the scheme. Despite the fact that it contained proposals most unpalatable to each of the disputing factions in Ireland, both sides agreed to accept it, and to do their best to work it loyally.

I wish the story could end there. But it cannot. The plan which held out such promise for a settlement of the ancient grievance of Ireland, and which was accepted by both parties in Ireland itself, was thereafter deliberately smashed by extremists on both sides. My first warning of this opposition came in the shape of a memorandum sent to me on

June 11th, 1916, by a prominent Unionist member of the Cabinet — the day before my scheme was accepted without opposition by the Ulster Unionist Council, and a week before it was also unanimously approved by a gathering of Nationalists at Belfast. The memorandum was as follows:

"Information reaches me from both England and Ireland, North and South, that there is no disposition to come to a settlement, that the line taken by the leading Unionists, as the result of their interviews in London, is that the Unionist Party in Ireland are being driven by the Prime Minister and Minister of Munitions into accepting a situation which they know to be morally wrong and wrong politically, that the Nationalist Party are sullen and hostile and have no intention of abandoning their policy and programme whatever may be the decision of their leaders.

"At the same time I hear the gravest accounts of the condition of Ireland. If one half of what I have heard is true it seems to me to be quite clear that this is not the moment to embark upon any political experiment. The situation is very different from what I believed it to be when we first discussed this question, far graver and more serious, and unless I am wholly misinformed I don't think it would be possible for me to give my assent to any agreement including the adoption of Home Rule, the more so as I have excellent authority for the opinion I hold very strongly that, whatever may be said or written, the U.S.A. will not interfere with the supply of munitions or other supplies."

This unexpected communication by one of my own Cabinet colleagues, who had been a party to the decision authorising me to carry out the negotiations, and who had talked over with me my scheme before I finally submitted it to the leaders of Irish opinion, was characteristic of the type of bitter partisan hostility which the prospect of a settlement of the Irish trouble called forth from extremists who would rather see no settlement at all than one which did not fully conform with their ideas. On June 23rd — the very day on which final approval of the proposals was recorded by a representative Conference of the Ulster Nationalists — a manifesto denouncing it was issued by five Unionist Peers — Lords Balfour of Burleigh, Cromer, Halsbury, Midleton and Salisbury. Two days later Lord Selborne, the President of the Board of Agriculture, resigned from the Cabinet as a protest against the scheme.

Lord Lansdowne, the veteran Tory leader, fired the next shot. On June 28th I received the following note from Mr. Asquith:

"10, Downing Street,
Whitehall, S.W.
June 28, 1916.

"My dear Lloyd George,

"Please look at enclosed which has just come from Lansdowne.

Yours,
H. H. A."

The enclosure was the following letter:

"Lansdowne House,
Berkeley Square, W.,
28 June, 1916.

"My dear Asquith,

"You will, I am sure, have noted that my consent to the postponement of further discussion as to the Irish settlement was given with considerable reluctance and not without misgivings. I agreed, not because I was convinced that further inquiry was likely to produce satisfactory results, but because it seemed to me that, having regard to the extreme gravity of the situation, no suggestion which gave us breathing time ought to be put aside.

"The discussion towards the close was hurried, and I am not sure that we were *ad diem* as to the scope of the enquiry. I may, therefore, perhaps be allowed to make my own views clear.

"What we want to know is, not merely whether, under a Nationalist Government, Sir John Maxwell, with his 40,000 men, will be able to put down another Sinn Fein rebellion, or whether our military and naval resources would be sufficient to prevent a German-Irish landing. The question seems rather to be whether, with a Nationalist executive, it would be possible to deal effectively and promptly with domestic disorder, *e.g.*, with sporadic but organised disturbances, occurring simultaneously all over the country. Could we deal with them as effectively and as promptly as we could if they were to occur now?

"Another point which it seems to me requires to be cleared up is this. Do Messrs. Redmond and Devlin understand that, if a Nationalist Government is set up, we shall still make use of the Defence of the Realm Acts, and that their suggestion that under the new dispensation the ordinary law will suffice cannot be entertained?

"And do they understand that Mr. Devlin's promise of an immediate amnesty for the persons who are now imprisoned owing to the part which they took in the recent rebellion is not one which can be entertained?

"I understand that you advised the S. W. Unionists yesterday to formulate their demands as to the safeguards which they considered indispensable.

"Would it be possible to press them to put in a statement of their requirements, and, if we find that they are reasonable — could the Nationalist leaders be required to accept them as one of the conditions of settlement?

Believe me,
Yours sincerely
LANSDOWNE."

On July 10th Mr. Asquith made a statement in the House of Commons in which he set out the main features of the agreement which had been reached. The following night Lord Lansdowne spoke in the House of Lords about the proposals, in terms which Mr. Redmond characterised as "a gross insult to Ireland . . . a declaration of war on the Irish people, and the announcement of a policy of coercion."

On July 17th a meeting was held at the Carlton Club of Conservative members of both houses of the Imperial Parliament, at which an "Imperial Unionist Association" was formed to "watch negotiations as to the Irish question between the Government and the Nationalist Party." This Association proceeded to adopt a resolution calling for stern measures of repression in Ireland, and opposing any idea of immediate Home Rule. In conformity with the wishes of their followers, the Unionist members of the Coalition Cabinet insisted on serious modifications in the terms which had been agreed on between me and the Irish leaders, when a Bill was being drafted to carry them into law.

This situation was exposed by Mr. Redmond on July 24th, when he raised the question on a motion for adjournment of the House of Commons. Sir Edward Carson, placated by the proposed exclusion of the six counties from the scheme, urged strongly that a settlement should be made with the South. But the other Conservative members of the Cabinet were obdurate, and mangled the terms which I had originally put forward until Mr. Redmond was no longer willing to accept them.

The matter was concluded by Mr. Asquith's announcement in the House of Commons on July 31st that Mr. H. E. Duke, the member of Parliament for Exeter, was to be appointed Chief Secretary for Ireland. With this step we reverted to the old and unsatisfactory system of control — of which the Royal Commission on the Rebellion of Ireland had already stated in its report, issued on June 26th and published on July 3rd, 1916, that:

"If the Irish system of government be regarded as a whole, it is anomalous in quiet times and almost unworkable in times of crisis."

The revival of that "anomalous" and "almost unworkable" system led to the persistent growth of further disaffection, culminating in the chaos of the immediate post-war years, and the ultimate settlement of the problem on lines which involved far bigger concessions to Southern Ireland than would have been made in the scheme I had proposed. The last word has not yet been spoken in this unhappy feud that Britain has inherited from a foreign foe, who, having conquered England first, then proceeded to annex Ireland.

CHAPTER VI

THE COMING OF CONSCRIPTION

A big army not originally contemplated — British dislike of conscription — Early success of voluntary recruiting — Change in the position — Prospect of a long war — Voluntary system becomes inadequate — Difficulties caused by party feeling — My own attitude — Attempts to work the voluntary system — "Householders' return" — Lord Haldane on the Common Law position — National registration — Results of national registration — Findings of Cabinet Committee in August, 1915 — My evidence before the Cabinet Committee — Mr. Runciman's view — Mr. M'Kenna's financial objections — Lord Kitchener declares for compulsion — Questions posed by the Committee — Divisions in the Cabinet — Lord Kitchener's scheme — Men at the front want conscription — The Derby scheme — Pledges given to the married men — Unsatisfactory result of the Derby canvass — First step in conscription: single men called up — Resignation of Sir John Simon — Reassurances to labour — The second round: protests by older married men — Cabinet dissensions — Man-power shortage: Sir William Robertson's warning — Secret sessions of Parliament — Universal military service enacted — My speech in the House on the principles at stake — My part in the controversy: Sir William Robertson's letters — Hostility roused among a section of Liberals: my speech at Conway — Tribute to Mr. Asquith — Enthusiasm in France — Achievements of voluntary recruiting — The King's message.

Apart from the proposals I placed before the Liberal and Conservative leaders in 1910 for a National Militia, no statesman had ever contemplated that the military contribution of this country to a European war should exceed the limits of our normal regular army. Our ideas were embodied in the Expeditionary Force created by Mr. Haldane. After the declaration of war an appeal was made for 100,000 men. Their main use was intended to be as units for filling gaps in the ranks. It was only when the numbers who volunteered reached a figure which was beyond the highest hopes of enthusiasts that the Cabinet and Parliament widened their view of the part we were destined to play on the battlefields of Armageddon.

We had always visualised Britain playing her traditional rôle in Continental wars. Our Navy would keep the seas for the Allies. Our wealth would help them to finance their foreign purchases. Our Army would play a subordinate part in the struggle.

But why was not conscription adopted from the moment the Cabinet decided to raise an army on the Continental scale? Obviously it would have provided the most effective method for organising the man-power of this country.

To the British people the idea was unfamiliar, and we move slowly in these islands. Bred on a soil for centuries inviolate, we were accustomed to send abroad only small, professional armies, the ranks of which, in so far as they were British, could be filled by the recruiting sergeant on a voluntary basis, with the allurement of uniform and the King's shilling. Our national defence had been the fleet, which requires far fewer men than does an army, and for whose needs in the darkest moments of the Napoleonic struggle, the press gang — long since passed into the limbo of forgotten evils — had troubled only the seaport towns and their vicinity.

Not only were we unused to the idea of universal and compulsory national service for war; we also had a strong traditional objection to the creation of large armed forces, as potential instruments of tyranny and an infringement of personal liberty; and, moreover, among wide sections of the nation there was a tendency to look down on the common soldier's vocation.

Besides, in the early days, few conceived that the war would be a long-drawn-out affair. It was surmised that no nation could sustain war on the modern scale for more than a short time. Pacifist and militarist writers agreed about that. "Over by Christmas" was the popular slogan, which was used to excuse the corresponding cry, "Business as usual."

For these reasons it was thought by all those who had the supreme responsibility of interpreting public opinion that it would have been impossible at the outset of the war to carry through a scheme for the mobilisation of the whole country, such as was adopted in France. And to add to these negative arguments against such a procedure, there was the positive fact that recruits during the first months were pouring in, on a voluntary basis, far more rapidly than the military authorities could handle them. In the first three months of the war, nine hundred thousand new recruits were enlisted, at an average of three hundred thousand a month, in addition to the reservists recalled to the Colours and the Territorials already enlisted. The army authorities had neither barracks in which to house these men, uniforms in which to clothe them, nor weapons with which to drill and train them. Far from needing to adopt special measures to secure men for the forces, we were driven to raise and stiffen the physical standard for recruits, in order to check this unmanageable spate.

As time passed, however, a series of developments occurred to modify the situation.

The military authorities, for their part, improvised by the time the first rush of recruits was over a technique for handling supplies of men on this unprecedented scale. The stream itself dwindled by the end of the year to an average of thirty thousand a week.

Already before the close of 1914, it was becoming clear that the unregulated process of voluntary recruiting had swept into the Army large numbers of men who were vitally necessary in the workshops, for the production of munitions of war and in other civilian avocations essential even in war.

Many of them, from their skill, intelligence and experience, were pivotal men and irreplaceable. Efforts were made to get some of them back, but the salvage operations were not very successful. The obvious lesson was that if the war were not to be bungled and lost, our resources of man-power must be more intelligently applied.

The war had not ended by Christmas. On the contrary, it was settling down into a long-drawn-out struggle, which would demand from us not only a far bigger military force on the Continent and elsewhere than had at first been expected, but would require a continuous stream of fresh men to replace casualties and keep the armies up to strength.

As the magnitude of the struggle, and its life-and-death importance for us, was borne in upon the nation, the popular antipathy to military service died away, and was replaced by a healthy impatience at the spectacle of sturdy young men "skrimshanking" at home while fathers of families were in the trenches.

These developments weakened the case for persistence in the voluntary system, and helped to prepare men's minds for its abandonment when eventually it proved incapable of furnishing the Army with an adequate supply of fresh recruits.

Not the least of the difficulties which had to be overcome before conscription was eventually adopted was the hostility engendered by its advocates. There were associated before the war in the popular mind with extreme Jingoism, and in consequence opposition to any suggestion of national military service had become an article of faith with some Liberals and Socialists. An agitation for conscription was begun early in the struggle from the same quarters, which kept alive the feud and gave it the semblance of a party issue. It would have been far easier for the Government to introduce national service at an early date, if the matter had not taken on such a violently controversial colour, so that its adoption looked like a chauvinist triumph.

My own attitude to this question has never been based on considerations of political orthodoxy. Long before the war I had formed the opinion that there was much to be said in favour of some system of national training, and of universal liability to military service for national defence. I have told how I advanced this suggestion when talking with the German Ambassador, years before the war, and how the matter was also discussed as a practical proposition with the leaders of the Conservative Party by the Liberal Government in 1910.

Looking backward, there is no doubt at all that we should have been able to organise the nation for war far more effectively in 1914, and bring the conflict to a successful issue far more quickly and economically, if at the very outset we had mobilised the whole nation on a war footing — its man-power, money, materials and brains — and bent all our resources to the task of victory on rational and systematic lines. Towards the end, something approaching this condition was in fact reached, but there had intervened a long and deplorably extravagant prelude of waste and hesitation. But a majority of the Cabinet opposed conscription not only as inexpedient, but because at that time they were strongly antagonistic to it on principle and there was no pressure from the Conservative opposition to apply conscription.

A decision having been reached, with something like national unity, to rely as long as possible upon the voluntary principle, every effort was made to stimulate its successful working. At first, recruiting meetings, posters, literature, and other forms of popular appeal were employed. The recruiting crusade was well organised. The services of expert propagandists, political agents, advertising agents, and public speakers, lay and clerical, were requisitioned, and their combined work in agitation and enlistment was a triumphant success. By degrees, other more systematic approaches to the manhood of the nation were improvised, and only after these repeated promptings and combings proved unavailing to maintain our supply of recruits did we turn of necessity to compulsory service.

The first of these systematic steps was the "Householders' Return", organised early in November, 1914, by the Parliamentary Recruiting Committee. This was a return of men eligible and willing to serve, and was secured by means of forms sent to every householder in the Kingdom, with a covering letter signed by Messrs. Asquith, Bonar Law, and Arthur Henderson, the leaders of the three political parties, appealing to every eligible man to hold himself ready to enlist in the forces of the Crown.

This scheme, reinforced by the appeals of poster and public meeting, helped to maintain the steady flow of recruits well into 1915. At the beginning of the year, on January 8th, 1915, when conscription was being debated in the House of Lords, the official attitude of the Government at that time was stated by Lord Crewe in the following phrase: "We do not regard the possibility of compulsion as being within the landscape, as we now see it." More than three months later, on April 20th, I myself stated in reply to a question in the House of Commons that: "The Government are not of opinion that there is any ground for thinking that the war would be more successfully prosecuted by means of conscription." Both of these statements as to the Government's attitude were determined by the fact that as yet the voluntary system was continuing to yield as adequate a flow of recruits as could be absorbed by our training and equipping facilities at that date.

That the attitude of some of us on this issue was purely

realist, and not doctrinaire, is illustrated by a weighty pronouncement which Lord Haldane made in the course of the debate on January 8th, 1915, to which I have already referred. After declaring that hitherto the voluntary system was proving adequate, and showed no signs of breaking down, he added:

> ". . . By the Common Law of this country it is the duty of every subject of the Realm to assist the Sovereign in repelling the invasion of its shores and in defence of the Realm. That is a duty which rests on no Statute but is inherent in the Constitution of the country. It has been laid down . . . that any subject at a time of emergency may be asked to give himself and his property for the defence of the nation. Therefore compulsory service is not foreign to the Constitution of this country. Given a great national emergency I think it is your duty to resort to it. I can conceive a state of things in which we might resort to it. . . . At a time of national necessity every other consideration must yield to national interest, and we should bar nothing in the way of principle if it should become necessary."

This statement was of importance, not only for its value as a summary of the Common Law position with regard to compulsory national service, but as showing that Lord Haldane himself and others like-minded in the Cabinet were approaching the issue purely on a basis of practical expediency, and held no theoretic objection or prejudice against its adoption. I may also refer here to the statement made by me at Manchester on June 3rd, which I have already quoted in my account of the Ministry of Munitions, where I emphasised that there was nothing anti-democratic in conscription; on the contrary, every great democracy had resorted to it in times of national danger as a fit and proper democratic weapon for self-defence; and if necessity arose we ought without hesitation to apply the same weapon ourselves in this present conflict.

As a matter of fact, I had become painfully aware, long before I actually became principally responsible for creating a Ministry of Munitions, that the haphazard results of the voluntary system in a national emergency of this magnitude were leading to deplorable waste and mismanagement of our available man-power. I was eager to press forward some scheme for a more systematic coördination of these resources, and one of the first acts of the new Cabinet formed by Mr. Asquith at the end of May, 1915, when he established the first Coalition Government, was to instruct Mr. Walter Long to draft a Bill for the setting up of a National Register. The aim of this Register was twofold. By providing a complete record of the number and distribution of men at different age levels throughout the country it would enable us to calculate our available resources of men for military service, and also inform us what supplies of men were available for production of munitions.

Some time was lost in discussion of the points raised, but ultimately on the 5th of July the National Registration Bill was laid before Parliament and carried by a large majority. Opposition to it, based mainly on the presumption that it was a preliminary to conscription, came from a small group of Liberal and Labour Members, and, of course, Messrs. MacDonald and Snowden, who throughout the war persistently opposed every effort to secure recruits for the national defence. Indeed, three months earlier, the Independent Labour Party, of which Mr. Ramsay MacDonald was the leading light, had carried in their Norwich Conference a resolution censuring the official Labour Party for its work on behalf of recruiting.

The returns obtained by the National Register showed that there were about five million men of military age in Great Britain who were not already serving with the Forces. Of these, there were, of course, a considerable number physically unfit for military service, and, further, a number in "barred" occupations who were held non-recruitable because indispensable to the maintenance of national industry and in particular of munitions. It was estimated that Great Britain contained a residue of 1,700,000 to 1,800,000 fit men available as recruits not yet serving with the Forces. This figure was proved later on to be an underestimate of our reserves of man-power.

While this register was being compiled a Cabinet Committee on our national resources in men and money had carried out in August, 1915, an investigation into the situation, and in a Report dated September 2nd, 1915, it pointed out that voluntary recruiting was not enabling us to make a military effort comparable to the resources of the country. Lord Kitchener was aiming at an army of 70 divisions in all theatres by the latter part of 1916. The Committee held that "a 100-division army would bear a truer relation both to our dangers and to the exertions of our Allies." After making all allowance for our naval, financial, and industrial contributions, "it cannot be claimed that an army of 70 divisions represents our true proportionate contribution of men to the Allied line of battle."

Taking the 70-division scheme, however, as the standard to be reached, the Committee showed that present methods would be insufficient. In addition to the regular reserves and territorial forces mobilised at the beginning of the war, the fresh recruits accepted and passed into the Army in 13 months totalled 1,888,000. "The recruiting records for the last six months show an average yield of 20,000 a week, resulting in an effective yield to our military forces of probably 19,000 men." Lord Kitchener was asking for at least 30,000 a week — a figure which a month later he raised to 35,000. "Even the yield of 20,000 a week can only be maintained by repeated canvassing of individuals and by every form of social, and in some cases of economic, pressure upon all classes of men (except munition workers) from 17 to 45, whether married or single, whether usefully employed or not, and whether or not they can be spared from their trade or district."

The Committee reported the evidence it had received in statements to it by the President of the Board of Trade, the Chancellor of the Exchequer, Lord Kitchener, and myself. From its record of my own evidence I cull the following extracts:

Asked by the Committee what form of compulsion the Minister of Munitions considered necessary, "Mr. Lloyd George said he would take the same powers exactly as were taken in France. He would make everybody between certain ages liable to serve in the Army at home or abroad, and only during the duration of the war. With this general and basic authority 'you could work the rest all right.' " And in my concluding remarks I am reported as saying:

"You will not get through without some measure of military compulsion or compulsion for military service. The longer you delay the nearer you will be to disaster. I am certain you cannot get through without it. I do not believe, for instance, that you can keep your armies at the front without it, unless you are going deliberately to cut their numbers down to a figure which will be inadequate, and which is known to be inadequate in advance. The number of men you should put at the front does not depend on us in the least. It is going to depend on the Germans and what the Germans are going to do during the next three months in Russia. If they succeed in putting the Russians out of action during 1916 as a great offensive force, for us simply to keep 70 divisions at the front is suicide.[1] Not only that, it is murder, because to send a number of men who are obviously inadequate is just murdering our own countrymen without attaining any purpose at all. . . ."

[1] In 1918 we had 89 divisions, including Dominion, etc., troops.

The President of the Board of Trade, Mr. Runciman, argued to the Committee that on the basis of the statistics he had at his disposal there would, after leaving a sufficient number of men in industry, be less than half the number available for the army which Lord Kitchener considered indispensable to maintain his seventy divisions, and not more than half of these could be secured by voluntary recruiting. The Committee felt that this argument "would appear to lead directly, if unconsciously, to compulsory military service" (of which Mr. Runciman was a leading opponent). But they did not agree with his sweeping exclusion by whole classes of large numbers of potential recruits from his calculations.

The statement of the Chancellor of the Exchequer, Mr. M'Kenna, was to the effect that Britain could not afford to carry on her financial aid to her Allies and at the same time maintain an army of seventy divisions in the field.

One or other of the two tasks we might compass, but not both. The Committee found his arguments ingenious but unconvincing, and reminded the Cabinet that "whereas a few months ago the possibility of raising a substantial loan in the United States was scouted altogether, and whereas a few weeks ago we were assured that £20,000,000 was the utmost limit, the Chancellor of the Exchequer now hopes to borrow £100,000,000 sterling from this quarter during the present year, and to repeat the operation in a subsequent year."

Lord Kitchener told the Committee that "it would be his duty to ask Parliament before the end of the year for a Bill giving him compulsory powers." He added, however, that he regretted the raising of the question of compulsory service at the present time, because he had intended to choose his own time for rushing it on the country as a non-party measure of military emergency, whereas it was now being revived as a party issue. Before deciding on his scheme for compulsion he wanted to see the results of the National Registration.

The Committee concluded in their Report dated September 2nd, 1915, that "the men are available for the 70-divisions army, but the number cannot be obtained on a voluntary basis." They posed as questions for the Cabinet:

> "First: Whether the 70-divisions scheme is to be cut down to the limits which can be supplied by voluntary enlistment, or whether it is to be carried out by compulsory measures.
>
> "Secondly: Assuming that the 70-divisions scheme is to be carried out and that compulsion is to be used, whether a decision should be taken now or some time later in the year."

At this time the Cabinet was broadly divided into three sections on the question of conscription. There was the group of those who had come to regard a measure of compulsory national service as vitally necessary for the successful prosecution of the war, and in consequence were anxious to bring it in with the smallest possible delay. At the other extreme stood those who through principle or prejudice were as strongly opposed to it, and prepared to fight it to the last ditch. Between them were some who were not opposed in principle, and admitted that we might have to resort to compulsion, but were loath to admit the need for so radical a change of system until it was proved to be unavoidable, and only then if they were sure it would command general approval by the mass of the people. They anticipated that any attempt to carry and enforce compulsory service would excite such opposition as to make the proposal unworkable.

On October 8th, 1915, Lord Kitchener laid before the Cabinet a memorandum on "Recruiting for the Army", which began with the ominous statement:

"The voluntary system, as at present administered, fails to produce the number of recruits required to maintain the armies in the field."

He proposed that a scheme of conscription by ballot should be introduced, based on the returns of the National Register. Each district should be expected to furnish a quota of recruits in accordance with the numbers of men available within the area, as shown by the Register. If voluntary recruiting failed to produce the full quota, the balance would be obtained by a ballot of the eligible men not yet enlisted.

This scheme was, however, severely criticised as clumsy and unworkable, and it was not further proceeded with. It was recognised that if the voluntary system could not be continued the alternative must be a national measure of compulsory service.

The opponents of this argued in the Cabinet and outside that conscription was impracticable because the volunteers already enlisted would be unwilling to serve alongside pressed men, and while a separation of conscript and volunteer armies was unworkable, their mingling would be disastrous. Lord Curzon took the trouble to have extensive enquiries made from officers and men of all ranks in France on this question, and the quite unanimous verdict returned was that these fears were without foundation. The army in the field felt strongly that those at home who would not come out otherwise should be fetched, and while it was suggested that the conscripts might at first have to put up with a certain measure of chaff and ragging, this would soon pass, and the difference in their conditions of enlistment be forgotten.

Actually, of course, this was what took place when conscription was put into force. Here again it turned out that those who raised imaginary objections to a firm policy were flinching at shadows. Our bane throughout those early periods of the war was the incurable tendency of a number of people in high places to argue that measures vitally necessary for the success of our effort could not, for some reason or other, be taken. Thus we were told that the outside firms could not learn to make munitions; that the finances of the country could not stand the strain of our total effort; that the men needed for our Army could not be spared from industry; that gunners could not be trained to operate our programme of big guns; that the country would not stand conscription; that volunteers would not fight beside pressed men, and so on. Every one of these arguments was falsified by the event. Unhappily, each one of these objections served for a greater or less time to hold up and paralyse the efforts we should have been making to win the war. The advice of these prophets of the impossible cost us months and years of prolonged warfare, and hundreds of thousands of British lives.

In deference to the objections of the anti-conscriptionists, and to the hesitations of the middle group of the Cabinet, one final effort was made, in the form of the Derby Scheme, to galvanise the voluntary system into renewed vigour. It was generally recognised, both in the Cabinet and in the country, that if this failed, conscription would be inevitable.

The Derby Scheme owes its name to the fact that Lord Derby, although for many years a strong supporter of the introduction of Universal Military Service, consented to become Director of Recruiting and to carry through a last canvass of the country's man-power, in order to give the Voluntary System the utmost opportunity of furnishing the men needed for the Army. He was appointed on October 5th, 1915, and the post carried, at his request, no pay and no military rank.

The authorship of the plan which he set himself to administer has not hitherto been made public.

The main feature of the Derby Scheme was a personal canvass of every man in the Kingdom between the ages of 18 and 41, working on the basis of the National Register. Each man was asked to attest — to pledge himself to join up when called for — subject to the undertaking that all attested men would be divided into two classes, the single and the married, and each of these into 23 groups according to age; that the military authorities would call the men up by class and group as wanted for the Army, beginning with the younger single men, and would call up none of the married men till all the single men had been summoned to the colours.

The married men were encouraged to put down their names in the light of an asurance that not only would they be left at home till the single men had all been called in, but that if the single men did not attest in adequate numbers the married men would not be bound by their attestation pledge. This was stated by Mr. Asquith in a speech he delivered in the House of Commons on November 2nd, 1915:

> "I am told by Lord Derby that there is some doubt among the married men who are now being asked to enlist as to whether they may not be called upon to serve, having enlisted, while younger and unmarried men are holding back and not doing their duty. Let them disabuse themselves of that notion at once. So far as I am concerned, I would certainly say that the obligation of the married men to enlist is an obligation which ought not to be enforced and ought not to be held binding on them unless and until we can obtain, I hope by voluntary effort, but if it were needed, and as a last resort by other means, as I have stated, the unmarried men."

This position was rendered still more definite and explicit by correspondence between Lord Derby and Mr. Asquith, which confirmed the pledge that no attested married men should be called up unless and until the unmarried men had been recruited voluntarily or conscripted by Act of Parliament.

Every possible effort was made to ensure the full success of the Derby Scheme. His Majesty the King wrote a special appeal: "To My People", supporting the scheme, which was issued on October 23rd. The instructions to the local Recruiting Committees as to carrying out the canvass were jointly considered, approved and signed by Lord Derby, by the Chairman of the Parliamentary Recruiting Committee, and by Mr. Arthur Henderson, Chairman of the Labour Recruiting Committee. The Closing Day for the canvass, originally fixed as November 30th, was extended to December 15th.

The result was rather what might have been anticipated. Married men attested in considerable numbers, secure in the assurance that they would not be expected to fulfil their promise unless and until all the single men had been called up. The single men attested much less generally. Out of 2,179,231 single men of military age not enlisted before October 23rd, 1915, the number presenting themselves under the Derby Scheme, and enlisted, attested or medically rejected, was 1,150,000, leaving 1,029,231, or nearly half the total, outside the scheme. Of those who put down their names, so many were either the medically unfit or "starred" men — men employed in jobs from which it was held that in the national interest they could not be spared for the Army — that Lord Derby estimated the net number of single men he would actually get for the Army through his scheme would be only 343,386 out of the total of 2,179,231 in the country.

In face of these figures, it was obviously impossible to pretend that Mr. Asquith's pledge to the married men had been fulfilled. Over a million single men had refused to attest, and the policy of recruiting them compulsorily was the inevitable sequel. As regards popular support for such a policy, all the attested married men were naturally insistent on it. They protested that it would be a breach of the promise made to them to summon them to the Colours while so many unmarried men were left at home.

Accordingly, on January 5th, 1916, after much heated discussion in the Cabinet, the first definite measure of conscription was introduced, when Mr. Asquith laid before Parliament a Military Service Bill to compel the attestation of all unmarried men, and widowers without children or dependents, between the ages of 18 and 41. Defending the Bill against the objections of anti-conscriptionists inside and outside the Government, he urged that it was necessary in redemption of the pledge he had given to Lord Derby — a pledge which he certainly considered to be within the limits and upon the general line of policy which had been agreed upon by the Cabinet. He was himself of the opinion that no case had been made out for general compulsion, and he thought the Bill would be sincerely supported by those who either on principle or — as in his case — on the ground of expediency were opposed to compulsion.

This line of argument failed to convince some of his opponents. Sir John Simon resigned from the Government rather than support conscription in any form, and rallied about three dozen other Liberal members into an opposition to attack the measure.

Sir John Simon, speaking on January 5th, 1916, in the debate on the Military Service Bill, declared that his opposition to any measure of conscription was one of fundamental principle, and he added that there were other members of the Government who had not resigned whose views on the matter were indistinguishable from his own. The reference was, of course, recognised as being to Mr. M'Kenna and Mr. Runciman, who had both opposed the measure strongly in the Cabinet. They did not, however, carry their principles to the point of resigning. When it came to the direct issue they based their objection, not on the fundamental principle with which Sir John Simon credited them, but on the argument that we could not spare from our national industries as many men as would be taken into the Army through conscription, nor afford to keep them under arms when we had got them. During the days immediately prior to the introduction of the measure it was thought that they also might resign if they could not get the Bill so modified as to limit and reduce the numbers liable to be called up under it.

Mr. Redmond and his Irish Nationalists opposed the Bill on its first introduction, but when they knew definitely that Ireland would be excluded from its scope they withdrew their opposition. The reason for the exclusion of Ireland was that the Bill was intended to implement the pledge given in connection with the Derby Scheme, and this scheme had not been worked in Ireland.

Mr. Arthur Henderson and the Labour Party were placed in a rather difficult position by a resolution of the Trades Unions at their Bristol Conference on January 5th condemning the Government's proposals. Mr. Asquith was, however, able to give Mr. Henderson official assurances that nothing in the nature of industrial conscription was contained in or implied by the Bill, and in consequence Mr. Henderson spoke and voted in support of the Second Reading. A minority of the Labour Party, led by Messrs. Ramsay MacDonald, Snowden, and Thomas, opposed the measure.

Carried through all its stages by overwhelming majorities, the Bill became law on January 27th, 1916. At midnight on March 1st all single men who had not already joined up were automatically reckoned as enlisted in His

Majesty's forces for the period of the war. The single men attested under the Derby Scheme had already been all called up, and a first call was now made on the attested married men, of whom the groups aged 19 to 27 were summoned to the colours.

So ended the first round. But the issue could not rest there. Forces were at work which, with a march as inevitable as destiny, pressed the nation forward into a complete system of compulsory service.

With the advance of the spring of 1916 there came a call from the military authorities for more recruits. This meant summoning the older groups of attested married men. But at the rumour of this a violent agitation broke out. These fathers of families declared that before they were called for, a much closer comb-out ought to be made of the single men, very many of whom were still at home, exempted from military service because they were in starred occupations. Further, it was insisted that the younger unattested married men ought to be called up before their elders were sent to the trenches. And the older men, with serious responsibilities for children, for houses, for businesses, ought to have some arrangements made to relieve them of their financial difficulties — leases, mortgages, and so on — before they were taken for the Army.

Fierce and long were the debates in the Cabinet on this issue. The calling up of the older classes of married men was postponed while the new phase of the problem was being studied. Mr. Asquith promised that on April 18th he would make a statement about recruiting, but on that day he had to announce a postponement because of Cabinet disagreements; and he followed this on the 19th by announcing a further postponement, as disagreement in the Cabinet was so serious as to threaten the break-up of the Government. He adjourned the House of Commons till April 25th, on which date a secret session of the House was held to thrash out the problem.

The existing shortage of men for the Army was proving itself serious, and the methods so far available for securing new recruits were proving insufficient. A month previously, on March 21st, 1916, the Chief of the Imperial General Staff, Sir William Robertson, had submitted a memorandum in which he stated that:

> ". . . As regard personnel we are not now in an appreciably better position for making that 'maximum effort' . . . than we were when I raised the question nearly three months ago. At the present time the infantry serving abroad is 78,000 below its establishment; the 13 Territorial Divisions at home are also deficient of 50,000 men. . . . Of the 193,891 men called up under the Military Service Act no fewer than 57,416 have failed to appear. . . ."

A note by the Army Council on the 15th of April, 1916, showed that the estimated deficit would on June 30th be 179,000 men, and that while as yet there were only 52 divisions abroad instead of the intended 62, there was a deficit of 66,000 men in their establishment.

At the secret session of Parliament on April 25th the situation was passed under review, and the Prime Minister put forward the Government proposals to deal with it. These were officially announced afterwards to include the extension of service of time-expired men, transfer of recruits from territorial to regular units, prompt enlistment of men whose exemption certificates had expired, and recruitment of all youths as they reached the age of 18. Further efforts were also proposed to enlist unattested married men, and if in a month's time 50,000 of these were not forthcoming, and 15,000 a week thereafter, then compulsion would be resorted to.

A second secret session was held on April 26th, and on the following day Mr. Walter Long introduced a Bill embodying the Government's proposals; but it was so adversely criticised that Mr. Asquith withdrew it. There was by now a quite general impatience with any further paltering or half-measures, which Mr. Asquith, with his usual good sense, clearly recognised. On May 2nd he announced that the Government would bring in a measure to impose general and immediate compulsory military service. This was introduced on the following day, and on May 25th it received the Royal Assent. The opposition to it was of quite a trivial nature. Sir John Simon's band of non-coöperators had sunk to twenty-seven, and Mr. Ramsay MacDonald's Labour group to ten.

I was in charge of the measure on its second reading in the House of Commons, and speaking on that occasion I challenged the appeal to principle made by its opponents:

"I have waited for this great overriding principle and I have not heard it yet. Is this Bill inconsistent with the principles of either Liberalism or democracy? Is it inconsistent with the principles of democracy that the State should demand the services and help of every man to defend its life when it is at stake? There is not and never has been a country yet faced with a great military peril that has ever saved itself without resort to compulsion. Never. It is true of autocracies, it is even more true of democracies. Where is the principle? I have a personal interest in finding out, because I have been told that I am a traitor to Liberal principles because I supported conscription; therefore I am personally interested in seeking it out. I cannot find it. Every great democracy which has been challenged, which has had its liberties menaced, has defended itself by resort to compulsion, from Greece downwards. Washington won independence for America by compulsory measures; America defended its independence in 1812 by compulsory measures. Lincoln was not merely a great democrat, but his career was in itself the greatest triumph that democracy has ever achieved in the sphere of government. He proclaimed the principle of 'Government of the People, by the People, for the People,' and he kept it alive by conscription. In the French Revolution the French people defended their newly obtained liberties against every effort of the autocracies of Europe by compulsion and by conscriptionary levies. France is defending her country to-day by conscription. In Italy the Italian democracy are seeking to redeem their enthralled brethren by compulsion. In Serbia the Serbian peasants defended their mountains by compulsory measures, and they are going to win them back by the same means. When honourable members say that conscription is contrary to the principles of liberty and true democracy, they are talking in defiance of the whole teaching of history and of common sense."

I also remarked that in face of the national emergency which made this measure imperative, I would submit to be driven out of my party, and out of public life altogether, rather than refuse it my support.

I had in fact been pressing the need for compulsory military service on the Government for a considerable time, and the importance of the part I had played in finally carrying it through was attested by two letters which I received at the time from Sir William Robertson. The first of these was of some length, and in it Robertson was good enough to comment in warm terms on my "great courage and patriotism", and wound up with the assertion that "but for you it would not have been done." The second was shorter, and I transcribe it in full:

"War Office.
2/5/1916.

"Dear Mr. Lloyd George, —

"The Bill introduced to-day should more than compensate you for the rubbishy Press attacks of the last week or two. The great thing is to get the Bill, and for it the Empire's thanks are due to you — alone.

Yours very truly,
WM. ROBERTSON."

These expressions of appreciation are perhaps the more important, because Sir William Robertson was not always in as cordial sympathy with my ideas. But if my zeal for this cause won me some approval in quarters not uniformly favourable to me, it added a fresh edge to the bitterness of those who held that my determination to fight the war through, without hesitation or reserve, was a most improper and, indeed, unholy attitude. The distrust and hostility of this section of Liberal opinion was henceforward confirmed and ineradicable. Speaking at Conway on May 6th, 1916, in advocacy of the Military Service Bill, I found myself compelled to reply to a series of attacks which had been directed against me by a prominent Liberal journalist who was at that time in close touch with some of my colleagues, for "abandoning Liberalism", "throwing such fervour into the prosecution of the War", and "having differences of opinion with my chief." To the first charge, the fact that a vast majority of Liberals in the House of Commons had supported the Conscription Bill sufficiently gave the lie. To the second charge I pleaded guilty on the ground that while I hated war, I held, once we had decided to wage war, that we must wage it effectively. "That is why I have had no sympathy with those who seem to think that because war is hateful, you ought to fight it with a sort of savour of regret in your actions. Doubting hand never yet struck firm blow."

Of my relations with Mr. Asquith I declared:

"I have worked with him for ten years; I have served under him for eight. If we had not worked harmoniously — and we have — let me tell you here at once it would have been my fault and not his. I have never worked with anyone who could be more considerate, and I disdain the things they have said. But we have had our differences. Good Heavens! What use would I have been if I had not differed? I should have been no use at all. He has shown me great kindness during the years I have worked with him. I should have ill requited them if I had not told my opinions freely, frankly, independently, whether they agreed with his or not.

"Freedom of speech is essential in everything, but there is one place where it is vital, and that is in the Council Chamber. The councillor who professes to agree with everything that falls from his leader has betrayed him."

Looking backward after the event, no one can now doubt that the adoption of conscription was vitally necessary for carrying the war through to victory. Without it we should have been overwhelmed when Russia, Roumania, and Serbia had all cracked and the French Army was threatening mutiny.

The effect on our Allies was heartening. Lord Esher in a memorandum dated May 4th, 1916, reported an interview he had just had with M. Briand, and stated:

"M. Briand spoke with enthusiasm and deep content of yesterday's proceedings in the English Parliament. He is certain that it will have far-reaching results in Germany, and will accentuate the uneasiness, growing fast among the Central Powers, as to the ultimate issue of the War. . . . The adoption of compulsory service in England will, he thinks, have a lowering effect on German mentality and morale.

"The effect in France will be even greater.

"In spite of all that England has done, which is well known to the French Government, there are many people in France in whose minds doubts still linger as to the determination of England to go through with the War to the bitter end. To these people the adoption by the English Parliament of a procedure so foreign to the traditions and habits of the English people will be a '*coup de massue*.' The whole French nation, he says, will now recognise that England means to make every necessary sacrifice, and any doubts that existed will be at once dispelled."

While recognising the necessity for the introduction of compulsory service, I have always emphasised and paid tribute to the magnificence of the voluntary effort which the manhood of the country put forward in 1914 and 1915. In my speech at Conway on May 6th, to which I have already referred, I said:

"The achievement of the nation in raising by voluntary methods those huge armies is something of which we may very well be proud. It is almost unparalleled in the history of war, and nothing which has happened since in the way of compulsory measures can ever detract from the pride we possess in the fact that we are the first nation in the history of the world that has raised over three millions of men for any great military enterprise purely by voluntary means. Young men from every quarter of this country flocked to the standard of international right as to a great crusade. It was a glorious achievement, and well may Britain be proud of it!"

According to a memorandum of the Committee of Imperial Defence, dated April 17th, 1916, the number of men who had by that date actually gone into service with the forces, naval and military, including those already serving at the outbreak of war, was 3,769,659, to which there should be added those in attested groups of married men not yet called up, and single men attested but retained in starred occupations, to a total of 697,000, making a grand total of 4,667,000 men as our full volunteer force, exclusive of contingents from the Dominions and India, which would bring the sum to well over 5,000,000.

On the day when the Military Service Bill received the Royal Assent, the King issued a "message to his people" in the following terms:

"Buckingham Palace,
25th May, 1916.

"To enable our country to organise more effectively its military resources in the present great struggle for the cause of civilisation, I have, acting on the advice of my Ministers, deemed it necessary to enrol every able-bodied man between the ages of eighteen and forty-one.

"I desire to take this opportunity of expressing to my people my recognition and appreciation of the splendid patriotism and self-sacrifice which they have displayed in raising by voluntary enlistment, since the commencement of the war, no less than 5,041,000 men, an effort far surpassing that of any other nation in similar circumstances recorded in history, and one which will be a lasting source of pride to future generations.

"I am confident that the magnificent spirit which has hitherto sustained my people through the trials of this terrible war will inspire them to endure the additional sacrifice now imposed upon them, and that it will, with God's help, lead us and our Allies to a victory which shall achieve the liberation of Europe.

GEORGE R.I."

CHAPTER VII

DISINTEGRATION OF THE LIBERAL PARTY

First dissidents in August, 1914 — Growth of anti-war feeling among political sectaries — Malcontents in the clubs: I find myself ostracised — A message from Theodore Roosevelt — Anti-conscriptionists' hostility breeds a split — Characteristics of Mr. M'Kenna — Liberal guerrilla war against second coalition — Tragedy of Mr. Percy Illingworth's death — War fatal to Liberalism — National safety more important than party issues: condition for honest coalition — My colleagues in the war.

THE fissures which showed themselves in the ranks of Liberalism during the debate on conscription were not of sudden growth. They had been steadily forming and widening during the previous twelve months. At the first challenge in 1914 a gust of patriotic fervour had swept the party forward in united resolve, and there were very few who felt compelled by their principles to join with Lord Morley, Mr. Trevelyan, and Mr. Burns in withdrawing from the Government and deciding to hold aloof from the conflict. The leaders of the National Liberal Federation issued on August 8th a circular announcing the indefinite suspension of party propaganda and calling on Liberals to sink political differences and give themselves to the service of the country; and the *Liberal Magazine* declared, "In the great war in which we are engaged, at whatever cost we must win."

But as the war went on the men brought up on the peace-loving precepts of Cobden and Bright and Gladstone disliked it more and more. They had no doubt or hesitation as to the justice or inevitability of our part in it. But they gradually became depressed at the sight of the dread machinery which thrust itself upon them in the highways and byways, and at the evidence of the accumulating horror which spread desolation throughout the land. The larger and more sagacious half of the party treated the war as a disagreeable necessity forced upon us in the defence of liberty, and to be brought to an end all the sooner by a vigorous organisation of all our available resources into a great national effort. But the real political sectary in his heart argued thus: "War is a hideous thing. You must show your aversion by waging it half-heartedly. Wield the sword with your left hand, and let your right nurse its strength until the blessed day arrives when it will be needed once more for swinging the sword of the Lord and of Gideon in the eternal fight for the principles to which we are attached." The men who threw the whole of their strength and spirit into waging war effectively were disliked and distrusted more and more by the sectarians. Every cannon and shell turned out by these men weighed them down deeper into perdition. Hence the heavier the guns they turned out the deeper their damnation. The men who won their admiration and trust were those leaders who proved the sincerity of their horror for war by waging it nervelessly. The more ineffective they became the greater was the trust which was placed in the integrity of their leadership by these high-minded followers. Even under the accommodating Premiership of Mr. Asquith there were ominous growls and occasional outbursts of impatience from the straitest of his supporters. They resented conscription, which had consequently to be carried in two steps. There is no greater mistake than to try to leap an abyss in two jumps.

The Opposition Lobbies, it is true, were not overcrowded with malcontents, but there were sinister grumblings in the corridors and tea-rooms. The activities of the Ministry of Munitions in turning out guns, rifles, shot, and shell on an unprecedented scale provoked irritation and even resentment amongst certain Liberals in Press, Parliament, and Club. The personal attitude of old political friends towards me changed and chilled after I became Minister of Munitions. It found petulant expression in speeches and articles, and I felt myself shunned and even spurned by men who once had greeted me with cordiality and enthusiasm. I was treated as one tainted with the leprosy of war. I had a sense of political isolation more complete than I had ever experienced during the whole of my lifetime. My old friends were turning their backs on me. The Conservatives had not yet forgotten the part I had played in the bitter controversies of the last few years, and the Liberals were resentful and sulky.

This attitude hurt me deeply, but it did not slow down by one pulsation my resolve to work energetically and to the limit of my power at the terrible task to which I had been called. I had assented to the declaration of war with tenacious reluctance, but once I was persuaded of its inevitable justice I threw myself with all my energy into the task of helping my country to vindicate the right. I was encouraged during these difficult times by a message which I received, early in 1916, from Theodore Roosevelt through a friend of his, Colonel Arthur Lee (now Lord Lee of Fareham), who acted as my military liaison officer at the Ministry of Munitions. Roosevelt's letter ran as follows:

"Dear Arthur,

"Your letter was most interesting, and I am more pleased than I can say that you are so hard at work and in so congenial and useful a way. Give my heartiest regards to Lloyd George. Do tell him I admire him immensely. I have always fundamentally agreed with his social program, but I wish it supplemented by Lord Roberts' external program. Nevertheless, my agreement with him in program is small compared with the fact that I so greatly admire the character he is now showing in this great crisis. It is often true that the only way to render great services is by willingness on the part of the statesman to lose his future, or, at any rate, his present position in political life, just exactly as the soldier may have to pay with his physical life in order to render service in battle. In a very small and unimportant way I have done this myself during the last eighteen months. I have paid no heed, and shall not pay the slightest heed, to the effect upon my own fortunes, of anything that I say. What I am trying to do is to make this country go right, and I don't give a damn as to what my countrymen think of me in the present or the future, provided only I can make them wake up to the sense of their duty. In an infinitely greater emergency, Lloyd George seems to me to be following the same line of conduct in trying to serve Great Britain at present.

"Don't make any mistake about me. I don't believe there is any chance of my being nominated, because, as I wrote Lodge the other day, it would be utter folly to nominate me, unless the country was in heroic mood. If they put 'Safety First' ahead of honour and duty, then they don't want me, and they need not expect that I will pussy-foot in any shape or way on the great issues that I regard as vital, and to which I regard all others as subordinate.

"I hope you have by this time seen a copy of my book. Read the first chapter and the conclusion. Perhaps Lloyd George might be interested in looking at two or three sentences that you may care to show him. . . ."

As long as the party was united there was no organised secession. Sir John Simon's feeble efforts to lead a "cave" on conscription were a ridiculous failure. He is a very able man, but he commands neither the boldness, the breadth, nor the inspiration that are essential to great leadership. But apart from these issues there was inside the Cabinet a definite group which sought to drive a wedge between the Prime Minister and myself. As long as I was at the Exchequer I saw Mr. Asquith almost every morning before the Cabinet and discussed with him matters of urgency.

Interviews were easily arranged when I worked at the Treasury Buildings, which had a door opening into 10 Downing Street.

On my way to the Treasury from 11 Downing Street I passed through the Prime Minister's residence. We invariably got on well and pleasantly together when we met. But when I went to the Ministry of Munitions I had to be there by nine o'clock and I found it difficult to leave until late in the evening. I thus saw much less of Mr. Asquith. In fact I saw very little of him alone for months. That was the opportunity of the mischief-makers and they took full advantage of it. When I left the Exchequer and Mr. M'Kenna took my place it was understood that his appointment was to be provisional. I was to return to my post at the Treasury as soon as I had set munitions going. This arrangement was a mistake and did much harm. The very possibility of its ever materialising made of Mr. M'Kenna a bitter enemy and poisoned his personal relations towards me. Ever afterwards they remained septic. This condition made business transactions in which I was engaged as Minister — all involving finance — very difficult. I ought to have assured him from the outset that I had no intention of ever claiming the redemption of the Prime Minister's pledge. Mr. M'Kenna possessed many of the gifts that make a good administrator in times that do not call especially for imagination, breadth of vision, or human insight. He knew the details of his job as Chancellor, he was a competent arithmetician, a ready reckoner (Mr. Balfour once said he was "an adroit accountant"); he was, in fact, a master of finance in blinkers. His chief defect, as I have already pointed out, was that he was apt to divide his more conspicuous colleagues into those he liked and those he viewed with distrust, suspicion, and jealousy. This peculiarity made him a source of weakness and danger in a team. His was the most active personal element in the disintegration of the Asquith Coalition. A lady with a gift of satirical analysis of character once said to me that he was like one of those shilling paint-boxes given to children. The blocks were hard and angular, the colours were all very definite and crude. He possessed none of those delicate tints which you find on an artist's palette.

From June, 1915, to June, 1916, I was so immersed in the hurrying on of munitions for our hard-pressed Army that I had very little time to watch the political situation or to keep in touch with politicians in or out of the House of Commons and I did not quite realise how far hostile intrigues had gone. When, later on at the end of 1916, the definite split came in the party and most of the Liberal members of the Cabinet declined further responsibility for the conduct of the war except under conditions of personal leadership which were unacceptable to the nation, all restraint disappeared, and no likely opportunity was missed for criticising and occasionally embarrassing the Government of the day. The attacks were generally left to guerrillas, but the sympathy and encouragement of leaders to these snipings were not wanting and were barely concealed. On two or three conspicuous occasions which appeared to be propitious, leaders and all joined in the assault, horse, foot, and artillery. The official organisation set to work energetically in the country to spread suspicions and undermine confidence in the War Cabinet which was prosecuting the war with such excessive zeal. Multitudes of true Liberals did their best to save Liberalism from the eternal reproach of presenting this factiousness as the only contribution which their party was able to make to the security of the nation at a time of unparalleled danger in its history. For this they were persecuted, and for this they have never been forgiven by those whose futility in a grave emergency has doomed Liberalism to a generation of querulous impotence.

What would have happened had the party kept together to the end? It is impossible to surmise. There was one man who, if he had survived the war, might have kept the Liberal leaders from separating — the late Mr. Percy Illingworth. Without his powerful help as Chief Whip, Mr. Asquith was unequal to the task of reconciling personal differences and imposing unity. Percy Illingworth was the best type of Englishman — straight, competent, fearless, with a complete subordination of self to duty. He was devoted to Mr. Asquith as his leader — he was proud of him as a Yorkshireman. He was attached to me as a friend. He was loyal to us both, and we both knew and trusted him implicitly. He had a thorough cognisance of the intrigues of little men who plotted incessantly to separate us, and as long as he was there he kept a vigilant eye upon their activities and intimidated them with his Yorkshire bluntness of speech. In January, 1915, he died of typhoid acquired by eating a bad oyster. Had he been alive in 1916 there would have been no split between Mr. Asquith and myself. Of that I am convinced. What trifling incidents often precipitate important events! A rotten mollusc poisoned the whole Liberal Party for years and left it enfeebled. Later on the bite of a monkey in Greece altered the whole course of events in the Levant and had its reactions much farther afield.

War has always been fatal to Liberalism. "Peace, Retrenchment, and Reform" have no meaning in war. Moreover, a nation, to make war effectively, must be prepared to surrender individual right and freedom for the time being. If the war is prolonged, that submission becomes a habit. Victory is the triumph of force and not of reason. After every great war there is a period during which belligerent nations incline to divide into two extreme camps — roughly known as revolutionary and reactionary. In that temper

Liberalism is at a disadvantage. That is why it is to-day at a discount throughout Europe. Even in America its doctrines assume the form of a dictatorship. The collapse of the Liberal Party in this country was inevitable from the moment it became responsible for the initiation and conduct of a great war. The instinct of the ordinary Liberal in that respect was sound. The War therefore made him uneasy.

1914 was a catastrophe for Liberalism. That was unfortunate, but the issues at stake were too big for treatment in terms of party interests. The challenge to international right and freedom was so tremendous that Liberalism — above all Liberalism — could not shirk it. When millions of men placed their lives at the disposal of their country without giving a thought to the political complexion of the Government or Minister to whose call they were responding or whose decrees they were obeying, it would be but a sorry boast for politicians who face no such danger to claim that they also had forgotten party interests in their country's peril. But there are certain obvious principles which should govern politics in such circumstances. Any combination of parties in a national emergency, if it is to be effective, involves a readiness in all the parties concerned to give and take. The moment it becomes a blind or subterfuge for the attainment of its aims by one party in the combination, then it is a selfish fraud practised on the nation. The two war Coalitions were honestly worked for patriotic ends. I saw Mr. Asquith at the head of two war Governments, one Liberal, the other Coalition, and from a close acquaintance with him during both administrations, I am able to say, and do say unhesitatingly and without qualification that, once war was declared, in neither of his Governments did he give any thought to party advantage. Indeed, so completely did he forget even party principles during his second administration that, in his desire to propitiate old opponents and so ensure unity, he assented to a Protectionist Budget, and even went so far as to pledge the country, by an agreement entered into with its Allies at the famous Paris Conference, to a drastic and far-reaching policy of protection after the war.

Whether general danger to a community comes from flood, fire, or war, the instinct that leads to common action rather than to divided counsels is the same. It is evinced primarily by a readiness to coöperate with anyone who is willing and fit to climb the ladder, play the hose, handle the axe, or in any useful way face and fight the fire.

This elementary parable represents my views on the correct position of the party system during a war great enough to demand the undivided attention and whole energy of a nation.

For my own part, throughout the whole war, I never made inquiries as to a helper's political past. And when I knew the party to which he belonged, that fact exercised no influence whatever on my judgment of his qualification. I only wanted to ascertain his fitness for his job.

The two men of whom I saw most during the last two years of the war, when I had supreme direction, were Mr. Bonar Law and Lord Milner, both of whom belonged to the political side opposed to my own. And yet at our numerous conferences and consultations I was never even remotely conscious of their party associations. Why should I have been? When specialists are called into consultation on a case of serious illness, foolish indeed would be the relative and even criminal would be the doctor who thought more of the political views of these experts than of their qualifications to assist in pulling the patient through the crisis. Unhappily for the Liberal Party it included, at that supreme time of trial, many doctors and kinsmen who took another and narrower view of their responsibilities, and who protested stoutly that consultants tainted with political heresy should be excluded from the sick-room. And these bigots have never forgiven those who adopted a different attitude.

CHAPTER VIII

LORD KITCHENER: A CHARACTER STUDY

Conflicting estimates of him — Flashes of greatness — Fixed ideas — Contempt for democracy — Opposition to Nonconformist chaplains — Fight over the Welsh Division — Attitude to Irish Division — The two Irish flags — A Welsh prisoner's adroit complaint — Gifts of organisation — Long view of war's duration — Immense value of his personal appeal — Accurate forecast of German strategy — Unreceptive to new developments of warfare — Decline of his authority — Crushing effect of news of his death.

To me Lord Kitchener is one of the unsolved mysteries of the war. Was he a great man, or was he a great disappointment? There were many competent observers who knew him well, but took different views of his character — there were many who held conflicting estimates alternatively and simultaneously. But no one who ever saw him regarded him as an ordinary man, for his very appearance had a distinction all its own. What he did well he did with a sway that was peculiar to himself. When he saw, his vision was penetrating. Even his failings were not ordinary. He held childish opinions on some matters, but they were not commonplace. When he did silly things, as the wisest men occasionally do, they were extraordinarily silly. His intuitions, his improvisations, his visions — yes, even his stupidities — were all far removed from the average.

A lady with a pernicious gift for stinging epigram described him as "Not a great man, but a great poster." He was, indeed, the greatest "poster" since Boulanger, but he was far more. He was certainly not a Boulanger, for he was conspicuously free from the vice of the *poseur*. After having been in close touch with him and having seen him at work every week and almost every day, for nearly two years, I could not even then quite make up my mind about his qualities. Of this I feel certain, he had flashes of greatness. He was like one of those revolving lighthouses which radiate momentary gleams of revealing light far out into the surrounding gloom and then suddenly relapse into complete darkness. There were no intermediate stages. Now and again he would express an opinion or give utterance to an illuminating phrase that penetrated the fog of war, and then sometimes he would indulge in a garrulousness which displayed the greatest ignorance of the elementary conditions with which he had to deal. He had an ineffable contempt for the Territorials and a puerile fear of the Senussi. I heard him talk of the Territorials as if they were a worthless rabble of make-believes. On the other hand, I heard him talk with woe of the possibility of a million Senussi horsemen sweeping into the Egyptian Delta. Whether he had always been so, or whether the tropical sun had scorched and parched some of his intelligence, leaving merely oases of verdure and fertility, I cannot judge, for I only met him once previously, some three years before the war. He was then full of admiration for the German Army and pitying contempt for the French Army. "They will walk through them like partridges," was one of his phrases. I discovered that his opinion was not based on military but on political reasons. There is no greater fatuity than a political judgment dressed in a military uniform. What convinced him of the superiority of the German to the French soldier was that the latter had been demoralised by democratic views and concomitant ideas of liberty which were utterly incompatible with true discipline, whereas the former was trained to obey his superiors. He was right and he was wrong. The German system proved superior for the short course, but French democracy was the better in the long run. The autocratic system of the German Empire crashed hopelessly when it had to bear the burden of a great defeat.

Kitchener's rigid point of view and its reactionary arrogance showed itself in other directions. Some of his mental veins had hardened and any pressure on them produced apoplectic results. He vehemently opposed the recognition of Nonconformist denominations not already included in the Army List, and his refusal to appoint chaplains of what he evidently thought were superfluous and eccentric sects provoked the most angry scenes I have ever witnessed at a Cabinet. The Army only recognised three or four denominations. The others, not being on the Army List, had no existence for him. He did not realise that with an army that was being multiplied tenfold and drawing recruits from classes, or rather types, untapped by the ordinary recruiting sergeant, the variety of religious beliefs held must necessarily be greater. To his mind the religious services provided for the regulars of the old Army ought to be good enough for these amateur soldiers. The vital importance of encouraging national coöperation by deferring to all legitimate susceptibilities did not occur to him. This showed the light occulted. When he gave way, however, he did it thoroughly. I well remember how, when he had been overruled by the Cabinet on the question of chaplains, he took a piece of paper, started writing, and turning to me said: "Come now, tell me the names of these sects for which you want padres. Is this list right? 'Primitive Baptists, Calvinistic Wesleyans, Congregational Methodists' — ?" It was not intended to cast ridicule; he simply had never heard the correct names of these great religious bodies. I gave him the right titles. He wrote them all down carefully. As soon as he returned to the War Office he took steps to invite representatives of all these denominations to attend a Chaplains Committee there. It functioned right through the war without any friction.

A smaller man, according to the wont of small men, would have pretended to signify agreement, and then have placed every obstacle in the path of execution. Lord Kitchener may or may not have been a great man, but he certainly was not a small one, and here his action was that of greatness, for having been overruled, he loyally accepted defeat.

His attitude towards the various nationalities that constitute the people of the United Kingdom was more obdurate, and his obstinacy had far-reaching and fatal results. Scotchmen had by tradition established a military title to their nationality, and it was a title Lord Kitchener respected and honoured. But although Welshmen and Irishmen had also their separate national regiments, he declined to encourage their national sentiments when it came to the point of raising separate Welsh and Irish divisions. The case of the Welsh Division was one with which I was naturally particularly concerned. In order to encourage recruiting in the Principality, a number of influential Welshmen, with the Earl of Plymouth at their head, decided to form and raise a purely Welsh Division. Colonel Owen Thomas took a very active part in this effort. But when the proposal came before Lord Kitchener he promptly vetoed it. The question was thereupon raised by me in the Cabinet, and there was a fierce fight. In the end the cause of the Welsh Division was carried. Lord Kitchener came to me afterwards and said: "What was the name of the officer who pressed this scheme forward?" I told him it was Colonel Owen Thomas. "Can you bring him along to me?" asked Kitchener, and I promised to do so. The Colonel was summoned posthaste to London, and I took him round to Kitchener, at the War Office. Kitchener bent on him a terrific frown, and Thomas, though a stout-hearted fellow, visibly quailed on seeing that imposing personage with his stern face and his terrifying eyes. Lord Kitchener rumbled forth: "I understand you are a Colonel." Thomas timidly signified assent. "Would you like to become a Brigadier-General?" Thomas could not find his tongue, and I answered promptly for him, "Of course he would!" "Then I will make you a Brigadier-General for this Welsh Division. Carry on!" said Kitchener.

In the case of the Welsh Division he thus made a handsome surrender. But unhappily for the country, he maintained his dislike for the Irish Division. This formation represented poor John Redmond's last effort to bring Ireland effectively into the war. He addressed recruiting meetings throughout Ireland, and his eloquence won thousands of young Irish Nationalists and Catholics to fight under the standard of freedom and justice raised by the British Empire. His brother, William Redmond, one of the best-loved members of the House of Commons, took a commission in this new unit, and he subsequently fell fighting under the British flag in France. But Lord Kitchener did his best to damp the ardour of the Redmonds. He refused commissions to educated young Irishmen of the class and type who were being made officers in England, Scotland, and Wales for no conceivable reason, except that he distrusted and disliked their nationalism. The culminating incident will take an invidiously prominent place in the tragic history of Irish relations with Great Britain. Nationalist ladies, fired with enthusiasm for the new Irish Division, for Mr. Redmond and for the cause to which they were devoting themselves, embroidered a silken flag with the Irish harp emblazoned upon it. At the same moment the patriotic ladies of Ulster were embroidering the Red Hand of Ulster on the flag which they designed to present to a division which was being raised in Ulster. In due course the two flags were presented to the respective divisions. One was taken and the other was left. When Lord Kitchener heard of the green flag and its Irish harp, he ordered that it should be taken away. But the Ulster flag was allowed to fly gloriously over the heads of the Orange soldiers of the Protestant North. Ireland was deeply hurt. Her pride was cut to the quick, her sense of fair play was outraged, her sympathy with the Holy War against the military dictatorship of Europe was killed, and John Redmond's heart was broken. He ought to have appealed to Parliament, but he probably knew it was too late to avert the evil. From that moment the effort of Irish Nationalism to reconcile England and Ireland by uniting the two peoples in a common effort for the oppressed of another land failed, and Lord Kitchener's sinister order constituted the first word in a new chapter of Irish history.

Like all great men he had a sense of humour. Amongst my papers I came across a pleasant reminder of this fact. A Welsh mariner interned at Ruhleben had sent home a letter in which he had sought successfully to convey without censorship, to his relations at home, some notion of the severity of the conditions in that camp. The letter was sent on to Kitchener. Here is the letter:

"Englisches Lager,
Barake 11,
Ruhleben,
Bei Spandau,
Berlin.

"Dear Wife and Children,

"I have your letter of the 1st, and am pleased to know you are all well. I am afraid we are here for a long time and we dread the winter. I wish I were at home with you.

"I am still keeping well and I cannot say any more. My love to you all, and my respects to Cig, Tan, Menin, and Siwgr, whom I have not seen this long time, but hope to see when I get home.

&c., &c."

A footnote by Lord Kitchener's correspondent explains that:

"The words as above (Cig, Tan, Menin, Siwgr) are Welsh, and the interpretation of them respectively is:

Meat
Fire
Butter
Sugar."

A copy was sent on by Lord Kitchener to Sir Edward Grey and myself with this endorsement:

"Sir Edward Grey
"Mr. Lloyd George.

"The value of the Welsh language in dealing with the cultured Teuton.

K."

When I met him subsequently at the Cabinet he chortled over the incident.

His was a hypnotic personality and the impulse of his magnetism moved multitudes of men to willing action. Was he a great organiser? I cannot tell, even though I saw his greatest tasks. He undoubtedly possessed some of the rarest qualities of the great organiser — the gifts of improvisation, of drive, of leadership. But he had developed two patent defects, a reluctance to delegate and, more serious still, an inability to choose the right men.

Lord Kitchener was one of the first to realise the magnitude of the war. When most men talked of peace before Christmas he predicted a three years' struggle and set out — as far as men were concerned — to prepare for it. He made a call first for half a million and then for a million more. He knew that with the means at his disposal not one half of them would be available for the field for a full year. As a matter of fact the first battle of the first divisions of the "K" army was fought in September, 1915. His views as to the duration of the campaign changed somewhat from time to time, and in the spring of 1915 he predicted that the German reserves would be exhausted by September. But nothing can rob him of the credit for the vision that foresaw in August, 1914, a three years' campaign, and for the energy and wisdom with which he set out at once to prepare for it.

I doubt whether any other man could at that moment have attracted the hundreds of thousands who rallied to the flag at his appeal. And those who were responsible for placing the striking portrait of Lord Kitchener's strong face on the appeals to fight for "King and Country" had a genius for publicity. It was eminently the face of a commander. The resolution of its firm lines, the mixture of calm penetration and determination in the steady eyes, the intelligence of the broad, square brow, all gave an impression of irresistible strength that inspired everyone who saw it. And in those stormy days who was there who did not gaze on those granite features with a confidence of the kind that led the nation to heights of sacrifice? He was cast in nature's mould for a hero.

Another proof of Lord Kitchener's military vision was given in August, 1914, when the intention of the Germans to advance through Belgium was still unknown. General Joffre and his advisers were confident that the real blow would come from the Ardennes and that no serious German forces would advance in the Mons direction. Their view was that the roads in that quarter were not suited for the progress and maintenance of a great army. Lord Kitchener took a different view; and I have a distinct recollection of his expressing his opinion to the Cabinet. The event proved he was right. The French Commander's mistake was very nearly fatal to the Allied cause.

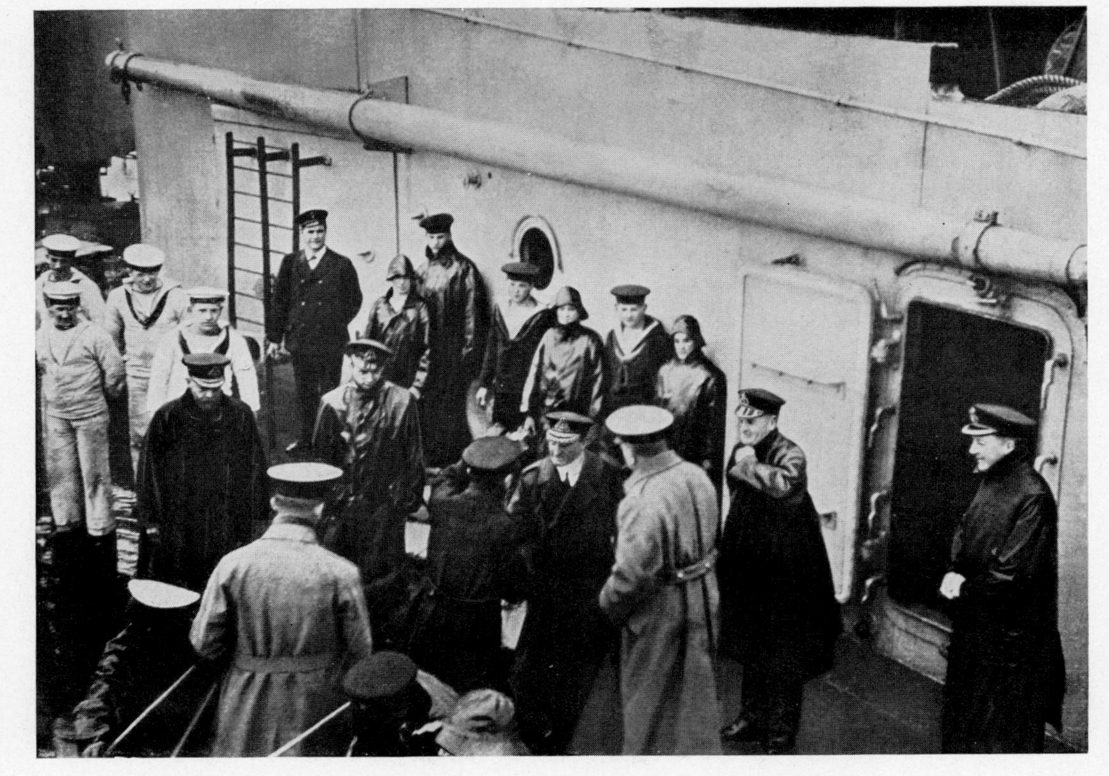

ADMIRAL OF THE FLEET EARL JELLICOE BIDDING GOOD-BYE TO LORD KITCHENER ON BOARD *HAMPSHIRE*

Within half an hour of the taking of this photograph Hampshire *struck a mine and Lord Kitchener was drowned*

Kitchener had not the mind for directing a great war conducted along lines to which he was completely unaccustomed either by training or experience. He never took to the manufacture of heavy guns for field warfare and he was sceptical of the prodigal expenditure of shells in trench warfare. He did not realise the part which the machine gun was destined to play in the war.

As the operations developed on lines which were farther and farther removed from his conception of warfare he became less and less effective and his judgment was less and less trusted by his colleagues. It is not too much to say that during the last few months of his stay at the War Office he was a *roi fainéant*. Sir William Robertson was appointed to the position of Chief of the Imperial General Staff with powers that reduced Lord Kitchener's position to that of a signatory Minister. He held the Seals of Office, but so far as war direction was concerned he had to use them under Sir William Robertson's orders. It was no doubt a humiliating position for a great soldier, because he was in every respect a greater man and a greater soldier than the keeper of his seals. Nevertheless, his hold on the public never diminished, and to the end there was always a small crowd waiting outside the War Office watching to catch a glimpse of him. And when the sad news broke upon London that he had gone down with the *Hampshire* in the cruel waters of the North Atlantic, a pall of dismay descended on the spirit of the people. Men and women spoke of the event in hushed tones of terror. The news of a defeat would not have produced such a sense of irreparable disaster. The tidings of the German advance of March, 1918, did not send such a shudder of despair through Britain as did the news of the tragic end of this remarkable man. I am not capable of analysing Lord Kitchener's attributes or gifts. But he was one of the great personalities of the war who exercised an indubitable effect on its course and thus on the destiny of the whole world. Great Britain and her Allies owe to the memory of Lord Kitchener the undying gratitude and the enduring fame which are the due of great service rendered greatly in a great cause.

CHAPTER IX

AT THE MINISTRY FOR WAR

News of Kitchener's fate — My ministerial situation — Not attracted to War Office — Draft memorandum of my views on the situation — Powerlessness of War Secretary — Need to mobilise civilian ability — Military distrust of brilliancy — Failure of War Office strategy — Success of Ministry of Munitions — Lack of sympathy with war direction — Plan to form a "ginger" opposition — I am persuaded to withdraw opposition — I take over the War Office — Two chief tasks: Transport and Mesopotamia — The Russian issue — Sir William Robertson invited to go — My letter to Mr. Asquith of 26/9/16 — Sir William Robertson refuses to go: his letter — Bad news from Russia — War weariness growing — Effects of German propaganda — Too late.

On the sixth day of June, 1916, I walked across from the Ministry of Munitions to attend a War Council at 10, Downing Street. Before I entered the Cabinet Chamber the Prime Minister's Secretary, Mr. Bonham Carter, beckoned me into his room and jerked out something about the *Hampshire*. Usually quiet and composed, he was obviously labouring under some suppressed emotion which rendered his speech scarcely articulate. At last he was able to convey to me the startling news that the cruiser in which Lord Kitchener had sailed for Russia had struck a mine off the Orkneys and that Lord Kitchener and his staff had all been drowned. When I entered the Cabinet Room I found the Prime Minister, Sir Edward Grey, Mr. Balfour and Sir Maurice Hankey sitting at the table, all looking stunned by the tragedy. One realised how deep was the impression made by the personality of this extraordinary man on all who came in contact with him. Sir Maurice Hankey and I quite forgot for the moment that had it not been for the Irish negotiations we also would have shared the same fate.

The passing of Lord Kitchener left an empty place at the War Office. I realised that this post might be offered to me.

But I was far from eager to go to the War Office under present conditions. Although the post of Secretary of State for War was a much more exalted one than that of the Minister of Munitions, and during the present hostilities came second in importance only to that of Prime Minister, it had during recent months declined very much in real influence. Lord Kitchener had lost much of his grip, and, as I have related above, the effective direction of War Office matters had been delegated by a special order in Council to his Chief of Staff. I had no liking for the prospect of finding myself a mere ornamental figurehead in Whitehall. It is a part I would play grudgingly and gracelessly. Had the Secretaryship of State been a live office, where the Minister exercised supreme control subject to Prime Minister and Cabinet, I should have welcomed the promotion. It would have afforded the opportunity to pull things together and alter the direction of affairs. I was becoming increasingly dismayed and dissatisfied at the course along which affairs were drifting, and seriously considered whether I could not render more effective help to our country by resigning office altogether, in order that, as an independent critic, not bound by the traditions of Cabinet unity, I might urge in Parliament and in the country a more vigorous and intelligent prosecution of the war.

Among my papers I find the draft of a memorandum which I prepared on June 17th, 1916, for the purpose of laying before Mr. Asquith my views, in reply to his offer of the Secretaryship for War. This is what I had set down:

"I wrote you the other day asking you to let me have an opportunity of placing before you certain serious considerations before you made up your mind finally about the War Office. Let me at once relieve your mind of one possible anxiety. During the eight years I have had the privilege of serving under you I have no doubt given you from time to time a good deal of worry, but it has never been due to any personal claims I have ever pressed upon you. You were good enough to admit that, when the present Coalition Administration was formed. I do not now propose to ask you for any personal consideration or advancement, as you will realise later on. I have made other plans. But that emboldens me to place before you one or two considerations of a very urgent character. . . .

"1. If the Allies are to be pulled together and to be induced to coöperate, you must have a Secretary of State for War who, apart from possessing personality, will possess real power and influence. No statesman with any self-respect would consent to occupy office under the humiliating conditions to which poor Kitchener had been reduced during the last few months of his life. Many a time I have seen him wince under the indignity of his position. Unless the Secretary of State has the ultimate say in patronage he will be treated with supreme contempt in his own department, and by the whole of the Army. Such a man would have no weight in the councils of the Allies, at a time when it is most urgent that his voice should be cast on the side of unity and coöperation.

"2. There are many important spheres of activity in the British Army which would be better placed under civilian than under military direction. It is no use referring to what is done in Continental armies. Those armies numbered millions, and the best brains of the nation were attracted by the great prizes which were to be won by service in them. Ours was a small thing. The rewards were necessarily limited in number and scope. Where good brains are to be found in the British Army they ought to be put into tasks which civilians cannot discharge. They are wasted on mere business and contractual jobs. On the other hand, if the brains devoted to that class of work are not good, the Army suffers very severely and there is extravagance without efficiency. I never can get a soldier to realise this; he has a rooted prejudice against giving what has always been regarded as a military job to a civilian.

"3. Soldiers are not very eager to promote brilliant subordinates, who may, if very successful, dim their lustre. They are not consciously influenced by such rivalries, but unconsciously they undoubtedly are. They prefer a safe, second-rate man in a position affording great opportunities, to running the risk of creating formidable rivals by choosing men of exceptional powers. This undoubtedly accounts for one or two appointments in the British Army, and still more for two or three non-appointments. A civilian on the other side would have no sense of rivalries in military promotion and he would insist upon the best man being appointed.

"4. No wise civilian would ever dream of embarking upon strategy. A man who did that would be fit for no post in any ministry. He would be a danger. There you must be advised by the expert. But the expert must also have his schemes checked by the common sense of the civilian. That is what happens in the War Committee. Great strategical enterprises ought to be submitted not merely to the Secretary of State, but to the War Committee. The soldiers in this war have not been a conspicuous success. Up to the present there has not been a plan conceived and carried out by them which has not ended in bloody failure.

"These are some of the thoughts I wanted to put before you determined your action. As I have already stated, I have no personal interest in the matter. I propose now to take a course which I had determined upon long ago. I have been profoundly dissatisfied for a long time with the progress and conduct of the War. I have expressed my dissatisfaction in writing and orally to you, the War Committee and the Cabinet. Had it not been for the fact that I had undertaken a task the carrying out of which was vital to the success of our Army, I should long ago have joined Carson, with whom I have been in the main in complete sympathy in his criticisms of the conduct of the War. But when there was trouble with labour, when the organisation which I had with the help of others created had not yet borne fruit, I felt as if I were running away from the post of difficulty. But now the Munitions Department has been an undoubted success. Ammunition is pouring in. When I came in we were manufacturing in this country 70,000 shells a week; that is about one-sixth of what we spend now in a single week of ordinary trench warfare activity. The whole ammunition reserve was under 75,000; we produce more than twice that per day now. The guns are coming in by the hundred. The policy for which I was mainly responsible in respect of heavy guns — a policy, by the way, which I heard described by one of my colleagues as "sheer lunacy," and which has been consistently opposed by him and by others for months — has now been demonstrated by the facts of the war to be the only one that can possibly achieve success. Our Army in France is now sending in a requisition for hundreds more of heavy guns than had ever been ordered by the War Office. Had it not been that I had in defiance of all authority high and low made arrangements for the manufacture of these guns, the requisition would be in vain.

"I am only pointing out these things in order to show that the Munitions Department ought almost to be able to run itself now. I therefore feel that my position in the Ministry is an anomalous one, as I am completely out of sympathy with the spirit and the method of the war direction. I feel we cannot win on these lines. We are undoubtedly losing the war, and nothing can save us but the nation itself. The people do not realise how grave the situation is. I feel they ought to be told. They ought to have a chance of saving themselves, otherwise they have a right to turn round on those who hold these views and say when disaster comes: 'Why did you not tell us in time?' I know you have always taken a more optimistic view of the prospects, but I think you will agree that up to the present my gloomy forebodings have been realised. I hope to God I am wrong; but if I am not, I should feel I had been guilty of a gross neglect of duty if in order to retain a pleasant office I had chosen to muzzle myself and not warn them in time of the danger impending their country. This is no newly formed resolution on my part, as the Lord Chief Justice can tell you, for I intimated to him many weeks ago my intention on the subject. There are things which must be said not merely to our own countrymen, but to the Allies, which cannot be said by one who is still a member of the Cabinet, and yet it is essential to the winning of the war that these warnings should be uttered. I have found it very difficult to refrain from expressing my opinion in conversations, and I am conscious that to do so whilst I am still a member of the Government lays me open to the charge of disloyalty, so that I find myself in the unhappy position of having to choose between disloyalty to my colleagues and the betrayal of my country.

"It is with deep regret that from an overwhelming sense of public duty I feel that I must sever my association with you and with some of my other colleagues who have shown me great kindness and goodwill, but I am profoundly convinced that I can render better service to my country in a very dark hour by standing outside and telling them what I know. I believe the Government is rapidly losing the confidence of the nation. It cannot retain it by artificially prolonging the life of Parliament. The nation ought to have an opportunity of choosing its own policy and its own representatives to expound it, and I specially feel that the men in the trenches ought to have an opportunity of choosing the Parliament and the policy on which their lives depend. Here again I am conscious of being out of touch with several of my colleagues and I cannot help seeing that there is an attempt being made to put off a decision on this important question until it is too late to act.

"As to Ireland, as far as I am concerned it must be either through or off in the course of the next few days; but I feel that outside the Government I can be more helpful even in the settlement of that question."

That memorandum gives a pretty definite indication of the views I had formed by that time about the situation; and it shows some of the reasons why I was loath to take on the position of Secretary of State for War. However, after further talks with Mr. Asquith, with Lord Reading, who was strongly opposed to resignation, with Mr. Bonar Law and also with Lord Beaverbrook, who was present at all my conversations with Mr. Bonar Law on the subject of the conduct of the war, from this time onward to the reconstruction of the Government, I was persuaded to give up the idea of resignation. I also consulted a very old and always a very good friend of mine, the late Sir Edward Russell (afterward Lord Russell) of the *Liverpool Post.* I sent my memorandum on to him, but he advised against resignation. Mr. Bonar Law urged that if I resigned and joined Carson in criticism it would make his position in the Government quite intolerable. He also would have to retire. Thus we should break up the national unity. I therefore decided not to send in my memorandum, and to postpone for the time my intention of leaving the Government. I accepted the War Office with considerable misgivings, partly on the ground of general war policy and partly because I disliked working in fetters.

On July 6th, 1916, therefore, Mr. Asquith, who had been once again in temporary charge of the War Office, pending the appointment of Lord Kitchener's successor, handed it over to me.

I was at the War Office for only five months — too short a time to effect much change in its internal organisation and policy, particularly since the Chief of Staff, Sir William Robertson, regarded any effort to exercise authority on my part as an impingement upon his special powers, so he thrust out all his prickles whenever he suspected I might be about to attempt any rash civilian interference with the sanctities of military matters. The two chief tasks which I was able to carry out during my brief tenure — tasks of which I give some account in following sections — were the tidying up of the appalling muddle in Mesopotamia, and the reconstruction of the transport system on the Western Front. I also stirred up recruiting in the Empire outside these islands.

In these problems, which I inherited with my new office,

I claim to have achieved a good measure of success. In the case of another inherited problem I was less happy. This was the matter of a military mission to Russia. I had from time to time since the war began pressed the Government to establish closer relations between the Western Allies and Russia. I was anxious not only to secure a more effective coördination between East and West, but also to find out what could be done towards reëquipping and thus reorganizing the Russian Armies.

Lord Kitchener was on his way to Russia when he lost his life. It was a mission of extreme urgency, for the critical state of affairs in that Allied country could hardly be exaggerated, and if she were to be saved from collapse it was vital that we in the West should come to a good understanding with her on matters of strategy, finance, and equipment supply.

Lord Kitchener had preëminently possessed the right qualifications for this mission. Now that he was gone, it became a question of finding someone suitable to replace him.

The obvious and in fact inevitable person for this mission was Sir William Robertson. As Chief of the Imperial General Staff he possessed the necessary status, prestige, and qualifications. The only conceivable alternative would have been General Haig, the Commander-in-Chief, who clearly could not be spared from France in the middle of a great offensive. True, Robertson was not an authority on finance, but this could be got over by sending Lord Reading with him to deal with questions of that nature which needed to be settled.

Robertson made difficulties. The Somme offensive was in full blast, and he was very busy with the arrangements it involved. Time slipped by, and when we reached the latter part of September I felt it was imperative to bring matters to a head; for Archangel was ice-bound in winter, and winter would soon be here.

Accordingly I wrote the following letter to Mr. Asquith:

"War Office,
26th September, 1916.

"CONFIDENTIAL.

"My dear Prime Minister,

"Before you come to a final decision on the suggestion that I made to you this morning, as I attach very great importance to something being done on those lines, I should like to put before you once more the considerations which convinced me that action on this matter is essential. I have thought so for some time.

"(1) The tone of some of the communications from Petrograd indicates a good deal of irritation against us in Russian official, and specially in Russian military circles.

"(2) The Germanophile influences have been considerably strengthened in the Russian Government by recent changes. Our friends have disappeared one by one and there is no man now of any influence in the Russian Bureaucracy who can be said to be favourable towards this country.

"(3) The Russians, like all peasant peoples, are very suspicious of a trading and financial community. They always imagine that we are trying to get the better of them in a bargain. The mere fact that their suspicion is a ridiculous one to a business man does not in the least affect the peasant mind. They have undoubtedly got it into their heads that we are anxious to make money out of them. This suspicion must be removed.

"(4) It is not a question of terms but of atmosphere. The Russian is a simple and, I think, a good fellow, and once we win his trust there will be no difficulty in doing business with him. We must therefore take some striking action which would clear away these suspicious vapours that obscure the real issues. I therefore urge the importance of sending immediately to Russia emissaries of high standing with full powers to clear up the situation. It is a misfortune that Bark and Bylaeff left before an agreement was arrived at. But that is past.

"(5) Whoever is sent must not merely possess authority, but must be known by the Russians to be a person or persons of high standing and influence in this country. I would strongly urge that Sir William Robertson and Lord Reading be asked to go. As to Sir William Robertson, his standing here is known to the military authorities in Russia, and for the moment they are the only people who count in Russia. The bureaucrats are poor creatures. He could discuss with General Alexeieff the military dispositions for next year. It is important these two men should meet. Up to the present the Russians have never conferred with the Western Powers as to military plans. Men like General Gilinski, who represent the Russian Armies in Paris, are worse than of no account; and I am afraid that if there is a second Chantilly conference Alexeieff either cannot or will not send anyone who will have full power to decide the outlines of the next campaign. The eastern generals probably concentrate their minds too exclusively on the east, and I am not sure that the western generals are not inclined to commit a similar error by limiting their views too much to the countries where their forces are operating. It would be a good thing for both General Robertson and for General Alexeieff that they should interchange views, and the decision arrived at by these two great soldiers after such an interchange might very well be decisive.

"As for Lord Reading, he has the high standing and the necessary diplomatic gifts and the knowledge of finance which would enable him successfully to achieve an understanding with Russia.

"I am afraid of the present misunderstanding developing into strained relations. It would probably not produce a rupture during the progress of the war, but it would certainly have a very sinister influence upon the peace negotiations.

Ever sincerely,

D. Lloyd George.

"P.S. There has already been a delay of some months in ordering essential military material for Russia, and I am apprehensive that Russian generals will attribute failures — due to their own shortcomings — to our delay in furnishing them with financial assistance."

My proposal in regard to Sir William Robertson was shattered against the rock of personal suspicions. He was already predisposed to imagine that I would welcome his absence from the War Office, and there were those in the Cabinet who were resolutely hostile to anything I did or suggested, who deliberately encouraged Robertson to refuse the proposed mission. Indeed, one of them subsequently admitted that he had advised Robertson not to go. As a consequence, I received on the next day this letter from the C.I.G.S.:

"War Office.
27/9/16.
6.15 P.M.

"Dear Mr. Lloyd George,

"The Prime Minister has just sent for me to discuss the Russian visit. I have thought it well over since you spoke to me this morning and have concluded that it is impossible for me to make the visit without losing entire control over the war, and this at an important time. I quite realise the force of what you say, but if I went I should be away for at least a month and that is much too long if I am to keep my hand on the many problems we are dealing with.

"I am honestly very sorry not to be able to fall in with your proposal, and as I told the P.M., if I am asked to go — I shall go, but my opinion is that I ought *not* to go, if I am of any use as C.I.G.S.

"Callwell got on well when he went. He would be better than no one!

"Believe me, I am sorry, but I must tell you what I feel about the necessity for my remaining at my post.

Yours very truly
W. R. Robertson."

With this refusal the proposed mission to Russia collapsed, and our chance of coming to a real understanding with our great Ally in the East was lost until it was too late to save Russia from its final collapse.

Such news as came through to us during the autumn of 1916 from Russia showed what a fatal blunder the abandonment of the mission was proving. All the omens were pointing to a breakdown of the Russian military effort and to a separate peace with Germany. At the end of July, Sazonow, faithfully pro-ally, had been intrigued out of the Russian Foreign Ministry, and been replaced by Sturmer, who was suspected, not without reason, of pro-German leanings. The King of Sweden (who was pro-German in sympathy) had remarked to the British Ambassador at Stockholm, on hearing this news, that there would be peace between Russia and Germany in two months! Though this prophecy was unfulfilled, it was based on a true insight into the trend of affairs in Russia.

Sir George Buchanan, the British Ambassador in Petrograd, mentioned in a private letter to Lord Charles Beresford on October 17th the prevalence of rumours of a separate peace, which Sturmer had officially denied, and reported the growth of a pro-German sympathy in influential circles. In a further letter of October 28th he stressed the progress which pro-German and anti-British propaganda was making, and added: "The losses which Russia has suffered in this war are so colossal that the whole country is in mourning; and so many lives have been uselessly sacrificed during the recent unsuccessful attacks against Kovel and other places that the impression seems to be gaining ground with many people that it is useless going on, more especially as Russia, unlike Great Britain, has nothing to gain by prolonging the war . . . with the people becoming every day more discontented and with a man like Sturmer at the head of the Government, I cannot help feeling anxious."

On November 30th, Lord Rhondda sent me a series of memoranda written by a British officer stationed at Archangel, recording his impression gleaned on a visit to Petrograd and Moscow. He, too, was impressed with the strength of German propaganda and war weariness among the mass of the nation. "From the highest to the lowest all are of opinion that the spirit of the Russian populace in the big cities of late has fallen very greatly," he wrote. "The chief cause, of course, of this change in national morale is the extreme difficulty of getting the first necessities of life, even at any price, and the now universal necessity of standing in long queues in the big towns to get a small supply of such articles as milk, black and white bread, butter and/or cheese, sugar, tea and coffee, meat, fish, etc. . . . These queues form an excellent field of operations for agents of German propaganda, where it is subtly hinted and often even openly asserted by people standing waiting their turn that all this misery is merely being suffered for the aggrandisement of England. . . ."

Then came the following prophetic sentences: ". . . The next three months are the critical period. . . . Either the Government will yield or there will be a *coup d'état*, or, if neither of these things happen, Russia will have to stop fighting and make peace, with disastrous results."

This informant urged that measures of counter-propaganda should be initiated with the utmost dispatch. "It is only with the most assiduous and patient nursing that the Russian Government and people can be led through another one or two years of war and hardship, and no effort or comparatively trifling expense should be spared in achieving this. . . ."

But the warning was too late. The ice had already closed round Archangel. Before it melted again in the spring, Russia had crashed into revolution, and all hope of reinforcing her as an Allied Power was at an end.

CHAPTER X

SIR WILLIAM ROBERTSON

A remarkable career — Administrative ability — First impressions — Distrust of foreigners — General "Non-non" — Admiration for the Germans — Defects as C.I.G.S. — Comparison with Sir Douglas Haig — Dislike of arguments — View of General Lyautey — Geniality and humour.

Sir William Robertson was one of the enigmas of the war. He was not a great soldier, but that he possessed an outstanding personality is beyond question. The fact that there was such a wide diversity of opinion and such an acute controversy as to his gifts and character is sufficient proof that he was no common man. No one in so exclusive a profession as the Army, where social prestige and accomplishment count for so much, could have risen from the humblest upbringing and the lowliest rank to the topmost heights which he occupied unless he possessed talents well above his fellows. He was industrious, steady, intelligent; all the administrative tasks entrusted to him, whether as ranker, N.C.O., or commissioned officer, he discharged competently and with distinction. He was an excellent organiser. He had, during his military career, few opportunities, if any, of leading men in the field. His experience had been of an administrative kind, and here he was a conspicuous success. In that respect amongst all the generals, he was second only to Sir John Cowans. He had other qualities which made for speedy promotion in the Army. He was cautious and discreet. His massive reticence made a deep impression on all whose duty it was to seek his opinion.

A laconic sentence, or often a mere grunt which might

signify anything, was all that he vouchsafed in answer to the most anxious searcher after truth on our military position. He was noncommittal but he was sternly orthodox. Such mistakes therefore as he committed were all of the negative kind, and as these were always in accordance with Army regulations and traditions they counted in his favour and helped his promotion. He understood the Army better than any of his rivals.[1]

Such men always get on in any vocation. These qualities of circumspection in judgment and speech lead even shrewd and experienced observers of all sorts and conditions of men to infer that there is a vast mental hinterland unexplored and unrevealed, Mr. Asquith declared Robertson to be "the greatest strategist of the day." That he most certainly was not. But his oracular monosyllables and grunts misled much abler men than himself. Of his abilities I have already spoken. Some of his limitations I have indicated. His mind was sound but commonplace. He was cautious to the point of timidity. There lay his strength — that also accounted for his drawbacks. A general who takes no risks or leaves them to others never won a difficult campaign.

When I first met him he had reached a very considerable position in the military hierarchy. He was Chief of the Staff to the Commander-in-Chief of the Expeditionary Force in France. I was certainly impressed at my first acquaintance with him. I saw a good deal of him later on in the war and I came gradually to understand his powers and his limitations.

[1] Extract from *Times* obituary leading article:

". . . he was not a genius, except in Carlyle's definition. There was no meteoric brilliance about him; his imagination was commonplace . . . That is the true lesson of Robertson's career. Genius dazzles by its splendour; but it is possible to see this man exactly as he was, to watch each of the struggles which he made, and to understand completely the reasons why he triumphed. There is excuse in genius for failure to emulate it: Robertson's career offers no excuse. What he did any man or boy of ordinary attainments can do also, provided that he is willing to make the necessary sacrifices of immediate leisure and comfort."

He had a profound and disturbing suspicion of all foreigners; if I may use a fruit-grower's vocabulary, Robertson had the canker of xenophobia in his very sap and that vitiated the quality of his product. In a war conducted by an alliance of several nations it was essential to victory that there should be a sound and broad interpretation of the policy of the single front. In the order of his distrust came Frenchmen, first and deepest of all, then Italians, Serbians, Greeks, Celts, and last of all — if at all — Germans. The Austrians had no existence for him except in his arithmetical tables. They were not near the Western Front and did not otherwise obtrude their hostile presence into his strategical conceptions. The French always irritated him and brought out all his stubbornness. That is why they called him General "Non-non"; that represented his first impulse towards all their requests and proposals. Briand once said to me: "Rob-berrt-son says 'non' before he has heard what your proposal is about."

Of the Germans he had a very high opinion and no dislike. In 1916, when the German Army was making its stubborn defence of the slush on the Somme plateau, he said to me: "If we and the Boche were together, we would have beaten the whole lot of them long ago." When the fighting was at its worst he did not hesitate to express his opinion in a discussion on Peace Terms, that a strong Germany in Central Europe was vital to the preservation of peace. His memorandum on that subject rose in parts to the heights of statesmanship. After a week's reflection on his own temerity he withdrew the memorandum and cancelled it. He would have been much more effective as a politician than as a soldier. Since he has already passed away I can express this opinion without inflicting the hurt it would inevitably have caused him.

I shall have a good deal to say later on as to his fitness

Photo. by Elliott & Fry

FIELD-MARSHAL SIR WILLIAM ROBERTSON, D.S.O.

Chief of Imperial General Staff, 1915–1917

for the position of Chief of the Imperial Staff. I do not believe he ever visualised the full significance and responsibility of that great position. His function ought to have been that of Chief Military Adviser to the Cabinet on War as a whole. Sir Douglas Haig, Sir Archibald Murray, Sir John Maxwell, General Milne and General Maude were all sectional generals, and their minds were bound to be concentrated in the main, if not entirely, upon the problem of defeating the army immediately in front of them, but the C.I.G.S. ought to have realised that it was his duty to supervise and to coördinate efforts on all the battlefields. He came into full authority when the British contribution to the war in men, material, money and ships, had grown to vast dimensions and was still growing. We were therefore entitled not indeed to impose our ideas upon our Allies or to dictate to them, but to impress and insist much more than we did. Our chief failure in the first three campaigns of the war was in coördination of forces and resources, in a full realisation of what the united front meant strategically. Robertson rendered no help in overcoming this calamitous defeat. From the moment he became C.I.G.S. he hindered and thwarted at every turn every effort to concentrate or distribute the aggregate power of the Allies in such a way as to achieve the surest and speediest results. I felt profoundly that in this respect he completely failed the statesmen whom he derided, but ought to have guided.

Sir Douglas Haig was a stronger man. I doubt whether he was abler than Robertson but he had better fighting qualities. He was a man of more indomitable will and courage. He was also Robertson's senior; that counts in every profession but most of all in the Army and Navy. Other qualifications being fairly equal, seniority has always the say. That is why, whenever I saw these two men together, I felt that Haig dominated, overawed and almost bullied his junior. Robertson was not endowed with that intrepidity in thought and action that makes great generals.

There was a rigidity about Robertson's physical movements which gave an indication of his lack of mental suppleness and adaptability. He did not argue, he shrank from being involved in argument and he hated contention; one reason being that he was very sensitive about any challenge to his personal or official dignity in word or deed. When the Woolwich workers were making some trouble on a question of time or wages, Dr. Addison invited Sir William Robertson to address them on the urgency of their work. He thought that a few words from so distinguished a soldier might appease them. When, however, the two reached the hall they found it filled with a raging and noisy crowd who hurled questions at the visitors without respect to stars or stripes. The Chief of the Imperial Staff was offended at that kind of reception. He felt his dignity would be impaired by arguing with a tumult, so he declined to speak and left the meeting to Dr. Addison.

He rarely intervened in Council and I never heard him take much part in discussion with Allied generals. At these conferences between the soldiers and sailors of the Allies, Robertson usually sat at the table in gruff silence. His protests were frequent, but generally inarticulate. He thoroughly disapproved of Foch, Nivelle, Joffre, and Lyautey, but he never condescended to dispute with them. He seemed bored, if not overpowered by the voluble confidence of the French generals. When I attended the Rome Conference in 1917, M. Briand and General Lyautey, who was then Secretary of State for War in France, travelled by the same train. Late at night Lyautey sent for Sir William Robertson and myself to come to his saloon. He had a map of Palestine in front of him, and from this he proceeded to deliver a very lengthy lecture on the strategy of a campaign for the conquest of Jerusalem. Robertson never uttered a word of approval or dissent; he let out an occasional grunt, and when Lyautey had concluded his address, he turned to me and said: "Has he finished?" I told him I thought he had. We got up, and on our way back to the British carriage he said to me: "That fellow won't last long." Nor did he, for his demission ensued in a very few weeks.

Robertson's appearance gave no idea of the essential geniality and kindliness of the man. In repose his facial expression was sullen, if not rather morose; in conversation he melted and often became entertaining, so long as you did not venture on a topic on which he disagreed with you. In that case he found refuge in glumness.

He could be full of fun. I recollect returning from a visit to Paris with him and Lord Kitchener. In the train there was a good deal of pleasant chaff interchanged between us. Lord Kitchener was giving an account of his house down in Kent, to which he was very attached. He complained, however, that there was no water in the particular valley in which he had built his residence, but it added to his grievance that there was plenty of water in the valleys on either side. Robertson said: "Then why don't you make a tunnel from one of these valleys to draw water into your own?" The idea amused the great sapper.

Personally I was attracted by Robertson and would have liked to have been able to work with him to the very end. That is a story I must tell in another volume.

CHAPTER XI

TRANSPORT

The "three M's" — Immense task of army transport for B.E.F. — Transport problem in Woolwich Arsenal — Problem of transport in France — Block in ammunition transport — Efforts to get Sir Eric Geddes invited to G.H.Q. — My visit to Sir Douglas Haig — Sir Eric comes over — His friendship with Haig — A programme prepared — Geddes appointed D.M.R. at War Office — Call for his services in France — Sir Douglas Haig's letter to Geddes — My exchange of letters with the Commander-in-Chief — Establishment of "Geddesburg" — Assembling yards organised — Light railways constructed — Programme for standard-gauge lines — Road construction — Work of Sir Henry Maybury — Chinese coolies — Sir Douglas Haig's tribute.

Sir Douglas Haig once told Sir Eric Geddes that the problem of warfare consisted of "three M's": Men; Munitions; Movement. I tell elsewhere in this story the way men were supplied to our military authorities by civilian organisers, and the use or misuse that was made of them; I have shown how those same authorities proved unable to organise the production of their munitions, and had to remit this task to politicians and men of business. Now I have to show how the professional soldiers who fought so valiantly in the stricken area also found themselves unable to cope with the vast problem of Movement which this unprecedented war set before them, and how here again disaster was narrowly averted by the aid of the civilian expert. I am not arraigning the professional soldier, but only the supercilious folly miles behind the shell area which stigmatised all civilian aid in the construction or direction of the war machine as unwarranted interference by ignorant amateurs.

It is of course hardly surprising, when one recalls the

gigantic scope of the transport problem — the millions of men with their equipment, baggage, horses, etc., which had to be moved to and from France and from one front to another; their colossal daily supplies of food, fodder, ammunition, tools, trench warfare supplies; medical and surgical stores and evacuation of wounded — that elderly officers who had reached seniority after years of service under the rather rigid conventions of a small army, and with no practical experience of traffic on a large and continuous scale, would not necessarily be competent to work out the best method of dealing with this vast tangle of unanticipated transport. It required an exceptional experience which they had never obtained, and exceptional organising ability which the process of their selection could not guarantee.

Quite early in the work of the Ministry of Munitions I encountered this failure of the military to organise unprecedented transport, and that no farther away than within the walls of Woolwich Arsenal. When I took over Woolwich in August, 1915, and I put Mr. Vincent Raven in charge of it, he found himself responsible for a bewildering range of factories and departments, occupying an area of about 3½ miles long by 2½ miles wide, with about 150 miles of internal railway track for bringing in and distributing its supplies of raw material and evacuating its output. There was not enough rolling stock. The system was so confused that it was impossible to get the raw material into the Arsenal, to get the finished goods out, or to move stuff efficiently from place to place within the Arsenal itself. Traffic was hopelessly congested. He had to get a special expert in from one of the railway companies to take charge, and organise the system of transport. He speedily got things on to an efficient footing.

But the real crux of the transport problem was the connecting links between the French ports and the front line. On this side, the movement of foods and men in Britain, and their despatch to the French coast, were organised by our own highly efficient railway chiefs and shipping services. Once landed in France, they came on the French railway system, badgered and disorganised by inexpert officers who were trying to wring from it services on a scope hitherto unconceived. As might have been expected, the result was confusion, congestion, and delay.

While I was Minister of Munitions I sent Geddes over to France on one occasion, with the permission of the War Office, to look into some matter of the recovery and transport of salvage. The account he gave me on his return of the transport situation was so disquieting that I suggested to Lord Kitchener that he should be sent to make an investigation and report, with a view to its better organisation. But Lord Kitchener now held the opinion that these were purely military matters, into the sanctity of which no profane civilian must be allowed to intrude. He was by this time suffering from that growing inertia and ossification of the mind which so gravely impaired his usefulness during his last months of office.

Shortly before I left the Ministry of Munitions it was reported to me from France that there was a shortage of ammunition. On enquiry I found that this was in no way due to failure on our part to produce it. In fact our munition factories were becoming choked up with completed output because the base depots in France were too congested to receive it.

On the day on which the death of Lord Kitchener was reported, Sir Eric Geddes, whose special work had been so much hampered by the failure in transport facilities, came to see me on the subject of transport. It appeared that in reply to a request from the War Office for an estimate as to output of artillery ammunition from July 1st, onwards, the figure of 1,000,000 rounds per week had been given. Of the possibility of this production the War Office was frankly sceptical, and stated that even if it were produced it could not be conveyed either across the Channel or to the front, owing to the congested state of the ports and roads, and that in any event the guns could not fire it. In view of the fact that the last advance estimate of the Ministry had been exactly fulfilled, and of all our efforts to produce what the Army wanted, this attitude was, to say the least of it, somewhat exasperating.

As soon as I became Secretary of State for War in July, 1916, I sent through Lord Derby, who was then my Undersecretary, a request to Sir Douglas Haig that he should invite Sir Eric Geddes to go over and look into the matter of transport. But my suggestion was not favourably received. The day after I learnt this I was going over myself to France to visit the whole of the front from Verdun to Flanders. When I reached Paris I saw Lord Esher, who was located there in his usual post of general adviser to everybody and liaison officer between everybody and anybody — a most useful kind of person if he possesses tact, discernment, and experience. Lord Esher had these qualities in a superlative degree. He was a friendly and helpful personage, with a great knowledge of military things and people. I told him all my misgivings about transport and Haig's polite snub to Derby. I said that I had sent Derby because I thought he was a special favourite of the Commander-in-Chief! He did not confirm that impression and said: "Go there yourself and talk quite frankly about the whole position. Talk to Haig himself about it and refuse to be referred to his staff. Your only difficulty will be that although Haig is not a good judge of men, he stands by them with stubborn loyalty to all, whatever their quality. But if you can show him that essential supplies are being kept from his army during the progress of a great battle, he will listen and look into the matter." I took his advice, drove straight to G.H.Q. and stayed the night at Sir Douglas Haig's château. He received me with great cordiality, and gave me the usual sanguine estimate of the progress and prospects of the Somme offensive. Casualties were omitted from the narrative. When I approached him on the subject of transport I decided that it would be better not to discuss merits or details, but to ask him to see Sir Eric Geddes and afford him an opportunity for seeing the transport arrangements and reporting to him on their condition. To this suggestion he assented with alacrity, as it enabled him to get out of what might turn into a disagreeable discussion with the new Secretary of State for War. I was equally pleased because I felt assured that he would now treat the proposal for a change not as an arraignment of his organisation of the war front but as a method of helping him at a critical moment. With his agreement I wired Sir Eric Geddes an invitation to pay a visit to G.H.Q. and inspect transport arrangements.

Sir Eric went over and spent two days there. He was treated, needless to say, with perfect courtesy. At the end of the time the Commander-in-Chief asked him if he had seen everything, and Geddes answered that he had seen enough to think about, but did not know what to think yet. He stayed a few days longer, but then had to tell Haig that he had been shown nothing which the ordinary distinguished tourist would not have been shown; and that what he wanted was a month, in which time he would analyse the problem and produce a report and programme.

Very fortunately, Sir Eric Geddes and Sir Douglas Haig had by this time taken warmly to each other. Sir Douglas later on stated that he "recognised in him the very qualities which the army in the field required." The upshot was that the Commander-in-Chief invited the railway expert to come and spend a month making a thorough investigation and evolving a programme for the transport system. Sir Eric went as a civilian, with a small expert civilian staff to assist him. There never was a more efficient group. He also took with him Sir George Beharrell and General Mance, D.D.M., at the War Office, whom I lent him for the purpose, and Sir Philip Nash, who with Beharrell had been working under Geddes in the Ministry of Munitions. In France he further added to his staff General Freeland, who was on the staff of the Director of Railways at G.H.Q. With these assistants he prepared a programme of transport improvement, including a light railway system for serving the forward areas behind the front line.

On Sir Eric's return I appointed him Director of Military Railways at the War Office. This brought me to my first conflict with the military members of the Army Council. The appointment had to be sanctioned by the Council. One of the generals sitting around the table, speaking obviously on behalf of the rest, protested against a civilian appointment which overrode or circumscribed the authority of experienced and respected generals already discharging these functions to everybody's satisfaction. I challenged this statement and submitted facts which proved serious confusion and congestion, from the ports to Amiens, at Amiens, and from Amiens to the front. Sir William Robertson sat glum during the discussions. Ultimately the appointment was sanctioned. The military members met and decided to send me a formal written protest. Immediately I received it I summoned another meeting of the Army Council and asked the protestors to state their case. The same spokesman repeated his arguments — the rest were silent and once more the appointment was confirmed. The following morning Sir John Cowans came to see me. He looked a little shy and embarrassed. He told me the military members of the Council had met and drawn up a document which they had asked him to present to me. He put on his great horn spectacles and drew a foolscap paper from his pocket. I stopped him and asked him whether it had anything to do with the Geddes appointment, and when he answered in the affirmative I told him that this matter was finally settled and I declined to reopen it. He smiled and said, "I thought you would say so. This paper is therefore of no use." He then tore it up and laughed. Thus ended my first encounter with the military members. I got on much better with them afterwards.

No sooner had Geddes taken up his post than Sir Douglas Haig wired that he wanted Geddes to join his staff in France as Director-General of Transportation. This created a difficult situation, for I did not want to lose him, in view of the important transport reforms I wished him to inaugurate at the War Office, and Geddes himself was by no means eager to go to France, knowing as he did what bitter jealousy of the interloper would be felt by some of the staff officers who had hitherto had charge of transport there. However, General Butler, who had come over from the Commander-in-Chief as a special emissary to secure the services of Geddes in France, was so insistent and persuasive that we eventually made a compromise. It was agreed that Sir Eric should hold the two positions simultaneously; while remaining Director of Military Railways, he should also become Director-General of Transportation in France, and thus be in a position to place his railway experience and remarkable gifts of organisation alike at the service of the War Office and the Expeditionary Force. He had two deputies, Sir Guy Garnet at the War Office and

Sir Philip Nash at G.H.Q. in France, two experienced railway managers.

There was the inevitable and anticipated disgruntlement in some quarters among the staff at G.H.Q. over this appointment. Certain indignant generals tendered their resignations. They started a rumour — only too readily believed in some quarters — that I was up to the politicians' trick of forcing unwanted civilians on the Army, and interfering with military authorities.

To dispose finally of the suggestion that I exercised my authority to force Sir Douglas Haig to dismiss a competent military staff in order to substitute civilians who knew nothing of war conditions, I would like to quote a letter written to Sir Eric by the Commander-in-Chief:

"General Headquarters of British Army in France,
Friday, September 22, 1916.

"My dear Geddes,

"Butler has told me of his interview with you, and I am very pleased to think that you are prepared to join me here and help in beating the Germans for the good of the Empire.

"I should be grateful if you would come over and see me in order that there may be no misunderstanding as to the conditions on which you are prepared to help.

"After full consideration of the organisation which you proposed to me on your last visit, I am most willing and anxious that you should take over complete charge of TRANSPORTATION services of the Army in France. That is to say that you would have under your control:

(a) Broad gauge railways.
(b) Narrow gauge railways.
(c) Inland water transport.
(d) Roads

and that whilst working under instructions from my Q.M.G. you will have direct access to me, and will be in the closest touch with me and my General Staff in order to know our plans so as to look ahead *in time* and provide for our future needs. . . .

"Looking forward to seeing you,

Believe me,

Yours very truly,

D. HAIG."

The appointment also called forth the following exchange of letters between the Commander-in-Chief and myself:

"War Office,

27th September, 1916.

"My dear General,

"Geddes has told me that you have asked him to become your Chief Executive Officer for Transportation in France. I had as you know already appointed him to a similar position in this country. I have told him that I would approve his undertaking complete responsibility for the work upon both sides of the Channel if you wish him to do so. The main thing, to my mind, is that he should be given a very free hand and the personal support of yourself and myself. If you decide to appoint him on your Staff I hope you will find it possible to make these conditions so far as France is concerned. I am doing so in England. He will have direct access to me and then I shall be able to take a close personal interest in supporting the full development of your transportation policy.

Yours sincerely,

(Signed) D. LLOYD GEORGE.

"General Sir Douglas Haig, G.C.B., etc."

The General's reply was as follows:

"General Headquarters,

British Armies in France,

1st October, 1916.

"My dear Mr. Lloyd George,

"I thank you for your letter of the 27th September. I am writing officially to the War Office on the subject of Geddes' appointment, but reserving various details for further discussion here with my Quartermaster-General and Inspector-General of Communications.

"It is my intention to give Geddes as free a hand as possible and to give him my personal support, but it is essential that changes shall be made gradually and without upsetting the existing organisation, which has done excellent work under very difficult conditions and has never failed me up to date.

Yours very truly,
D. HAIG."

Within a month Sir Eric had established his headquarters for the B.E.F. Transport at a little place three miles from Montreuil, called Monthouis, and before long destined to become famous under the sobriquet of "Geddesburg." From this centre Geddes organised the improved transport system which functioned so splendidly during the latter part of the war.

For a man of Sir Eric's railway experience the problem was not a very difficult one. It called chiefly for expert knowledge in the handling of traffic and the capacity to think on an adequate scale and then act promptly. The military transport authorities had been trying all along to "make do" with a totally insufficient transport system. The French railways in the area had been placed at their disposal, and over these and over French country roads, neither of which had been designed to bear a tithe of such weight and volume of traffic, they were trying to move their troops and stores. Naturally the machine broke down. There was an efficient service from depot or factory in Britain up to the French port. But the assembling yards behind the ports were the point of greatest weakness, having become a real bottle-neck which strangled the traffic flow. When the goods finally got past and on to the railheads, which were placed perhaps as much as fifteen miles behind the front line, they had to be conveyed forward this distance over broken-down roads which were simultaneously being used for movement of troops.

Putting experienced railway men in charge of the assembling yards helped to relieve the congestion there. But the first big innovation which Sir Eric undertook was the construction of light narrow-gauge railways in the forward areas to move supplies from the broad-gauge railheads up to the line. Till this time there were no light railways at all. He framed a programme for an eventual 1000 miles of light railway with rolling stock to correspond. The first stage in the execution of that programme involved an order for 1000 miles of light steel rails, and one stormy autumn night I was awakened in the small hours at the Crillon, where I was staying on a visit to France, by a despatch rider bringing Sir Eric's report setting out the proposal for this requisition. I read and initialled it, and it was rushed back to "Geddesburg" in time for Beharrell to fly with it to Boulogne and catch the 9 o'clock boat in the morning. He arrived in London and dismayed Sir Ernest Moir with the size of the requisition. But Sir Ernest duly produced the goods, and by June, 1917, the whole 1000 miles of light railway were complete. The dimensions of the task may be judged when I say that the 1000-mile narrow-gauge track involved 60,000 tons of steel for rails and sleepers, apart from the requirements of rolling stock. I may add here that in the autumn of 1917 a further 900 miles of light railway were ordered, and that up to the end of the war the total length supplied reached well over 4000 miles.

The congestion behind the ports in France could only be removed by increasing the capacity of the standard-gauge lines to clear the imported goods away. Sir Eric made arrangements with Sir Ernest Moir about the provision of supplies for this purpose.

At the end of November he put forward his programme for additional standard-gauge lines. Hitherto the Army had relied mainly on the existing French lines, and though in the two years 1915-16 Britain had supplied the French Government with over 150 locomotives and 2300 tons of railway material for maintenance of its railways, very little had been done to supplement the existing system with any British military railway additions. Sir Eric's new programme was for 1200 miles of standard-gauge line, 300 new large main-line locomotives, and about 9000 wagons. Sir Douglas Haig backed this up by paying a personal visit to this country at the beginning of December, and on December 12th wrote asking for means to carry out large schemes of doubling lines and building new lines, connecting lines, depots and extensions.

When I say that 1200 miles of standard-gauge track involved 160,000 tons of steel, or 6000 tons a week for six months, it will be seen that Sir Eric was not afraid to "think big." The support accorded to him by the Commander-in-Chief shows also that he had taught G.H.Q. to share his outlook. By June, 1917, nearly all this huge order had been completed, and a requisition for a further 1000 miles had been received.

With the expansion of the railways, the congestion at the ports was reduced. It was possible to clear the quays and speed up the discharge of cargoes when the bottle-neck beyond had been broadened.

The roads were another vital link in the transport system. They are, of course, the first requisite for organised military operations, a fact of which the Romans were well aware when they constructed their great military highways. Throughout the war, the roads of France were subject to terrific strain, and in the forward area, before the light railways were constructed, they were the only means of movement for both troops and stores. Of course, they got knocked to pieces, and for some time no proper effort was made to keep them in repair.

Sir Eric Geddes made arrangements for the systematic repair and construction of roadways. The stone for them was mainly quarried in France. The work was done to a large extent by prisoners of war.

Before leaving the subject of roads, I should like to pay a tribute to the fine work which Sir Henry Maybury did in organising this branch of our transport facilities. On the formation of the Transportation Department at "Geddesburg" Sir Henry Maybury was brought over to take charge of the road construction work — the maintenance of the existing roads, and building of new ones, particularly where the front moved forward. The mobility of our road transport in the latter part of the war was due in a high degree to his efforts.[1]

[1] To illustrate the dimensions of motor transport used by the Army, I quote the following figures showing the total numbers of mechanical transport vehicles acquired by the War Office from the outbreak of war to September 1st, 1916, and the numbers supplied by the Ministry of Munitions between the latter date and the end of December, 1918:

(a) Lorries: heavy and light		
Acquired by War Office from every source before 1/9/16	21,705	
Supplied by M. of M. from 1/9/16 to Dec., 1918	37,785	
		59,490
(b) Cars, vans, and ambulances		
Acquired by War Office, &c	9,630	
Supplied by M. of M.	24,170	
		33,800
(c) Steam Wagons		
Acquired by War Office, &c	440	
Supplied by M. of M. &c	714	
		1,154
(d) Tractors		
Acquired by War Office, &c	936	
Supplied by M. of M. &c	2,505	
		3,441
(e) Motor Cycles		
Acquired by War Office, &c	18,750	
Supplied by M. of M. &c	22,300	
		41,050

These figures are, of course, exclusive of the motor vehicles supplied to our Allies.

Photo. by Press Portrait Bureau

THE RT. HON. SIR ERIC GEDDES, G.C.B.

Closely connected with the transport developments was the recruitment of the Chinese Auxiliary Corps by Sir Eric Geddes, who sent an officer to China to recruit 15,000 Chinese labourers for work in France, out of whom some 6000 were required for work on the railways, and 1000 for inland water transport, the others being employed at various tasks on the road, railheads, dumps, etc.[1] They were immensely powerful fellows, and it was no uncommon spectacle to see one of the Chinese pick up a balk of timber or a bundle of corrugated iron sheets weighing three or four hundredweight and walk off with it as calmly as if it weighed only as many stone!

At times, of course, these Chinese coolies came under aërial bombing or long-distance shelling. That did not greatly perturb them; they were far less nervous under fire than the British West Indian Auxiliaries, who were similarly engaged on Labour Corps duties. But it tended to disorganise their work in another way, because if they suffered any fatal casualties, they would all break off work to attend the funeral, and neither threats nor cajolery had the least effect on them, nor would bombing or shelling by the enemy scatter their cortège, until the obsequies had been duly completed.

The whole story of British achievement in the sphere of transport during the war has never yet been told. It would be well worth telling in detail, and would reflect very high credit on those who were responsible for its development, most of all on Sir Eric Geddes. The following extracts from Sir Douglas Haig's final despatch, while it exhibits some remarkable reticences about certain points in the story, pays

[1] I am told that when I was asked to sanction the recruitment of "Chinese Labour" for the British Army in France I replied, "For Heaven's sake don't give it that name! What about Chinese Auxiliary Corps?" The former appellation would have recalled an unpleasant political controversy still fresh in party memory on both sides.

a merited tribute to the "civilian experts" whose advice I persuaded him to consider in 1916:

"The successful coördination and economic use of all the various kinds of transportation requires most systematic management, based on deep thought and previous experience. So great was the work entailed in the handling of the vast quantities, of which some few examples are given above, so complex did the machinery of transport become and so important was it that the highest state of efficiency should be maintained, that in the autumn of 1916 *I was forced to adopt an entirely new system for running our lines of communication.*[1] The appointment of Inspector-General of Communications was abolished, and the services previously directed by that officer were brought under the immediate control of the Adjutant-General, the Quartermaster-General, and the Director-General of Transportation. The last-mentioned was a new office created with a separate staff composed for the greater part of civilian experts to deal specifically with transportation questions.

"The Director-General of Transportation's branch was formed under the brilliant direction of Major-General Sir Eric Geddes during the autumn of 1916, as above stated. To the large number of skilled and experienced civilians included by him on his staff, drawn from the railway companies of Great Britain and the Dominions, the Army is deeply indebted for the general excellence of our transportation services."

[1] My italics. D. Ll. G.

CHAPTER XII

THE MESOPOTAMIA MUDDLE

Reasons for describing Mesopotamia campaign — The Paradise of the Brass Hat — History of the expedition — Capture of Basra — Control by Indian Army — Expedition reinforced — Home Government warns against extended operations — Kut captured — Attack on Baghdad authorised — Repulse at Ctesiphon — Siege and fall of Kut — I transfer control to Home Government and order an investigation — A story of amazing incompetence — Conditions in Mesopotamia — Requirements for a campaign — Indian military authorities starve the expedition — Inadequate artillery and munitions — Shortage of river transport — Orders for boats muddled — Fresh boats refused — Incompetence of Indian marine — Simla out of touch with situation — A red tape blunder — Mismanagement at Basra — Sir George Buchanan frozen out — Appalling failure of medical services — Peace-time incompetence of Indian military hospitals — Conditions worse in war — Wounded left on battlefield — No ambulances — No transports for sick and wounded down river — Arrival of wounded at Basra: Major Carter's description — Major Carter threatened for reporting conditions — Outside help refused — Findings of the Commission — Deception about available reserves — Sir John Cowans takes charge — A classic account of official circumlocution — My first impressions of Cowans — The laundry books — A born organiser — Complete efficiency in his department — Spokesman for the generals.

THERE are three reasons why I incorporate a chapter on the Mesopotamia scandal in my reminiscences of the war. One is that I opposed the initiation of the campaign. I quote the following minute from the War Council held on February 24th, 1915:

"Mr. Lloyd George suggested that the Mesopotamia Expedition was merely a side issue. The Turks knew how far-reaching the effects of a disaster there would be and would spare no efforts to bring it about. The Mesopotamia force ought, in his opinion, to be withdrawn and concentrated on the Dardanelles."

The second is that when I became Secretary for War on July 6th, 1916, the first urgent task which I found awaiting my attention was the problem of dealing with the mess and muddle of the British Expedition to Mesopotamia. My last reason for telling it as part of my war story is that it is a perfect example of what military administration is capable of, if entirely freed from civilian "interference." It was an ideal professional soldiers' campaign, lacking even a minimum of supervision from the meddlesome politician. Tradition places the Garden of Eden in the land between the Euphrates and the Tigris. In this blissful enclosure there reappeared in 1916 the Paradise of the Brass Hat. He reigned alone in unfettered and unrestricted sway over this garden for nearly two years. There was no serpent or consort to mislead or meddle with him. Where there were any politicians roaming about they were as meek as any beast in the ancient Garden. He ran his Eden alone. Let us see what kind of a Paradise he produced.

It is a gruesome story of tragedy and suffering resulting from incompetence and slovenly carelessness on the part of the responsible military authorities. Attempts had been made to smother the story through a campaign of secrecy and deliberate misrepresentation, but despite these efforts enough had leaked out early in 1916 to make it clear that strong action on the part of the Home Government was demanded.

The history of the expedition up to that date can be briefly outlined as follows. Towards the close of September, 1914, it became evident that Turkey was likely to join the enemy powers. This made it at once important to take steps for safeguarding the oil supplies in the Persian Gulf, which were owned by the Anglo-Persian Oil Company, a concern in which the Government had become large shareholders as a means of ensuring supplies of oil fuel for the Navy.

Troops were at the time being dispatched from India to France, and the Imperial Government — through Lord Crewe, who was then Secretary of State for India —

arranged with the Government of India for one brigade to be diverted to the Persian Gulf, to occupy the island of Abadan at the mouth of the Euphrates, and protect the oil tanks and pipe lines. This force was duly sent, and landed on October 23rd, 1914.

Within a fortnight after this, on November 5th, 1914, war was declared on Turkey. Thereupon two fresh brigades were dispatched to Mesopotamia, and on November 22nd, the town of Basra was captured and occupied. Basra was the seaport of Mesopotamia, and was on the west bank of the Shatt-el-Arab (the wide joint stream of the Tigris and Euphrates) about seventy miles up river from the open sea.

This expedition, though sent by arrangement with the British Government at home, and subject to the general agreement whereby all expenses of the Indian Expeditionary Forces beyond their ordinary cost of maintenance should be borne by Imperial Funds, was in respect of its administration under the sole control and responsibility of the Indian Army authorities.

Under threat of Turkish attacks, the Indian Government reluctantly sent another brigade in February, and when the danger to the force grew more acute they were peremptorily ordered in March to send a fourth. Meantime the expedition had extended its area in December by capturing the town of Kurna, where the Tigris and Euphrates join, fifty miles above Basra. It had thus occupied the whole length of the Shatt-el-Arab.

The Indian Government decided on April 1st, without obtaining the consent of the India Office at home, to organise the expedition as an army corps. They sent two more brigades to complete a second division, and sent General Nixon to be Commander-in-Chief of the force. He was instructed to make plans for occupying the whole of the Basra Vilayet, and eventually advancing on Baghdad.

The oil field lay to the east of the Shatt-el-Arab, up a tributary, the River Karun, and the pipe line ran down its left bank to the island of Abadan. On April 19th, the Home Government asked the force to move against the Turks in this region. General Nixon asked on the same day for more forces, which were refused by India. The Home Government concurred, and added a warning against extensive operations, saying, "Any proposal involving possible demands for reinforcements of undue extension is to be deprecated. . . . Our present position is strategically a sound one and we cannot at present afford to take risks by extending it unduly. In Mesopotamia a safe game must be played."

General Nixon then sent part of his force, under General Gorringe, up the Karun River, and the other part under General Townshend, to capture Amara, ninety miles up the Tigris, getting a last-minute sanction from the British Government. Both operations were successful, and on June 3rd Amara was taken. Then, in boiling heat, an advance was made up the Euphrates to Nasariyeh, sixty-eight miles beyond Kurna. The Indian Government now became eager for more progress, and got the consent of Sir Austen Chamberlain, who was then Indian Secretary, for Townshend to advance on Kut, one hundred and fifty miles up the Tigris beyond Amara. Kut-el-Amara was entered after severe fighting on September 29th, 1915.

In November, 1914, the idea of an eventual advance on Baghdad had been turned down both by the India Office and by the Viceroy of India, who gave strong reasons against it. But subsequent successes had led the Indian Government to favour the project, and they sought permission from the Home Government for General Nixon to carry out his plan for this advance. On October 6th, 1915, it was definitely vetoed by Sir Austen Chamberlain, but later he relented to the point of saying that if the General

Staff approved and thought the operation feasible, with the aid of two fresh divisions which might presently be placed at the disposal of the Mesopotamian force, the India Office would be prepared to consider it. The Indian General Staff, also after some hesitation, agreed that with two fresh divisions Baghdad could be taken and held. In the end General Nixon told General Townshend to go ahead and capture Baghdad with the tired men he had at his disposal, on the strength of the hope that presently another two divisions would arrive in Mesopotamia.

Townshend advanced as far as Ctesiphon, a few miles from Baghdad, where he found the enemy strongly entrenched, and numerically equal or superior to his own exhausted troops. After a fierce fight the British forces retired, and had to retreat down the river, compelled by lack of supplies and medical accommodation for casualties, and fighting a series of rearguard actions till they reached Kut, which they prepared to hold until relieved and reinforced by the further troops which were expected. More than 30 per cent. of the force had been killed or wounded.

General Townshend reached Kut on December 3rd, where he was told by the military authorities to defend himself till relieved. By December 7th, the town was fully invested by the Turks. After suffering severely in attempts to take it by storm, they settled down to beleaguer it.

The remainder of the British forces hastily improvised efforts to relieve the town. They were reinforced by the two promised divisions from France. These were Indian divisions, already severely punished in the French fighting, and they arrived piecemeal during December at Basra, where 12,000 troops were immobilised through lack of transport to take them to the front. The attempts of the Tigris force to relieve General Townshend were heavily defeated. They made some progress in their attacks on the beleaguering lines, but owing to lack of reinforcements they abandoned the attempt to break through. Ultimately, on April 29th, 1916, after having gallantly defended the town for one hundred and forty-seven days, Townshend's brave men were starved into surrender.

Long before this tragic climax, it had become clear that the expedition was being hopelessly mismanaged in some way or other, and early in February, 1916, the War Office took charge of the expedition. The forces there were, however, parts of the Indian Army, and immediately under the Indian General Staff in Simla. It was not until July, 1916, when I went to the War Office, that the administration of matters connected with the expedition were transferred to the control of the Home Government.

That was my first step towards clearing up the muddle. My second was to promote the appointment of a Commission to make an investigation into the muddle and its causes. This Commission was set up in August, 1916, and issued its report on May 17th, 1917. The report was signed by seven of the eight Commissioners, while Commander J. Wedgewood put in a separate report, substantially agreeing with the other, but emphasising more forcibly certain aspects of the blunders and errors which had been committed, particularly by the Viceroy and Commander-in-Chief in India.

The facts revealed by this Commission's report cast a baleful light upon the mismanagement, stupidity, criminal neglect and amazing incompetence of the military authorities who were responsible for the organisation of the expedition, and on the horrible and unnecessary suffering of the gallant men who were sent to failure and defeat through the blunders of those in charge.

The General Staff in India knew perfectly well the nature of the country to which the force was being sent, and the kind of equipment which would obviously need to be supplied to it. Mesopotamia is a flat, alluvial tract, largely covered by floods in the wet season, while in the summer the rivers dwindled to very shallow streams. There are no proper roads, and water transport was the principal means of moving either men or supplies. It is a country of torrid heat in summer, though the nights throughout a considerable part of the year are cold, and during the winter and spring the country is subject to cold winds and icy storms. It was a primitive and backward country, some distance by sea from the nearest civilised base.

Obviously, therefore, the first essential for sending any expedition to Mesopotamia was to ensure that it was very well found; that it had an ample supply of suitable river boats for its transports; that clothing and food should be suited to the conditions of the country; that medical equipment, especially for the wounded and the sick, should be above the average, to meet the dangers of a sterile and disease-ridden land; that provision was made for establishing a well-equipped base at the port of Basra; and that arrangements for reinforcements should be carefully planned and promptly executed.

Every single one of these obvious duties was not merely done badly, but left undone to the point of incredibility. In the opening months of the war the Indian Government showed an extraordinary tardiness in rendering any help at all to the Empire in its struggle. Only under strong pressure would it send a single soldier to the front, and despite its enormous population it declared itself incapable of recruiting substantial additional forces. It would not spend an extra *pice* on the war; indeed, in the budget debate of March, 1915, at Simla, a member boasted that although it was a war budget, military expenditure had not been increased, and was, in fact, below the original estimate. The Indian troops which came to France came under the control of the British authorities; but those which were sent to Mesopotamia were entirely in the hands of the reluctant and parsimonious authorities at Simla, and were stinted and starved of every kind of equipment and support. "Every General who appeared before us agreed," said the Commissioners, "that the Mesopotamian Expedition was badly equipped."

It was short of artillery, particularly of heavy guns. The Indian Military Authorities do not appear to have thought of asking for any. It was not till December, 1915, when the ill-starred attack on Baghdad had been already attempted and failed, and General Townshend was beleaguered in Kut, that the first request was received for heavy guns for Mesopotamia, and not till May 26th, 1916, that India sent a definite statement of its requirements for these weapons.

Even as late as the spring of 1916 the expedition was deficient in many things which India could have supplied, such as wire cutters, rockets, Véry lights, water carts, tents, mosquito nets, sun helmets, bombs, medical supplies, and even blankets and clothing. The Commander-in-Chief in India excused himself before the Commission by saying that some of these articles had not been heard of before the war, at least in India. But they were not supplied to this expedition when the war had been in progress eighteen months. Even the Turks were using Véry lights in Mesopotamia before our troops had any.

Despite the severities of the weather at certain seasons, the military authorities proposed at first to leave the provision of warm clothing for the troops entirely to private benevolence, sending them out with nothing but "shorts" and tropical clothing. The Viceroy himself protested against this.

There were no aëroplanes at all for the first six months, though the need for them in that wide, roadless land was obvious. For this failure the authorities at home must share the blame.

But it is when we come to the question of river transport that the blundering and incompetence of the military authorities is seen in its full functioning. So long as the expedition was confined in its objectives to the original landing on the island of Abadan, or the port of Basra, it was mainly dependent on ocean-going transport. But from the moment when, in December, 1914, it advanced, with the approval of the authorities at Simla, up river to Kurna, special river transport became a vital necessity, and with each further advance, which lengthened the line up the river, the need for transport vessels increased.

As early as November 23rd, 1914, after the capture of Basra, General Barrett was advised by Commander Hamilton, R.I.M., who knew the Tigris intimately, to apply at once for twelve special steamers, as they would have to be built to an unusual pattern, and would take twelve months to construct. But the general and his staff did not think the matter urgent, and did nothing about it till in January they were asked by India what further transport they needed. He then asked for seven steamers and two lighters. In February he asked for four tugs. These were obtained in India in March, and sent out; but when in May General Nixon took over, he found that they were useless for the hot weather, when the river ran low. He asked for vessels drawing not more than 3 feet or 3 feet 6 inches.

After delays in India, this request was ultimately incorporated in a requisition telegraphed to the India Office on August 4th, 1915. Nothing was done till confirmation in writing turned up in September. Then the officials at the India Office made enquiry of the firm recommended to them for this work, but rather than pay them a commission amounting to one-third of one per cent. for supervising the execution of the order they turned to their expert naval architect who, without special knowledge of the conditions of the Tigris, proceeded to secure them the building of vessels differing in a number of respects from the type ordered — vessels which were sent out in sections between April and December, 1916. It may be briefly stated that on account of the alterations of the pattern these boats were useless for the purpose of up-river transport; that the fact that they had to be assembled at Basra meant considerable further delay after they reached Mesopotamia; and that owing to lack of facilities for shipbuilding at Basra, and the large size of some of the sections, they were very difficult to handle — particularly as no drawings, descriptions or instructions came with them. Some sections sank in thirty feet of water, and the rest had to be towed to Bombay to be erected there. The Commission remarks:

> "More inept proceedings than those connected with the purchase and shipment of river craft in England in 1915 and early in 1916 would be hard to find."

When in October, 1915, General Nixon learnt that the paddle-steamers wanted would take a year to build, he asked for stop-gap boats from India. The Indian authorities replied, as they had done previously in June, that no suitable tugs were available. A month later they admitted that there were thirteen available. The Commission gives a picture of the circumlocution and red tape which created the long delays before any request from Mesopotamia got even a negative reply. Correspondence was usually conducted between the G.O.C. in Mesopotamia and the Chief of the Staff in Simla or Delhi. From the latter office, anything about river craft would be transmitted to the Quartermaster-General, who could thereafter communicate what he thought necessary to Captain Lumsden, R.N., the

Director of the Royal Indian Marine at Bombay. How that officer spent his time is thus described by the Commission:

"The Director of the Royal Indian Marine was not granted — at any rate did not exercise — any initiative in maritime or nautical matters. . . . The time of the Director and Senior Officers of the Indian Marine is much taken up with mere office or desk work. The amount of writing which they have to get through — or at all events do get through — can only be described as enormous. . . . The Director of the Royal Indian Marine gave to the Commission a list of the duties, the discharge of which he considered rendered it impossible for him to visit Mesopotamia and see for himself the actual state of things there. Most of the duties specified required neither maritime experience nor nautical knowledge, and could have been performed by any alert business man, even though he may never have been on blue water in his life."

The report, in fact, makes several references to the fact that the Indian officials never went to look at things for themselves, and when they were told of conditions, refused to pay attention to the reports. Worse, they blankly misreported the facts. "So much out of touch was Simla with the actual situation in Mesopotamia that we find the Indian General Staff, in 'appreciations' in June and September, 1915, definitely stating that the expedition was well supplied with river craft, and using this among their arguments for the advance to Baghdad."

The lack of river transport up to the spring of 1916 was a direct cause of the failure of military operations carried out by the troops with the utmost bravery. On account of the shortage it took nearly two months to concentrate troops and supplies for the advance from Amara to Kut, and the advance to Baghdad was fatally delayed through the same cause. It seems almost certain that, but for the shortage of river transport, the Turkish Army would have been destroyed between Amara and Ctesiphon; and the evidence shows conclusively, according to the Commission, that shortage of river transport was the chief cause of the failure to relieve Kut.

Since the vital importance of such transport was clearly understood both in India and at home, it is natural to ask what on earth possessed the military authorities to allow the advance up the Tigris in face of the shortage. The report of the Commission brings out that General Nixon, the commander on the spot, when he found the Indian authorities unable or unwilling to provide the needed transport, was optimistically ready to try his luck with what he had; and the Indian authorities themselves, having failed to provide what they must have known was necessary, made no effort to impress the gravity of the shortage on the India Office at home. This Office was allowed to get the impression that all was well, an impression perpetuated by a typically official incident. General Nixon's appeal for more vessels, sent to the India Office by the Indian Government, was not laid before the Secretary of State. The Military Branch of the India Office sent it on to the Stores Branch as an indent; and though it was forwarded to the War Office, no letter was sent drawing attention to the shortage of transport it revealed. Thus military officials both in India and in London suppressed or ignored facts which, had they been known by either the War Council or the Cabinet, would have prevented the granting of consent to the ill-fated advance on Baghdad.

Allied to the failure to furnish river transport was the neglect to develop wharfage and storage facilities at Basra.

The boats available had their usefulness heavily reduced through this failure. General Gorringe stated that "no improvement in the unloading wharves for ships was made until December, 1915 . . . although the accommodation was bad and congested for stores of every kind being unloaded." To the physical drawbacks was added the incompetence of the military officials. The Commission reports that delays to steamers were at first occasioned, not so much by inability to get cargoes out into lighters, as by inability or unwillingness of the military departments ashore to receive it rapidly.

"It is clear that management of the traffic of a port and discharge of cargo was not work to which officers of the Royal Indian Marine had previously been accustomed. . . . Men with these qualifications were known to be employed in one or other of the great Indian and Burmese river ports. Their advice was not asked for: and their assistance was not utilised until more than a year after the landing of the expedition in Mesopotamia when conditions in Basra had become serious."

In January, 1916, the Indian Government at last sent an expert civilian, Sir George Buchanan, formerly in charge of the Port of Rangoon, to become Director-General of Basra and reorganise its traffic and facilities. Characteristically, they omitted to define his status and duties; and General Nixon proceeded to limit and circumscribe these in such a way that Sir George Buchanan found it impossible to carry on, and soon returned to India. In his report to Simla he said:

> "I found it difficult to realise that we had been in occupation of Basra for a year, as the arrangements for the landing and storing of goods of every description were of the most primitive order, and in the absence of roads, the whole area was a huge quagmire. To a newcomer appearances were such that troops and stores might have been landed, for the first time, the previous week. . . . The military expedition to Basra is, I believe, unique, inasmuch as in no previous case has such an enormous force been landed and maintained without an adequately prepared base."

But if the neglect of transport by the military authorities was directly responsible for the failure and defeat of the expedition, their neglect of medical equipment turned disaster into horror.

Tales of the atrocities resulting from inadequate provision for the wounded and sick were so widespread that even Sir Beauchamp Duff, the Commander-in-Chief of the Army in India, felt himself compelled in March, 1916, to set up a Commission to inquire into the matter. Their report was, however, such a sickening exposure of official negligence and incompetence that the Indian Government would not publish it. The Mesopotamia Commission appointed by the Home Government had this report before them, and published it as an appendix to their own report. It was known as the "Vincent-Bingley" Report, as Sir William Vincent and General Bingley were the chief members responsible for it.

The evidence of both reports is that the expedition was systematically starved by the Indian military authorities in regard to every vital medical provision, and that protests were stifled, and outside offers of help refused.

The standard of the Indian Army in this respect was low to begin with. A witness from the Indian Medical Service told the Commission: "I doubt whether you gentlemen would consider that the Sepoys' Hospitals in peace-time India are hospitals at all." Sir Alfred Keogh, Director-General of Army Medical Services at the War Office, said:

> "I have no hesitation whatever in saying that the medical arrangements connected with the Army in India have been for years and years most disgraceful. . . . Anything more disgraceful than the carelessness and want of attention with regard to the sick soldier in India it is impossible to imagine."

But if things in India were bad, they were far worse in Mesopotamia. The expedition was sent out with a medical establishment, even according to its organisation orders, lower than that laid down for a frontier campaign; and "the actual amount of medical personnel in Mesopotamia was during long periods far below even this meagre scale."

There was at times a serious shortage of essential drugs. Necessary appliances for the hospitals were scanty or altogether lacking. Often there was no ice. For months there were no electric fans. There were not enough bandages, blankets, bed-pans, and splints. Even when the wounded got to the military hospital at Bombay it was to find there an appalling state of neglect — no X-ray apparatus, a lack of splints and surgical appliances, a shortage of doctors, surgeons, nurses, and attendants.

The doctors and ambulance staffs with the expedition performed miracles of heroic work, but there were very few of them. At the first Battle of Kut some of the fighting units were without stretcher bearers, and wounded men were left on the field of battle all night, some of them being stripped, mutilated, and killed by the Arabs.

No wheeled transport for seriously wounded cases was sent out. Instead, a number of riding mules were supplied! The Commissioners say: "We have no evidence that these riding mules were ever used by the wounded, though their presence on one occasion in a very restive state is recorded by a witness. They are obviously useless for serious cases."

In default of wheeled ambulances, the medical officers were forced to move the more seriously wounded in springless army transport carts, drawn by mules, ponies, or bullocks. The A.D.M.S., 3rd Division, said that this cart, "which is without springs, has no cover to give protection against rain or the direct rays of the sun; and the bottom of which consists of bars of iron which, even when liberally covered with mattresses or other padding, renders the placing of a wounded man, especially in cases of fracture, in such a conveyance, a practice which can only be designated as barbarous and cruel."

In some cases, we learn, dead bodies were used as cushions on these carts, in default of any other means of padding them.

But it is when we come to the transport of wounded and sick men down the river to Basra that the story reaches its culminating horror. There were no river steamers at all fitted as medical transports, nor any personnel to attend to casualties on the journey. Use had to be made of the scanty river transport employed in bringing men, stores and animals up stream, and as congestion grew it became impossible to clean or disinfect these boats in any way before sending the wounded, thickly packed in them, down to Basra, and detailing from the scanty and over-worked field ambulance staffs a few men to accompany them — too few to give proper attention to them or even to feed them.

> "Wounds which required dressing and re-dressing were not attended to, and the condition of many of the patients who travelled by these steamers was, when they reached Basra, deplorable. There the wounds of many were found to be in a septic condition, and in urgent need of re-dressing. In some cases bed sores had developed, more than one patient arrived soaked in fæces and urine, and in a few cases wounds were found to contain maggots."

The Commission quote a description, by Major Carter, I.M.S., which I cannot repeat without apologising for its repulsive horror, of how the wounded after Ctesiphon arrived in Basra. Yet it is necessary for us to face frankly the record of what actually happened to a number of valiant men who fought for Britain and her Empire in the Great War. Our soldiers had not merely to read of, but to suffer this. Here is the account:

"I was standing on the bridge" [of the hospital ship *Varela* from Bombay] "in the evening when the *Medjidieh* arrived. She had two steel barges without any protection against the rain, as far as I can remember. As this ship with two barges came up to us I saw that she was absolutely packed, and the barges too, with men. The barges were slipped, and the *Medjidieh* was brought alongside the *Varela*. When she was about 300 or 400 yards off it looked as if she was festooned with ropes. The stench when she was close was quite definite, and I found that what I mistook for ropes were dried stalactites of human fæces. The patients were so huddled and crowded together in the ship that they could not perform the offices of nature clear of the edge of the ship, and the whole of the ship's side was covered with stalactites of human fæces. This is what I then saw. A certain number of men were standing and kneeling on the immediate perimeter of the ship. Then we found a mass of men huddled up anyhow — some with blankets and some without. They were lying in a pool of dysentery about 30 feet square. They were covered with dysentery and dejecta generally from head to foot. With regard to the first man I examined . . ." — [I omit a still more terrible passage of the description] — ". . . The man had a fractured thigh, and his thigh was perforated in five or six places. He had apparently been writhing about the deck of the ship. Many cases were almost as bad. There were a certain number of cases of terribly bad bed sores. In my report I describe mercilessly to the Government of India how I found men with their limbs splinted with wood strips from 'Johnny Walker' whisky boxes, 'Bhoosha' wire, and that sort of thing.

" 'Were they British or Indian?'

" 'British and Indian mixed.' "

This procedure was thus described by the G.O.C. of the Expedition:

"Wounded satisfactorily disposed of. Many likely to recover in country comfortably placed in hospitals at Amara and Basra. Those for invaliding are being placed direct on two hospital ships that were ready at Basra on arrival of river boats. General condition of wounded very satisfactory. Medical arrangements under circumstances of considerable difficulty worked splendidly."

What about Major Carter's report to the Indian military authorities? The Commission gives the following account of its reception:

"He [Major Carter] was treated with great rudeness. Surgeon-General Hathaway, in writing to the D.M.S. in India on this subject, says: 'The Army Commander, realising the injustice, ordered the D.A. and Q.M.G. and myself to deal with him [Major Carter] with reference to his objectionable remarks.' And General Cowper, then D.A. and Q.M.G., told us: 'I threatened to put him under arrest, and I said that I would get his hospital ship taken away from him for a meddlesome, interfering faddist.' "

General Cowper was passing on treatment he had himself received, for the Commander-in-Chief in India, Sir Beauchamp Duff, had threatened to dismiss him for sending to India too insistent demands as to need for river transport.

Not only would the authorities do nothing themselves; they would let no one do anything to help them. On August 11th, 1915, the Secretary for India wired the Viceroy with an offer from the Lord-Lieutenant of Hampshire to raise funds for the sick and wounded soldiers in Mesopotamia, and send out doctors, nurses, medicines, and hospital comforts. After consulting with the Commander-in-Chief, the Viceroy answered that money was ample and sufficient for supplying comforts for sick and wounded in Mesopotamia and in India; that everything necessary was being done, and that his Government had arranged for doctors and nurses. Electric fans were offered by the Madras Fund in December, 1914, for installation in the hospitals of Basra, but by the middle of 1915 none had been actually installed. The British Red Cross Society cabled

General Nixon to accept two petrol-driven motor-launches. The offer was repeated on December 28th, and the reply was:

> "Nothing required at present. If anything needed in future will not hesitate to ask you."

This was just after the total breakdown of medical services, following the battle of Ctesiphon.

I need not particularise further the failures of the military authorities to deal with other medical and sanitary issues; the insufficient and inappropriate food they supplied, which led by 1915 to an outbreak of scurvy among the troops, and a much more serious outbreak the following spring; the neglect of water supply, so that the troops were reduced to drinking from the nearest river, and an outbreak of cholera resulted. The report of the Commission makes it clear that on every hand there was utter failure to make the most elementary provision for the obvious needs of the expedition. In their "Findings", they remark:

> "Looking at the facts, which from the first must have been apparent to any administrator, military or civilian, who gave a few minutes' consideration to the map and to the conditions in Mesopotamia, the want of foresight and provision for the most fundamental needs of the expedition reflects discredit upon the organising aptitude of all the authorities concerned."

I need not refer to the way in which the military authorities in India starved the expedition of drafts and reinforcements — although they were in charge of a country of 315,000,000 people, of whom 50,000,000 belonged to fighting races. But one amazing incident deserves mention. When in October, 1915, the advance on Baghdad was in prospect, and the need for reinforcements to support the force there was urgent, the Imperial Authorities asked the Indian Government to provide a division temporarily, as the two divisions from France might not get there in time. "With the intention of evading this liability," says the Report, "the Indian Government resorted to procedure which, to say the least of it, was disingenuous." There were, in fact, certain artillery batteries, cavalry regiments, and infantry brigades which could be spared in India, but the Home Government was not informed of this, and the reason given in a minute from the Military Secretary of Sir Beauchamp Duff to the Viceroy's Military Secretary ran as follows:

> ". . . It is proposed by the Chief that the force he has named should be assembled . . . for eventualities, but that the Home Government should not be informed of this. . . . The Home Government are very anxious that Baghdad should be taken, and they will send us the required force if we hold out, but they will give us nothing if the least sign of willingness to find reinforcements is shown by us."

So the Viceroy cabled on October 17th: ". . . In no case could I undertake to supply from India, even temporarily, a further force of the strength of a division."

The Indian Government, as Commander Wedgwood remarks, "held out" while Serbia was being overrun, and while our last man was being put in at Loos.

It is hardly necessary to add that the Commission passed severe censures upon the Commander-in-Chief in India, Sir Beauchamp Duff, and the Viceroy, Lord Hardinge; on the Surgeon-General, the Director of Medical Services, the Indian Marine, and the Commanding Officer in Mesopotamia, General Nixon. It further condemned the whole military system of administration as "cumbrous and inept", and recommended its drastic reform.

When I was appointed Secretary of State for War in July, 1916, my first task was to take in hand the Mesopotamian situation. The most urgent call was for improved transport and medical arrangements. It was my good fortune to secure the assistance of the Q.M.G., Sir John Cowans, a man whom I have always considered to be the most capable soldier thrown up by the war in our Army. I shall never forget the quiet efficiency with which he detailed the steps that he thought should be taken. He had no hesitation in utilising experienced civilian assistance and some of the ablest of his transport officials in the Barge department were promoted civilians. All that could be done from this end was put in hand and pressed through without delay and there were no further scandals in the administration of the Mesopotamian Army.

The Commission also stated that "it was not until London took over the sole charge that there was any marked improvement in the management of the campaign. The improvement and success since effected are a striking illustration of the all-importance of unity of control in time of war." A number of references are made through the report to the better state of things which had supervened since July, 1916.

I feel that I cannot conclude this rather gruesome chapter without quoting a first-rate example of official circumlocution. It might serve a useful purpose to insert it here as a warning.

The Report of the Mesopotamian Commission gives a graphic description of the cumbrous procedure and circumlocution which at that time hedged round any proposal to make provision for the needs of the Army. It was supplied by Mr. Brunyate, Financial Secretary to the Indian Government, and for some years Financial Adviser to the Commander-in-Chief and Military Member of Council. When asked to give a concrete case of how a paper relating to a proposal for army equipment would pass through the two departments, he replied:

"The Quartermaster-General, it may be supposed, wishes to have more mules. Probably before putting forward the proposal at all he sees the Commander-in-Chief personally as Commander-in-Chief and ascertains from him that he is willing to have that proposal ventilated. He then writes a note stating his facts, probably supported by a note from the Director of the Army Remount Department, makes a definite recommendation, estimates the cost, and marks his note to the Army Department of the Government of India. The office clerks of the Army Department note on the case, the Assistant Secretary notes, the Deputy Secretary may note, and it reaches the Army Secretary — we will call him General Holloway, though he is not actually Army Secretary now. He criticises the proposal if he thinks fit . . . the Office of the Financial Adviser then note upon it . . . the clerks in the Finance Adviser's office note, the Assistant or Deputy Financial Adviser notes, now Mr. Fell. Mr. Fell may be prepared at once to accept the proposal on behalf of the Finance Department, and may intimate that he does not intend to refer it to the Finance Member. The file then goes back to the Army Secretary, and in that case he at once arranges for the necessary orders to be issued to give effect to the Quartermaster-General's proposal, unless he thinks the case of sufficient importance to refer it to the Army Member.

"Such reference will, of course, practically always be required if the proposal is one requiring the sanction of the Secretary of State. In that case the Army Secretary would take the Army Member's orders at this stage, and a despatch to the Secretary of State would then be drafted in the Army Department. . . . Or again, Mr. Fell, when the case first reached him, might have criticised the proposal, and indicated a desire to see it modified or rejected. In that case the file would still go back to the Army Secretary, and he would doubtless at that stage take the orders of the Army Member unless before doing so he wished to have the opinion of the Quartermaster-General on the criticisms and suggestions which had been made in the Military Finance Branch. Mr. Fell, when criticising the proposal, would probably have indicated whether he intended to refer the case eventually to the

Finance Member. Thus when the Army Secretary brought these criticisms before the Army Member, the latter would know that if he decided to override the Financial Adviser's criticisms, he might have to face opposition from the Finance Member. The Army Member would then pass his orders. If he adhered to the scheme as put forward by the Quartermaster-General and the Army Department he would record a note to that effect. The file would then go back to the Financial Adviser, and the latter would not note again, but would submit the case to the Finance Member. If the Finance Member decided not to press the objections raised by Mr. Fell, the proposal would become a fully accepted proposal, and orders would be issued for putting it into effect. If, however, the Finance Member definitely objected to the scheme, the case would then go back to Mr. Fell for return to the Army Secretary for re-submission to the Army Member. The Army Member might then defer to the Finance Member's objection, in which case the whole proposal would be dropped with the Army Member's concurrence, though a reluctant concurrence. If, however, the Army Member, in spite of the Finance Member's objections, considered that the proposal was a necessary one, he would intimate to the Army Secretary that the case should be referred to His Excellency the Viceroy, under our Rules of Business, which prescribe that when two Members of Council differ the case must be referred for the orders of the Viceroy. The Army Secretary would then lay the case before the Viceroy. The latter might very possibly indicate a personal opinion that, in the circumstances, as a particular case, he thought it perhaps desirable that the views of the Army Member should be deferred to, and any expression of the Viceroy's wish in an ordinary case is very frequently — I might almost say generally — deferred to. Or the Viceroy might, pursuing the ordinary procedure under our Statutory Rules of Business, simply instruct the Army Secretary that the case was to be brought up in Council, the following week. It would then be discussed in Council, the Army Secretary being present, but not taking any part in the discussion, and would be settled by the views of the majority of the Council."

Asked how long a disputed case might take, he replied:

"At the best a disputed proposal would, I think, ordinarily take a good many weeks. I cannot put it more exactly than that, but a great deal depends on whether the responsible secretary takes a grip of the case and prevents it being constantly remitted backwards and forwards between the Financial Adviser on the one side and the Administrative Authority, the Quartermaster-General, or whoever he may be, on the other, inviting each in turn to reply to the other's rejoinders and criticisms. Where a case was not taken hold of and put to an end, I have known it very lamentably protracted from this cause. . . ."

This fantastic picture is not a page from some Dickensian work of fiction. It is a sober account by a highly responsible official of the actual procedure adopted up to 1916 by the military authorities at Simla — procedure to which any request for vitally necessary supplies for the Mesopotamian Expeditionary Force would be subjected. It helps to explain the tragedy which befell that gallant company.

As Sir John Cowans was the General Officer who undertook the reorganization of the transport system in Mesopotamia, and as his work was a triumphant success, it would not be out of place here to give my impressions of this genial and competent soldier.

The first time that I recollect seeing Sir John Cowans — "Jack" Cowans, as he was known to all his numerous friends — was at the first meeting of the Munitions Committee which was set up at the end of 1914. We met at the War Office, in the Secretary of State's room, and when the discussion on the supply of munitions had come to an end, and our interviews with General von Donop and others were over, Lord Kitchener suggested that we might like to see the man who was responsible for the other war supplies — the Quartermaster-General. General Cowans was sent for, and my first impression was that of a large, rather ungainly, awkward and weather-beaten man with a stolid face and shrewd eyes. He did not in the least resemble my idea of a Staff General. He had rather the visage and demeanour of a successful corn merchant in an agricultural town. He sat down without a glimmer of expression on his face, and when asked for particulars as to food supplies for the Army, he slowly and clumsily pulled out a shabby spectacle case and extracted a pair of horn-rimmed glasses. When these were adjusted he pulled out of his pocket a worn notebook that bore a distinct resemblance to a laundry book, and casually gave us extracts from the notes therein for the answers. Then the clothing — another book. We listened and gradually realised that we were being given a lucid summary of the organisation of supplies which was so completely satisfactory that when Lord Kitchener inquired of us whether we wanted to put any questions, we all felt there was nothing left to ask. This perfunctory soldier surprised me with his quiet, unostentatious efficiency. It was borne in upon the committee that here was a man who understood organisation — that he was an organiser to his finger tips. When I came to know him better I realised that under his rough exterior and stolid look there was a simple and kindly nature and an inexhaustible fund of good humour and joviality. Once you knew him it took little to awaken the twinkle in his eye and to provoke his hearty, noisy, infectious laugh.

With an appearance of being extraordinarily casual, Cowans was an excellent business man. His own department was perfectly ordered, and he himself was thoroughly acquainted with all the workings of it. He discharged his duties throughout the four and a half years of the war in such a way as to give complete satisfaction to everybody concerned, soldiers and civilians. Whatever doubts and grumbles there were about the deficiencies and shortcomings of other war leaders, there never was a murmur from any quarter as to the efficiency with which Sir John Cowans did his work. That is more than can be said about any other prominent figure in the war, military or civil.

I have already described the appalling state of affairs in Mesopotamia when Cowans took the job in hand. Quickly, with almost incredible speed, the state of affairs changed completely. Without fuss and apparently without effort he straightened things out and no more was heard of scandals in Mesopotamia.

When as Secretary for War I came to grips with the Army Council because I insisted upon putting civilians into jobs which soldiers had hitherto been responsible for, it was Cowans who was sent as representative of the irate generals to put their protests before me. He was certainly the best person for the job as far as I was concerned, for his efficiency and good humour made him an acceptable mediator. You could not quarrel or get angry with Jack Cowans. He smiled wrath away.

CHAPTER XIII

THE KNOCK-OUT BLOW

Peace kites in 1916 — Sir William Robertson's peace proposals — Strong position of the Central Powers — Outlook in France and Italy — Russian collapse and approach of revolution — Growth of submarine menace — Figures of shipping losses — The French attitude: M. Briand's speech — Germany's outlook less favourable than her position — Rumours of a peace move by President Wilson — My determination to go through with the fight — Interview with Mr. Roy Howard — No outside interference before victory is won — Tribute to France — Effect of interview — Viscount Grey's letter — My reply — Grey's fears falsified by events — Spring-Rice's reports of American attitude.

THE latter half of 1916 saw a succession of sporadic and untraceable attempts in certain quarters to bring about an inconclusive peace. Kites were flown and hints broadcast in Holland, in Spain, at the Vatican, in Sweden and the U.S.A. There was good reason to think that some at least of these movements were being stimulated by German agents, as this was a propitious moment for securing favourable terms for the Central Powers. In the early months of the war, Germany with her elaborately prepared and highly efficient military equipment and organisation had pressed her attack upon the Allied Powers who were far less skilfully directed, less adequately equipped, and, in the case of the British forces, only just beginning to improvise their military resources. That tide of German conquest had now reached its height, but there was a good deal in the military and naval situation to engender misgiving and even despair of a clear, unmistakable victory being secured on either side.

The uneasy stirring of this peace talk brought to the fore the question of the aims with which we were pursuing the war, and the terms on which we hoped to end it. In August, 1916, the matter was raised in the War Committee, and Sir William Robertson, amongst others, was asked by the Prime Minister to prepare a memorandum setting forth the views of the General Staff on the peace terms desirable from the military point of view. Sir William Robertson's memorandum, dated August 31st, 1916, is in many respects a very remarkable document to have been written in the circumstances of the time. It reads:

1. Although the end of the war is yet by no means in sight, negotiations for peace, in some form or other, may arise any day, and unless we are prepared for them we may find ourselves at a great disadvantage, not only as compared with our enemy but as compared with our Allies. It is not unlikely that M. Briand already possesses very decided views on the subject, carefully worked out for him under his general direction by the clever people who serve him, and who do not appear on the surface of political life. At a hastily summoned council we should have no chance against him, armed with a definite policy to which he may beforehand, and unknown to us, have committed the Russians and perhaps other Powers of the Entente. If this should happen, the Germans might take advantage of it to drive in a wedge between us and the other Entente Powers, with the result that we might find ourselves without support in those claims which we may be compelled to make, more especially in regard to the disposal of the captured German colonies. We need therefore to decide, without loss of time, as to what our policy is to be; then place it before the Entente Powers and ascertain in return what are their aims, and so endeavour to arrive at a clear understanding before we meet our enemies in conference.

2. For centuries past — though unfortunately by no means continuously — our policy has been to help to maintain the balance between the Continental Powers which have always been divided by their interests and sympathies into opposing groups. At one time the centre of gravity has been in Madrid, at another in Vienna, at another in Paris, and at another in St. Petersburg.

We have thwarted, or helped to thwart, each and every Power in turn which has aspired to Continental predominance; and concurrently as a consequence we have enlarged our own sphere of imperial ascendancy. As part of this traditional policy we have aimed at maintaining British maritime supremacy, and at keeping a weak Power in possession of the Low Countries. In more recent years a new preponderance has been allowed to grow up, of which the centre of gravity has been in Berlin, and the result of it is the present War.

3. It is submitted that the basis of peace negotiations must be the three principles for which we have so often fought in the past and for which we have been compelled to fight now, namely:

(a) The maintenance of the balance of power in Europe.

(b) The maintenance of British maritime supremacy, and

(c) The maintenance of a weak Power in the Low Countries.

4. If and when these general principles, and such others as are deemed necessary, are accepted by His Majesty's Government it will be possible to formulate the conditions upon which, and upon which only, we would be prepared to negotiate. No useful purpose would be served by discussing these conditions until the general principles have been settled, but some of the many questions demanding examination may be mentioned by way of showing how important it is to commence investigation with as little delay as possible. It may be added that this paper is written mainly from a military standpoint, and in this connection it cannot be too often remembered that the conditions upon which peace is concluded will govern, or at any rate ought to govern, the size and nature of the army subsequently required by us.

5. If the balance of power in Europe is to be maintained it follows that the existence of a strong Central European Power is essential, and that such a State must be Teutonic, as a Slav nation, the only other alternative, would always lean towards Russia, which would accordingly obtain a preponderant position and so destroy the very principle which we desire to uphold. On the other hand, as Germany is the chief European competitor with us on the sea, it would be advantageous to make such terms

of peace as would check the development of her navy and of her mercantile marine. In other words, it would be to the interests of the British Empire to leave Germany reasonably strong on land, but to weaken her at sea. The full extent to which His Majesty's Government have already been committed is not known to the General Staff, but apparently it is the intention to break up Austria-Hungary. By the Roumanian Political Convention a large part of Eastern Hungary will be transferred to Roumania; Italy will no doubt insist on retaining Trieste with Istria and some of the neighbouring districts; and Serbia is to be given part at least of Herzegovina, Bosnia and Slavonia. The chief problems to be determined are the disposal of Austria proper, of the Magyar district of Hungary, of the Northern Slav provinces of Bohemia, Moravia and Galicia and finally, whether there shall be access to the Adriatic from the north otherwise than through Italian or Serbian territory. It is clear that all these provinces cannot become independent States. Galicia may be absorbed in a new Polish Kingdom, but Bohemia and Moravia on the one side and Hungary on the other will be difficult of disposal. Acting on the principle of maintaining a strong Germany, it might be advantageous if Austria proper were incorporated in that Empire, more especially as thereby ten million South Germans would be brought in as a counterpoise to Prussia. The other alternative, which has the advantage of settling the question of the disposal of the various provinces, is to maintain a diminished Austria-Hungary, and in that case an Adriatic port, Fiume for choice, should be allotted to it. This new Austria-Hungary would very probably form a very close union with Germany, but such a union might be not altogether to our disadvantage on land as limiting the power of Russia and the Slav States, and on sea as preventing the Mediterranean from becoming a French and Italian lake.

6. As regards the western boundaries of Germany we will presumably be obliged to agree to the wishes of the French with regard to Alsace and Lorraine. Belgium must be restored to her pre-war condition, and it may be desirable that the Grand Duchy of Luxembourg should be added to her territories. It would be

advantageous if Belgium could be given free access from the sea to Antwerp by transferring to her that part of Seeland which lies south of the Scheldt. In this case Holland might be given compensation in East Friesland and in the East Frisian Islands.

7. On the north it is to be wished that the whole of Schleswig and possibly a part of Holstein should be restored to Denmark. From a naval point of view it would be of the highest importance to take away from Germany the Kiel Canal — which might be internationalised — the Harbour of Kiel, the North Frisian Islands, and the eastern shores of the Heligoland Bight. These questions, as all others of a naval nature, are of course matters for the Admiralty to advise upon.

8. On the east the boundaries of Germany will depend on those that may be given to Poland. A difficulty in the way of creating this new State is to provide it with a seaport. The Poles themselves are desirous of having Dantzig, and state, in support of this claim, that sixty per cent. of the population of West Prussia is Polish. It would, however, scarcely seem feasible in any circumstances to cut off East Prussia from Germany, and it is hard to believe that Germany will ever be so crushed as to consent to the transfer of Posen to Poland, unless the latter were to form a State of the German Empire under a German Prince, a contingency which presumably could only occur in the event of a German victory. As regards Poland, we shall probably be obliged to conform to Russian wishes.

9. Bulgaria may either secede from the Central Powers and be allowed to retain her existing territories, plus the uncontested zone of Macedonia, or she may fight on to the end. In the latter case, if and when Russia is established in Constantinople, it is possible that she may try to annex Bulgaria, and eventually to link it up with Bessarabia by wresting the Dobrudja from Roumania.

10. The principal suggestions here made for examination are that Germany should be reduced on the west and north by the cession to other Powers of parts of Alsace and Lorraine, East Friesland, Schleswig, and part of Holstein; that there should

be some rectification of frontier due to the creation of Poland; and that in the south she should be strengthened either by the incorporation of Austria proper, or by a close union with a much diminished Austria-Hungary; and that her naval power should be shaken by taking away from her the Kiel Canal and various districts on the North Sea and Baltic which are of great maritime importance.

11. It is apparently the intention to break up the Turkish Empire by handing over Constantinople and the Straits to Russia, and by dividing up Mesopotamia, Syria, and parts of Asia Minor. This intention does not affect the question of the future boundaries of Germany in Europe, but it is of importance as preventing German development in the Near East.

12. In Asia outside the Turkish Empire, our main concern is with Persia, and there seems no reason why any agreement that it may be necessary to make with Russia concerning that country should be discussed at the Peace Conference.

13. Our future relations with our Allies demand as close consideration as our relations with our enemies. What is our policy to be towards the French in Salonika, towards the Italians and French in Albania, towards the Italians in Asia Minor, towards the Russians in the Balkans, and towards the Slav world generally in connection with the creation of Poland? It is well to remember that the present grouping of the Powers is not a permanency, and indeed it may continue but a very short time after the war is over.

14. With regard to her colonies, Germany will have lost the whole of them when the campaign in German East Africa has been completed. They are:

Kiauchau
Togoland
The Cameroons
German Southwest Africa
German East Africa
German New Guinea
The Bismarck Archipelago

The Caroline, Marshall, Marianne, Solomon and Samoan Islands, in the Pacific.

Germany is certain to make strenuous efforts to recover all or most of these Colonies in order that she may keep her "place in the sun" and preserve at least the semblance of a position as a world power. She is therefore likely to put forward tempting bargains to those Powers who are not interested in order that pressure may be brought to bear upon those Powers who are interested to relinquish their claims. We alone are interested in all these Colonies, and France only in the Cameroons, Belgium in East Africa, and Japan in Kiauchau and the Northern Pacific Islands. It is easy to see therefore that if the cession of a portion of, say, Poland to Russia, or of Alsace-Lorraine to France, or even the complete evacuation of Belgium is made conditional by Germany upon our giving up Togoland, Southwest and East Africa, and the Southern Pacific Islands, we may be placed in a difficult position.

15. Kiauchau, the Marianne, Caroline and Marshall Islands have been occupied by, and are being administered by, the Japanese, and Japan is unlikely to release her hold on them without a substantial *quid pro quo,* which it will not be easy to find.

16. The Samoan Islands were occupied by, and are now administered by, the Government of New Zealand, which is likely to attach a high sentimental value to this, the first conquest of a young people. The same applies to German New Guinea, the Bismarck Archipelago and the Solomon Islands, which were occupied by and are now in the hands of the Australian Government, who have the further inducement, to keep what they have got, that these islands form a valuable buffer between the mainland and possible Japanese encroachment.

17. In Africa the difficulties are even greater. The Union of South Africa, with the experience of this war behind it, is unlikely to tolerate the neighbourhood of a great foreign power. They have conquered German Southwest Africa with their own resources, and taken a leading part in the campaign in East Africa. We are, therefore, likely to enter the Peace Conference

with Togoland as the only possession which we can use freely for the purpose of bargaining.

18. The many problems which the future disposal of the German Colonies involve require very full consideration, and no time should be lost in obtaining the views of the Dominions, and in deciding on the attitude to be adopted in regard to the other Entente Powers.

19. Another question requiring discussion and settlement, as far as possible, is that of enemy proposals for an armistice pending negotiations for peace. The existence of the Entente blockade makes it extremely difficult to suggest any equitable terms on which an armistice could be arranged. From the point of view of the Entente the maintenance of the blockade during the armistice is absolutely essential, as otherwise the Central Powers would be able to provision themselves during the armistice and would consequently be in a much better position to recommence hostilities if the negotiations for peace were to collapse. The enemy would no doubt strongly oppose a maintenance of the blockade because it would progressively weaken him every day that it continued, with the result that at the end of the armistice he would be in a worse position than at the commencement. But we may hope that during the same period his position would, if there were no armistice, become worse, and we cannot allow him to reap an advantage from an armistice which he would not obtain if there were no armistice. In fact we need not concern ourselves with him. The last thing Germany would do, in similar circumstances, would be to give the least consideration to the difficulties of her enemy. Moreover, our desire will be to conclude the negotiations as quickly as possible, whereas the removal of the blockade will almost certainly tend to lengthen them indefinitely.

20. There seem therefore to be three courses which require consideration:

(a) Refuse an armistice altogether and continue fighting during peace negotiations or until the enemy surrenders unconditionally.

(b) Limit the armistice to land and air operations; mari-

time operations, whether submarine or otherwise, being continued.

(c) Agree to some kind of rationing policy during the armistice, calculated to leave the Central Powers in the same economic position at the close as at the beginning of the armistice.

21. All three courses have their objections. As regards *(a)* it would not be easy to conduct peace negotiations while active operations were in progress, as the constant fluctuations in the fighting might have a corresponding influence on the negotiations. It must also be remembered that the negotiations would necessarily take a long time, as so many different Powers are concerned, to say nothing of the conflicting interests and large areas involved.

22. On the other hand it will be difficult to draft satisfactory terms for an armistice even if it is confined to land and air operations alone, for unless the terms are most precise and can anticipate all possible contingencies, constant complaints will be made as to infringements of its conditions and innumerable disputes may in this way arise. Further, if it were decided to grant an armistice as in *(b)*, and submarine attacks on passenger and merchant vessels were continued, the Conference proceedings might become embittered and a settlement rendered the more difficult. Course *(c)* is not recommended. The more hungry the enemy is kept the better, and after all he probably has enough to live upon. Also, it would be difficult to arrange a scale of rations that would be acceptable to all parties.

23. It is quite evident that the question is beset by numerous difficulties and therefore its examination is the more urgent. On the whole it seems hardly possible to refuse an armistice, but it is necessary that we should have some definite guarantees of good faith, and therefore it is suggested that the granting of an armistice should at least be made conditional on:

(a) The immediate withdrawal of all enemy troops inside their pre-war frontiers.

(b) Immediate release of all prisoners of war held by the enemy.

(c) Tentative surrender of a certain portion of the enemy fleet.

W. R. Robertson.
General Chief of the Imperial General Staff.

War Office
31st August, 1916.

Apart from the interest of this document as setting out the ideas of the military authorities upon the territorial measures that should be taken to limit the perils of a recurrence of the German menace, it is of value in that it reflects the expectation current at the time that peace negotiations might not be far distant on the horizon.

There were, however, marked differences in the attitude adopted by various influential people to this prospect. Many who had entered the war reluctantly felt that once it had been forced upon us, it would be a real disaster if peace were made before it had been demonstrated clearly that no military machine, however perfect, could prevail in the end against the roused conscience of civilisation. But this view was by no means fully appreciated and shared in all quarters. In face of our dubious military position and unsatisfactory outlook, there were those who felt attracted towards the possibility of a prompt if inconclusive peace.

The third campaign of the war was now drawing to a close and the Allies seemed farther than ever from achieving a favourable determination of the issue. At the end of the first campaign, Belgium had been almost entirely occupied by the enemy; a large and important section of Northern France had also been overrun by the Germans, and even after the retreat from the Marne ten of the richest provinces of France remained in enemy occupation. At the end of the second year's campaign Serbia had fallen entirely into the hands of the Central Powers, and Bulgaria with its brave army had joined the enemy and thousands of square miles of Russian territory had been conquered and were adding to the resources of the enemy in food, timber and labour.

By the end of the third summer Roumania had been crushed and most of its territory, including its capital, was in enemy occupation. Invaluable reserves of oil and corn were added to the enemy stores of essential supply. The Balkans were thus almost entirely in the hands of the Central Powers, for whose munitions the road to Constantinople had been cleared. Turkey had been resuscitated and was making a formidable contribution to the military strength of its allies. She was holding up at one point or another hundreds of thousands of British and French troops. We had been driven by Turkish forces out of the Dardanelles, and a British Army had surrendered to the Turks in Mesopotamia. In the West, attempts made with colossal losses to release the fierce grip of the German Army on the soil of France had not succeeded in producing any tangible result. The Germans had been hammered by the most formidable artillery ever mobilised on a battlefield and they had suffered severely, and had to abandon some territory, but their casualties were not comparable with those inflicted on the French and notably on the British Army, and the territorial gain was insignificant whether computed in superficies or strategy. The German attack on Verdun had failed, but the French had even there lost considerably more men than the Germans.

The French nation was bleeding at every pore and no one could visit France without feeling that although the courage of this gallant people was undaunted and its spirit unbroken, its ardour was being quenched in the blood of its sons. Official reports from Italy were far from encouraging. The Italian people were by no means as united in their decision to enter the war as the other belligerents. Their inadequately equipped troops had, since May, 1915, performed prodigies of valour and triumphs of engineering skill in scaling fortresses drilled and blasted out of the great mountains that lowered over the Italian plains, but progress had been slow, and losses had been heavy. Recently, there had been a serious setback. The Cabinet were informed early in November by Sir Rennell Rodd, our Ambassador in Rome, upon the accuracy of whose reports on the Italian position we all placed implicit confidence, that "there were already in Italy certain symptoms of war weariness and discontent at the protraction of the struggle. Great Britain is represented as the only country anxious to prolong the struggle *à outrance* for her own ends. It would be wrong to pretend that there exists here the same grim determination to carry through as prevails in France and in the British Empire."

The Russian armies were broken and quite unable to offer any effective resistance to the German attack, and although their position in respect of ammunition and rifles was supposed to have improved during the year it was quite clear that their equipment would not enable them to stand up much longer to the formidable artillery at the disposal of Hindenburg's armies. Ten thousand tons of ammunition stacked at Archangel had, either through carelessness or treachery, been blown up. The whole administration was slack, incompetent, and drenched with corruption. No wonder that the Russian people were seething with discontent. The peasantry were permeated with sullen disaffection. The workers in the towns were becoming more difficult and insubordinate. Strikes multiplied and street demonstrations were becoming a menacing feature. The soldiers had ceased to believe in the possibility of victory and whether they were called upon to advance or to resist they obeyed mechanically, but their response lacked spirit or confidence. Discipline alone held them in the trenches.

Food everywhere throughout Russia was becoming scarce. Revolution was only a question of time. It was taken for granted on all hands. Although we were assured by our representative in Russia that it would not occur until the war was over, the Allies could not rely upon a population saturated with a spirit of disgust with its Government to go on risking precious lives at the behest and for the sake of an autocracy which no longer commanded respect, and which in fact had become universally despised among all classes high and low. There were hopes that Russian resistance might last long enough to hold up a considerable proportion of the Central Powers' armies until the Allies on the Western and Italian fronts had at last achieved the long-expected "break through." But that hope was becoming increasingly precarious and in the event it proved to be illusory. A complete collapse of the Russian resistance meant two or three million German and Austrian troops, with their formidable train of artillery, released for the Western and Italian fronts, to attack an exhausted France and discouraged Italy.

There was another impending peril which threatened the very life of Britain — the sinking of our merchant ships by enemy submarines. The German Admiralty had set itself the task of increasing its submarine fleet fourfold in numbers. The increase in size and power of these elusive vessels of destruction was more menacing than the augmentation in their numbers. It meant that the area of attack was widened. The newer types could travel into the ocean and hunt far and wide for their prey. The difficulties of organising effective protection were thereby considerably enhanced. The output of the German yards was multiplying at an alarming rate, and the figures of our losses leapt up steeply, week by week. The defence was by no means equal to the assault. It had to fight an invisible foe — an enemy who left no spoor behind but who destroyed and then disappeared, pursuing his course in the trackless depths, unseen, unseeable, and untraceable, leaving nothing behind to indicate direction or distance.

The following table shows the rate at which British merchant vessels were being sunk by submarines during 1916:

Date	No.	Tonnage.
January, 1916	5	62,288
February "	7	75,860
March "	19	99,089
April "	37	141,193
May "	12	64,251
June "	11	36,976
July "	21	82,432
August "	22	43,354
September "	34	104,572
October "	41	176,248
November "	42	168,809
December "	36	182,292

This is how the position appeared at that time to Lord Robert Cecil, who was then an influential member of the Cabinet:

"One thing is clear. Our situation is grave. It is certain that unless the utmost national effort is made it may become desperate, particularly in the matter of shipping. The position in Allied countries is even more serious. France is within measurable distance of exhaustion. The political outlook of Italy is menacing. Her finance is tottering. In Russia there is great discouragement. She has long been on the verge of revolution. Even her man-power seems coming near its limits."

This was a situation that must necessarily invite doubt in the stoutest hearts and recruit patriotic and humanitarian sentiment to the side of immediate peace. But for reasons which I give later on I felt that any attempt to make peace at a time when the Germans were at the climax of strength and achievement, whilst we were only just beginning to mobilise our full power, would necessarily be unsatisfactory and inconclusive.

The attitude of France towards any peace overtures at this stage was one of uncompromising hostility, despite the gloom of the outlook. It was set out very clearly at a sitting of the French Chamber in a speech of exceptional power by the Prime Minister, M. Briand. A Socialist by the name of M. Brizon had delivered a speech on September 19th, 1916, in the course of which he dwelt upon the losses of France and ended by asking if France had not suffered enough, and whether she could not now negotiate peace. M. Briand in reply delivered one of the most eloquent speeches of his life. I quote an extract from that speech. When he sat down he received from the Chamber what is said to be "such an ovation as has never been accorded to a Prime Minister" and the House by four hundred and twenty-one votes to twenty-six ordered the speech to be placarded throughout France. It may therefore be assumed that it represented the determined and even fierce resistance of the country which had suffered most from the war to any premature efforts to make peace.

"Look at your country, M. Brizon. It has been violently attacked. It stands for something in the world as a propagator of those ideas which have done work for the world's progress. When your country, which has for two years had the honour to be champion of right, has stayed the invader, and defends the whole world, when its blood flows, you say 'Negotiate peace.' What a challenge, what an outrage to the memory of our dead! [Loud cheers, and a shout *"Débout les morts!"*] What, M. Brizon! Ten of your country's provinces are invaded. Our old men and women and children have been carried off. They bear their misery bravely, awaiting deliverance at your hands. Is it then that you come to us saying, 'Negotiate, go and ask for peace'? You little know France if you imagine that she can accept economy of milliards, or even of blood in such humiliating circumstances. What peace would you get for France? It would be a peace of war. If you wish that peace should shine upon the world, M. Brizon, if you wish the idea of liberty and justice to prevail, ask for victory, and not for the peace obtainable to-day, for that peace would be humiliating and dishonouring. There is not a Frenchman who can possibly desire it."

On the other hand Germany had her troubles. A blockade had been tightly drawn around the Central Powers, while on the other hand the Allies had developed very extensive arrangements for securing their own essential supplies. Austria and Turkey were broken reeds. Germany could not lean her hopes too heavily upon them. In Britain the work of the Ministry of Munitions was now bearing copious fruit, and the adoption of national service was securing hundreds of thousands of men for our armies.

It was natural, therefore, that Germany should be ready to welcome and foster suggestions from any quarter urging an early peace settlement, while her strength remained intact and her position on the war map lent colour to the suggestion that she was substantially a victorious Power. Rumours indeed reached us that her emissaries in the United States were angling for intervention by President Wilson with a view to an early and favourable peace.

The President himself would not have been without his own reasons for being attracted by the suggestion of proposing such an intervention. The presidential election was at hand — it was due at the beginning of November — and there was the very large and influential German-American vote to consider. He was, moreover, standing on his reputation as the man who had kept America out of the war, and anything he could do to reduce the very real danger — a danger which not long after took concrete form — that America would after all be drawn into the conflict, would obviously help his election campaign. The moment was, however, in my view utterly inappropriate for the discussion of any peace terms which would be remotely satisfactory to the Allies. I will not pretend that my opinion was shared by all members of the British Cabinet. There were those among them who had grave doubts about the military position and the outlook for our shipping, our food supplies, and financial reserves. Lord Grey, Lord Lansdowne, Mr. M'Kenna, and Mr. Runciman in particular were obviously uneasy about the prospect. They had misgivings as to the possibility of continuing the war beyond Christmas, 1916. It has become clear from statements which have since been published that a similar impression was widely held abroad.

I felt it vitally important to throw out a sharp challenge to the defeatist spirit which was working from foreign quarters to bring about an inconclusive peace, and which appeared to find an echo even in some responsible quarters in our own country.

I was no friend to war. It was only with the utmost reluctance that I had at the last minute agreed to the ultimatum of Britain. My pacifist attitude was very well known, and had it not been for Germany's violation of Belgian neutrality, I should up to the last have refused to remain in a Cabinet which implicated the country in war with all its carnage and organised barbarism. But once having entered on the war, I was no less resolute to pursue it until at least the object of our sacrifice had been achieved. It was not merely a question of abiding by the Shakespearian counsel.

> "Beware
> Of entrance to a quarrel: but being in
> Bear't that the opposed may beware of thee."

A conference under existing conditions might have involved a peace which would have been a virtual and practical abandonment of the cause which compelled us to take up arms.

Accordingly, copying an example which had been set shortly before by Lord Grey himself, I granted, on September 28th, 1916, an interview to an American correspondent — in this case Mr. Roy W. Howard, the President of the United Press Associations of America — in which I outlined my views as to the attitude this country and her Allies should adopt towards any talk of an immediate peace.

I began by pointing out that Britain had only now got into her stride in her war effort, and was justifiably suspicious of any suggestion that President Wilson should choose this moment to "butt in" with a proposal to stop the war before we could achieve victory. "There had been no such intervention when we were being hammered through the first two years, as yet untrained and ill-equipped. Our men had taken their punishment without squealing. They had held grimly on while the winning Germans talked of annexing Belgium and Poland as their spoils of victory, and of making it a fight to a finish with England.

"The whole world — including neutrals of the highest purposes and humanitarians with the best of motives — must know that there can be no outside interference at this stage. Britain asked no intervention when she was unprepared to fight. She will tolerate none now that she is prepared, until the Prussian military despotism is broken beyond repair."

It was idle for people now to deplore the horror of continued conflict, when their pity had not moved them to stop it while British troops were being gassed, and exposed to an overpowering attack that used ten shells to their one.

"But in the British determination to carry the fight to a decisive finish there is something more than the natural demand for vengeance. The inhumanity and pitilessness of the fighting that must come before a lasting peace is possible is not comparable with the cruelty that would be involved in stopping the war while there remains the possibility of civilisation again being menaced from the same quarter. Peace now or at any time before the final and complete elimination of this menace is unthinkable. No man and no nation with the slightest understanding of the temper of the citizen army of Britons, which took its terrible hammering without a whine or a grumble, will attempt to call a halt now."

"But how long do you figure this can and must go on?" I was asked.

"There is neither clock nor calendar in the British Army to-day," was my reply. "Time is the least vital factor. Only the result counts — not the time consumed in achieving it. It took England twenty years to defeat Napoleon, and the first fifteen of those years were black with British defeat. It will not take twenty years to win this war, but whatever time is required it will be done.

"And I say this, recognising that we have only begun to win. There is no disposition on our side to fix the hour of ultimate victory after the first success. We have no delusion that the war is nearing an end. We have not the slightest doubt as to *how* it is to end."

"But what of France?" I was asked. "Is there the same determination there to stick to the end; the same idea of fighting until peace terms can be dictated by Germany's enemies?"

"The world at large has not yet begun to appreciate the magnificence, the nobility, the wonder of France," I replied. "I had the answer to your inquiry given me a few days ago by a noble Frenchwoman. This woman had given four sons — she had one more left to give to France. In the course of my talk with her I asked if she did not think the struggle had gone far enough. Her reply, without a moment's hesitation, was: 'The fight will never have gone far enough until it shall have made a repetition of this horror impossible.' That mother was voicing the spirit of France. Yes, France will stick to the end."

I pointed to the defence of Verdun as evidence of French staying power. While the British were buoyed up by a sporting spirit, the French were burning with an unquenchable patriotism. The motto of the Allies was "Never Again!" I was myself fresh from a visit to the battlefields, and the ghastliness I had witnessed was something which must never be rëenacted. The war must make that certain.

This was the substance of my interview, which was given very wide currency, and was discussed in every country. The "Policy of a Knock-out Blow", as it was called, caused great exasperation, not only to the Central Powers (as witnessed by the constant reference to it in their Press and in the speeches of their politicians) but even to several of my colleagues in the British Cabinet, who, if not exactly pacifists, were leaning towards an early peace of accommodation. Several of my colleagues regarded the interview as provocative, and many held that it did not accurately represent the attitude of the Government towards the idea of an immediate peace.

It was not long before I discovered that this interview had caused a great deal of perturbation and animadversion amongst the members of the Cabinet. I received the following letter from Viscount Grey: [1]

"29th September, 1916.

"My dear Lloyd George,

"The more I think of it the more I am apprehensive of the possible effect of the warning to Wilson in your interview, and I want to explain why this is so.

[1] Sir Edward Grey, created Viscount Grey of Falloden, July, 1916.

"1. Briand's speech, and I think steps taken in Washington, has made any further warning to Wilson unnecessary for the present.

"2. We shall now be held responsible in America for warning Wilson off the course. He will now point to your words as the reason why he can do nothing, and this will tend to bring him and Bethmann-Hollweg together.

"3. Wilson will be more disposed to put upon us the pressure that Congress has urged him to put, which may be very inconvenient.

"4. The extreme submarine warfare will be precipitated by Germany, who will tell Wilson that as he can do nothing because of us, Germany must use every means against us. Wilson and his supporters will be less inclined than before to resent submarine warfare against us.

"5. It has always been my view that until the Allies were sure of victory the door should be kept open for Wilson's mediation. It is now closed for ever as far as we are concerned. I am still anxious about the effect of submarine warfare.

"I hope you won't think me captious in questioning one point in our interview of which the rest not only draws my assent but my admiration. I may be quite wrong in my view, but a public warning to the President of the United States is an important step, and I wish I had had an opportunity of putting these considerations before you and discussing them with you.

"No answer needed now as nothing more can be done till we see the effect.

Yours sincerely,

GREY of F."

To this I replied:

"October 2, 1916.

"My dear Grey,

"Thanks for your letter. I wonder whether you are still of the same opinion after reading M.I.I.'s secret information? Have you seen it?

"Spring-Rice's telegram 2943 seems to be also very significant. If the hands of Wilson had been forced — and there is every indication that the Germans and Irish coöperation could do so — then we should be in a very tight place. Any cessation of hostilities now would be a disaster; and although we could always refuse or put up impossible terms, it is much better that we should not be placed in that predicament. *You* could not have warned off the United States without doing it formally. I could commit a serviceable indiscretion; you could not. It would ruin you; I am inoculated!

". . . In so far as callous impenitence will allow me, I am genuinely sorry for adding one dram to your cup of anxieties.

Ever sincerely,
D. LLOYD GEORGE."

Lord Grey committed himself to a series of forecasts in this letter all of which were falsified by the event. He predicted that it would encourage Wilson to "do nothing and would tend to bring him and Bethmann-Hollweg together." A few months later, when I was Prime Minister, Wilson broke off diplomatic relations with Germany, and a few weeks after doing so entered into the war on the side of the Allies. Grey predicted that another result of my letter might be an increase in the pressure which the President would bring to bear upon us. That also turned out to be an unrealised apprehension. He foresaw that my interview would precipitate an extreme submarine warfare by Germany and that President Wilson as a result of it would be less inclined to resent submarine warfare against us. Germany had decided at the beginning of 1916 to increase fourfold the number and potency of her submarines. At the end of August she had already launched a large number of these new, more powerful craft. And so far from Wilson and his supporters being less inclined than before to resent submarine warfare, it was the intensification and extension of the submarine campaign that provoked America to declare war against Germany early in 1917.

As to Grey's prediction that the door against Wilson's mediation would, as a result of my interview, be "closed for ever as far as we are concerned", two or three months later President Wilson issued his famous Peace Note.

It is, however, significant of Lord Grey's frame of mind at this time that he seemed to have a doubt as to the victory of the Allies — and that he was relying as a means of escape from the consequences of defeat upon the mediation of the President of the United States.

How little Lord Grey's estimate of the probable effect of my interview corresponded with reality is made clear by the reports which came to hand from our Ambassador in the United States, Sir Cecil Spring-Rice. In a telegram to the Foreign Secretary, dated October 4th, 1916, Spring-Rice said:

"I am informed from a very reliable source that the President has no intention of making peace proposals. The Secretary of State for War's statement has had a great effect.

"I have also reason to believe that action will not be taken on the Retaliatory Clauses. . . ."

He followed this up with a letter dated October 6th, 1916, in which he wrote:

"Mr. Lloyd George's statement, which had an immense and instantaneous effect in this country, put a stop to the peace rumours which for some time have been prevalent here. It seems generally acknowledged now that the President has no intention of offering his meditation at any rate in the near future."

The letter also said that the American Government was maintaining uncompromising opposition to Germany in regard to any extension of the submarine campaign, and explained that the peace rumours emanating from German sources were being used by them to assist their deals on the stock market.

"The publication of a peace rumour is at once followed by a general decline on the Stock Exchange, and the authoritative quarter which launches such a rumour is in excellent position to profit by its power."

In a later telegram, dated October 20th, 1916, Sir Cecil Spring-Rice reported: "Lloyd George's interview had the most excellent effect here." There is in fact no evidence that my "Knock-out Blow" interview did anything to injure our cause in the States. On the contrary, it steadied opinion there and helped to increase the sympathy felt with us in our desperate fight.

CHAPTER XIV

THE LANSDOWNE PEACE MOVE

Peace discussed by the Asquith Cabinet — Lord Lansdowne opens the discussion — His memorandum — Doubt of Allied victory — Mr. Runciman's pessimism — The food problem — Naval shortage of destroyers — Man-power running short — Cost of prolonging the war — A stocktaking needed of Allied resources — Disbelief in "Knock-out Blow" — Danger of political trouble in France and Russia — Trouble with the neutrals — We should not discourage peace moves — Objection to my insistence on victory — Comments on the Lansdowne memorandum by Robertson and Haig — Lord Grey's contribution — Only Mr. Balfour frames concrete peace terms — The Balfour memorandum — Allied victory assumed — Strip Central Powers of non-German territory — A new map of Europe — Problem of Poland — Schleswig-Holstein — No internal interference with Germany or Austria — Napoleon's failure to crush Prussia — Possibility of German-Austrian unity — Slav races too divided to threaten Europe — Germany will still be strong — Need to secure access to sea for Central Powers — Problem of indemnities — Mr. Henderson's views — Lord Robert Cecil's memorandum — Mr. Asquith decides against peace move — Importance of these peace discussions — Mr. Asquith's speech in the House — Lord Grey against peace without victory — Peril of an inconclusive peace — Why it was impossible to open negotiations.

SHOULD we make or encourage peace overtures whilst the issue of the war was still in doubt and the enemy had good reason to claim that he had won on points? The British Cabinet was brought by the intervention of one of its most respected members to a searching and considered examination of the question.

The type of partisan pacifist who maintains that an honourable and satisfactory peace could have been negotiated long before November, 1918, is generally anxious to cast the whole of the blame for prolonging the war on the Coalition that came into existence at the end of 1916. In order to sustain their criticism they assume that 1917 afforded the first real opportunity for making peace. The discussions which took place in the Asquith Cabinet on the desirability of encouraging peace overtures and the decision arrived at by the Cabinet are either unknown to these critics or are wilfully ignored by them.

The first serious peace movements in Europe started immediately after the termination of the sanguinary battle of 1916. The horrible and futile carnage of the Somme following on the ghastly losses of Verdun had sent a thrill of horror through all the belligerent lands and there was a distinct movement for an interchange of views as to the possibility of a settlement.

In the middle of November Lord Lansdowne startled the Cabinet by a memorandum which he circulated amongst members with the consent of the Prime Minister. It was written the day before Mr. Asquith and I left England for the Paris Conference and was in the hands of members of the Cabinet on our return. This bold document frankly suggested doubts as to the possibility of victory. It was at least courageous, and proved that he, at any rate, was quite alive to the perils of the Allied situation. It was clear that Lord Lansdowne thought a condition of stalemate had been reached and that there was no prospect of any improvement.

The text of this memorandum was as follows:

MEMORANDUM BY LORD LANSDOWNE RESPECTING PEACE SETTLEMENT

The members of the War Committee were asked by the Prime Minister some weeks ago to express their views as to the terms upon which peace might be concluded. I do not know whether there has been a general response to this invitation, but the only reply which I have seen is one written last month by the First Lord of the Admiralty, in which he deals at some length with the problems which might have to be discussed at any Peace Conference. Mr. Balfour observes truly that these questions cannot be profitably examined except upon an agreed hypothesis as to the military position of the combatants at the end of the war, and he proceeds to assume, though merely for the sake of argument, that the Central Powers, either through defeat or exhaustion, have to accept the terms imposed upon them by the Allies.

I venture to suggest that the attention of the War Committee might with advantage be directed to a somewhat different problem, and that they should be invited to give us their opinion as to our present prospects of being able to "dictate" the kind of terms which we should all like to impose upon our enemies if we were in a position to do so.

We are agreed as to the goal, but we do not know how far we have really travelled towards it, or how much nearer to it we are likely to find ourselves even if the war be prolonged for, say, another year. What will that year have cost us? How much better will our position be at the end of it? Shall we even then be strong enough to "dictate" terms?

It seems to me almost impossible to overrate the importance of these considerations, because it is clear that our diplomacy must be governed by an accurate appreciation of them.

We have obtained within the last few days from the different Departments of the Government a good deal of information as to the situation, naval, military and economic. It is far from reassuring.

From the President of the Board of Trade we received on the 26th October a most interesting and carefully compiled memorandum tending to show the daily growing shortage of tonnage and its consequences. Mr. Runciman comes to the conclusion that our shipbuilding is not keeping pace with our losses, and that, although the number of our vessels is down, the demands on our tonnage are not diminished. We must look forward to depending more and more on neutral ships, but we can be under no illusions as to the precarious nature of that resource. I do not think I exaggerate when I describe this most important document as profoundly disquieting. But in a later memorandum, dated 9th November, the President paints the picture in still gloomier colours, and anticipates, on the advice of his experts, "a complete breakdown in shipping . . . much sooner than June, 1917."

The President of the Board of Agriculture has recently presented to the Cabinet his report on Food Prospects in 1917. That report goes to show that there is a world's deficit in breadstuffs, that the price of bread is likely to go higher, that there has been a general failure of the potato crop, that the supply of fish is expected to be 64 per cent. below the normal, that there is considerable difficulty in regard to the supply of feeding-stuffs, that the difficulties of cultivation steadily increase, that land is likely to go derelict, the yield to decline, and the number of livestock to diminish greatly.

Lord Crawford's later note, dated 9th November, on Home Food Supplies, shows that these anticipations were not unduly pessimistic. The position has, he tells us, become much worse, and, owing to the inroads made upon the agricultural population by the demands of the Army, it is in some parts of the country "no longer a question of maintaining a moderate standard of cultivation but whether cultivation will cease."

Turning to our naval and military resources, we have a report from the First Lord of the Admiralty, dated 14th October, from which we learn that, in spite of the tremendous efforts which we have made, the size of our Home Fleets is still insufficient, that we have nearly reached the limit of immediate production in the matter of capital ships, that we have not got nearly enough destroyers to meet our needs for escort and anti-submarine work, that we shall certainly not have enough for our Allies, and that the position in regard to light cruisers is not much better. From the same report we may infer that the submarine difficulty is becoming acute, and that, in spite of all our efforts, it seems impossible to provide an effectual rejoinder to it. The increasing size of the enemy submarines, the strength of their construction (which will apparently oblige us to rearm our merchantmen with a heavier gun), and their activity in all parts of the world, point to the same conclusion.

The papers which we have from time to time received from the General Staff and from the War Committee prove that in the matter of man-power we are nearing the end of our tether. The last report of the Man-Power Distribution Board seems, in particular, to sound a grave note of warning. The unexhausted supply of men is, they tell us, now very restricted, and the number available can only be added to by a still further depletion of industry. In the meanwhile Ireland still declines to add to the available supply the 150,000 men who would be obtainable from that country, and I am not aware that any serious attempt is to be made to secure them.

All these seem to me to be very serious factors in the calculation which it is our duty to make. It will be replied, and no doubt truly, that the Central Powers are feeling the pressure of the war not less acutely than we feel it, and I hope we shall also be told that our staying powers are greater than theirs; but, even if this be so, it is none the less our duty to consider, after a careful review of the facts, what our plight and the plight of the civilised world will be after another year, or, as we are sometimes told, two or three more years of a struggle as exhausting as that in which we are engaged. No one for a moment believes that we are going to lose the war; but what is our chance of winning it in such a manner, and within such limits of time, as will enable us to beat our enemy to the ground and impose upon him the kind of terms which we so freely discuss?

I do not suppose for an instant that there is any weakening in the spirit of the people of this country, and I should hope, although I do not feel absolute confidence on the subject, that the same might be said of our Allies; but neither in their interests nor in ours can it be desirable that the war should be prolonged, unless it can be shown that we can bring it to an effectual conclusion within a reasonable space of time.

What does the prolongation of the war mean?

Our own casualties already amount to over 1,100,000. We have had 15,000 officers killed, not including those who are missing. There is no reason to suppose that, as the force at the front in the different theatres of war increases, the casualties will increase at a slower rate. We are slowly but surely killing off the best of the male population of these islands. The figures representing the casualties of our Allies are not before me. The total must be appalling.

The financial burden which we have already accumulated is almost incalculable. We are adding to it at the rate of over £5,000,000 per day. Generations will have to come and go before the country recovers from the loss which it has sustained in human beings, and from the financial ruin and the destruction of the means of production which are taking place.

All this it is no doubt our duty to bear, but only if it can be shown that the sacrifice will have its reward. If it is to be made in vain, if the additional year, or two years, or three years, finds us still unable to dictate terms, the war with its nameless horrors will have been needlessly prolonged, and the responsibility of those who needlessly prolong such a war is not less than that of those who needlessly provoke it.

A thorough stocktaking, first by each Ally of his own resources, present and prospective, and next by the Allies, or at all events by the leading Allies, in confidential consultation, seems indispensable. Not until such a stocktaking has taken place will each Ally be able to decide which of his desiderata are indispensable, and whether he might not be prepared to accept less than 20s. in the £ in consideration of prompt payment. Not until it has taken place will the Allies as a body be able to determine the broad outline of their policy or the attitude which they ought to assume towards those who talk to them of peace.

I think Sir William Robertson must have had some such stocktaking in his mind when he wrote the remarkable paper which was circulated to the Cabinet on the 31st August. In that paper he expressed his belief that negotiations for peace in some form or other might arise any day, and he urged that "we need therefore to decide without loss of time what our policy is to be, then place it before the Entente Powers, and ascertain in return what are their aims, and so endeavour to arrive at a clear understanding before we meet our enemies in conference." The idea may, for all I know, have been acted on already.

Many of us, however, must of late have asked ourselves how this war is ever to be brought to an end. If we are told that the deliberate conclusion of the Government is that it must be fought until Germany has been beaten to the ground and sues for peace on any terms which we are pleased to accord to her, my only observation would be that we ought to know something of the data upon which this conclusion has been reached. To many of us it seems as if the prospect of a "knock-out" was, to say the least of it, remote. Our forces and those of France have shown a splendid gallantry on the Western Front, and have made substantial advances; but is it believed that these, any more than those made in 1915 with equally high hopes and accompanied by not less cruel losses, will really enable us to "break through"? Can we afford to go on paying the same sort of price for the same sort of gains?

Judging from the comments supplied by the General Staff, I should doubt whether the Italian offensive, however successful, is likely to have a decisive effect.

At Salonika we are entangled in an extraordinarily difficult enterprise, forced upon us, against our better judgment, by our Allies, and valuable only because it occupies enemy troops who would otherwise be fighting the Russians and the Roumanians. On the Russian and Roumanian frontiers we shall be fortunate if we avoid a disaster, which at one moment seemed imminent. General Brussiloff's language is inspiring, but is it really justified by the facts? The history of the Russian operations has been very chequered, and we shall never, I am afraid, be free from the danger of miscarriages owing to defective strategy, to failure of supplies, to corruption in high places, or to incidents such as the disastrous explosion which has just lost us 10,000 tons of munitions at Archangel.

Again, are we quite sure that, regarded as political rather than military assets, our Allies are entirely to be depended upon? There have been occasions upon which political complications have threatened to affect the military situation in France. I quote the following sentences from a letter written a few days ago by a very shrewd Frenchman: "*Rappelez-vous bien que la Démocratie française n'est pas menée par son gouvernement; c'est elle qui le mène: un courant d'opinion publique en faveur de la cessation de la guerre pourrait être irrésistible. . . . Au feu, le soldat français se battra toujours comme un héros; derrière, sa famille pourra bien dire: en voilà assez!*" Italy is always troublesome and exacting. Sir Rennell Rodd, in a despatch dated the 4th November, asks us to take note of the fact that there are already in Italy "certain symptoms of war weariness and discouragement at the protraction of the struggle. . . . Great Britain is represented as the only country anxious to prolong the struggle *à l'outrance* for her own ends. . . . It would be wrong to pretend that there exists here the same grim determination to carry through as prevails in France and the British Empire." The domestic situation in Russia is far from reassuring. There have been alarming disorders both at Moscow and in Petrograd. Russia has had five Ministers of the Interior in twelve months, and the fifth is described as being by no means secure in his seat.

Our difficulties with the neutrals are, again, not likely to diminish. It is highly creditable to the Foreign Office that during the last two years we have escaped a breakdown of our blockade policy, which, in spite of continual obstruction and bad faith, has produced excellent results; but we have been within an ace of grave complications with Sweden and the United States. As time goes on the neutrals are likely to become more and more restive and intolerant of the belligerents, whose right to go on disturbing the peace of the civilised world they will refuse to admit.

I may be asked whether I have any practical suggestion to offer, and I admit the difficulty of replying. But is it not true that, unless the apprehensions which I have sketched can be shown, after such an investigation as I have suggested, to be groundless, we ought at any rate not to discourage any movement, no matter where originating, in favour of an interchange of views as to the possibility of a settlement? There are many indications that the germs of such a movement are already in existence. One cannot dismiss as unworthy of attention the well-substantiated reports which have come to us from time to time upon this subject from Belgian, Scandinavian, Japanese, and Russian sources, or such circumstantial stories as those told in Sir Esmé Howard's despatch of the 24th August as to the meeting held at Prince Lichnowsky's house, and in Lord Eustace Percy's memorandum as to the intimations made by the Rector of the Berlin University. The debates in the Reichstag show that the pacifist groups are active and outspoken. From all sides come accounts of the impatience of the civil population and their passionate yearning for peace.

It seems to me quite inconceivable that during the winter we shall not be sounded by someone as to our readiness to discuss terms of peace or proposals for an armistice. Are we prepared with our reply? Lord Crawford has dealt with the question of an armistice. I am not sure that I agree with some of his suggestions, but I am sure that he is right in holding that an unconditional refusal would be inadmissible.

As to peace terms, I hope we shall adhere steadfastly to the main principle laid down by the Prime Minister in the speech which he summed up by a declaration that we could agree to no peace which did not afford adequate reparation for the past and adequate security for the future, but the outline was broadly sketched and might be filled up in many different ways. The same may be said of the not less admirable statement which he has just made at the Guildhall, and of the temperate speeches which the Secretary of State for Foreign Affairs has from time to time delivered.

But it is unfortunate that, in spite of these utterances, it should be possible to represent us and our Allies as committed to a policy partly vindictive and partly selfish, and so irreconcilably committed to that policy that we should regard as unfriendly any attempt, however sincere, to extricate us from the *impasse*. The interview given by the Secretary of State for War in September last to an American correspondent has produced an impression which it will not be easy to efface. There may have been circumstances of which I am unaware, connected perhaps with the Presidential election, which made it necessary to announce that at the particular moment any intervention, however well meant, would be distasteful to us or inopportune. He said, indeed, that "the world must know that there can be no outside interference *at this stage*" — a very momentous limitation. For surely it cannot be our intention, no matter how long the war lasts, no matter what the strain on our resources, to maintain this attitude, or to declare, as M. Briand declared about the same time, that for us, too, "the word peace is a sacrilege." Let our naval, military and economic advisers tell us frankly whether they are satisfied that the knock-out blow can and will be delivered. The Secretary of State's formula holds the field, and will do so until something else is put in its place. Whether it is to hold the field, and, if not, what that something else should be, ought surely to depend upon their answer, and that again upon the result of the careful stocktaking, domestic and international, which, I hope, is already taking place. — L.

November 13, 1916.

The above note had been written before the discussion, which took place at to-day's Cabinet, from which we learned that the War Committee had already decided to take important steps in the direction which I have ventured to indicate. — L.
November 13, 1916.

Coming from a statesman of Lord Lansdowne's position and antecedents, this document made a deep impression. No one could accuse him of being a mere "pacifist." He was the author of the Entente Cordiale in 1904. He was an unflinching advocate of the policy of standing by all the implications of the fateful Treaty.

Before the Cabinet came to any conclusions on the Lansdowne memorandum, the Prime Minister invited the opinions of the military and naval authorities on the suggestion of a possible stalemate. The Chief of Staff, Sir William Robertson, truculently repudiated such a possibility. Ultimate victory was assured the Allies, provided the advice of the War Office was obediently followed in every particular and its demands patriotically fulfilled in every detail. There must be more men and material hurled at the enemy, and the hurling must be done exclusively on the Western Front. It was made quite clear that there would be still heavier casualties than those already suffered. From that Sir William Robertson did not shrink, but this further slaughter of British lives must occur in France and Flanders and not elsewhere.

Sir Douglas Haig put in a memorandum on similar lines. In this note, which Sir William Robertson appended to his answer to the Lansdowne memorandum, the Commander-in-Chief stresses the difficulties of maintaining any offensive in France during the winter, but points out that the conditions of which he complains represent only the normal situation at that time of the year. On the other side of the picture, the Germans had been badly defeated on the Somme, and their losses, he stated, had been undoubtedly heavy — far heavier than those of the Allies. Their *morale* had been lowered seriously. Indeed, he reached the conclusion that an "appreciable proportion of the German soldiers are now practically beaten men, ready to surrender if they could find opportunity, thoroughly tired of the war, and hopeless of eventual success." The Allied troops, on the other hand, were all confident of victory.

"It is true that the amount of ground gained is not great. That is nothing. Our proved ability to get the enemy to move at all from his defensive positions was the valuable result of the fighting."

Sir Douglas Haig further said that he regarded the prospects of success on the Western Front in 1917 as most favourable. For this, however, he wanted many more troops, and an ample supply of munitions — of which "the enormous quantities required have been furnished this year with unfailing regularity." More aircraft, more road and railway material, etc., were also wanted. Given these supplies, he and his army were confident of being able to achieve ultimate victory. From the memoranda put in by the Chief of the Imperial Staff and the Commander-in-Chief there could be no doubt as to military opinion about our prospects.

Lord Grey's contribution was characteristic. His position as Foreign Secretary was pivotal when it came to a question of making peace or continuing war. We all anxiously awaited his guidance. He always was the most departmental of Ministers, and he had always been buried in his office, with hardly a thought for anything else. He scarcely ever expressed any opinion on any Cabinet questions outside his own department. His aloofness was monumental. He had a habit — entirely his own — of drafting his despatches at the Cabinet table whilst discussions were proceeding on home affairs. This lofty detachment he carried into the War Cabinets. In the discussion bearing on the most effective methods of prosecuting the war he had little to say or suggest. Having been forced to declare the war from which he had failed to save his country it was for others to direct it and find the means for its successful prosecution. But here was a question preëminently affecting his department. Should any peace approaches be encouraged or entertained? The initiative had been taken by one of his immediate predecessors at the Foreign Office — Lord Lansdowne.

In spite of the confidence manifested by the military authorities, Lord Grey expressed his misgivings as to the effect of the submarine campaign and said he thought it had not been mastered and for the present seemed to be getting more and more beyond our control. He went, however, so far as to say that as long as the military and naval authorities considered that the position of the Allies was likely to improve, even though it might not result in the ultimate and complete defeat of Germany, it would be premature to make peace. Should it at any future time become evident that the Allies could not further improve their position, they should proceed forthwith to make the best peace terms they could.

Ever noncommittal and hesitating, he neither associated

himself with Lord Lansdowne nor did he dissent from his views. He neither approved nor disapproved. Whatever the decision or the event his intervention would conform to either. Was he in favour of the Lansdowne thesis? If it were turned down and its author and his supporters were taunted with faint-heartedness no one could fairly quote one sentence of unequivocal commendation from Lord Grey. On the other hand, if either then or later Lord Lansdowne's brave memorandum were justified, then no one could say that Lord Grey had offered any hostile criticism to its purport.

Sir William Robertson in his memorandum had arraigned the Foreign Secretary's diplomacy both before and during the war and had ascribed to its feebleness most of our misfortunes. The attack occupied one short paragraph in Sir William Robertson's contribution. Sir Edward Grey devoted pages to an explanation and defence of his failures — his failures to avoid war; to keep Turkey out of the war; to secure the timely help of Greece, and to lure Bulgaria on to our side. He had done everything of which diplomacy was capable without adequate military support. The failure was military and not diplomatic. All very interesting, but having no bearing on the momentous issue raised by Lord Lansdowne — whether it was better to make peace now or to fight on in the hope that we might be in a better position later on to dictate terms.

It is rather surprising that no constructive suggestions for peace were ever put forward by him either now or at any time. If he gave any thought to the terms of peace which he had in his mind as the end and aim of the war he never favoured his colleagues with his ideas. The only concrete proposals as to peace terms submitted to the Asquith Cabinet came from another pen. It was shortly before the Lansdowne discussions that the Government for the first time had submitted to its judgment any categorical and concrete and comprehensive scheme of a peace settlement. This was the document, to which reference has already been made, which came from the pen of Mr. Balfour, then First Lord of the Admiralty. Lord Balfour's is a truly remarkable document and will bear careful perusal. The sentences in which he refuses to commit himself to any expression of opinion as to the possibility of future wars are ominous, coming from such an experienced statesman and so clear and penetrating an intellect. Apart from that it is the first time any statesman of the first rank committed himself to a written forecast of the conditions of peace.

"THE PEACE SETTLEMENT IN EUROPE

MEMORANDUM BY MR. BALFOUR

"The Prime Minister asked the Members of the War Committee to express their views on the peace settlement; and the present paper is an attempt — a very tentative and halting attempt — to comply with this request.

"Even the most tentative suggestions must, however, proceed upon some hypothesis with regard to the military position of the combatants at the end of the war. What this will be no human being can foresee with any assurance. But inasmuch as it is convenient to proceed upon a hypothesis which is clear and determinate, I shall assume in what follows, though merely for the sake of argument, that the Central Powers, either through defeat or exhaustion, have to accept the terms imposed upon them by the Allies.

"Let me add this further preliminary observation. The number of questions which will have to be discussed at any Peace Conference is obviously very large. In what follows I desire to do no more than to offer some stray reflections upon the most important group of these questions — that which is concerned with the redistribution of population in the European area. By this limitation will be excluded not merely such subjects as the restriction of armaments, the freedom of the seas, and the revision of international law, but also Heligoland, the Kiel Canal, strategic modifications of frontiers,[1] and the extra-European problems connected with Asia Minor and Germany's Colonial Empire.

"On some of these subjects I may perhaps trouble the Committee at a later date.

"The principal object of the war is the attainment of a durable peace, and I submit that the best way of securing this is by the double method of diminishing the area from which the Central Powers can draw the men and money required for a policy of aggression, while at the same time rendering a policy of aggression less attractive by rearranging the map of Europe in closer agreement with what we rather vaguely call 'the principle of nationality.'

"The second of these methods, if successfully applied, would secure many objects which are universally desired by the Allies. It would give Belgium her independence, restore Alsace and Lorraine to France, provide some kind of home rule for Poland, extend the frontiers of Italy, and establish a Greater Serbia and a Greater Roumania in South-East Europe; I should greatly like to see it applied in Bohemia also. To Bohemia, Germanic civilisation is profoundly distasteful. The Czechs have been waging war against it for some generations, and waging it under grave difficulties with much success. Whether an independent Bohemia would be strong enough to hold her own, from a military as well as from a commercial point of view, against Teutonic domination — surrounded as she is at present entirely by German influences — I do not know; but I am sure the question deserves very careful consideration. If the change is possible it should be made.[2]

"Now, a map of Europe so modified would not only carry out the second of the two methods of preserving peace which I have described above, but would also help to carry out the first. The resources of men and money on which the Central Powers

[1] Of course such strategic modifications might involve transfers of populations, which could not properly be described as negligible. But their object would not be to acquire territory, but to increase security by making frontiers more defensible.

[2] I presume that arrangements will be made by which the frontier of Bohemia would, to some small extent at least, become coterminous with the New Poland.

could draw for purposes of aggressive warfare would be greatly diminished. Alsace-Lorraine, Austrian Poland, with possibly parts of German Poland, Transylvania, Italian Austria, Bosnia and Herzgovina would cease to be recruiting grounds for supplying German or Austrian Armies; and the men of military age thus withdrawn from the Central Armies would be added to the nations with which the Central Powers are now at war; thus, as it were, counting two on a division.

"The populations thus transferred would, I suppose, be more than 20 millions. I take no account in this argument of the non-Italian population which Italy will no doubt obtain if the Allies are successful; nor do I discuss the uncontested zone coveted by Bulgaria. If the principle of nationality be rigidly applied, I suppose that, without doubt, Bulgaria ought to have it. Whether she deserves it, and whether, in view of Serbian sentiment we can give it to her, is quite another question.

"I conceive that this general scheme is, broadly speaking, what public opinion in this country would desire to see carried out. The point on which there might be most difference of opinion would perhaps be the fate of Poland — since the fate of Constantinople and the Banat is already settled so far as the Allies can settle it. Almost the only thing on which Russia and Germany seem to be agreed is that the status of Poland should be altered by the war, and that, while receiving some measure of autonomy, it should remain dependent upon one of its two great neighbours. But as to what the limits of the new Poland should be, and on which of its two great neighbours it is to be dependent, there is, it need hardly be said, a fundamental divergence of opinion between Petrograd and Berlin.

"Looking at the Polish question from a purely British point of view, I should like to see the new State include not merely Russian Poland, but as much of Austria and German Poland as possible. This, of course, is in strict accord with the two principles laid down earlier in the paper. But I should *not* like to see the old Kingdom of Poland restored. I should fear that the new Poland would suffer from the diseases through which the old Poland perished; that it would be a theatre of perpetual intrigues between

Germany and Russia; and that its existence, so far from promoting the cause of European peace, would be a perpetual occasion of European strife.

"Moreover, even if such a Poland were capable of playing the part of an efficient buffer State (which I doubt), I am not sure that a buffer State between Germany and Russia would be any advantage to Western Europe. If Germany were relieved of all fear of pressure from Russia, and were at liberty to turn her whole strength towards developing her western ambitions, France and Britain might be the sufferers; and I am not by any means confident that cutting off Russia from her western neighbours might not divert her interests towards the Far East to an extent which British statesmen could not view without some misgivings. The more Russia is made a European rather than an Asiatic Power, the better for everybody.

"I therefore conclude that the solution of the Polish question which would best suit our interests would be the constitution of a Poland endowed with a large measure of autonomy, while remaining an integral part of the Russian Empire — the new State or province to include not only all Russian Poland, but also Austria's and (part at least of) Prussia's share in the plunder of the ancient kingdom.

"Personally I should like to see the Danish portions of Schleswig-Holstein, filched by Prussia and Austria from Denmark in 1863, again restored to their former owner. But Denmark would hardly accept the gift unless it was accompanied by some form of territorial guarantee which she would think effective; and even then the memory of Belgium might act as a deterrent. But the question should be seriously considered. I ought, parenthetically, to add that unfortunately the region through which the Kiel Canal passes is German both in language and sentiment.

"So far I have indicated the kind of changes which I should like to see attempted when peace comes to be discussed. But there are some projects advocated by those who believe in the complete victory of the Allies which I regard with great suspicion. Among these perhaps the most important are the projects for breaking up or reconstituting the German Empire. If I had my way, I should rule out any attempt to touch the internal affairs either of Germany or of Austria. It may be that, under the stress of defeat, ancient jealousies — forgotten in the hour of victory — will revive. South may be divided from North, Roman Catholic from Protestant, Württemberg, Bavaria, and Saxony from Prussia, or from each other. A revolution may upset the Hohenzollerns, and a new Germany may arise on the ruins of militarism.

"Any or all of these things are possible, but I would certainly deprecate any attempt on the part of the victorious enemy to bring them about. One of the few recorded attempts to crush militarism in a defeated State was Napoleon's attempt to destroy the Prussian Army after Jena. No attempt was ever less successful. As everybody knows, Napoleon's policy compelled Prussia to contrive the military system which has created modern Germany. It may be — I hope it will be — in the power of the Allies to strip Germany of much of her non-German territory; but, whatever be the limits of the new Germany, I hope no attempt will be made to control or modify her internal policy. The motto of the Allies should be 'Germany for the Germans — but only Germany.'

"This formula, however, even if it be accepted, does not solve the problem of Central Europe. It says nothing, for example, of the future relations between Germany and Austria. I should myself desire to see the Dual Monarchy maintained, shorn indeed of a large portion of its Slav, Italian, and Roumanian territories, but still essentially consisting of Austria and Hungary. If this were to occur, we should have in the future, as we have had in the past, a German Empire and an Austrian Empire side by side and probably kept in close alliance — political if not also economic — for purposes of mutual protection. Other possibilities, however, have to be considered. The result of the war may be the complete break-up of the Dual Monarchy; and if the Dual Monarchy breaks up, it is reasonable to suppose that the German portion of it would coalesce with the German Empire, leaving Hungary either isolated or dependent. Apparently such a change would create a great German-speaking State more formidable than Germany before the war: and this may be, in fact, what would happen. On the other hand, it must be remembered that such a change would profoundly modify the position of Prussia. The Roman Catholics and South German elements would become overwhelmingly strong; and if the driving force behind German aggression be due, as most observers think, to Prussian organisation and Prussian traditions, the change might in its ultimate effect be a defeat for German militarism.

"But I do not disguise from myself either that the dangers of such a Teutonic reorganisation are considerable, or that the likelihood of its occurring may be increased if the result of the war is to convince the German-speaking peoples that their only hope of national greatness lies in their consenting to forget all causes of difference and welding themselves into a single powerful State. Those who think the future must necessarily resemble the past may perhaps be disposed to remind us that for the five centuries preceding the Bismarckian era the political tendencies prevailing in Germany have been, on the whole, centrifugal and separatist. They will argue that this inveterate tradition, interrupted though it has been by forty-five years of a united and triumphant Germany, nevertheless represents the real tendencies of the race; and that to this tradition it will revert after a war for which Prussian policy and a Prussian dynasty have been responsible.

"Personally, I am inclined to doubt this conclusion, plausible as it seems; nor do I believe that anything which we and our Allies can accomplish will prevent the Germanic Powers, either united by alliance or fused into a single State, from remaining wealthy, populous, and potentially formidable.

"For this reason I do not share the fears of those who think that the triumph of the Slav countries is likely to menace German predominance in Central Europe. When we remember that the Slav populations are divided by language, religion and government; that they fought each other four years ago; that they are fighting each other at this very moment; that the only one among them which can count as a Great Power is Russia; and that Russia, according to most observers, is likely to be torn by revolutionary struggles as soon as the pressure of war is removed; when (I say) we remember these things, we shall probably be disposed to think that the Germanic States will be very well able to take care of themselves, whatever be the terms of peace to which they may have to submit.

"This is a fact (if it indeed be a fact) which is sometimes ignored. Many of those who speculate about the future of Europe seem to fear that Germany will be so weakened by the war that the balance of power will be utterly upset, and Britain will be left face to face with some other Great Power striving in its turn for universal dominance. I doubt this. In any case it seems to me quite clear that, measured by population, Germany — and still more, Germany in alliance with Austria — will be more than a match for France alone, however much we give to France, and however much we take from the Central States. If, therefore, Europe after the war is to be an armed camp, the peace of the world will depend, as heretofore, on defensive alliances formed by those who desire to retain their possessions against those who desire to increase them. In that event the Entente is likely to be maintained. Germany may suffer a spiritual conversion; Russia may break up; France and Britain may be rendered powerless by labour troubles; universal bankruptcy may destroy universal armaments; international courts may secure international peace; the horrors of 1914, 1915, 1916, and 1917 may render the very thought of war disgusting to all mankind. On these subjects it is vain to speculate. All I would for the moment insist on is that the greatest territorial losses which the Allies can or ought to inflict on the Central Powers will leave them powerful both for defence and offence. Whatever trouble Russia may give us in Mesopotamia, Persia and Afghanistan, I do not think she will attempt the domination of Europe, still less succeed in securing it.

"There are two subsidiary points on which I may say a word before concluding — rights of way and indemnities. If the shores of the Adriatic are in Italian hands, if Salonika is in Greek hands, how are we going to provide the Central Powers with commercial access to the Mediterranean and the South? That they should not be denied such access seems to be fairly clear. It is one thing to cut off Germany from her megalomaniacal designs upon Asia Minor, Mesopotamia, Persia, and India; it is quite another to put the commerce of Austria-Hungary with the Eastern Mediterranean and the Suez Canal at the mercy of the States which lie between it and the sea. There could, it seems to me, be no more powerful incentive to new wars. Some method of guaranteeing to States which have no convenient seaboard the free flow of commerce through selected channels is therefore urgently required. I have had no time to give to the subject, but I have sometimes idly wondered whether the treaties which apply to navigable rivers flowing through different States might not — with the necessary modifications — be applied also to ports and railways.

"My last topic is war indemnities. I have, for the sake of argument, assumed that the success of the Allies is going to be complete. On this assumption — ought indemnities to be demanded?

"Germany has never made any secret of her intention of beggaring her enemies and reducing them, if she got the power, to complete commercial subservience. My own inclination would be strongly against imitating Germany's behaviour in 1871 and imposing a commercial treaty on my opponents for my own advantage. Such treaties are needlessly humiliating, even when they are not onerous. When they are, they are sure, sooner or later, to be broken.

"But there are two things I should like to do, and which in the interests of international morality I think ought to be done. I think the Central Powers should be made to pay for the damage they have done in Belgium, Northern France, and Serbia; and I think they ought to surrender shipping equivalent in amount to that which they have sent to the bottom in the course of their submarine warfare. These are charges which it should be within their power to meet; and if within their power to meet, then certainly within our right to demand. Whether more can or ought to be exacted is a point on which I feel incompetent to give an opinion; but it may be worth remembering that to take territories from the Germans or Austrian Empires free of debt, is in effect to increase the burdens on the States from which they are taken, and to relieve the burden on the States to which they are added.

"Oct. 4, 1916. A. J. B."

Mr. Henderson, one of the ablest and most influential of Labour leaders, at this time publicly as well as in private, threw in the whole weight of his great influence with organised labour against "a premature peace." His words are worth quoting:

"The war has gone on too long for some of the people of this country. It is possible that in the military situation of the case we may become war-weary, and I want to warn everyone of the danger of a premature peace. I am as strong for peace as any man or woman can be, but I must be satisfied that the peace we expect places us, above any doubt, beyond the recurrence of such a catastrophe. . . . We are in the War, and to talk about peace with all the most unscrupulous military forces against us would be a step to having the whole thing fought over again. That would not be ending the War by a permanent peace. A peace under such conditions, with Belgium and France, Serbia and Roumania, in the condition they are! No! We want not a dishonourable peace, but a lasting, permanent peace, peace based upon national right and national honour, and I say these two words in spite of the fact that one of my own colleagues has described them as platitudes."

This speech fairly expressed the view I also took at the time as to the mistake of encouraging peace overtures until the military situation had considerably improved.

Another member of the Government whose attachment to the cause of peace is above suspicion, Lord Robert Cecil, came to the conclusion that in view of the military estimates of our prospects:

"A peace now could only be disastrous. At the best we could not hope for more than the *status quo* with a great increase in the

German power in Eastern Europe. Moreover, this peace would be known by the Germans to have been forced upon us by their submarines, and our insular position would be recognised as increasing instead of diminishing our vulnerability. No one can contemplate our future ten years after a peace on such conditions without profound misgiving. I feel, therefore, that we are bound to continue the War."

He then proceeds, in the memorandum from which I am quoting, to make certain practical suggestions as to the organisation of the nation. Lord Robert Cecil's memorandum has a further interest because it contains a review of the military position at that date by a very able observer:

"Whether we agree with Lord Lansdowne's conclusions or not, one thing is clear. Our situation is grave. It is certain that unless the utmost national effort is made it may become desperate, particularly in the matter of shipping. The position in Allied countries is even more serious. France is within measurable distance of exhaustion. The political outlook in Italy is menacing. Her finance is tottering. In Russia there is great discouragement. She has long been on the verge of revolution. Even her man-power seems coming near its limits.

"On the other hand, our enemies, though badly injured, are not disabled. The economic position of Germany may or may not be alarming. It is certainly not yet desperate. No certain information as to her supplies is available. There is no trustworthy ground for thinking that she is starving, although she may be — very possibly she is — in want of other necessaries, such as wool, cotton, lubricating oils, rubber, which will hamper and diminish her military strength, and there is great political discontent. In Austria the position is probably worse."

The Prime Minister, having, according to his wont, carefully gathered or received opinions amongst his colleagues without attempting to influence them, decided ultimately that the time had not yet arrived for peace feelers. No member of the Cabinet expressed his dissent from this conclusion.

I have given a fairly exhaustive account of the Lansdowne episode because I am anxious to demonstrate that the Governments that conducted the war never lost sight of the importance of seizing any favourable opportunity that might offer itself to make an honourable peace. The Lansdowne discussions have also their special value because they are the first occasion on which any of the belligerent Governments courageously faced the possibility that peace might have to be considered without victory. The Asquith Government examined the whole position with great care and came to the unanimous conclusion that to enter into peace negotiations with Germany before inflicting a complete defeat upon her armies would be disastrous. The principle of President Wilson's subsequent dictum in favour of peace without victory was carefully studied and emphatically repudiated in advance by the Asquith Government. What is more to the point, when one considers the kind of criticism levelled at the Government of 1917, is the conclusion come to by the Asquith Administration that without acknowledgment of defeat on the part of the Central Powers overtures of peace should not be encouraged, as they would settle none of the issues raised by this colossal struggle and might and probably would be dangerous to the *morale* and solidarity of the Allies.

Mr. Asquith himself gave no countenance to a timorous or defeatist attitude. A fortnight after my "knock-out blow" interview had been published, he delivered, on October 11th, 1916, a speech in the House of Commons, in the course of which he said:

"The strain which the war imposes on ourselves and our Allies, the hardships which we freely admit it involves on some of those who are not directly concerned in the struggle, the upheaval of trade, the devastation of territory, the loss of irreplaceable lives — this long and sombre procession of cruelty and suffering, lighted up as it is by deathless examples of heroism and chivalry, cannot be allowed to end in some patched-up, precarious, dishonouring compromise, masquerading under the name of Peace. No one desires to prolong for a single unnecessary day the tragic spectacle of bloodshed and destruction, but we owe it to those who have given their lives for us, the flower of our youth, the hope and promise of our future, that their supreme sacrifice shall not have been in vain. The ends of the Allies are well known; they have been frequently and precisely stated. They are not selfish ends, they are not vindictive ends, but they require that there shall be adequate reparation for the past and adequate security for the future. On their achievement, we in this country honestly believe depend the best hopes of humanity."

Here we had a fine and firm resolve expressed in the splendid eloquence of which Mr. Asquith was a master. The fact that his eldest son, Mr. Raymond Asquith, a young man of great brilliance and promise, had fallen in action a few weeks before the delivery of this speech, gave tragic force to this passage.

Hardly less emphatic was a statement made less than a fortnight later by Lord Grey. It is indeed somewhat curious to note that while Prince Max of Baden in his "Memoirs" describes Germany watching through the late autumn of 1916 what it regarded as the approach of a "trial of strength between Lloyd George and Lord Grey", for and against the policy of the "knock-out blow", Lord Grey himself, speaking on October 23rd to a gathering at the Hotel Cecil, was declaring:

"There must be no end to this war, no peace except peace which is going to ensure that the nations of Europe live in the future free from that shadow and in the open light of freedom.

For that we are contending. It is our determination, which the progress of the war but deepens, in common with our Allies, to continue the war till we have made it certain that the Allies in common shall have achieved the success which must, and ought to be theirs, till they have secured the future peace of the whole continent of Europe, till they have made it clear that all the sacrifices we have made shall not have been made in vain."

These valiant words lend little colour to the rumour which for some reason or other was then evidently widespread, not only in this country but even more throughout Central Europe, that Lord Grey was one of those who were angling for an inconclusive peace.

Can anyone doubt now, on a calm review of the position, that Mr. Asquith and his colleagues were right in the conclusion to which they came? Could we have made a peace at that time which would not have recognised Germany as a victor? Could we have made it at any time before the final breakdown of Germany's prowess? Would Germany have agreed to restore the complete independence of Belgium? Even if she consented to evacuate Belgium, would she have agreed to impose no military and commercial conditions which would have meant the practical incorporation of Belgium in the sphere of German domination and military and trading expansion? All the evidence is in the negative. The few far-seeing German statesmen who foresaw the perils which encircled the Fatherland and were anxious that peace should be made whilst the German military power was intact, never ceased to urge the German Chancellor to make an unequivocal statement about the full restoration of Belgium. Their efforts and urgent appeals were in vain right up to the final collapse. Prince Max of Baden, who later on became Chancellor, pointed out to the German leaders that even so pronounced a pacifist as Mr. Ramsay MacDonald, speaking in the House of Commons in the spring of 1916, had insisted that a declaration by Germany of her intention to restore a complete Belgian sovereignty and every "portion of it" was a condition precedent of any peace settlement. That declaration never came.

Would Austria have given up her conquests in Serbia? Would there have been no terms imposed as to the fortification of the Serbian capital, which would have left Serbia helplessly at the mercy of Austria, and thus reduced her to a state of vassalage to the Austrian Empire? Would no part of Serbian territory have been carved out to requite Czar Ferdinand's loyal rapacity? Then what about the Baltic provinces of Russia and Russian Poland? Would Germany have given up all her marvellous conquests in Russia and added nothing to her territories in that quarter? A suggestion that Alsace-Lorraine be restored to France as a condition of peace would have been greeted throughout the Fatherland with a Teutonic guffaw. France at the end of 1916 was certainly not in a position to ask for more than the restoration of the German conquests of 1914. Even then were the German industrialists prepared to give up the Briey mines? All the contemporary evidence points the other way. Apart from that there was not one chance in a million that peace negotiations could produce a settlement in the East or West satisfactory to the most moderate Allied statesmen.

Would real disarmament have been any part of the 1916 peace? Would Germany have consented to dismantle the redoubtable military machine that had placed her in such a commanding position in the world? And if Germany did not disarm, no other country could have afforded to do so. To quote again the words then used by a statesman whose name is a guarantee for pacific intentions — Lord Robert Cecil: "A peace now could only be disastrous. At best we could not hope for more than the *status quo*, with a great increase in the German Power in Central Europe." The only result would have been a bigger Germany, better armed, confident that her armies were unbeatable in the field even by overwhelming numbers, and with a military staff which had learned how war under modern conditions could be best and most effectively conducted.

It is often said now by men who are seeking busily to find fault with those who shouldered the terrible responsibilities of decision in the war, that no harm would have been done had the Allies taken the initiative in approaching the Central Powers with a view to the Convocation of a Peace Conference in 1916, even if such a conference failed. It is urged that if Germany and Austria made unreasonable conditions the Allied populations would have firmly supported their representatives in rejecting these terms and would then have continued the fight with renewed zeal and conviction. Would they? If Germany had offered to withdraw all her forces from Northern France and from Belgium, merely imposing certain conditions in the case of Belgium as to the uses of the ports of Belgium and as to the dismantlement of her frontier fortresses, could the Allied Governments have roused once more the spirit of 1914 to the pitch of facing for more than two years the horrible losses of the preceding two and one-half years, merely in order to restore Alsace-Lorraine to France or to hand back Courland and other conquered territories to the incompetent hands of Russian autocracy? The inhabitants of these lands are no more Russian than they are German. Once the carnage of war had stopped, would Britain have consented to renew it and send her sons to fight other bloody battles like the Somme in order to restore the useless fortifications of Belgrade or to rescue some obscure vilayat in Macedonia from the clutches of the Bulgarian king? At any rate, the risk that nations would have accepted any humiliations inflicted upon foreigners, rather than send millions more of their own kinsmen to the wholesale slaughter of modern warfare, were too great for those who looked forward to the permanent triumph of international right, justice and peace as a result of the sacrifices of this generation. We should have met at the Congress a Germany which had victoriously held up Europe for two and one-half years, shattered completely the power of three of her enemies, Russia, Roumania and Serbia, and was still in occupation of the territory of two more, and had successfully defied every effort to dislodge her hold on her conquests. The best that could be hoped for would be a completely liberated France and Belgium, with a Germany swollen through its eastern conquests by scores of thousands of square miles and tens of millions of population. With a war so ended we should have been confronted with a triumphant Prussian militarism which had demonstrated its invincibility in the field against overwhelming odds in numbers, material and wealth. Mr. Asquith and his Cabinet were emphatically right in refusing to assent to the Lansdowne proposition. Had they done so, even if they had secured the adhesion of France, it could not have ended in a great and workable peace. France would not have agreed readily to make any overtures, because no peace possible at that time would have satisfied her essential conditions — the restoration of her lost provinces and reparation for her damaged towns and villages. Italy would have been fooled, for she had banked on Allied success for the redemption of the Italian valleys in the Austrian Empire, and notwithstanding her heavy losses she would have had nothing out of any peace settlement which was attainable in 1916. It would have been said that Britain was anxious for peace and was prepared to sell her Allies to attain it. Such an impression would have had a shattering effect on Allied *morale* — east and west. The failure to make peace or a refusal by France to follow a peace initiative from Britain would have distracted and divided opinion in America, at the moment when opinion in that great country was being driven rapidly in our direction by the reckless and indiscriminate methods of the submarine campaign.

CHAPTER XV

THE MILITARY POSITION AT THE END OF THE 1916 CAMPAIGN

A talk with Sir William Robertson — Summary of his memorandum — Position on the Western Front — Superiority of the enemy — No end in sight — Allied and enemy man-power — A dinner discussion — Further memorandum by Sir William Robertson — Difficulty of forecasting duration of war — Non-military factors in the problem — Allied weaknesses — Victory on Western Front unlikely till 1918 — Steps to be taken — My statement to War Committee — A conference of East and West needed — Decision to hold Paris conference — Difficulties of arranging conference in Russia — Telegram to Paris — Political and military conferences in France — My memorandum on the situation — The outlook — Aims of the Somme offensive — Verdun — Our blunders of strategy — Dardanelles — Serbia — Roumania — Salonika — Greece — Hopeless outlook in the West — Southern front — Eastern front — Problem of attrition — Submarine menace — Financial difficulties — Possibilities in the Balkans — Proposal for a conference in the East — Our visit to Paris — Briand clawed by the "Tiger" — Reception of the memorandum — Asquith and Briand — First session of Paris Conference — M. Briand's introductory speech — Governments, not army staffs, ultimately responsible — Combined action on all fronts essential — Value of a Balkan campaign — Mr. Asquith urges a Russian conference — Italy non-committal — Russian ambassador approves conference — My plan for prompt action — Russia must be supplied with munitions — My proposals for conference in Russia — Italy asks for financial assistance — M. Briand urges pooling resources — Situation in Greece — Venizelos not to be recognised hastily — Proposals of the military chiefs — Second day of conference — Salonika effectives exaggerated — Transport lacking at Salonika — Italian engineers for Balkan roads — Italian finance — Poland — Paris conference a farce — Stupidities of 1917 campaign — Military chiefs ignore their Governments' views — Lost opportunities in the Balkans — A walk with Sir Maurice Hankey — Need for a small committee.

If we were resolved to continue the war, it was vital that we should fight in a way that would give us a reasonable chance of achieving victory. But when I surveyed the outlook both on land and sea in the closing months of 1916, I saw the gravest grounds for disquietude. There was as yet little sign that the efforts and sacrifices we had made were leading us towards a victorious conclusion; and the information which came either to the War Office or to the Admiralty was by no means reassuring.

In October, 1916, at one of the stilted and formal morning interviews which the Chief of the Imperial Staff, in the course of his duty, accorded to me as his civilian chief, after he had exhausted the few secondary and trivial matters upon which he had gone through the form of consulting me, I probed him as to the position on the Somme, the terrible casualties, and the insignificant gains. He returned the familiar answers to the effect that the German losses were greater than ours, that the Germans were gradually being worn down, and their *morale* shaken by constant defeat and retreat. All the same it struck me that his answer was not given with the usual rigid confidence. I then asked him whether he would mind telling me whether he had formed any views as to how this sanguinary conflict was to be brought to a successful end. For the time being the question took him aback, and he looked like a general in full dress who thought to himself, "This is one of those fool questions that ignorant civilians always fire at you, and they must not be encouraged." He just mumbled something about "Attrition." I asked him whether he would mind giving me a memorandum on the subject. In due course it was written, and here is a summary of it:

The Western Front is still held to be the main theatre of operations for the British forces.

As to the secondary theatres: In Mesopotamia the British force is improving its position, and will be in a condition to meet any effort the Turks can make against us by the time they are ready to attack. In Egypt there is similarly reason to expect that the western front against the Senussi will be safe by the end of the year, and arrangements complete for an advance on the east into the Sinai desert.

At Salonika the Allied forces have held the Bulgarian-German Armies. General Milne has asked for a reinforcement of 15 divisions and heavy artillery to achieve a victory on the Macedonian front, but the C.I.G.S. considers such a transfer from the main theatre of the Western Front undesirable. He thinks the only decisive campaign in the Balkans this winter must be on the Roumanian front. He regrets that the Allies have agreed to send reinforcements of 39,000 rifles to Macedonia.

In German East Africa we hold the coast line, and have driven the German forces into the unhealthy interior.

On the Western Front we are now superior to the Germans in numbers, in aircraft, in artillery, and probably to some extent also in the supply of ammunition. The effect of the Somme offensive has been to unsettle the enemy and weaken their *morale*. They are not actually demoralised, and we cannot expect them to collapse, but their prospects are worse than ours when we were being subjected to similar assault in 1914, as they have not behind them the undeveloped resources we had then. So our relative superiority is growing greater every day. But the C.I.G.S. holds that we must keep up the western pressure as, if the Central Powers can transfer more of their troops to the east, the result will be disastrous. He gives figures to show the extent to which such transfers have taken place in the last five months. Since June 1st, the German forces have increased by 27½ divisions, most of which have been added to the Eastern Front, where the number of battalions has risen (between June 1st and October 23rd) by 221 while on the west it has been reduced by 74.

He then went on to show how we have increased our mechanical strength on the Western Front. The following figures show the growth of British artillery in France:

	1st January, 1916.	End October, 1916.
Field guns	1,938	3,060
Howitzer & heavy guns	785	1,879
Daily income of ammunition	30,000 rounds	210,000 rounds

Howitzers and heavy guns would number over 2000 by the end of the year, and the increase in machine guns, trench mortars, etc., has been on a corresponding scale. But in man-power the Army in France is 80,000 below establishment, and should be reinforced. There should be a further comb-out, and the Home Defence Force should be reduced after the Navy had been induced to make more effective arrangements to prevent invasion. The greatest possible force should be available in France by the spring of 1917.

The Entente Powers are suffering from bad communications and defective coöperation, apart from France and England. The value of the Entente troops of Roumania, Belgium, Serbia, Portugal and Russia is low — in the case of Russia, through lack of equipment. The enemy troops were more mobile and have a moral superiority. The duration of the War depends on the staying power of Germany's allies. Austria and Turkey are growing exhausted, and Bulgaria is weakened by its previous wars. Germany is, however, fighting with undiminished vigour, and can continue the War for as yet an indefinite period. But her supplies of food would become very short in another six months.

The C.I.G.S.'s conclusion was that the end of the war could not yet be predicted. We must be prepared to put our whole effort, tighten the blockade, rally every available man, and face still greater strain and sacrifice, to secure the peace we desired.

Sir William Robertson ended his memorandum with a table setting out the estimated numbers of troops and of still available reserves at the disposal respectively of the Allies and of the Central Powers. It is worth studying, for it contains ominous figures, upon which I comment later on. The following is a summary of this table:

	Entente Armies, including troops, in home territory and excluding coloured troops	Reserves still available
British	3,517,000	?
French	2,978,000	775,000
Russian	4,767,000	6,500,000
Italian	1,676,000	1,250,000
Roumanian	590,000	380,000
Belgian	128,000	10,000
Serbian	117,000	22,000
Portuguese	65,000	
	13,838,000	8,937,000
	Enemy Forces	
German	5,470,000	2,000,000
Austro-Hungarian	2,750,000	800,000
Turkish	500,000	300,000
Bulgarian	400,000	112,000
	9,120,000	3,212,000

The C.I.G.S.'s picture did not present a cheerful outlook. We could now hold our own against the Turks in Mesopotamia and Egypt — but nothing more just yet. At Salonika we could stand up to the Bulgarians if they attacked, but we were in no position to attack them. On the Western Front we were doing better. We were shaking the German *morale*. His solitary proof of it was disturbing. Several German divisions had fled from the western battlefield to the east. Why? Not because they were beaten but because they felt they could hold their own with seventy-four fewer battalions. What a commentary on the smashing triumphs of the Somme!

The statistical table showed that so far as existing effectives and reserves at any rate were concerned, we had an overwhelming majority of men compared with the enemy powers. But our superiority in numbers depended entirely on Russia and Roumania remaining effectively in the war. That was becoming increasingly problematical. Once they were eliminated the numerical superiority passed over to the enemy countries. Equality of numbers then would only be attainable by a further heavy drain on our man-power. It was an ominous fact that of the 13,838,000 Allied troops, 5,357,000 were Russian and Roumanian; and of the reserves 6,880,000 were Russian and Roumanian. Roumania, with her 970,000, was about to disappear from the Allied schedule. Russia, with her 11,000,000, was to follow soon after.

As to the general military position I have summarised it in a preceding chapter. It was not encouraging.

The conviction was borne in upon me that a much more serious effort must be made to coördinate the Allied efforts in east and west; Sir William Robertson admitted the Allied weakness in that respect. In thinking this matter over I made up my mind to have a confidential talk with the Prime Minister about the situation and I accordingly invited him to come round one evening to dinner at my house.

The invitation was accepted and the dinner duly took place. Besides Mr. Asquith there were present Lord Crewe, Viscount Grey, Mr. Balfour, Lord Curzon and, I think, Lord Lansdowne. I laid before them my views as to the seriousness of the situation and as to the steps which should be taken. Mr. Asquith heard me sympathetically and recommended me to bring the matter forward for discussion at the next meeting of the War Committee.

This meeting took place on November 3rd, 1916, and in anticipation of it, I secured from Sir William Robertson a further statement setting out his views as to the probable end of the war, which I reproduce here:

"1. You tell me the War Committee wish to have my opinion with respect to the probable duration of the War, and I must at once confess that I feel it very difficult to express any opinion which can usefully be relied upon. Hindenburg is alleged to have stated recently that no man can foresee the end of the War, and I certainly cannot. This inability to forecast events is not peculiar to this war, but is more or less common to all wars. It is, in fact, greatly accentuated in the present war both by the colossal scale of the War and the conditions under which it is waged Never before, for instance, have such large questions of international finance and commerce been involved.

"2. Further, we are not fighting for some comparatively minor object which we might hope to attain after giving the enemy a sound beating, but we are to continue the War, 'until the military domination of Prussia is wholly and finally destroyed.'

"3. The question you ask me is by no means merely, or even mainly, a military one. For example, I am ignorant of:

(*a*) Probable solidarity of the Allies and of enemy countries.

(*b*) Social and economic conditions in the enemy countries.

(*c*) Comparative staying power in money and commerce of the two opposing sides.

(*d*) Possible submarine developments.

(*e*) The power of our Navy to keep open sea communications and preserve adequate mercantile marine for the supply of ourselves, our Allies, and the Allied armies overseas.

(*f*) Advantages and disadvantages which may accrue from Allied diplomacy.

"4. The staying power in men counts for very much, but I do not know what men we ourselves are capable of putting into the field or when they can be put there. Nor do I think, for reasons explained in my paper of the 26th ultimo[1] that in the case of the other belligerents any really useful purpose would be served by attempting to find the answer to your question by the manipulation of figures. In the first place the figures we use are to a great extent guess-work. Secondly, although the Entente have on paper more men than the enemy, they cannot be nearly so easily liquidated in practice. Russia is corrupt, badly armed and administered, and will not improve her communications; Italy refused to move men from her own country; Roumania is in retreat. Finally, Germany's interior position and complete control over the policy and operations of the Central Powers give her an advantage worth many hundreds of thousands of men.

"5. On the Western Front we and the French have been steadily gaining a moral and material ascendency over the enemy, and as regards ourselves it is still within our power to put more men and more guns and munitions into the field. If we do this, and if we do not fritter away our efforts in non-vital theatres, and if Russia can be supplied with a reasonable amount of heavy artillery and other necessary war material, we may hope that in the future the pressure upon the enemy on both fronts will not be less severe than it has been in the past. How long we can continue to apply this pressure, and when we may expect to derive decisive results from it are questions which mainly depend upon the factors mentioned in para. 3. It also depends upon the strategy of the Entente, over which my control is very limited. I am, therefore, quite unable to form any opinion as to when the end of the War may be, but I think we shall be well advised not to expect the end at any rate before the summer of 1918. How long it may go on afterwards I cannot even guess. One thing is quite certain, as I have many times said during the present year, and that is that we cannot hope for a conclusion in our favour unless and until we make full and appropriate use of all our resources. We have not yet taken the steps to do this and we ought to take them at once. I referred to some of them in the final paragraph

[1] Summarised on pages 318–321.

of my paper of the 26th ultimo, and I may add here that we must:

Have a full day's work from every man and woman.

Make all possible use of foreign labour.

Check present waste and extravagance in the national life.

Become as self-supporting as possible.

Clearly explain to the nation the grave nature of the task in front of us.

Secure a control over the War in all its aspects equivalent to the contribution we are making towards it. (I emphasised this in January last, but little, if any, improvement has been effected.)

W.R.R.
C.I.G.S."

"November 3, 1916."

Basing myself upon this document, I made a statement at the War Committee, of which I give the following extracts from the summary contained in its minutes:

"Mr. Lloyd George . . . read to the War Committee a minute by the Chief of the Imperial General Staff, dated the 3rd November, 1916, regarding the probable duration of the War.

"Mr. Lloyd George said that this was one of the most serious documents on the War that he had read. We were not getting on with the War. We were now at the end of the third campaign of the War, yet the enemy had recovered the initiative. He had in his occupation more territory than ever before, and he had still some four millions of reserves. At no point had the Allies achieved a definite clean success. . . .

" 'How then,' Mr. Lloyd George asked, 'is the War to be brought to an end?' "

I then summarised the facts of the Allied military position in terms which were subsequently embodied in the memorandum which appears later.

The minute then goes on:

"So far as the public was concerned, the responsibility for the conduct of the War attaches to the politicians, and more especially to the Cabinet Ministers who compose the War Committee. The public will forgive anything except inaction and dritt. He urged that the politicians responsible for the conduct of the War in the principal Allied countries, ought to meet together to take stock of the situation. In the first place, the representatives of France, Italy, and Great Britain should confer together. . . .

"He suggested that the first object of the Conference should be to insist that West should confer with East. . . .

"Mr. Lloyd George concluded by urging:

(1) A small conference composed of two ministers each from France, Italy, and this country.

(2) A military conference to take place subsequently in the East, which should be attended by the principal generals from the West, preferably Generals Robertson, Joffre, Castelnau, and Cadorna."

In the discussion which followed, so the minutes state, a general agreement was expressed with the tenor of my remarks, though they were criticised by some members as unduly pessimistic in regard to the general situation of the Allies.

It was generally agreed that the offensive on the Somme, if continued next year, was not likely to lead to decisive results, and that the losses might make too heavy a drain on our resources, having regard to the results to be anticipated. We decided, therefore, to examine whether a decision might not be reached in another theatre. As a preliminary step my proposals were approved in principle, and it was left to Lord Grey and myself to draft a telegram to Paris and one to Rome with regard to the proposed conference in Paris.

The War Committee agreed that before the meeting of the military conference at Chantilly, arranged for

November 15th, it was essential that there should be consultation between the heads of the principal Allied Governments, in order to take stock of the situation and of the broad principles of policy and strategy that should decide the next phase of the campaign and the operations next year. They considered that the question should be first discussed by the statesmen, who had the real and ultimate responsibility for the whole conduct of affairs, and that the presence of expert advisers at this stage of the conference would be undesirable. They regarded a large conference as useless and suggested that it should be limited to two statesmen each from this country, France, and Italy, the British representatives being the Prime Minister and Mr. Lloyd George. The difficulty about Russian representation appeared insuperable, as no one could take the place of the Emperor and his chief political and military advisers, who could not leave Russia at present.

The War Committee further agreed that, if the Paris conference arrived at important conclusions, these should be discussed with Russia, and that this could probably best be done by sending representatives of the Allies to Russia, where they could be received by the Emperor, and confer with the chief persons who, under the Emperor, directed policy and strategy. Without a visit to Russia, no final agreement affecting both West and East could be adopted, and in no other way than a visit to Russia could full consultation and effective discussion be assured.

It was arranged that Lord Grey and I should concert a telegram to Paris and Rome on these lines.

The military conference at Chantilly, to which reference is made in the above quotations from the War Committee minutes, was one that had already been arranged to take place in November between representatives of the military staffs of the Allied Armies. While there would be obvious advantages in arranging our conference of statesmen at a time when we could have these military authorities available for consultation, it seemed no less important to claim priority for the political conference, since, as was pointed out at our Committee, we were the authority ultimately responsible for decision.

At the next meeting of the War Committee, on November 7th, it transpired that there appeared to be some difference of opinion among our Allies as to the proposal for a further conference in Russia. Italy was dubious about the possibility of sending representatives to such a conference. Further, it seemed that the military chiefs were proposing to hold their meeting at Chantilly a week before the Paris conference could be held, and this I considered to be undesirable; for as I pointed out to the Committee, there would be a tendency among the generals to commit themselves at this conference as to their strategical views, before the responsible heads of the Governments had been able to reach a decision as to what they felt it necessary to take in hand in the way of preliminary consultation with our Eastern Allies, and there might be difficulty subsequently in inducing the generals to modify or reconsider their opinions.

A telegram was accordingly despatched on that day to Rome and Paris in the following terms:

"We are of opinion that the only way to secure effective consultation on the future conduct of the War ensuring the best coöperation in east and west and the coördination which is essential to success, is for a conference to be held in Russia and preferably at the Russian General Headquarters if the Emperor would allow it.

"We regard conference at Paris as preliminary to conferring on the spot in Russia and the main object at Paris should be to arrange this. To postpone consultation at Paris as suggested by Italy would involve very considerable delay. The Prime Minister and Secretary of State for War will, therefore, go to Paris on Monday in order to have informal conversation with M. Briand on Tuesday, the day which he has chosen. After this we hope it will be agreed to ask the Russian Government to fix a conference in Russia at the earliest possible date at which Great Britain, France and Italy should be represented. We consider that the conference to be of any use must be small in number and be in Russia. The other Allies can be called into conference subsequently at Paris if need be.

"Meanwhile we urge that military conference at Chantilly should be postponed for a week. We think it would serve no useful purpose till the considerations which we wish to put before M. Briand have been examined and without these considerations before it the conference at Chantilly might be committed to conclusions that it would be necessary to revise."

The views here expressed were ultimately agreed to by our Allies, and the Paris conference was arranged to take place on Wednesday and Thursday, the 15th and 16th of November, 1916; but General Joffre refused to postpone the military conference at Chantilly and it was held on the same date as the Inter-Allied conference. In the event it dominated and to large extent stultified the political conference. The soldiers successfully torpedoed our efforts to secure a joint examination by soldiers and statesmen from the east and west of the strategy of the Allies for the campaign of 1917. The disastrous military offensives of that year were hatched at Chantilly by the generals, and their selfish action in precipitating momentous decisions without consultation was largely responsible for failure to avert the Russian crash.

In preparation for this Paris conference, I drafted a statement setting out my view of the military situation, and of the need for a further conference in Russia to coördinate the Allied efforts in east and west. This statement was revised and very extensively abridged by Mr. Asquith, and the condensed version of it, rendered into French, was taken by us to Paris. I give below a copy of this document, re-inserting, in italics, the principal passages in my original draft which were blue pencilled by Mr. Asquith from the memorandum as laid by him before M. Briand. The omissions were due not so much to disapproval about the accuracy of the statement, as to the Prime Minister's reluctance to append his signature to a document which the French might regard as critical of the higher commands in both countries. In effect he took all the sting out of the document.

"The time has come for the Allies, in their innermost counsels, to look the facts of the situation in the face. The war environment is always peopled with illusions, many of them deliberately fostered in order to keep up the spirit of the combatants, many others created by the electric atmosphere engendered by all great wars.

"We are at the turning-point of the campaign. *Upon the decisions we take now will depend the ultimate issue. In 1914–15–16 we could afford to blunder without throwing away the chance of final victory. If we take the wrong turning in 1917, I do not believe that our fortunes can be retrieved.* The situation is undoubtedly grave.

"We are approaching the end of the third campaign. After months of hard fighting we have made no appreciable impression on the strongholds of our enemies. On land they hold all their conquests, with hardly any diminution in the area of the conquered territories. At sea they are more formidable and destructive than they have ever been since the commencement of the War. On land they have recovered the initiative which some months ago they lost. Our new ally, Roumania, whose irruption into the field on our side was *confidently predicted by one of the highest military authorities* to mark the end of Austria, is now fighting for very life on her own soil, and *is barely holding her own with the help of Russia. Nearly 50 per cent. of the army with which she entered the field has already been put out of action. She has been deprived of hundreds of square miles of her territory and* the German forces are within twenty miles of the richest oil wells in Europe.

"At sea, the British Allied and neutral shipping, on which depends not merely the active coöperation of England in the alliance, but the very life of the English people, its food, its munitions, and those of its Allies, is being destroyed at an alarmingly increasing rate.

"On land, what is the prospect? We were confidently assured in February, 1915, by a high military authority[1] *that in a few months' time the Germanic federation would have exhausted its reserves. This is the end of 1916. The Germans since June have added twenty-seven new formations to their gigantic armies; this week they have added another. Their army has increased since June by 300,000, and our military advisers, after careful investigation of the facts, now inform us that the reserves of man-power available for Germany and her allies exceed 3,000,000 men, without reckoning the additional 1,000,000 of young men who march every year into military age.*

"As to the blockade, Germany will be saved from famine, and will even be able to make headway against every difficulty, so far as its most essential war needs are concerned, if it succeeded in securing the Roumanian cornfields. On the Somme, the Allies have achieved a succession of brilliant victories, but what has been the result of these operations? What were the results which the Somme offensive was designed to provide?

1. To draw closer the bonds of the Franco-British Alliance. That has been achieved beyond all doubt.

2. To raise the siege of Verdun. We have succeeded there.

3. To break through the German lines, and roll the enemy back to the Meuse. Here we were not successful.

3a. *The capture of some important strategic position then*

[1] Lord Kitchener.

held by the enemy and the occupation of which by the Allies would have placed him at a serious disadvantage in the next push — something comparable to what the capture of Verdun would have been for the Germans. That object has failed.

4. To divert great forces from the Eastern Front so as to enable the Russian offensive on that front to succeed. The movement of enemy troops has been the other way. *Since the Somme offensive began, nineteen divisions have left the West for the East, and as a result,* the Russian offensive, which started so brilliantly in the spring, and from which so much was hoped, has been stopped, and has given place to complete immobility.

Another object has been recently added to the occupation of such a number of German divisions as to make it impossible for the Germans to concentrate such forces on Roumania as would crush that country. That event is still doubtful. All we know is that Germany has as many troops and guns there as the difficult terrain will permit.

"The most brilliant success scored by the Allies this year has been the recapture of the Verdun forts by a single *coup de main,* without great losses to the assailants. This is a feat of arms, the planning and execution of which displayed the highest qualities of generalship. In barely fifteen days the French Army completely wiped out the results of the grim and costly German attacks, which have gone on for eight months. In consequence, the western line is a little more favourable to the Allies than it was at the end of 1915. *If anyone this time last year had ventured to predict the actual position to-day he would have been denounced as a morbid and malignant pessimist.*

"We must now take such measures as will prevent the situation next year from being only a repetition, if not an aggravation, of the present situation. Time is no longer in our favour.

"The outstanding features of the conduct of the war which give me the greatest concern as to the future are twofold:

1. That in the main decisions taken during the last three campaigns every military estimate of what could be accom-

plished with the resources at our disposal has not only been mistaken, but conspicuously falsified by events.

2. That the same mistakes are repeated time after time without any reference to the disastrous experience gained by the failure of the preceding ones.

"Let us take the campaign of 1915 as an example. This campaign was ruined by two obsessions.

"The first was that the Germans intended a great attack on the Western Front.

"As a matter of fact their great attack was on the East and South-East.

"The second was that by frontal attack, backed up by such artillery preparation as the Allies were then capable of, their forces would break through the German lines. This mistake was committed at Neuve-Chapelle, repeated at Artois, Festubert, Loos, and Champagne. When the attack failed to accomplish its full purpose, it was always thought to be due to the absence of something which could easily be supplied if a second attack of the same kind were made. Then when the second failed, it was said that it came very near success, and that a few more guns or more divisions of infantry would have ensured complete triumph.

"The failure to conceive what was possible and what was not under present conditions of warfare was responsible for the failure of the experiments, which were repeated each time with greater forces, and consequently ended each time in enormously greater losses. Still the same old obsession has taken a firmer grip than ever of the military brain.

"There is no fundamental difference in the character of any of these attacks. There is no essentially novel form of strategy or attack introduced.

"The nearest approach to a new resource or device has been the employment of the tanks, and that came from entirely non-military sources.

"Another example of the failure to estimate the real obstacles in the path of victory was the Dardanelles. The military attack

on Gallipoli was entirely conceived and planned by soldiers, and the greatest soldier amongst them told me shortly before the attack that Gallipoli would be carried with the forces then at the General's command with losses not exceeding 5000. How lamentably the military diagnosis failed is now a matter of history, but in each succeeding attack there was the same under-estimate of obstacles, the same conviction that we could butt through by throwing great masses of men and guns on the enemy lines as though we were fighting in the eighteenth century and not in the twentieth.

"I hold in the history of 1915 the case of Serbia to be the most unpardonable and, I fear, the most irreparable of all the Allied failures. We realise now how important it was for us to block the German road to the east. We could have cut off their supplies. We should have given the German people the sense of being hemmed in, and what would have been more destructive to their morale than the consciousness of that fact? We could have won Bulgaria and organised a great Balkanic Federation with a reserve of 2,000,000 fighting men, which we could have gradually equipped and made formidable armies out of for attacking the Germanic Powers on their southern flank. We could have encircled the Powers in a ring of flame. Turkey, with very little ammunition and hardly any power to manufacture it, would soon have collapsed from sheer exhaustion. This could have been accomplished by the timely occupation of the Vardar Valley with half the forces which are now in Salonika, and a third of the men who fell in fruitless and fatuous attacks on German barbed-wire entanglements in the Western campaigns of 1915. Instead of this, what has happened? The German road to the east is open from Belgrade to Baghdad; she is supplied with corn, cotton, coffee, tea, copper and, what is still more important, with first-class fighting men. These facts have given her people new hope. Bulgaria is equipped, Turkey is reorganised; Greece is overawed with a third of her people hostile to the Allies; Serbia is destroyed; Roumania is fighting for her life. An attempt was made to occupy the Vardar Valley in November, 1915. We realised at last how vital it was to seize the bridge to the east. But

it was then too late. The Balkans, which might have been an asset, are now a heavy burden.

"In 1916, we have repeated in the case of Roumania the fatal error of 1915 in the case of Serbia. The volcanic energy which Russia has displayed in retrieving the blunder made may yet redeem the situation. Nevertheless, it was a blunder of the most inexplicable character. What are the facts? We all knew exactly what the Roumanian equipment consisted of. We knew that the Roumanian Army had no heavy guns, and that her supply of ammunition even for field guns was quite unequal to the stress of a sustained attack or defence. As long as the Austrian Armies were engaged elsewhere Roumania might be all right; but our military advisers must have known that if the Germans chose to withdraw their forces from the attack on Verdun and send a few of their reserve divisions to Roumania, Roumanian guns and ammunition were quite unequal to facing such a concentration. This, however, does not seem to have been foreseen by any of the advisers of the Allies; at least, no one seems to have made any provision against this contingency. Either no Government contemplated it as possible, or each Government thought it was the business of the other to make plans for meeting that eventuality. It was only after the German attack had developed that the Allies improvised hurried expeditions to rescue Roumania from her doom. It is no exaggeration to say that Roumania may be the turning-point of the campaign. If the Germans fail there it will be the greatest disaster inflicted upon them. Afterwards it will only be a quesion of time. But should Germany succeed I hesitate to think what the effect will be on the fortunes of the campaign. Eight hundred thousand men who constitute excellent fighting material if well equipped will have been thrown away.[1] *The Germans' stores, much depleted, will be stocked with great quantities of oil and corn, which will place the Central Powers above any anxiety in these two important respects — and yet no one seems to have thought it his particular duty to prepare a plan which would bring such triumph to the Allies if it*

[1] Sir William Robertson's memorandum placed the Roumanian effectives and reserves at 970,000 men.

succeeded, and which would certainly avert a possible disaster of the first magnitude to their cause. And this is the third year of a campaign which has seen many muddles of the same sort committed through this fatal lack of coöperation and forethought.

"The Salonika expedition is another illustration of the two fatal defects which have pursued the Entente — tardiness and lack of coöperation. The Salonika expedition launched in time would have saved Serbia and given us the Balkans. At best all that can be said for it now is that it is holding 250,000 Bulgarians and Turks with a force which is nominally at any rate double that number. Why so many Bulgarians should think it necessary to confront it I am at a loss to know. General Milne's figures show that the aggregate number of Allied rifles available do not very much exceed 100,000. The equipment in guns and in transport of these troops is ludicrously inadequate even for the modest rôle which it is supposed to play. Neither General Foch nor Sir Douglas Haig would ever dream of attacking the tiniest Somme village defended by a single German regiment with the guns and ammunition General Sarrail and General Milne have at their disposal for the storming of over 200 miles of the strongest positions in Europe held by over 200,000 of the finest infantry. The ammunition of the two combined forces would hardly last out a couple of days in a Somme bombardment. No wonder when the Roumanians came to discover the depleted condition of our ammunition they concluded that we had not altogether kept the spirit of the bargain into which we had entered with them. The whole state of the Salonika Army gives the impression that the generals in command had as a matter of policy been deprived of every temptation to make too effective a use of the armies under their control. It is true that we have recently sent large reinforcements of men and a few batteries of heavy guns, and a further stock of ammunition. If they had been despatched two months ago — and it is just as difficult to spare them now as it was then — General Sarrail might have really threatened the Bulgarian flank on the Monastir side and compelled them to withdraw perhaps a couple of divisions from the Roumanian Front in order to save Macedonia. Sarrail failed

for lack of transport, lack of troops, lack of guns, and what the Roumanians and Russian public know now about this, the French and British public will know soon.

"The history of our dealings with Greece is a dreary picture of paralysing indecision. The Greek people are with us, and have indicated their sympathies repeatedly by their votes, but the King is now, and always has been, the Kaiser's friend and the Entente's foe. He has never missed an opportunity of serving the former and selling the latter. He gave valuable information to the enemy as to our troops, our positions, our intentions, and our movements. Under our very eyes, with our troops looking on, he handed over an important stragetic position like Fort Ruppel to the enemy — a fort which it would take us thousands of valuable lives to storm. He gave the Germans a whole division of infantry and most valuable mountain guns. He has fooled us all round the ring and made us the laughing stock of the East whilst we were writing lawyer's letters to his military advisers.

"It is only by a relentless scrutiny of our shortcomings in the past to find out wherein we have failed that we can hope to avoid failure in the future. Our first duty is to calmly face the facts of the situation, however painful, and to acknowledge, at any rate to ourselves, and in our own councils, wherein we are responsible for the unsatisfactory conditions with which we are now confronted. To attempt to ignore them or to gloss them over amongst ourselves is a sure guarantee of disaster. I quite realise the importance of keeping up the public faith in victory, and that it is not always necessary to call the attention of the people to the dangers and defects of our position; but in the War Councils of the Allies the facts must be exposed as they really are, and, unless this is done, someone must take the public into his confidence and give the people a chance of saving themselves before it is too late.

"But so far as the British Government can judge, the operations in the west, if continued on the present footing, hold out no hope of our inflicting on the German armies in 1917 a defeat sufficiently crushing to put an end to the War, unless we are able to reinforce them by much greater efforts in the other theatres of war.

"The position in the southern theatre does not offer any much greater hope of a decisive success. It is true that the Italian Army, by means of a campaign admirably conceived and well carried out, has made appreciable progress and gained considerable victories. All the same, trench warfare generally predominates on this front, and one can see no dawning of a day of big results.

"On the Eastern Front the Russian attack, starting under such happy auspices, has been brought to a full stop, and it is clear that on the principal Russian Fronts there will be great difficulties to overcome before serious progress can be made.

"As we have already said, the entry of Roumania on to the scene did not produce the decisive results which had been hoped for, and if the situation in this theatre is a little less grave than it has been, it continues, none the less, to be an object of serious pre-occupation for the Allies. As we foresaw, the difficulty of communications by land and sea has prevented a decisive success on the Salonika Front. The greater part of the Bulgarian Army, it is true, has been held there, and on the flanks there are slight advances to record. All the same, these operations do not allow us to count on a decisive success in that region, unless the operations are combined with others on other fronts in such a way as to divert a considerable part of the forces opposed to us. Even in that case, the lack of roads and railways will hold up our advance, which would, in any case, be difficult in face of the resistance awaiting us.

"The effect of our inability to obtain a decisive result on the Salonika front is that the Central Powers still keep open the route which leads them to their objectives in the East.

"What is the prospect in front of us? What is our policy? *Has anyone mapped out a road to victory? If he has, I have not yet been privileged to see that document. Words will not win. We must have a definite plan. I have only heard of one.* People talk of hammering, and of a war of attrition. The success of hammering depends entirely upon whether you are making a greater impression on the barrier or the hammer. The success of a war of attrition depends upon the time it takes, and who can last out the longest. In examining the chances of success of a war of attrition, certain essential factors must always be present to the mind.

"The first is the reserve man-power of the Central Powers and their allies. Our General Staff places these reserves at three or four millions. They reckon in addition that each year a million young men become available for service.

"We shall be wise not to conclude that even these appalling figures exhaust the man-power of the enemy. Polish conscription may well give him between 500,000 and 1,000,000 men. Prisoners, Polish and Lettish labour, are constantly releasing young men from essential trades. The German military leaders are also clearly giving a good deal of attention and thought to the substitution of machine power for man-power. They believe that owing to the perfection of their machinery they can reduce the numbers of their infantry men by several thousand in each division, and they have one considerable advantage over the Entente, that being in possession of enemy ground, they can gradually give way, selling land dearly as they retreat without any serious damage to their military position. This last point is illustrated by the difference between the fighting on the Somme and the fighting at Verdun. The French Army could not retreat five miles at Verdun without giving up something of considerable strategical value and of infinitely greater moral importance. They were consequently bound to defend every kilometre at the most appalling cost. On the other hand, the Germans could give up 5, 10, even 20 kilometres on the Somme without surrendering any point of much strategic or moral importance.[1] *The only thing that matters to them is that in reconquering French or Russian territory their enemies should pay more for its capture than it cost them in its defence.*

"Another factor, if we wish to measure the chances of a war of attrition, is the effect of the submarine campaign against our merchant shipping. The importance of this cannot be exag-

[1] This they did in the spring of 1917, thereby disarranging the whole of the Nivelle plans.

gerated. Undoubtedly during the last few weeks the destruction of Allied and neutral tonnage has taken on alarming proportions, and unless effective steps can be taken to check it, the consequences may be of the most serious character to the armies of the Allies. Our success depends so much upon our maintaining the unchallenged supremacy of the sea that if we fail to protect our transports and our supplies, it will be impossible for Great Britain to maintain her present forces either in the east or the west. It will become equally impossible for France and Italy, Russia or ourselves to keep up the present supply of munitions. We feel confident of being able to defeat this latest and most pernicious development of the German submarine attack, but it would be idle to pretend that it does not fill us with serious anxiety, when we contemplate the prospect of a campaign lasting over a period of years.

"The difficulties which we have experienced in making payment for our purchases from abroad must be as present to the minds of French statesmen as to ourselves. Our dependence upon America is growing for food, raw material and munitions. We are rapidly exhausting the securities negotiable in America. If victory shone on our banners our difficulties would disappear. *Success means credit: financiers never hesitate to lend to a prosperous concern: but business which is lumbering along amidst great difficulties and which is making no headway in spite of enormous expenditure will find the banks gradually closing their books against it.* The fall of Roumania would have a serious effect on our American credit. On the other hand, if Roumania succeeded in resisting the tide of invasion then the victories of Verdun and our advance on the Somme would have their maximum effect, and the Americans would open their purses and send us their merchandise. The problem of finance is the problem of victory . . . *not debatable victory, but unchallengeable victory; not victory won here countered by disaster there.*

Another consideration to be taken into account is the morale of the four nations behind the armies. As the War drags its weary and bloodstained path, the sacrifices and the sufferings must necessarily increase; the casualties will become heavier, and the gloom cast by the appalling losses over the homes of the country will become darker and deeper. Then food will become scarcer and costlier, the burdens of taxation will be heavier. Efforts will be made perhaps by powerful neutrals to patch up peace on what would appear to be specious terms, and there is a real danger that large masses of people, worn out by the constant strain, may listen to well-intentioned but mistaken pacificators; and, last of all, there is the danger, which one hardly likes to contemplate but which is ever present in our minds, of one of the four great Allies being offered terms which seem better than an indefinite prolongation of the horrors of war. No alliance has ever borne the strain of a protracted war without breaking. These are considerations which it would be well for us to bear in mind when we are urged to depend upon attrition as the sole means of bringing this terrible war to an end.

What, then, is our suggestion? It is that the responsible military and political leaders of the four great Allied nations should for the first time since the commencement of the War meet together to discuss the situation and to formulate their policy or strategy. The responsible leaders of the Central Powers and their Allies are constantly meeting to discuss plans, to devise new plans, to revise old ones. The real military leaders of Russia never had five minutes' conversation with the military leaders of the West. Such communications as I have read between them indicate a good deal of divergence in essential points of strategy. Take, for instance, General Alexeieff's despatches on the Balkans. These are questions not merely of strategy, but of equipment, which have never yet been discussed by the Higher Commands at the various conferences. I do not regard discussion about Russia with General Jillinski, or even General Palitzine, as an interchange of views between East and West. History will mock at us for our neglect to insist upon a meeting of the responsible military and political leaders of the various fronts for three whole campaigns. The whole policy of the Allies ought to be coördinated; there ought to be a complete understanding between the East and West. Surely Generals Joffre and Robertson have something to say about their experiences in the West which it would be worth General Alexeieff's while to hear. On the other hand, General Alexeieff must have had a good deal of experience and must have learned many lessons which it would be valuable for his Western colleagues to hear something of. There is no other business which would have been conducted for three years without some sort of interchange of opinions between the men that matter in the direction of affairs. If a conference is decided upon, it would be a farce to send anyone there except the men who matter; the men who represent France, Russia, Italy, and Britain must not merely be men of the highest capacity, they must also be men whose decisions could practically be accepted, not because they have been tied down by their instructions and therefore cannot assent to anything which their colleagues or superiors had not already given previous assent to, but accepted because of the high positions which the representatives hold.

"What, then, is our proposition? We have shown above all the importance of the rôle played in the present war by Roumania and the Balkan countries. We have shown that the conquest of Roumania would furnish the enemy with very considerable resources of man-power, and would be an incalculable aid to the reëstablishment of their economic equilibrium. On the other hand, we have shown that the elimination of Bulgaria would complete the encirclement of the Central Empires, would isolate Turkey, which would then be compelled to die of exhaustion, and would bring the Entente Powers markedly nearer to final victory.

"Although these advantages are so evident that they justify the greatest efforts for the achievement, we do not hide from ourselves the considerable difficulties to be anticipated. Our military advisers have more than once explained to our Government and to the French Government how difficult and uncertain every operation must be that is based on Salonika.

"Our proposition is that the statesmen and generals of the great Western Powers should confer with the statesmen and generals of the Eastern Front, taking for their programme the examination of the situation in its entirety, and more particularly the military situation in the east. The object of the conference must be to determine what it is possible to do on the Eastern Front, and what is the nature and importance of the help which the west ought to give to the east for those operations which are judged to be necessary. Moreover, the statesmen and generals of the west ought to explain clearly to the statesmen and generals of the east the limits which are imposed on our possible effort in the Salonika region. In Russia, since the dismissal of M. Sazonoff, there are only two men who can speak with authority: the Emperor and General Alexeieff. At the present moment it is impossible for either of these to come to the west. That is why — and we insist on this point — it is of capital importance that generals and statesmen competent to represent the Western Powers with the fullest authority should go to Russia as promptly as possible in order to discuss these questions, the interest of which is vital for the conduct of the War."

A meeting of the Cabinet was held on Monday, November 13th, and on the following morning the Prime Minister and I proceeded to Paris accompanied by Sir Maurice Hankey. He had arranged to have a private conversation with M. Briand on the morning of the 15th of November before the Allied Conference opened that afternoon, with a view to placing before him confidentially the opinions of the British War Cabinet. This private meeting was fixed for the Quai d'Orsay at 10.30 A.M. on the 15th of November. When Mr. Asquith, Sir Maurice Hankey and I arrived we found there was no M. Briand. We were informed that the President de Conseil had been unexpectedly detained at a meeting of one of the committees of the Chambre des Députés, to which he had been suddenly summoned, but that he expected to arrive soon. We waited for another half an hour and then came another message that he had found it impossible to get away, but that we might expect him in another quarter of an hour. Then Sir Maurice Hankey learnt from an amused official that the Chairman of this Committee was M. Clemenceau, and that he was subjecting the French Premier to a fierce cross-examination on certain unsatisfactory aspects and episodes in the conduct of the war and that M. Briand was having a very *difficile* time. We then realised that M. Briand was detained by circumstances over which he had not the least control, and that one of the circumstances was the redoubtable "Tiger" over whom no one had any control.

Another three-quarters of an hour passed and M. Briand hurried into the room, looking flustered, unhappy and altogether rather badly mauled. We learnt that he had escaped the ruthless claws of the great political cat this time, but with difficulty, and only by the exercise of every fibre and sinew of his renowned dexterity and suppleness. He was not, however, in a state of mind which would enable him to give cool and concentrated attention to our memorandum. We felt that the conditions were not propitious for a calm examination of the military position. The problems raised needed all the concentration and composure which every member of that small gathering could command. However, after an interchange of the usual civilities and conventional inquiries, Mr. Asquith explained the purpose of the informal meeting he had sought. He pulled out of his pocket the memorandum and read it, or rather rushed through it, without emphasis or pause. M. Briand, whilst preserving the pose of a courteous and attentive listener, was evidently too ruffled and distracted to take in ideas at such a speed. He asked Mr. Asquith to leave a copy and promised to study it all with great care before the afternoon meeting. That was all, and then we shook hands, and Mr. Asquith and I drove off to the Hotel Crillon, feeling like men whose proposals, to which weeks of thought and debate had been given, had been received with civil torpidity. Here was the country that had so far sustained the most serious damage in the war and had the enemy in occupation and control of its finest provinces, and yet there seemed no evidence of any racking preoccupation on the part of its leaders with the problems of liberation. That was the burden of M. Clemenceau's satire, and I felt that there was some justification for his bitterness. No man has a greater admiration for M. Briand's gifts, but as a War Minister he was much too easy-going. My mind inevitably travelled on to contemplate the obvious similarity between French and British leadership. Both Mr. Asquith and M. Briand were men of rare intellectual gifts, but unfortunately they both lacked driving power. Once again we were captained by men who were distinguished figures on the bridge in normal weather; skilful navigators in ordinary storms, but not qualified for command in the most raging typhoon that ever swept the seas. France as well as Britain were both led by men devoid of vigour and initiative. Yet the fortunes of the Alliance depended upon their leadership.

The first session of the Inter-Allied Conference from which so much was hoped took place that afternoon. The importance of these meetings is shown by the list of those attending, which included, for the British Government, Mr. Asquith and myself, accompanied by Lord Bertie and Sir Maurice Hankey; for the French Government, M. Briand, President of the Council and Minister for Foreign Affairs, Admiral Lacaze, Minister of Marine, with M. de Margerie, Director of Political and Commercial Affairs at Quai d'Orsay; for Russia, M. Isvolsky, Ambassador in Paris; for Italy, Signor Carcano, Minister of the Treasury, Senator Tittoni, Minister of State, and the Marquis Salvago Raggi, Ambassador in Paris.

The President of the Council (M. Briand), after welcoming those present, made a characteristic speech, eloquent but inconclusive, the minute of which I quote verbatim.

"M. Briand recalled that at the moment when the former Conference of March, 1916, met, the whole of Europe was still suffering from the anguish caused by the attack on Verdun. The advance made in the last days of February by the German armies had given rise to the keenest apprehension; but the Allies on that occasion reviewed the situation in all its aspects, and coördinated their efforts, and as a result of that coördination they had been able to carry out an offensive which had already given satisfactory results, and of which one of the first consequences had been to relieve Verdun.

"At the same time the Russian armies had taken the offensive on their side, and one of the effects of these operations had been to relieve the congestion on the Italian Front, and to allow our Allies to score a brilliant revenge against the Austrians.

"The results obtained, however satisfactory they might be, were not, strictly speaking, decisive, but they had at least the consequence of removing the initiative in the field from the Germans and transferring it to the Allied troops. But that was not enough to bring victory.

"The War was about to enter upon a serious — one might say a decisive — phase, and the Allies would have to close their ranks in order to bring the war to a speedy end by achieving a final victory over their enemies, since the patience of the nations could not be indefinitely submitted to such an ordeal.

"Before discussing this problem, a question of principle arose: What ought to be the attitude of the Governments towards the Generals Staffs; whatever might be their confidence in the General Staffs — a confidence indeed fully justified — ought the Governments to abandon absolutely to them the conduct of operations?

"The French Government did not think so. It held, on the contrary, that it was the Governments which, since they bore the whole responsibility for the conduct of the War, should take the initiative in regard to operations, it being always understood that the execution of the plan adopted should be left to the military authorities, who had the means to carry it out.

"If there was agreement on this point, the moment would seem to have come for the Governments to envisage the direction which it would be desirable to give to the War. On that very day the delegates of the General Staffs were studying at Chantilly the elements of the problem, and their labours would be of great service in enabling the Governments to take a decision in full cognisance of the circumstances.

"What struck the Premier first of all when studying the situation on the basis of the documents furnished by the military authorities and carefully checked by General Headquarters, was the fact that the Allies had altogether at their disposal effectives superior by at least 50 per cent. to those which the combined strength of the Germans, Austrians, Bulgarians and Turks could put against them. That was a consideration well calculated to give courage and to justify an absolute confidence in final victory.

"These hopes showed a still firmer foundation," added M. Briand, "if the present fighting value of the armies were compared. While our troops had not only lost nothing of their attacking qualities, but on the contrary had never ceased to improve, as the success of our last Anglo-French offensive on the Somme had demonstrated, the soldiers of the German Army were far from possessing to-day, even among their officers, the same qualities as at the time of their formidable attack on Verdun.[1]

"Furthermore, the Allied situation from the point of view of munitions was growing stronger and stronger every day.

"Such considerations should not, however, be allowed to lull our courage to sleep, or make us lose sight of the great goal we had to reach. They should, on the contrary, stimulate our ardour, encourage us to intensify our efforts, and make us understand the great advantages which we have reaped from putting into the common store our strength and our resources.

"And now, what course of action ought we to adopt on all fronts? It was on this point that it would seem worth while to deliberate, in order to discover the swiftest solution of the War. The French Government considered, and its opinion would doubtless be shared by the military authorities, that it was absolutely

[1] A few weeks later the 50 per cent. superiority had already disappeared and the mutiny in the French Army did not quite bear out M. Briand's claim as to the superior "attacking qualities" of the Allied troops.

necessary to manifest an incessant activity on all fronts. This activity could not bring about a decisive result all at once, but it was indispensable in order to retain the initiative in the Allies' hands. The offensives of the armies of General Brussiloff and General Lechnisky had frankly not been decisive, but they had enabled the Russians to take 400,000 prisoners and disorganize the Austrian Army.[1] On its front, the Italian Army had dealt the Austrian Army terrible blows, which had greatly weakened it; while on our front our valiant troops and those of our friends and Allies the English, had undertaken an offensive which had already had happy consequences which were familiar to his hearers.

"All these operations, without being decisive, had had the effect of preventing our enemies from continuing the tactics of which we had been the victims at the outbreak of war, and from dealing us blows, first on one front, and then on the other. Since our activity had shown itself everywhere, the Austro-German Armies had been everywhere condemned to act on the defensive. Let that lesson profit us and encourage us to keep on! But what operations could be undertaken in winter? The French Government considered, and it had made its views on this subject known to its Allies, that it was in the Balkans that the most effective efforts could be put forth. What, in fact, was Germany doing?

"Pressed on all sides, it was not hesitating to violate the rights of nations in an attempt to procure new reserves of men in Poland. It was said that it could find in this way 300,000 or 400,000 men. Suppose these figures correct, would it not take several months more to train these new recruits and make soldiers of them? Were we going to wait without doing anything until Germany and Austria were able to use these troops against us? Would it not be much more worth while to make straight away an effort to stop, or at all events to render useless, this violation of the rights of nations?

"But what could be done? Let us ask ourselves. *It seemed to him indispensable to try by energetic action in the Dobrudja*

[1] The greater numbers of Russian and Roumanian prisoners captured by the Central Powers are not mentioned.

and against Sofia to put Bulgaria out of action, and thereby Turkey.

"That effort was not impossible, and he thought that Russia would be disposed to make it, if we could second her action by an offensive on the Salonika Front. There could not be for the army of the east any question of undertaking an operation of large scope. The narrowness of its base rendered this task almost impossible. But it could, for instance, continue its pressure on the German-Bulgarian Armies, and try to recapture Monastir.

"The Salonika Army, although inadequately supplied with men, had at all events carried out the promise made to Roumania to immobilise the Bulgarian Armies on its front. Since the entrance of Roumania into the picture, not a single Bulgarian soldier had been able to leave the Salonika Front to take part in operations against our new Ally. That in itself was an appreciable result, *but it was necessary for those operations to continue so as to free Roumania, and at the same time the activity of the Allied Armies must be intensified on all the other fronts.*

"If Bulgaria and Turkey were put out of action before the end of the winter, public opinion in Germany and Austria would certainly be demoralised, and next spring we should be able to deal our enemies decisive blows.

"That was how the French Government saw the course of the war. If the Allied Governments were in agreement with it in deciding that it was the Governments which should take in hand the general conduct of the War, and if they shared its way of looking at things, he had the firm conviction that we should be able next year to obtain decisive results.

"We had come to a grave hour — maybe to a critical hour, if there was wobbling in the decisions of the Allies and a dispersal of their efforts.

" 'I have shown you the goal that we wish to reach,' said the President of the Council in conclusion. 'It is worth our while to give it serious study, for if we adopt a definite solution, we shall have rendered a signal service to the cause which we support.' "

It was then the turn of the British Prime Minister to urge upon the Conference the definite proposal set forth in our memorandum. The minute of the conference continues:

"Mr. Asquith thanked M. Briand, in the name of the British Government, for the eloquent words he had just uttered. 'But,' added the Prime Minister, 'to attain the goal which has been indicated with such precision, it will be needful for statesmen and generals from the Great Powers of the west to proceed to Russia to confer with the Russian statesmen and generals, to determine what it is possible to do on the Eastern Front, and what is the nature and the importance of the help which the Western Powers can render to Russia and Roumania, to bring to a favourable issue those operations which are considered necessary. This conference would have for its object the examining of the situation in its entirety, and more particularly the military situation in the east. It is necessary that this meeting should take place as soon as possible, and that the statesmen charged to represent the Western Powers should have full authority to discuss the grave problems on which the conduct of the war depends.'

"The British Prime Minister was of the opinion that it was not the military authorities but rather the Governments which ought to undertake responsibility for the political and strategical conduct of the War, and he proposed that the representatives of the Powers met here to-day should forthwith, and *without prejudice in any respect to the conclusion of the conference which would be held in Russia,* enter on an engagement to submit themselves to the decisions of this Assembly.

"The Chief Italian Delegate thought, like M. Briand, that as the Governments had the responsibility of power, it was to them that the right belonged of deciding the conduct of the War, but he was of opinion that no decision ought to be definitely fixed before there had been consultation with the competent military authorities. With this reservation, M. Carcano entirely associated himself with the point of view of the French Government. The Minister of the Treasury pointed out at the same time that he was in this expressing only a personal opinion, and that he did not think himself authorised to enter on an engagement in the name of the Royal Government. He would wish to refer the matter to the President of the Council, who had been unable through sickness to be present at the conference, but with whom the final decision rested.

"M. Briand pointed out that at present they were concerned only with an exchange of views between the delegates of the Allied Powers, and that the solutions arrived at by them did not bind their Governments, and were only taken *ad referendum.* It could not indeed be otherwise, since it was a question of summoning a conference in Russia, the principal theatre of war during the winter, to discuss these problems there and take the necessary decisions.

"M. Tittoni declared that the Italian Government had been in agreement with the French Government since the coming into power of M. Briand in considering that the Balkan Theatre was that in which the War would reach its decision. But when it was a case of discussing in what manner the Allies ought to concert their efforts to attain a definite result, it was evident that they would have to discuss in the first place among themselves the conditions of their joint military and financial coöperation.

"The President of the Council did not disagree with this, but he pointed out that it was necessary for the Governments to take into their hands the direction of the War. The front on which operations were taking place was so extended that it was difficult to embrace with a single glance, *and there was no army chief who would not be tempted — it was human nature — to consider the front on which he was in command as the most important, just as each soldier did — hence the necessity for the Governments to be the arbiters of operations.* Our enemies had shown that they would not hesitate, even at the risk of a sacrifice of *amour propre,* to keep in view only the end to be reached. Did they not, the moment that Roumania entered on the scene, give up the pursuit of their attack on Verdun, despite even a dynastic interest therein, to transfer their principal effort to the Balkans?

"That example should not be lost on us. *It was not a question of obtaining a success at one point or at another, but of envisaging the final result, and of coördinating our effort to obtain as soon as possible the ultimate victory.*

"The Russian Ambassador, although without instructions and without special powers, undertook to state that the proposal to hold a conference of the Allies in Russia would be met with the liveliest sympathy on the part of His Majesty and His Government. M. Isvolsky added that he personally considered that it was the Governments, and not the Staffs, which ought to have the direction of the War, but that the question did not arise in Russia, since the Emperor was at once the supreme head of the armies and of the Government.

"As to the question of the principal theatre of operations during the winter it was clear from all communications received from Russia that the Imperial Government and everyone in Russia were well aware of the capital importance of the operations in the Balkans.

"M. Briand noted with satisfaction that all the delegates were agreed in principle in recognising that the Eastern Front would be during the winter the principal theatre of operations. Since that was the case, and while leaving to the conference which would be held in Russia the task of deciding what should be done by the Russian and Roumanian Governments, we could examine straight away to what extent these efforts could be seconded by the army in the east.

"Mr. Lloyd George noted with satisfaction that all the delegates had approved in principle the proposition of the British Government for summoning a conference in Russia to decide on the general conduct of the War, and that they were in agreement as to the necessity of adopting a common line of action.

" 'But that is not enough,' added Mr. Lloyd George. *'We must not rest content with taking these decisions. We have still to see that they are carried out.* After having decided on the Salonika expedition, the English and French Governments entrusted its execution to persons who were not perhaps sufficiently convinced of the importance of this front, and have not given sufficient attention to it to know whether the effectives were adequate, whether the transport was well organised, and in particular whether the artillery corresponded to the needs of the operations. Certain military authorities had said, it is true, that heavy artillery could not be utilised in this theatre on account of the bad state of the roads and of the topographical conditions; but the Germans have shown us the contrary in the Carpathians. *When Governments have taken a decision, they ought to see that it is carried out.*

" 'The goal towards which our efforts ought to be directed has been indicated with much eloquence by the President of the Council. It is a matter of encircling Germany more and more every day, of cutting its communications with the East, of hindering the formation of new armies.

" 'To get there, we shall have to unite all our resources. One cannot in fact avoid the thought that the magnificent offensive of the Russian Armies, despite the valour of the troops and the skill of the generals, has not perhaps yielded all that was hoped for, solely because of the inadequacy of heavy artillery on the Eastern Front. These armies ought then to be given the cannon and the munitions of which they stand in need, and that without waiting until the French, English and Italian Armies have been furnished with all the material that is necessary to them. We have got to help Russia and Roumania, not by taking from the surplus of our production, but by drawing if it must be upon what is necessary for ourselves, for it would be a shortsighted policy not to put these armies straight away into a position to fulfill the task which falls upon them.'

"Mr. Lloyd George proposed, in consequence, that the Assembly should adopt the following resolutions:

1. The three Governments of France, Italy and Great Britain undertake to participate in a political and military conference which shall be held in Russia as soon as possible.

Each Government will send to this conference, as its representatives, statesmen and officers of high rank, possessing full authority to speak in the name of their respective Governments.

2. The aim of the conference will be to examine the political and military situation in all its aspects, and in particular to fix

the nature and the importance of the military effort which the Allies ought to carry out in the east during 1917. The object of the conference shall be at the same time to estimate the importance of the help which ought to be provided by France, Italy and Great Britain to Russia and Roumania, in order to enable these Powers to carry out the operations which shall have been decided on.

3. The Governments represented at the present conference shall enter into an engagement to furnish in the fullest possible measure to their Allies the full military equipment asked for by the conference, which will be held in Russia, even if this should result in a certain slowing down in the equipment of their own armies, and Russia shall on its side enter into an engagement to conform to the decisions adopted by this Conference.

This last phrase does not in any way imply that the conference will impose certain conditions on Russia; it simply means that Russia will take the necessary steps to enable her to make use as promptly as possible, and with all the desired intensity of the resources put at her disposal by the Allies. It turned out that 300 pieces of heavy artillery sent to Russia at the beginning of the year could not be used until a quite recent date through lack of artillery-men to serve them.

"M. Tittoni, after stating that the Italian delegates could only take part in these deliberations *ad referendum,* asked permission to tell the meeting the reflections which Mr. Lloyd George's proposition suggested to him. One could not doubt, said he, the good will of the Italian Government; its solidarity with the Allies was whole and entire; but he did not want to rest content with theoretical formulas, and was trying to do practical work. Now, it was no use hiding the fact that the realisation of the programme advanced by the President of the Council and by Mr. Lloyd George would come crashing against difficulties independent of the good will of men. He had to speak freely.

"Now, for the Italian Government, one of the principal difficulties at the present moment was the financial question, and that was one of the reasons for the journey of the Minister of the Treasury. The question of exchange was becoming almost acute, since, less rich than France and England, Italy was experiencing great difficulties in meeting its payments to foreign countries. Of course, the Italian Government was ready to make every possible effort, but it was necessary for its Allies to come to its aid as well with the help it might require from the financial aspect.

"So far as concerned the operations at Salonika, the Senator of the Kingdom of Italy could only express his personal opinion, this question being chiefly within the competence of the military authorities; but he was convinced that the Italian Government would be ready to make the effort asked of it, if it had the assurance that the Russo-Roumanian pressure would be so powerful and continuous that it would be impossible for the Austro-Germans to withdraw troops from the Balkans in order to send them to one of the other fronts. If this condition was not fulfilled, the Allies would be running a great risk in weakening the French, English and Italian fronts, to any extent, however slight. *An intensification of the effort at Salonika would seem useless, if it were not the consequence and the complement of a great Russo-Roumanian effort.*

"It should not be lost sight of that to realise this effort many difficulties would have to be surmounted, not only difficulties of a military order, but economic and financial difficulties as well. It would not be sufficient to send troops; we must also be able to ensure their transport, their artillery supplies, and their provisioning under all heads. The question of the reinforcement of the Eastern Army thus presented very great difficulties.

"M. Briand remarked that when the Allies envisaged a plan of campaign, it was, of course, understood to be subject to the reserve that what proves impossible should be abandoned, and that it was precisely the object of the conferences then being held, and of that which would take place in Russia, to discover the steps to be taken to secure unity of action on all fronts, regard being had to the resources and the means of each of the Allies.

"It would, for instance, be impossible to ask France, which had ten departments invaded, which had mobilised more than 6,000,000 men, which had taken part in the operations in the

Dardanelles and at Salonika, and had gone at the outset to the aid of Serbia — it would be impossible to ask her for a greater effort in men. *But if France were asked for artillery, machine guns, munitions, and if it were in her power to furnish them, she would give them at once.* France had already given a good deal of war material to her Allies, but she was ready to intensify still further her production if this was possible.

"The Allies ought to try and fill up the gaps wherever they appeared. If one country was embarrassed in regard to effectives, the others ought to come to her help; if there was another in a difficult financial situation, it was their duty to try to give her the resources which she needed. *In the grave circumstances through which we were passing, all our resources must be pooled, without making it a question of* amour propre. That was how the French Government, and assuredly also all the Allied Governments, understood the conduct of the War."

The remainder of the session was devoted to a consideration of the position in Greece. With regard to this country the discussions were confined mainly to the question of the recognition of M. Venizelos' Government. A new factor, which was brought out by M. Briand, was that the King, in his conversations with M. Benazet, had made some remarkable promises. He had said that he was ready to withdraw his troops from Thessaly on condition that the territory evacuated was not occupied by Venizelist troops. He had also offered to give us the whole of the Greek material of war, and even to put his fleet at our disposal. M. Briand said that, if this offer were accepted, the Allies would obtain the use of 200 mountain guns, with 1000 rounds a gun, as well as a vast amount of other war material.

Mr. Asquith pointed out that if one of the conditions of the King's offer to M. Benazet was the abandonment of M. Venizelos his proposals would have to be rejected. He explained at considerable length the sympathy and respect felt in England for M. Venizelos, and urged that the ideal solution was the reconciliation of the King with M. Venizelos, and that our policy should be directed towards that. He also urged the desirability of the official recognition of the Venizelist Government, particularly owing to the anomalous position of the Venizelist troops, and the danger they ran of not being accorded belligerent rights.

M. Briand did not dispute the desirability of reconciliation between King Constantine and M. Venizelos, and said that in France public opinion is as favourable to M. Venizelos as it is in England. Public opinion, however, he added, was not aware of the difficulties.

The general opinion of the conference was not in favour of the recognition of M. Venizelos at present. It was pointed out that, in order to obtain belligerent rights, it was necessary that the enemy, no less than the Allied Governments, should recognise M. Venizelos.

It was generally agreed, however, that the Allies should not let any opportunity pass to support M. Venizelos and his friends, and to protect them wherever necessary. The friends of the Entente, as M. Briand said, must be the victims of their favourable sentiments towards the Allies.

The question was left much where it stood, and no resolution was passed. M. Briand finally summed up the discussion as follows:

> "So the Allies may expect a development which does not seem as though it could be delayed much longer, and which should be of a nature to give them satisfaction; but it still goes without saying that if the King or his Government were to adopt measures against M. Venizelos and his friends, the Allies would intervene immediately with all necessary vigour to defend the great Greek patriot, who has always shown himself favourable to their cause."

Thus ended the first day's conference. Before our meeting on the afternoon of the next day, the military chiefs at Chantilly had completed their deliberations, and had agreed upon a programme which bears evident marks of having been settled for them in advance by the French Headquarters Staff, and which ran as follows:

General Headquarters of the French Armies,
Staff Office, November 16, 1916.

The members of the Conference give their approval to a plan of action by the Coalition, as it has been defined in the memorandum which has been submitted to them, a plan having for its object to give a decisive character to the campaigns of 1917. They adopt, in consequence, the following resolutions:

I.

(*a*) During the winter, 1916–17, the offensive operations now being engaged in shall be pursued to the full extent compatible with the climatic conditions on each front.

(*b*) In order to be as much as possible in readiness to face every new situation, and especially in order to prevent the enemy from recapturing in any way the initiative of operations, the armies of the Coalition shall be ready to undertake joint offensives from the first fortnight of February, 1917, with all the means at their disposal.

(*c*) From the time when the armies are ready to attack, the Commanders-in-Chief shall adapt their respective conduct to suit the situation of the moment.

(*d*) If circumstances do not prevent it, the joint offensives carried out with all the means which each army can bring into play, shall be unloosed on all the fronts as soon as they can be synchronised [1] to dates which shall be fixed by common accord between the Commanders-in-Chief.

(*e*) With a view to realising all accord necessary between these diverse hypotheses, the Commanders-in-Chief shall not cease to maintain a close contact with each other.

[1] It is admitted that synchronisation will be realised if there does not elapse a delay of more than three weeks between the initial dates of the offensives released on the various fronts.

II. ON THE BALKAN FRONT

(*a*) The Coalition shall seek to put Bulgaria out of action as soon as possible. The desire of the Russian High Command is to continue and intensify with this object the operations in hand.

(*b*) Against Bulgaria the Russo-Roumanian forces shall act from the north, and the Allied army at Salonika from the south, the action of these two groups of forces being closely combined, so as to obtain a decision on one or other front of action, following the development of operations.

(*c*) The Allied Army of the East shall have its effectives raised as soon as possible to 23 divisions. This figure for effectives corresponds on the one hand to the number of troops which can be manœuvred and supplied with provisions in the theatre of operations in question, and on the other hand to the contingents which can be spared from the Western theatres of operations. With the object of attaining this effective force the British Government will raise without delay its forces to seven divisions, the French Government to six divisions; the Italian Government, having been informed of the intentions definitely affirmed by the Russian High Command, shall be requested to raise to three divisions the Italian forces at Salonika.

(*d*) The Allied Army of the East shall be carefully maintained at the full complement of its effectives.

III. SECONDARY THEATRES OF OPERATIONS

On all secondary fronts, actions aiming at the immobilisation of the enemy forces shall be pursued with means as reduced as possible, in order to reserve the maximum forces for the principal theatres.

IV. MUTUAL SUPPORT

(*a*) The members of the Conference renew the undertaking for mutual assistance adopted by the Conference of 5th December, 1915, and fully observed by all throughout the course of the present year, that is to say:

If one of the Powers is attacked, the others shall come immediately to its help to the full limit of their resources, whether indirectly by attacks which the armies not assaulted by the enemy will unloose upon prepared zones, or directly by the despatch of forces between theatres of operations linked by easy communications.

(*b*) In readiness for this latter eventuality, studies of transport and of the employment of combined forces shall be undertaken between the French, English, and Italian Headquarters Staffs.

V. MAINTAINING THE EFFECTIVES OF THE SERBIAN ARMY

The effectives of the Serbian Army shall be maintained by voluntary enrolments of prisoners of Serbian race, in the hands of Italy and Russia, to the full extent and with all the precautions determined by these two Powers.

Signed by the Representatives of the Commanders-in-Chief of the Allied Armies present at this Conference and designated below:

For Belgium:

General Wielemans, Chief of the General Staff of the Belgian Army.

WIELEMANS.

For Great Britain:

General Sir W. Robertson, Chief of the Imperial General Staff of the British Armies.

W. ROBERTSON.

General Sir Douglas Haig, Commander-in-Chief of the British Armies in France.

DOUGLAS HAIG.

For Italy:

General Porro, Chief of the General Staff of the Italian Army.

PORRO.

For Roumania:

Colonel Rudeano, Chief of the Roumanian Military Mission at the French G.H.Q.

RUDEANO.

For Russia:

General Palitzine, representative of His Majesty the Commander-in-Chief of the Russian Troops and the Chief of the Russian Military Mission.

PALITZINE.

For Serbia:

General Rachitch, delegate of the Serbian Army at the French G.H.Q.

RACHITCH.

For France:

General Joffre, Commander-in-Chief of the French Armies.

JOFFRE.

Accordingly, at our meeting on Thursday afternoon, the 16th of November, the representatives of the Allied Governments were joined by the leading generals (Joffre, Robertson, Haig, and Perro), whose report formed the agenda for our discussion, and whose conclusions limited and for practical purposes defined our action. I extract the following passages from the minutes of this session.

After M. Briand, with Mr. Asquith's support, had proposed that for the moment no more could be done than to approve the Chantilly resolutions *ad referendum* to the Petrograd Conference, to which the plan of Eastern operations had been referred, I intervened as follows:

"Mr. Lloyd George wanted to know how the figure of 23 divisions was arrived at. According to the information supplied, there were only 19 — 7 English, 6 French, 3 Italian, and 3 Serbian, the effectives in the Serbian Army amounting, according to the information supplied by General Milne, to about 36,000 rifles, which only equalled three divisions on the basis of the standard of the Allied Powers.

"General Joffre explained that there was a Russian Division, and that the Serbian Army was counted as six divisions.

"Mr. Lloyd George expressed his astonishment at this valuation, and pointed out that the Serb effectives were being reduced all the time. The Serbian soldiers fought with a courage which could not be praised highly enough, but the Serbian Army had no reserves, and its losses were rather high. It was for that reason that he only reckoned there to be three divisions of effectives in that army.

"Admiral Lacaze recalled that 140,000 Serbians had been transported from Corfu to Salonika.

"General Joffre added that this figure of 23 divisions was the maximum of what the Salonika theatre of operations would permit of employment. We could only deal with practical propositions. Besides, to raise the effectives of the Army of the East to this figure would take a good deal more time yet, *for if there were at our disposal a sufficient number of boats, there were still lacking the railways and necessary facilities to enable us to utilise a more numerous army.*[1] This meant that we must immediately intensify the activity at Salonika, and for that it would be preferable to send there one division straight away, rather than send two or three in January or February.

"Mr. Lloyd George asked on what information the opinion was based that this figure of 23 divisions was the maximum that could be used at Salonika, and whether this attitude was shared by the Generals commanding the East.

"General Joffre replied that this advice was the result of calculations made at General Headquarters.

"General Robertson announced that the British Government had received a *report from General Milne in which he declared that the possibility of utilising thirty divisions at Salonika could only be contemplated if the means of communication, the roads, and railways could be expanded, and if two new ports could be brought into service.*

"General Joffre explained that the military authorities had had to base themselves on the existing state of affairs, *because it would take not less than 12 or 18 months to construct the roads and railways needed to enable thirty divisions to manœuvre.*

[1] The British War Council decided to take steps for this purpose in January, 1915, but the Military Authorities entirely ignored the decision. See Vol. I, p. 345.

Replying to Mr. Lloyd George he said that no report had been received from General Sarrail.[1]

"M. Briand pointed out that it was by taking for their basis the position as it stands with its present possibilities that the General Staffs had been led to consider that 23 divisions represented the maximum of what could be absorbed and used this winter on the Salonika front. That was not to say that they could not, by constructing new roads and new railways, use more important effectives, but that the General Staffs had primarily had in view the realisation as early as possible of the objective before them — namely the conquest of Monastir, and along all the rest of the front a continuous action designed to retain the enemy forces so as to prevent the Bulgarians from sending troops to the Roumanian front.

"General Joffre added that the means of *communication are not yet sufficient, and before being able to utilise the effectives that have just been spoken of, locomotives and waggons will have to be sent for the Greek railways.*

"Mr. Lloyd George paid a tribute to the remarkable skill of the Italian engineers, especially over country of such a character, and wondered whether the Allies could not approach the Cabinet at Rome to ask them for help in this task.

"General Porro stated that if necessary the Italian Government would be quite ready to send engineer officers to construct railways in Greece. *He added that the reports from General Pettiti confirmed all that General Joffre had said about the lack of means of communication and about the bad state of the roads, which were almost unusable.*

"General Joffre *explained that the roads were so bad that half the fighting troops were being used in maintaining them.*

"Mr. Asquith expressed pleasure at the assurance given by General Porro. He considered indeed that Italy could not render a more important service than that of improving the lines of communication in the Balkans.

"General Joffre remarked that if the Army of the East

[1] He was Commander-in-Chief of the Salonika expedition. Decisions had been arrived at without any previous consultation with or even report from him.

had not yet reached Monastir, that was largely due to the difficulty of transport of men and materials in those regions, and indeed to the all but impossibility of revictualling them in certain cases. *The first thing to do was to construct roads and railways:* but it must not be lost sight of that, to the extent to which the army advanced, the engineers and workmen would have to make new railways for it. Progress would thus be necessarily very slow, *and that was why the military authorities considered that not more than 23 divisions could be used on the Salonika front,* and preferred to retain the effectives that were at their disposal for the Western Front.

"M. Briand thought the question should be dealt with by stages. For the moment the concern was that the expeditionary corps should be able to realise its objective on the Monastir side, and hold the Bulgarian troops on its front.

"If later on, after the construction of new railways, and improvement of the means of communications, it appeared that the expeditionary corps could absorb new troops, the French Government, and no doubt also the other Governments, would be ready to send the necessary troops.

"The President of the Council pointed out, in passing, that the conclusions of the Military Conference were in agreement with the views exchanged on the previous day between the delegates of the Powers. The conclusion of the work of the General Staffs confirmed the importance of intensifying operations in the East, so as to put out of action Bulgaria and Turkey. These conclusions were only adopted, it need hardly be repeated, *ad referendum,* but each group of delegates could forthwith inform its Government, and support at the Petrograd Conference the resolutions which had been proposed.

"The President of the Council asked the delegates of the Powers to register the conclusions of the General Staffs while waiting for the possibility of going to meet the Russian Government and get them approved there in definite form."

After this the Italian representatives gave an interesting account of the economic and financial state of affairs in Italy and its connection with the military situation. They emphasised the vital need of imports and raw materials if the *morale* of the Italian Army and people, which remained high, was to be maintained. They described the difficulty of a country whose exports had shrunk to small dimensions owing to war conditions in paying for imports unless further financial assistance was forthcoming. Mr. Asquith, while pointing out that our own position was far from easy, promised to examine with the utmost good will any proposals the Italian Government could make for the improvement of the situation, and M. Briand gave a similar undertaking. If the Allies wished to be victorious, he said, it was essential that they should put all their resources into the common stock. Some had reserves of men, others produced a superabundance of war material, others again could dispose of important financial resources. But if the Allies established a balance of their general situation it would be easy for them, or at least possible, to fill up the gaps which might exist by one or the other.

In regard to Poland the Conference discussed the text of a protest to be made by the Allied Governments against the creation by the Central Powers of a Kingdom of Poland.

The text of the draft originally proposed was purely negative in character, merely consisting of a protest, on the grounds of international law, against the German action. Mr. Asquith pressed very strongly that it should not be purely negative in character, but should contain a reference to the promises made by the Grand Duke in regard to Poland in August, 1914.

It will be obvious from the records I have here produced that this Conference, on which so much store had been set, turned out from the point of view of securing a genuine examination of the military position and strategy, by a gathering at which both soldiers and statesmen were represented, to be little better than a complete farce. M. Briand's opening at the Wednesday afternoon session was characteristic of his strength and weakness — eloquent in phrase, inconclusive in decision — strong in statement, feeble in action. The Allies, he explained, were superior in numbers, equipment and valour to their dispirited foes. We must energise these superior forces of the Allies and promote such a coördination of effort as would overwhelm the inferior armies of the enemy. The only danger was that the patience of the Allied nations would be worn out. So we must attack on all sides with all our strength. Our resources were common; so must be the front. The Balkans were the point upon which this united strength should be concentrated in the coming months. He envisaged such energetic action from the Salonika base against Sofia as would free Roumania and put Bulgaria and Turkey out of action before the winter. He painted the result of this enterprise with a broad brush dipped in radiant colours — public opinion in Germany and Austria would certainly be demoralised, and next spring we should be able to deal our enemies "a decisive blow." And he ended up with the proposal of a local operation for the capture of Monastir — a feat achieved later on by the broken army of Serbia alone. He also laid it down in precise terms that the statesmen of the Alliance must make clear to the Chantilly warriors that the strategy and direction came from Governments and not staffs and that it was for the latter merely to carry out the instructions framed at the Political Conference. At that very moment M. Briand had obviously agreed in advance to accept General Joffre's plans, which went no further than Monastir. The idea of breaking through the Bulgarian lines in order to extend effective aid to Roumania was, in fact, abandoned in the very speech wherein it was advocated with resounding rhetoric.

As for the document submitted to the second session by the Generals, setting out their decisions at Chantilly, it was an intimation that the military leaders regarded the determination of the lines of the campaign for 1917 to be a matter for which they had the primary responsibility. To this attitude they adhered in spite of an elaborate appearance of deference to the wishes of the Governments. The 1917 campaign was theirs with all its disasters. It repeated all the bloody stupidities of 1915 and 1916 and extinguished finally the *morale* of the Russian Armies already shaken but not irretrievably shattered. It also temporarily broke the spirit of the French and Italian and British Armies.

The proposal for the conference of responsible political and military leaders to be held immediately on Russian soil to settle the future plans of the Allies was completely ignored by the generals. They had agreed to their plans at Chantilly and they had no intention of allowing General Alexeieff to alter them. Signor Tittoni's objection to agreeing to the meeting except *ad referendum* to a sick Prime Minister helped the Generals to avoid committing themselves to a conference. As to Salonika they made a concession to civilian obtuseness. An attack was to be staged in that quarter at an early date, but it must be done as cheaply as possible. The stupid politician must be deluded into the belief that it was a serious operation with a view to crumpling up Bulgaria — a preposterous piece of deception to anyone who had made any study of the comparative strength or numbers, equipment and position of the combatants on that front. The Generals knew that they had no intention of pressing the attack beyond Monastir. The storming of the Balkans they knew too well was far beyond the power of the badly equipped Salonika Army. But the strength of the Salonika force must be exaggerated for civilian ears. It was, or soon would be, an army of twenty-three divisions brought up to effective strength. They juggled and shuffled with "divisions" when they knew they were only sham divisions. As a matter of fact it was the equivalent of barely ten divisions, and no effort was contemplated to increase its numbers in offensive efficacy. In the matter of artillery and transport it was hopelessly below the standard of the Western Front. When their attention was called to the inadequacy of the forces, General Joffre and Robertson urged that the transport facilities were so defective that you could not feed a larger number of troops, let alone carry the necessary ammunition for more cannon. It would take twelve to eighteen months to improve these facilities. The Expeditionary Force had already been at Salonika for that period and these arrangements had not been attempted. As I have previously said, a decision had been arrived at by the British War Council as far back as January, 1915, to take immediate steps to increase transport facilities between Salonika and Serbia. Lord Kitchener promised to take the matter in hand at once. Here, at the end of 1916, a campaign which our military advisers considered essential to restore our failures in South-eastern Europe, could not be attempted because the port, rail, and road transport were so inefficient that no effective attack could be staged. It came out in one of the military reports that half the troops were occupied not in fighting but in road repairing. General Milne reported that with thirty-three divisions the Bulgarian Army could be beaten. Had the necessary thirty-three divisions been landed, backed by a powerful artillery, what a difference it would have made to the course of events. Bulgaria, now getting tired of the war, would have been eliminated. The Bulgarian peasantry never cared for the side they were forced by their King to take. The road to Roumania would have been reached. The Russian Armies and those of the west would have joined hands. Turkey would have been cut off from the source of her supplies. More heart and spirit would have been given to the depressed and disaffected Russian soldiers. The Revolution would have been further postponed. Austria would have been enveloped on the east, the south, and the west and would have fallen to pieces. 1917 might have seen the end of the war. What a difference that would have made to the world!

I left the conference feeling that after all nothing more would be done except to repeat the old fatuous tactics of hammering away with human flesh and sinews at the strongest fortresses of the enemy. If Russia and Roumania fell out, there was nothing that could be done.

When Mr. Asquith, Sir Maurice Hankey and I returned to the hotel and Mr. Asquith, after a short and perfunctory conversation, retired to his usual rest before dinner, Sir Maurice and I went for a walk together to talk matters over.

We both felt that nothing in the way of a change in the conduct of the war had been accomplished and that in the absence of some dramatic *coup* things would go on as before until we slid into inevitable catastrophe. We felt that if either Russia or Italy collapsed or if the submarine losses could not be checked, the balance of advantage in favour of the Allies would be lost and would pass over to the enemy. I was in favour of an immediate resignation. To this Sir Maurice was opposed until some other means of effecting a change in the war direction had first been attempted. I can recall that as we passed the Vendome Column, Sir Maurice paused and said: "You ought to insist on a small War Committee being set up for the day-to-day conduct of the war, with full powers. It must be independent of the Cabinet. It must keep in close touch with the P.M., but the Committee ought to be in continuous session, and the P.M., as Head of the Government, could not manage that. He has a very heavy job in looking after the Cabinet and attending to Parliament and home affairs. He is a bit tired, too, after all he has gone through in the last two and a half years. The Chairman must be a man of unimpaired energy and great driving power." We both agreed that it was important that Mr. Asquith should continue to be Prime Minister. His great prestige and his unrivalled authority in the House of Commons would be assets which were regarded as indispensable. It was decided therefore that on my return to England I should place the proposition before the Prime Minister; but that before I did so it would be best to sound Bonar Law, whose good will and approval it was essential to secure. I wired from Paris to Lord Beaverbrook, asking him to arrange a meeting between Bonar Law and myself the following evening.

CHAPTER XVI

THE FOOD POSITION

Food shortage grows serious — My proposal for a planned national effort — Growth of submarine menace — Outlook for food supplies gloomy — Central Food Department proposed — My memorandum: a food controller proposed — Further discussion in War Committee, 13/11/16 — Committee approves control in principle — Further warning of submarine danger — Warning by Wheat Commission — No steamers to bring wheat to Britain — Nothing done by first Coalition Government.

By the autumn of 1916 the food position was becoming increasingly alarming and grave, and its handling by the Government was a most conspicuous example of its hesitancies. The increasing shortage of shipping made the food position doubly grave, dependent as we were upon ships for most of our food supplies. As far back as September, 1915, Lord Selborne, in a memorandum which he submitted to the Cabinet, had urged that "We should appoint another committee of the Cabinet to consider the whole question of the food supply of the nation for the next eighteen months." In this document he had pleaded the value of an increased wheat production. "It is only about a month," he wrote, "since the Chancellor of the Exchequer (Mr. M'Kenna) showed an invincible repugnance to encouraging the growth of wheat in England by offering the farmers a guarantee. It is possible to increase the production of food in the United Kingdom by voluntary effort, but a guarantee of the price of wheat would be by far the most effective measure which the Government would take for that purpose." On March 10th, 1916, I raised this issue anew by urging on the

War Committee that the aim we ought to keep in view in the matter of food supplies was that this country should as far as possible be self-contained. To this end the Board of Agriculture ought to be armed with drastic powers to improve the production of food so as to reduce our dependence on imports. Every possible acre ought to be cultivated against extension of the submarine campaign. I suggested the utilisation of machinery on a large scale. The plan, however, must be a *national* one.

On March 23rd, 1916, I spoke again on the same subject in connection with the problem of the shortage of ships.

In the War Committee of October 31st, 1916, the Prime Minister had read a letter from the Commander-in-Chief of the Grand Fleet, who "expressed misgivings regarding the danger to the cause of the Allies from submarine attacks on merchant shipping, *which must be expected to increase in the spring, when the enemy would have more submarines.*" It was known that in this opinion the Admiralty were in complete agreement with the Commander-in-Chief. Lord Crawford was now Minister of Agriculture, and had circulated to the members of the Committee an urgent document showing the seriousness of the situation; and how the outlook grew more difficult as time went on. He pointed out that *our stocks of wheat and flour at that moment (October 30th) amounted to four months' consumption, and that there was a world deficit of wheat. The probable wheat requirements of importing countries during the twelve months ending September 1st, 1917, were 72,000,000 quarters, while the total available supplies were estimated at 63,000,000.*

The freight space required to carry the necessary imports of grain and feeding stuffs in the eight months, November–June, was 8,981,000 shipping tons. The potato crop, too, had failed in England, as in Germany and France. The forecasts indicated a shortage of some 1,800,000 tons (or 24 per cent.) as compared with 1915. Moreover, the crop was diseased and a shortage of seed potatoes was possible. Fish supplies were some 64 per cent. below normal, and the prices had risen from 100 to 400 per cent. The feeding of live stock was causing anxiety, as foodstuffs were costly and labour scarce.

Lord Crawford stressed the desirability of establishing some central food department to supervise and coördinate the varied relations of the State with the import, purchase and distribution of food. The whole field and the general prospects might be suitably submitted to the continuing and comprehensive survey of the central body. (This suggestion had now been before the Committee for at least seven months, but no advance had been made nor decision taken.)

Lord Crawford ended his memorandum by the statement *that not before August, 1917* (*i.e.*, when the harvest of 1917 had been gathered in) *would war policy be free to dissociate itself from the influence of home food supply.*

I supported Lord Crawford whole-heartedly in his efforts to obtain a decision as regards the food supply, and on November 10th I circulated a short memorandum embodying a few concrete suggestions which I thought would materially help in solving the food problem. These were as follows:

"That someone — who shall not be a member of the Ministry — be immediately appointed to organise the food supplies, including purchase, production, distribution and prices.

"That he should be equipped with all the necessary legislative, administrative and financial powers to enable him to utilise to the full the food-producing capacity of the United Kingdom.

"That *inter-alia* he should direct his attention to:

1. Securing adequate supplies of food — especially from home sources.

2. Keeping prices down.

3. Increasing the acreage of land in this country which produces cereals, potatoes, vegetables, and other food products.

4. The mobilisation and utilisation to the full and in the best way of

(*a*) All the available mechanical appliances for the cultivation of the soil.

(*b*) The manufacturing capacity of this country and the United States for the output of machinery for cultivation.

(*c*) The skilled agricultural labour of the country.

(*d*) The unskilled male and female labour capacity of the country for agricultural purposes.

5. The utilisation for animal fattening of the enormous waste of food products now consigned to the refuse heaps in the great towns.

"War Office, November 10th, 1916."

The same day (November 10th) there was a meeting of the War Committee, at which the question of shipping shortage was discussed. The President of the Board of Trade, in the course of his statement, said that the Wheat Commission were at present unable to find forty free vessels for the essential service of conveying the Australian wheat supplies. *The conclusion that he drew was that a complete breakdown in shipping would come before June, 1917.*

On November 13th the War Committee met to discuss the food position again. They had before them Lord Crawford's memorandum. The President of the Board of Agriculture, with the clarity and suavity which he always commands, urged his case. He gave a sketch of the immediate and prospective outlook as regards food. He pointed out that land was going out of cultivation, that labour was scarce. The harvest this year, he said, had been less by half a quarter per acre than had been anticipated, which was equal to a reduction from twelve to ten weeks' supply. He was apprehensive of next year's harvest unless immediate steps were taken. He again urged the necessity for a Central Food Controlling Authority. I realised that if the submarine menace were not checked (and there seemed at that moment no expectancy that anything could prevent it from increasing in gravity) the war as far as we were concerned might end in starvation for this country. It was now months since the proposition of a central authority had been put before the Government, but we seemed to be no nearer achieving it. I therefore pressed at this meeting for the appointment of a Central Authority (which I had also insisted upon in my memorandum of November 10th). I urged, however, *that the President should have real authority with complete control subject only to the War Committee. I considered, moreover, that the person appointed should not be a Minister of the Crown, as his time would largely be taken up with answering questions in Parliament. He need only attend the War Committee whenever he wanted a decision of the first-class importance. Above all, I impressed upon the Committee that the appointment should be made at once. The actual difference between ten and twelve might seem to be small, but in point of fact it was very serious. I therefore begged the Prime Minister to treat the necessity of obtaining a man to control all food supplies as one of immediate urgency. I said that I attached great importance to machinery and cultivation. I saw no reason why every village in the country should not be self-supporting, just as it was when I was a boy.*

The President of the Board of Trade pointed out that nearly all the statutory powers required to carry out my proposals already existed in the Defence of the Realm Act, and that he had recently circulated to the Cabinet new regulations under the Act of a most drastic kind.

In spite of these "full powers" and "drastic regulations",

the Government had not sanctioned the measures suggested by the Minister for Agriculture and no progress was being made with the increase of home production.

The War Committee approved of my proposal for a Food Controller, in principle, subject to the right man being found to control the great organisation contemplated.

There were enough provisos in this last paragaraph to prevent any action being taken immediately. As a matter of fact, no Food Controller was appointed under Mr. Asquith's Premiership.

On November 16th the First Sea Lord of the Admiralty and the Chief of the Admiralty War Staff circulated a note to the Cabinet stressing the increasing gravity of the submarine danger. They concluded the note with the following words:

> "The increasing danger to our supplies from the enemy's submarines has recently become so much more evident through their ruthless attacks on neutral shipping as to make this question need more serious reconsideration *before it is too late.*"

But no immediate decision was taken. The accumulation of problems requiring urgent attention had indeed become so great that there seemed to be no time for any one of them to be properly thrashed out and a decision to be arrived at. On November 22nd, the matter was still in abeyance. The question of shipping and food supply was reaching a crisis, and the President of the Board of Trade circulated a memorandum complaining that nothing had been decided at the Cabinet Meeting on November 10th, and calling attention again to the urgency of the matter from the point of view of tonnage. On the same day the Wheat Commission sent a communication (the memorandum of the President may have been written as a result of this), urging the provision of further tonnage for food supplies. "So far from adding," they said, "to the reserves in the country, the shipments during the last fortnight to arrive this year have been nearly 200,000 quarters a week less than requirements, and all the information of the Commission points to the conclusion that this low rate of shipment will be continued until a further supply of tramp tonnage has arrived for loading in the Northern Range."

On the same day (November 22nd) the Shipping Control Committee met and discussed the tonnage situation in relation to the serious position of the wheat supply in this country.

They reported: "The Committee are informed that the stocks of wheat are running down; that we are living from hand to mouth. In London there are only two days' supplies, and London has therefore to be fed by rail from other ports. In Bristol there are only two weeks' supplies. . . .

"The Wheat Commission have purchased 700,000 quarters in North America, *but there are no steamers to bring the wheat to England.*

"In normal circumstances there would be ships 'coming free' in the Mediterranean after discharge of coal." These ships, however, owing to war conditions, would not become available for four months, and the wheat position was dangerously acute.

On November 23rd (the next day) three Ministers (the President of the Board of Trade, Lord Curzon and the President of the Board of Agriculture) raised, as a matter of great urgency, our present and prospective critical situation in regard to grain supplies. They brought in support the letter from the Wheat Commission and the report of the Shipping Control Committee; and the President of the Board of Agriculture pointed out that we were *consuming 200,000 quarters a week more than we were receiving; that every week we were buying sufficient wheat for 15 days' consump-*

tion, but were unable to ship it; and that if the wheat we had purchased were not brought forward it would diminish our power to purchase.

It was decided that a conference should be held that afternoon between the Admiralty, Shipping Control Committee, and President of the Board of Trade, and that they should report next day to the War Committee.

In spite of these urgent messages showing the critical position of our food supplies none of the plans suggested either by the Ministry of Agriculture or myself for dealing with the situation were put into operation during the lifetime of the First Coalition. A paralysis of will seemed to have seized the Government. Whatever the subject, it was impossible to get a move on. I am not sure that this palsy did not account for the unanimity of the Cabinet on the question of rejecting overtures for Peace. These would have meant action. The pacifist element was easily persuaded to do nothing. The Government was getting into that nervous condition where they could neither wage war nor negotiate peace.

CHAPTER XVII

INTERLUDE: A CABINET OF INDECISION

A nightmare situation — Problems that were being paltered with — Shipping — The Russian issue — Aëroplanes — Mr. Montagu's memorandum — Conflicts in the cabinet — Talking out the issue.

It is hard for me to convey an adequate picture of the sense of frustration and tangled impotence which oppressed me during those closing months of 1916. There are nightmares in which one welters amid a web of fettering strands and obstacles, and watches, wide-eyed, some doom approaching against which the strangled throat cannot force a sound of protest or appeal. The ineffectiveness and irresolution of our leadership in those dark weeks bred something of this nightmare feeling.

There was at this time a whole series of developments and problems which were being paltered with or shelved. Some of the wider issues of general policy I have already described. Firm handling of them was vital to our prospects of success, and I grew increasingly convinced that it was my duty as a responsible Minister to break through this miasma of indecision and force these matters to a definite issue, even at the risk of resignation from the Ministry and a subsequent public exposure of the ineptitude of the Allied war direction. I have also told of the way in which two or three important questions were dealt with, and these afford an illustration of the general method of procedure adopted by the government in an emergency. One of them was the neglect to take competent strong measures to protect our merchant ships against submarine raiders. The alarming rate at which our ships were being sunk was rapidly increasing. The October sinkings had been nearly 70 per cent. above those of September, and the Admiralty wrung their hands in despair when reporting fresh disasters at our meetings, but offered no hope that they could grapple successfully with the rapidly developing catastrophe. Then there was our failure to take steps to coördinate our strategy with our Russian Ally — a failure intensified by the refusal of Sir William Robertson, backed and instigated by a member of the War Committee — to represent this country at the proposed Russian Conference. His refusal dealt a death blow to our prospects of saving our Ally from collapse and concerting our military strategy with her. It was prompted by a groundless apprehension that the whole idea was a manœuvre to shift him from his position in the War Office, and that the methods of the intrigue by which he had supplanted Lord Kitchener were to be practised in turn on himself — that Robertson, in fact, was to be "kitchenered" out of his position of high authority. This point of view was pressed upon him by a prominent Cabinet Minister and he was only too ready to listen. It is idle to vow that I had no such purpose in view, and that I had always urged a more authoritative touch between East and West than that which was represented by the appearance at our Conference of Russian generals, for whom their own army had no use at home. Those who are capable of such baseness in a great crisis will readily believe that others meditated it. I was pressing on my colleagues what I sincerely believed was the best course in the interest of my country. However, Sir William Robertson would not go and the Prime Minister was not prepared to order him to go. At that time there was no military substitute of sufficient authority. Sir Douglas Haig could not be sent. He was so committed by ideas and loyalty to the front for which he was responsible that he could hardly be expected to review impartially the battlefield as a whole. Sir Henry Wilson was thoroughly disliked and distrusted by the Prime Minister. So that when Sir William Robertson declined to undertake the mission it dealt a sinister blow at the whole project.

The situation in regard to aëroplanes was another of the vital issues which were being muddled and mishandled in a fashion all too symptomatic of the methods of the Government. At that time we had already been discussing for weeks the question of aëroplane production. There was a wasteful rivalry going on between the Army and Navy on the subject. Certain works had been captured by the Navy that ought to be assisting in increasing the much-needed output for the Army. On the Western Front the Germans had regained superiority, especially in attacking and raiding machines, and the military chiefs were clamouring for more aëroplanes of these types.

The Cabinet debates on this issue were so protracted that judgment upon it was never delivered during the lifetime of the Asquith Coalition. The question of responsibility for the manufacture of aëroplanes was raised by Mr. E. S. Montagu on behalf of the Ministry of Munitions in September, 1916. Mr. Montagu was anxious that his Ministry should undertake the manufacture of all the aëroplanes required by both the Army and the Navy. In a memorandum to the Cabinet, he pointed out that:

"The present organisation, under which the supply of aircraft material is the concern of two bodies — the War Office and the Admiralty — acting under the general supervision of a third — the Air Board — and in constant and inevitable competition with a fourth — the Ministry of Munitions — appears to me to be one for which no arguments can be adduced, and which cannot be expected to obtain satisfactory results. In my opinion it is necessary at once to adopt one of two plans —

either to set up a new Supply Department responsible for the entire supply of both Air Services, or to entrust the task of obtaining that supply to the Ministry of Munitions, which was created to meet a situation in regard to munitions similar to that which now appears to exist in regard to aircraft."

The Aviation Board had been set up with a view to coördinating the efforts of both Army and Navy. Over this Board Lord Curzon presided. He was strongly opposed to Mr. Montagu's scheme. He admitted that:

"At this moment a source of urgent anxiety to General Trenchard lies in the appearance on the German Front of two new machines better in certain respects than any which we now possess there. It is not the *number* of these available that concerns him, but the fact of their superiority."

But he claimed that:

"We are developing fresh engines and fresh aëroplanes which we believe will surpass the recent German production. But the question at issue is, will our machines in fact be superior and will they be developed in time?"

He was clearly of the opinion that a new department should be set up which would have sole and complete control over the production and to a certain extent, the direction of all machinery for aërial warfare.

When Lord Curzon put forward his plan on these lines, he was in turn challenged by Mr. Balfour in a very caustic and amusing memorandum. To this Lord Curzon replied in suitable terms. It was clear that if the controversy did not conduce to the provision of aëroplanes it at least provided excellent entertainment for those who were privileged to read these documents and to hear the discussions. The pleadings took some time. First, the statement of claim by Lord

Curzon. Time must be given for the First Lord of the Admirality to file his defence, then there was a rebutter and a surrebutter. An interpleader by the Ministry of Munitions. Then at last the case was set down for trial.

I have a melancholy recollection of Cabinet Committee discussions at this period. The aëroplane case was always first in the list after the usual preliminary reports from the Army and the Navy. Lord Crawford's urgent memorandum on the food position should have come next and shipping also would have to be discussed, but with such skilled protagonists as Mr. Balfour, Lord Curzon, and Mr. Montagu the time was generally occupied in thrashing out the merits and demerits of the conflicting claims championed by these trained dialecticians. When in despair of conciliating the antagonistic proposals the Prime Minister had a habit of turning round to the mantelpiece to see whether any temporary relief from his perplexities was indicated by the position of the hands on the clock. We all knew what that meant. He was making for a postponement of further discussion to the next meeting. Lord Crawford put in a despairing cry for a few minutes' consideration before lunch of his anxieties about the food of the nation. He pointed out each time that the position was getting steadily worse, that consumption was exceeding supply at a time of the year when the process ought to be reversed. On the other hand, the Prime Minister would point out that it was clear from the hour which had been reached that there was no time left for the discussion of so grave a problem. There was nothing left for Lord Crawford but to plead for a special meeting to consider his difficulties. That meeting never took place in the lifetime of that Administration. At our next meeting came again the aëroplane case (partly heard). At the last meeting ever held we all thought that a decision had been arrived at, but as we were dispersing, I saw Lord Curzon standing alongside the Prime Minister and challenging that fact. Mr. Asquith surrendered and said that the case would have to be re-argued at the next meeting. When the next Cabinet meeting took place in Downing Street it was under a different Government.

CHAPTER XVIII

THE CRISIS: DECEMBER, 1916

Need to coördinate Allied efforts — All vital questions left to departments — Coöperation of Bonar Law and Carson vital — Sir Edward Carson's view of Mr. Asquith — Lord Beaverbrook's account — Premiership issue: views of Carson and Bonar Law — My memorandum to the Prime Minister — Mr. Asquith's reply — The reply unsatisfactory — I appeal to Mr. Bonar Law — A talk with Mr. Asquith — His further letter: anger at *Times* article — I accept his proposal — An interview refused me — My exclusion from meeting of Liberal ministers — Mr. Asquith cancels our agreement — A breach of faith — My letter resigning office — Our further correspondence — Resignation of Mr. Asquith — Mr. Bonar Law urges Mr. Balfour to become Premier — Mr. Asquith refuses to join a Balfour ministry — I undertake to form a government — Attitude of Conservative leaders — Mr. Balfour's support for my policy — He accepts office under me — Cleavage with Liberal leaders — My case never stated to party — Lord FitzAlan's help — Preoccupations of new government — Campaign of misrepresentation — Mr. Asquith's one-sided statement — Mr. Runciman's disingenuous speech.

THE upshot of our November peace discussions in the Cabinet had been the decision of the Government not to make peace until the fortunes of the Allies were unchallengeably better than those of the Central Powers. But this decision made it incumbent upon them to take the necessary steps to improve those fortunes before the patience of the Allied nations became exhausted. We had not only to resolve on the prosecution of the war to the utmost limit of our resources, but to take steps to utilise those resources to the best advantage, and especially to see that the great combined strength of all the Allies should not be dissipated and wasted through lack of coördinated effort. We had also to make sure that one of the most powerful of the Allies should not retire out of the struggle in a spirit of despair.

At the Paris Conference, M. Briand had pointed to the

possibility of exhaustion as one of the perils of the situation. As a matter of fact, we were within only a few weeks of the popular uprising in Russia against continuing the sacrifices of the war. Yet in face of this nearing danger there was manifest among our leaders no clearness of vision as to their course, no firmness of leadership and no promptitude or boldness of decision. Their disposition was to leave all vital questions to the Military, Naval or Civilian Organisation in charge of some special war activity, and I felt in my bones that unless some new energy and inspiration were injected into the war direction, we should before long drift into irretrievable disaster. I therefore came to the conclusion that I must act without further delay.

Having regard to the political forces in Parliament, I realised that it was essential that I should carry with me two men — Mr. Bonar Law and Sir Edward Carson. Standing alone I could only bring pressure to bear upon Parliament, and through Parliament upon the Government, by means of a popular agitation conducted with the support of a section of the Press. This would necessarily take time, and might have the effect of discouraging and demoralising public opinion. Russia a few weeks later proved the danger of producing a sense of disillusionment in the public mind, even by justifiable and necessary criticism. It would have reacted on the Army, whose ardour had been temporarily damped by the Somme mud — even more than by the Somme carnage. It was therefore essential that if a change was to be effected in the direction of our war activities it should be achieved with as little disturbance and public agitation as possible.

Of Sir Edward Carson I had seen a good deal through the patriotic good offices of a friend and supporter of his — Sir Arthur Lee — now Lord Lee of Fareham. Sir Edward Carson was convinced that the war was being badly muddled. His few months in the Coalition Cabinet, with its Serbian collapse, its Dardanelles fiasco, and the bloody futilities of our strategy in France and Flanders had the result of deepening his distrust of the Prime Minister's capacity to direct the War. His view was that all the disasters which had befallen the Allies could have been averted but for the Prime Minister's slackness. Mr. Bonar Law, on the other hand, having the Scotsman's natural respect for brains, was a great admirer of the Prime Minister, and it took him many months' experience of his obvious tardiness, indecision, and lack of drive in action to come to the conclusion that whatever Mr. Asquith's mental equipment — and of that neither of us had any doubt — he did not possess the qualities that make a great War Minister.

The story of my negotiations with Mr. Bonar Law and Lord Carson has already been told by Lord Beaverbrook in his fascinating book on "Politicians and the War." It is frankly told not from my point of view, but as a vindication of Mr. Bonar Law. Making an allowance for that honourable personal bias, I am prepared on the main facts to accept his narrative. As between Mr. Asquith and myself he is clearly unbiassed. He has no personal interest in either of us.

Sir Edward Carson was for pushing Mr. Asquith out of the Premiership. He argued that any shifts like a War Committee, whatever its composition, must necessarily fail so long as the chief responsibility and authority was vested in Mr. Asquith. Certain Ministers whom he named would be constantly at his ear and poisoning him against the new committee, and postponing, modifying, and thwarting its decisions. Mr. Bonar Law was emphatically of the opinion that it was desirable for the sake of preserving the national unity that Mr. Asquith should retain his position of Prime Minister. He dreaded anything like a split in the Cabinet at such a juncture. He was also apprehensive that there might be a division in his own party if Mr. Asquith were driven out of the Premiership. Most of the Tory Ministers were devoted adherents of Mr. Asquith's leadership in the war. I was also in favour of retaining Mr. Asquith as Prime Minister provided he left the new committee full and unfettered powers to direct the war. It is rather significant that at this stage not one of us (except Sir Edward Carson) contemplated Mr. Asquith's retirement and consequently there was nothing said at any of our interviews as to his possible successor. I wish to confirm Lord Beaverbrook's statement that Lord Northcliffe was never, at any stage, brought into our consultations. He had taken sides with Sir William Robertson against me on my criticism of the military chiefs for the prolongation of the Somme fighting and the failure to avert the Roumanian collapse. He had threatened to attack me in his papers if I continued "to interfere with the soldiers." When he saw that something was going on, he made an effort to resume friendly relations. But he was not only left out of the negotiations, but as far as I know he was not informed as to what was actually taking place.

After a good deal of conferring and debating between Mr. Bonar Law, Sir Edward Carson, Lord Beaverbrook and myself, I drew up the following memorandum for submission to the Prime Minister:

"1st December, 1916.

"1. That the War Committee consist of three members — two of whom must be the First Lord of the Admiralty and the Secretary of State for War, who should have in their offices deputies capable of attending to and deciding all departmental business, and a third Minister without portfolio. One of the three to be Chairman.

"2. That the War Committee shall have full powers, subject to the supreme control of the Prime Minister, to direct all questions connected with the war.

"3. The Prime Minister in his discretion to have the power to refer any question to the Cabinet.

"4. Unless the Cabinet on reference by the Prime Minister

reverses decision of the War Committee, that decision to be carried out by the Department concerned.

"5. The War Committee to have the power to invite any Minister, and to summon the expert advisers and officers of any Department to its meetings."

I showed it to Lord Derby, who fully approved of its terms.

I then took it to Mr. Asquith, having first of all explained to him fully the reasons that had prompted me to come to the conclusions embodied in my memorandum. He promised to think it over and let me know his view later on in the day. In the evening I received from him the following letter:

"10, Downing Street,
1st December, 1916.

"My dear Lloyd George,

"I have now had time to reflect on our conversation this morning, and to study your memorandum.

"Though I do not altogether share your dark estimate and forecast of the situation, actual and prospective, I am in complete agreement that we have reached a critical situation in the War, and that our own methods of procedure, with the experience which we have gained during the last few months, call for reconsideration and revision.

"The two main defects of the War Committee, which has done excellent work, are (1) that its numbers are too large; (2) that there is delay, evasion, and often obstruction, on the part of the Departments in giving effect to its decision. I might with good reason add (3) that it is often kept in ignorance by the Departments of information, essential and even vital, of a technical kind, upon the problems that come before it, and (4) that it is overcharged with duties, many of subordinate bodies.

"The result is that I am clearly of opinion that the War Committee should be reconstituted, and its relations to and authority over the Departments be more clearly defined and more effectively asserted.

"I come now to your specific proposals. In my opinion, whatever changes are made in the composition or functions of the War Committee, the Prime Minister must be its Chairman. He cannot be relegated to the position of an arbiter in the background or a referee to the Cabinet.

"In regard to its composition, I agree that the War Secretary and the First Lord of the Admiralty are necessary members. I am inclined to add to the same category the Minister of Munitions. There should be another member, either without portfolio, or charged only with comparatively light departmental duties. One of the members should be appointed Vice-Chairman.

"I purposely do not in this letter discuss the delicate and difficult question of personnel.

"The committee should, as far as possible, sit *de die in diem,* and have full power to see that its decisions (subject to appeal to the Cabinet) are carried out promptly and effectively by the Departments.

"The reconstitution of the War Committee should be accompanied by the setting up of a Committee of National Organisation to deal with the purely domestic side of war problems. It should have executive powers within its own domain.

"The Cabinet would in all cases have ultimate authority.

Yours always sincerely,

H. H. Asquith."

The reply was entirely unsatisfactory. The Prime Minister's counter proposal would effect no improvement and hardly any change in the position as it stood. The Prime Minister was to preside over the Committee and any Ministers dissatisfied with any of its decisions were entitled to appeal to the Cabinet before any steps were taken to carry them out. Then what about the Committee of National Organisation which was to be set up quite independently of the War Committee to deal with the purely domestic side of war problems?

(1) Would food production and distribution be relegated to it?

(2) What about shipping and shipbuilding?

(3) Would the question of man power be left to it?

If these questions were taken out of the cognisance and authority of the War Committee it would have a more limited scope and less power than the existing body of that name. I felt convinced that Mr. Asquith was resolved not to agree to any change in the war direction. I therefore decided to act without further loss of time and I wrote to Mr. Bonar Law as follows:

"War Office, Whitehall, S. W.
2nd December, 1916.

"My dear Bonar,

"I enclose copy of P.M.'s letter.

"The life of the country depends on resolute action by you now.

Yours ever,
D. Lloyd George."

I had seen Mr. Bonar Law late on Friday evening and it was decided that we should go forward with our plan of reorganisation whatever the consequences. On Saturday and Sunday Mr. Bonar Law was entangled in a series of clumsy manœuvres in which his Conservative colleagues were engaged. They had lost confidence in Asquith, but they did not want me. They disliked Carson and had no fanatical belief in Bonar Law. What were the poor fellows to do? They had no clear idea themselves. The story is told in detail by Lord Beaverbrook. Much of what he relates I learnt for the first time when I read his book. I could make no further progress until Mr. Bonar Law knew exactly where he stood in reference to the other leaders of his party. However, on Sunday afternoon I was asked by the Prime Minister's secretary — Sir Maurice Bonham Carter — to come up from the country to talk things over with his Chief, who was returning from Walmer Castle specially with that object. At the interview which ensued, Mr. Asquith and I discussed the whole situation in the friendliest spirit and ultimately came to a complete understanding. The terms of that arrangement are given by Mr. Asquith in the letter he wrote me the following morning. As soon as the agreement was reached he sent for Mr. Bonar Law to inform him of the "complete agreement" arrived at. I met Mr. Bonar Law on my way out. The Prime Minister and I were to meet on Monday to discuss the personnel of the new committee. On that question I anticipated no insuperable difficulty. The Monday meeting never came off and I was never privileged to meet Mr. Asquith as Prime Minister again.

In the Monday morning papers there appeared the following announcement:

"The Prime Minister, with a view to the most active prosecution of the War, has decided to advise His Majesty the King to consent to a reconstruction of the Government."

Some time in the course of the morning I received the following letter from the Prime Minister:

"10, Downing Street, S.W.,
4th December, 1916.

"My dear Lloyd George:

"Such productions as the first leading article in to-day's *Times*, showing the infinite possibilities for misunderstanding and misrepresentation of such an arrangement as we considered yesterday, made me at least doubtful as to its feasibility. Unless the impression is at once corrected that I am being relegated to the position of an irresponsible spectator of the War, I cannot go on.

"The suggested arrangement was to the following effect: The Prime Minister to have supreme and effective control of war policy.

"The agenda of the War Committee will be submitted to him; its Chairman will report to him daily; he can direct it to consider particular topics or proposals; and all its conclusions will be subject to his approval or veto. He can, of course, at his own discretion attend meetings of the Committee.

Yours sincerely,
H. H. ASQUITH."

When I read that letter I felt the Prime Minister had completely changed his tone. There was none of the cordiality and friendliness which had characterised our Sunday conversation. I had not seen the *Times* article of which he complained and I certainly had no responsibility for it. I had not communicated any information as to the negotiations which were going on with Mr. Asquith or the agreement arrived at with him to the proprietor or editor of that paper either directly or indirectly.[1] I was frankly too pleased with the idea that a break had been averted on terms which gave some chance of putting new energy into our war activities to do anything that would imperil the completion of the new arrangement. I replied:

"War Office,
Whitehall, S.W.,
December 4, 1916.

"My dear Prime Minister,

"I have not seen the *Times* article. But I hope you will not attach undue importance to these effusions. I have had these misrepresentations to put up with for months. Northcliffe frankly wants a smash. Derby and I do not. Northcliffe would like to make this and any other rearrangement under your Premiership impossible. Derby and I attach great importance to your retaining your present position — effectively. I cannot restrain, or, I fear, influence Northcliffe. I fully accept in letter and in spirit your summary of the suggested arrangement — subject, of course, to personnel.

Ever sincerely,
D. LLOYD GEORGE."

[1] Lord Beaverbrook makes this quite clear in his narrative of these events. *Vide:* "Politicians and the War."

During that Monday I pressed for my promised appointment with the Prime Minister. I was constantly put off by his secretaries. At last I was promised an interview at six o'clock. That interview was never accorded. Here is a facsimile of a note sent in by my private secretary late in the afternoon to me in my room at the War Office:

"War Office,
Whitehall, S.W.

"Bonham Carter says that the Prime Minister does not think he will trouble you to come over to-night. He is going to write."

Meanwhile the Prime Minister was engaged in a series of interviews with all my colleagues (Liberal and Conservative) who were hostile to the new committee. He even summoned a formal meeting of all the Liberal Members of the Cabinet to discuss the situation. It was to take place at the hour fixed for my interview. Mr. Arthur Henderson was also invited to attend. I received no invitation to attend that meeting to explain my position, although I was still a member of the Cabinet and had done nothing to forfeit my right to be summoned to a conference of the Liberal section. My last act had been to agree with the Prime Minister on the very issue which was to be discussed at the meeting.

On Tuesday morning I received the following letter from the Prime Minister:

"10, Downing Street, S.W.,
December 4, 1916.

"My dear Lloyd George,

"Thank you for your letter of this morning.

"The King gave me to-day authority to ask and accept the resignations of all my colleagues, and to form a new Government on such lines as I should submit to him. I start, therefore, with a clean slate.

"The first question which I have to consider is the constitution of the new War Committee.

"After full consideration of the matter in all its aspects, I have come decidedly to the conclusion that it is not possible that such a Committee could be made workable and effective without the Prime Minister as its Chairman. I quite agree that it will be necessary for him, in view of the other calls upon his time and energy, to delegate from time to time the chairmanship to another Minister as his representative and *locum tenens;* but (if he is to retain the authority, which corresponds to his responsibility, as Prime Minister) he must continue to be, as he always has been, its permanent President. I am satisfied, on reflection, that any other arrangement (such, for instance, as the one which was indicated to you in my letter of to-day) would be found in experience impracticable, and incompatible with the retention of the Prime Minister's final and supreme control.

"The other question, which you have raised, relates to the personnel of the Committee. Here again, after deliberate consideration, I find myself unable to agree with some of your suggestions.

"I think we both agree that the First Lord of the Admiralty, must, of necessity, be a member of the Committee.

"I cannot (as I told you yesterday) be a party to any suggestion that Mr. Balfour should be displaced. The technical side of the Board of Admiralty has been reconstituted, with Sir John Jellicoe as First Sea Lord. I believe Mr. Balfour to be, under existing conditions, the necessary head of the Board.

"I must add that Sir Edward Carson (for whom personally, and in every other way, I have the greatest regard) is not, from the only point of view which is significant to me (namely, the most effective prosecution of the war), the man best qualified among my colleagues, present and past, to be a member of the War Committee.

"I have only to say, in conclusion, that I am strongly of opinion that the War Committee (without any disparagement of the existing Committee, which, in my judgment, is a most efficient body, and has done, and is doing, invaluable work) ought to be reduced in number; so that it can sit more frequently, and overtake more easily the daily problems with which it has to deal. But in any reconstruction of the Committee, such as I have, and have for some time past had, in view, the governing consideration, to my mind, is the special capacity of the men who are to sit on it for the work which it has to do.

"That is a question which I must reserve for myself to decide.

Yours very sincerely,

H. H. ASQUITH."

The letter was a complete repudiation of the agreement he had entered into with me on Sunday and confirmed in writing on Monday. He had reached his decision to go back on his word without giving me an opportunity of further discussion with him. He saw all the critics. He resolutely refused to see me although he had promised to do so. Had I gone back on my word I know the nature of the comment that would have been passed on me by those who worked with frenzy to persuade Mr. Asquith to break faith. How it would have fitted into the legend of distrust which they so assiduously worked up for years, and which seems to be their sole article of unwavering faith!

I therefore felt bound to send him the following reply:

"War Office,
Whitehall, S.W.,
December 5, 1916.

"My dear Prime Minister,

"I have received your letter with some surprise. On Friday I made proposals which involved not merely your retention of the Premiership, but the supreme control of the War, whilst the executive functions, subject to that supreme control, were left to others. I thought you then received these suggestions favourably. In fact, you yourself proposed that I should be the chairman of this Executive Committee, although, as you know, I never put forward that demand. On Saturday you wrote me a letter in which you completely went back on that proposition. You sent for me on Sunday and put before me other proposals; these proposals you embodied in a letter to me written on Monday:

" 'The Prime Minister to have supreme and effective control of war policy;

" 'The agenda of the War Committee will be submitted to him; its chairman will report to him daily; he can direct it to consider particular topics or proposals and all its conclusions will be subject to his approval or veto. He can, of course, at his own discretion attend meetings of the Committee.'

"These proposals safeguarded your position and power as Prime Minister in every particular. I immediately wrote you accepting them 'in letter and in spirit.' It is true that on Sunday I expressed views as to the constitution of the Committee, but these were for discussion. To-day you have gone back on your own proposals.

"I have striven my utmost to cure the obvious defects of the War Committee without overthrowing the Government. As you are aware, on several occasions during the last two years I have deemed it my duty to express profound dissatisfaction with the Government's method of conducting the war. Many a time, with the road to victory open in front of us, we have delayed and hesitated whilst the enemy were erecting barriers that finally checked the approach. There has been delay, hesitation, lack of forethought and vision. I have endeavoured repeatedly to warn the Government of the dangers, both verbally and in written memoranda and letters, which I crave your leave now to publish if my action is challenged; but I have either failed to secure decisions or I have secured them when it was too late to avert the evils. The latest illustration is our lamentable failure to give timely support to Roumania.

"I have more than once asked to be released from my responsibility for a policy with which I was in thorough disagreement, but at your urgent personal request I remained in the Government. I realise that when the country is in peril of a great war, Ministers have not the same freedom to resign on disagreement. At the same time I have always felt — and felt deeply — that I was in a false position inasmuch as I could never defend in a whole-hearted manner the action of a Government of which I was a member. We have thrown away opportunity after opportunity, and I am convinced, after deep and anxious reflection, that it is my duty to leave the Government in order to inform the people of the real condition of affairs, and to give them an opportunity, before it is too late, to save their native land from a disaster which is inevitable if the present methods are longer persisted in. As all delay is fatal in war, I place my office without further parley at your disposal.

"It is with great personal regret that I have come to this conclusion. In spite of mean and unworthy insinuations to the contrary — insinuations which I fear are always inevitable in the case of men who hold prominent but not primary positions in any administration — I have felt a strong personal attachment to you as my Chief. As you yourself said on Sunday, we have acted together for ten years and never had a quarrel, although we have had many a grave difference on questions of policy. You have treated me with great courtesy and kindness; for all that I thank you. Nothing would have induced me to part now except an overwhelming sense that the course of action which has been pursued has put the country — and not merely the country, but throughout the world, the principles for which you and I have always stood through our political lives — in the greatest peril that has ever overtaken them.

"As I am fully conscious of the importance of preserving national unity, I propose to give your Government complete support in the vigorous prosecution of the War; but unity without action is nothing but futile carnage, and I cannot be responsible for that. Vigour and vision are the supreme need at this hour.

Yours sincerely,

D. LLOYD GEORGE."

His reply and the further correspondence that ensued will explain the progress of events that terminated the life of the Asquith Coalition.

"10, Downing Street, S.W.,
December 5, 1916.

"My dear Lloyd George,

"I need not tell you that I have read your letter of to-day with much regret.

"I do not comment upon it for the moment, except to say that I cannot wholly accept your account of what passed between us in regard to my connection with the War Committee. In particular, you have omitted to quote the first and most material part of my letter of yesterday.

Yours very sincerely,
H. H. ASQUITH."

"In the meantime, I feel sure that you will see the obvious necessity in the public interest of not publishing at this moment any part of our correspondence."

"War Office, Whitehall, S.W.,
December 5, 1916.

"My dear Prime Minister,

"I cannot announce my resignation without assigning the reason. Your request that I should not publish the correspondence that led up to and necessitated it places me therefore in an embarrassing and unfair position. I must give reasons for the grave step I have taken. If you forbid publication of the correspondence, do you object to my stating in another form my version of the causes that led to my resigning?

Yours sincerely,
D. LLOYD GEORGE."

"As to the first part of your letter, the publication of the letters would cover the whole ground."

"10, Downing Street, S.W.,
December 5, 1916.

"My dear Lloyd George,

"It may make a difference to you (in reply to your last letter) if I tell you at once that I have tendered my resignation to the King.

"In any case, I should deprecate in the public interest the publication in its present form at this moment of your letters to me of this morning.

"Of course, I have neither the power nor the wish to prevent your stating in some other form the causes which have led you to take the step which you have taken.

Yours very sincerely,

H. H. ASQUITH."

On Mr. Asquith's resignation Mr. Bonar Law was summoned by the King and entrusted with the task of forming an Administration. His first suggestion to the Sovereign was that he should summon some of the leading figures in the recent discussions with Mr. Balfour and Mr. Henderson to Buckingham Palace to see whether it was not possible to avoid any break in the unity of the nation by constituting a National Government under the leadership of Mr. Balfour. It is now a matter of history how we expressed our readiness to serve under Mr. Balfour — all of us except Mr. Asquith, who asked indignantly: "What is the proposal? That I who have held first place for eight years should be asked to take a secondary position." This broke up the Conference. Mr. Asquith subsequently refused to serve in a Bonar Law Administration. Mr. Bonar Law then declined to undertake the responsibility of forming a Ministry and recommended the King to send for me. This course he took in spite of the advice given him to the contrary by Mr. Balfour, Sir Edward Carson, and myself. I neither sought nor desired the Premiership. I knew that in the circumstances my elevation to that position would be skilfully misrepresented and I also knew that a War Committee in a Bonar Law Administration from which the obstructive elements had been kept out had an excellent chance of working smoothly and effectively and I felt confident that Mr. Bonar Law would give me a free hand and extend to me the support of a loyal chief, which was all

I desired. However, Mr. Bonar Law refused to listen to our combined entreaties, and I had to undertake the terrible responsibility of Premiership in a muddled war, with at least half my own party and more than half the Labour Party bitterly hostile, and a considerable section of the Tory Party — including most of their leaders — suspicious and distrustful.

I surveyed the possibilities. I was assured of the support of something under one half the Liberal Members in the House. Every Conservative Minister in the Government, except Mr. Bonar Law, and as I subsequently discovered, Mr. Balfour, was hostile to my Premiership. The attitude of Labour was doubtful, but not altogether antagonistic. I was satisfied that I would receive the active coöperation of Mr. Bonar Law and Sir Edward Carson (much the most influential leaders in the Conservative Party as far as its rank and file was concerned) and Lord Milner — who carried great weight with the Tory intelligentsia and Die-Hards (not by any means identical groups). If I secured the adhesion of Mr. Balfour I felt that I could risk the opposition of the other Conservative mandarins. I felt he had neither the energy, initiative, nor the administrative gifts requisite for the position of First Lord of the Admiralty at such a critical moment. His elimination from the Admiralty was an unwritten demand I had submitted to Mr. Asquith. Mr. Balfour had been told by Mr. Asquith of the adverse view I had formed of his administration of the Navy, and of my request for his removal. Nevertheless, I have since discovered that he supported my demand for a change in the war direction and refused to join in a reconstruction of the Ministry under Mr. Asquith.

As he said in letters written at the time to the Prime Minister, after he had been informed of my objection to his retaining office at the Admiralty: "We cannot, I think, go on in the old way. I still think (*a*) that the break-up of the Government by the retirement of Lloyd George would be a misfortune; (*b*) that the experiment of giving him a free hand with the day-to-day work of the War Committee is worth trying; and (*c*) that there is no use trying it except on terms which would enable him to work under conditions which in his own opinion promise the best results." He ended by insisting that his resignation should be accepted and "that a fair trial should be given to the new War Council *à la* George."

I knew nothing of these letters at the time. I only knew that I tried to get Mr. Balfour out of the Admiralty and that as this disagreeable fact would in all probability be communicated to him, an approach to him under these conditions was not very hopeful. I confess that I underrated the passionate attachment to his country which burnt under that calm, indifferent, and apparently frigid exterior.

Mr. Balfour was then ill in bed. Mr. Bonar Law undertook to sound him. He went to offer him the post of Foreign Secretary. He accepted it without any of the hesitations and portentous declarations of his patriotic duty which smaller and less sincere men might have indulged in — and later on did. But as Mr. Bonar Law was leaving, Mr. Balfour suddenly turned to him and said: "Would you mind telling me why Lloyd George was so anxious to get me out of the Admiralty?" Mr. Bonar Law answered with his usual bluntness: "You had better ask him yourself."

Quite recently I discovered that my objections to his retaining office at the Admiralty were a source of hurtful perplexity to him up to his last days. He thought I resented the report he issued to the Press of the much debated battle of Jutland. That report undoubtedly conveyed the impression even to friendly minds that the victory was debatable. My reasons for thinking he was not the best selection for the

Admiralty had no reference to this episode. The First Lord during a Great War ought to be a man of exhaustless industry and therefore of great physical energy and reserve. It was an office that called for unceasing attention to detail. It meant long hours, early and late. Mr. Balfour was obviously unsuitable for such a post.

As I have mentioned previously, the story of the first five days of December, 1916, and the efforts I made to bring about a new system in the direction of war — efforts which, quite contrary to my desire and intention, culminated in a change of Government and the retirement of Mr. Asquith — has already been told very graphically and in considerable detail by Lord Beaverbrook in the second volume of his "Politicians and the War." His account presents the story from the point of view of himself and of Mr. Bonar Law. Naturally, the events were seen by me at the time from a somewhat different angle, but there is no difference of substance between us as to the main features and stages of that crisis.

There was a tragic bitterness about the situation which developed through those days, and which forced a cleavage between me and colleagues with most of whom I had for long years been working in the happiest and most fruitful collaboration — a cleavage later on aggravated and perpetuated by the malice of petty-minded men with baneful effects on the future political development of our country. But even at the worst it had its brighter aspects. One was that it brought Mr. Bonar Law and myself into a close partnership, and laid the foundations of a mutual understanding and real friendship which is one of the happiest of my political memories.

From the moment I was invited by the King to form a Government I was so overwhelmed with urgent affairs, which brooked no delay, that I found no opportunity for presenting to the public my reasons for the course of action which ended in the downfall of the Asquith Administration. It was not merely the time occupied in the actual formation of the Government. That took a few days of interviewing, negotiating and adjusting.

And here I would like to pay a tribute to the tact, the wisdom and loyalty with which both Mr. Bonar Law and I were assisted in this difficult and even dangerous task by Sir Edmund Talbot (now Lord FitzAlan). He smoothed many difficulties and probably averted many indiscretions.

The moment the Government was formed there were many pressing matters to attend to which ought to have been settled many months ago. The campaign for 1917 had already been settled before I became Prime Minister. But there were many urgent questions which demanded immediate decision and prompt action. The production of aëroplanes — the food supplies of the country — the protection of our ships and the development of shipbuilding — the better mobilisation of the man-power of this country — the mission to Russia, too long delayed — the German peace move — and afterwards President Wilson's Peace Notes; these constituted but a part of the calls upon the attention of the War Cabinet. In these circumstances Mr. Bonar Law and I could not enter into a controversy upon the causes that led to the recent crisis. Apart from that consideration, we came to the conclusion that it was not desirable to have discussions upon personal matters which might endanger the national unity and imperil national coöperation. Neither of us therefore issued any statement on the subject. Had we done so we knew we could not have left it there, as we should have been bound to reply to inevitable criticisms and comments from those who were now freed from the cares and burden of office and who had more time, and, as it turned out, more inclination to dwell upon these things.

As far as Mr. Bonar Law was concerned the decision was probably the right one. But there is no doubt that my influence in the Liberal Party suffered severely from my neglect to put my case before opinions had hardened and prejudices had been created. Misrepresentations were soon broadcast throughout the land, and time was given for them to strike root in the soil, and when I regained leisure it was too late to eradicate them. Most of this work was done privately at confidential gatherings of Liberal associations throughout the country. Missionaries were dispatched from headquarters at Abingdon Street to every district to spread tendencious reports of the origin, motives and methods of the crisis. At secret conclaves much could be said which the presence of a newspaper reporter would have checked. Some salient facts were suppressed; others were distorted, and when I resumed my political activities after the War was over I was amazed at the beliefs that were current as to what had really happened. When I asked Mr. Asquith for permission to publish the correspondence, he had, as is shown in the above correspondence, refused to accede to my request on public grounds; I was rather surprised to find, when he came to address Liberal Members a few days after his resignation and to explain to them why he resigned, that he summarised some of the passages from his own letters and actually quoted some in full, whilst he omitted altogether to communicate to his hearers the statements I made in reply. His reason for doing so was:

"I will not read his letter because it is private; it was written very confidentially."

He did not think it necessary in the interest of fair play to explain that I had asked him for permission to publish my letter, and that he had refused. He conveyed the impression to them that the Sunday agreement was not an agreement at all, but merely a proposal for further discussion. He never informed them that he told Mr. Bonar Law after our Sunday interview that he and I had agreed on terms, and that the only question left for further debate was that of personnel; that he had made the same statement that very evening to the late Mr. Montagu and to Lord Reading. He never informed the meeting that on Monday I had repeatedly asked to see him and that he had declined to give me an interview, nor did he inform them of the important fact that a meeting of all the Liberal Members of the Cabinet had been summoned on Monday night to consider the position and that I had not been invited to attend the meeting. He withheld from them the fact that at a conference at Buckingham Palace presided over by the King he had refused to serve in a National Ministry under the Premiership of Mr. Balfour, although Mr. Bonar Law, Mr. Henderson and myself were quite prepared to do so. Nor did he tell them that when Mr. Bonar Law was entrusted with the task of forming a National Government he had refused, after consultation with his Liberal colleagues, to join it. It was obvious that if these vital facts had been communicated to those Members who had assembled at the Reform Club, they would have taken a different view of the transaction. Unfortunately, we allowed a very one-sided statement to go by default, and the truncated statement, because it was unchallenged, was accepted by the majority of Liberals in the country as a fair account of what had happened.

I will give only one example of the kind of thing which influenced Liberals against me at that time. Here is a speech delivered by Mr. Runciman to his constituents immediately after he left office:

"In reforming the Government the present Prime Minister invited his Unionist colleagues to rejoin him. He invited the Labour Party to join him, and he gave an invitation to one

Liberal Minister. I was not that one. I have been asked by my constituents already why I did not join the new Government. I can only make the simple reply that it was impossible to accept an invitation which I had not received."[1]

Surely there never has been a better example of *suppressio veri*. Had Mr. Runciman told his constituents that he was one of those who had agreed at the meeting of Liberal Ministers on Monday night not to take office under anyone except Mr. Asquith, and that at the meeting when that decision was reached the question of my Premiership was discussed as the alternative; had he informed them that he was one of those who advised Mr. Asquith not to serve under any other Premier, quite a different impression would have been conveyed to the minds of his electors. He clearly wished them to believe that whereas I was inviting Conservative and Labour men to join my Government, I wantonly and deliberately ruled out all my former colleagues except one.

[1] How busy I was may be inferred from the fact that I read the speeches of Mr. Asquith and Mr. Runciman for the first time when I came to write this story.

CHAPTER XIX

SOME PERSONAL SKETCHES

1. Mr. Asquith

Temperament of a judge — Great intellectual gifts — Judicial but not constructive — A great peace-time Premier — Part of the politician in war — Qualities needed for war-time statesmanship — Mr. Asquith's decline of vigour.

I recollect Lord Morley once saying to me: "Asquith ought to have been a judge. He would have made a great one. I remember," he said, "a conversation I had recently with Arthur Acland about early days when Acland, Asquith and I used to meet together often to discuss politics and I said what a pleasant fellow he was. Acland replied, 'Yes, but did you ever hear him make any suggestions of his own?' I had to confess that although he discussed every proposition advanced by others with great intelligence and force, he never submitted any ideas of his own for our consideration." Asquith undoubtedly had not only the mind, but the temperament of a judge. I hardly ever met him before we entered the same Cabinet together. But during the eleven years we were members of the same Governments — Campbell-Bannerman's and his own Administration — I had ample opportunities of seeing him. I always had an unqualified admiration for his unrivalled gifts of lucid and logical statement — his command of choice words and his sledge-hammer rhetoric. When I came to know him as a colleague and especially when I served under him as my Chief, my admiration widened and deepened. His massive and well-ordered intellect worked with the precision and directness of a perfect and powerful machine. But he waited until propositions were submitted to him. He never drove or initiated, he decided on schemes when they were placed before him. He never surveyed the needs of the country and devised means for supplying them, in peace or war. He dealt with questions not as they arose but as they were presented to him. But there his judgment was beyond that of any political leader I ever met. He started no new plans, but he was not afraid of examining any projects if they were placed before him clearly, and left on his logical mind an impression of having been well-considered beforehand. He was always essentially the judge. When he accepted a plan he used his great authority to obtain for it Cabinet sanction. And when it came to commending the scheme to the acceptance of the House of Commons, there was such inevitability in the presentation that it left critics wondering why they ever doubted. Such a mind was invaluable in the conduct of affairs when peace reigned and there were no emergencies demanding originality, resource and initiative. It was specially useful for a Cabinet where there were several able men full of ideas to which they were anxious to give administrative or legislative effect. But for the deluge, Noah was better adapted than Gamaliel would have been. Had there been no war, the Asquith Administration would to the end have stood as high in the annals of wise, fruitful and beneficent rule as any Government that ever existed in this country, and its capable chief would have been a worthy figure on the pedestal of distinguished achievements, which, by his special gifts, he had made possible. Such a pedestal he will always occupy. The 1906–14 Cabinet was one of the ablest councils that ever directed the affairs of any great country in times of peace.

But war demands other attributes. The part which political chiefs ought to take in the conduct of a war is a very debatable question. The line of demarcation has never been drawn, probably because there ought not to be any rigid line. So much depends on conditions, which are never alike in any two wars and vary and fluctuate from time to time in the course of the same war. So much also depends on the personalities engaged, whether civilian or military. Lincoln interfered a good deal with McClellan, but he gave Grant a free hand. There never has been a war where civilian action and impulse were so essential to success as the Great War of 1914–18.

In these volumes I have indicated directions in which civilian aid in the organisation of our military strength was found to be indispensable, and some where civilian advice taken in time might have averted disaster. There are certain indispensable qualities essential to the Chief Minister of the Crown in a great war. I do not propose to give an exhaustive schedule of these essential qualities, but such a Minister must have courage, composure, and judgment. All this Mr. Asquith possessed in a superlative degree. He gave dignified but not rousing and vigorous leadership to the nation. But a War Minister must also have vision, imagination and initiative — he must show untiring assiduity, must exercise constant oversight and supervision of every sphere of war activity, must possess driving force to energise this activity, must be in continuous consultation with experts, official and unofficial, as to the best means of utilising the resources of the country in conjunction with Allies for the achievement of victory. If to this can be added a flair for conducting a great fight, then you have an ideal War Minister. Mr. Asquith at his best did not answer sufficiently to this description to make him a successful Chief Minister in a war which demanded all these qualities strained to the utmost. But apart from these shortcomings the nerve of the Prime Minister at this time was clearly giving out, and he gave the impression of a man who was overwhelmed, distracted and enfeebled not merely by the weight, but by the variety and complexity of his burdens. Whether he was ever fitted for the position of a War Minister in the greatest struggle in the history of the world may be open to doubt, but that he was quite unfitted at this juncture to undertake so supreme a task was not open to any question or challenge on the part of anyone who came constantly in contact with him at the time.

Asquith's will became visibly flabbier, tardier and more flaccid under the strain of the war. Then came the personal tragedy which shattered his nerve. The death of his brilliant son — Raymond — came upon him with stunning effect, and he visibly reeled under the blow. It came at a time when he needed all the calm poise and firmness of mind which man can command. For a crisis had arisen where statesmanship had to intervene, decide and direct. It was a misfortune for Britain that the great statesman who had the supreme responsibility was less equal to his task than he had ever been in the whole course of his distinguished career. Mr. Bonar Law, who was well disposed to him, was of that opinion and expressed it repeatedly in the course of the conversations I held with him.

2. Lord Haldane

Best War Minister since Cardwell — False repute for intrigue — Last memories.

Haldane was a baffling personality. In private he talked incessantly — in public he talked volubly and at interminable length on any subject. His speaking was a rapid, thin stream of involved wordiness tinkling along monotonously. Nevertheless, with all his loquaciousness he was a doer of things. He was essentially a man of ideas which he carried out, but could not explain succinctly. That accounted for his wordiness. In spite of that defect, this garrulous lawyer was a man of action. There was one gathering at which he hardly ever spoke, and that was the Cabinet. He was almost its most silent member. He was by common agreement the best War Minister since Cardwell. He organised the Expeditionary Force which helped to save Paris; he founded the Territorial Army which helped the remnants of our regular army to hold the sodden trenches of Flanders until the new recruits arrived; he was responsible for the Officers' Cadet Corps which gave the Kitchener Army its intelligent young lieutenants; it was he who had the idea that the War Office would be all the better if it had a thinking machine and so he worked out a General Staff. It was no fault of his that Lord Kitchener decided to dispense with it. On Education he was full of practical suggestions, some of which fructified. He had boundless energy. He always wanted to be doing something. A combination of ideas and energy is tiresome to the complacent. He was, therefore, viewed with distrust by that class of politician. Once Haldane had an idea he worked without cease and resorted to every device and expedient to put it through. The sterile and the indolent cannot distinguish between intrigue and action — so Haldane passed for an intriguer. Of all the great political personalities he was the kindliest I met. Although I liked him well, I was never one of his special friends. We belonged to different, and at one time, very antagonistic sections of the Party. He was a "Liberal Imp" and I was a "pro-Boer." But his abandonment by men who were his devoted friends — at least by men to whom he was devoted — at the instigation of the fussy and noisy patriots that always dance around the flag as if they owned it, was one of the meanest betrayals of British history.

The British people are fundamentally just. Had his powerful friends stood up for him, pointed out his record of service to his country in this war, shown how flimsy were the imputations of unpatriotic leanings against him,

Photo. by Walter Stoneman

VISCOUNT HALDANE OF CLOAN, O.M.

there would have been a reaction in his favour, and the Tory leaders could not have dared to refuse coöperation because the man who organised the Expeditionary Force and the Territorials remained in the Government. Haldane was a brave and unselfish man. He never whined or complained about his treatment. All the same, it shook him. I rarely saw him after he left office. But I have the memory of seeing a man bent and bowed, walking slowly from his house in Queen Anne's Gate towards the Privy Council, where he sat as a judge.

3. Lord Balfour

Reputation as Irish Secretary — Battle over Education Bill — Vagueness in Tariff Reform controversy — An Elder Statesman — Knack of stating both sides — Balfour and Clemenceau — Capacity for decision — Fearless but irresolute at Admiralty — A good Foreign Secretary.

When I first saw Mr. Balfour he was at the height of his popularity and unpopularity. It was when I entered the House of Commons in 1890. He was then easily the most acclaimed statesman on the Unionist side of the House and it follows that he was the most detested figure amongst the Home Rulers. To the former he was the embodiment of strength and to the latter the incarnation of brutality. The ruthlessness with which he ruled Ireland would not have given him his parliamentary preëminence had it not been accompanied by consummate dexterity in defending his actions on the floor of the House. He was confronted by a phalanx of brilliant Irish speakers who commanded every weapon of effective parliamentary criticism — eloquence, humour and invective — not forgetting imagination. With these weapons they had pierced and slashed all his predecessors and left them bleeding, exhausted and disfigured. Mr. Balfour proved to be more than a match for the best and for all of them. He beat them at the game at which they were such masters. I am told that on the platform he was always a halting and ineffective speaker, but from 1887 up to the end of his Premiership in 1905 he was the most skilful of all the House of Commons speakers of his day, with the exception of the greatest of all parliamentary gladiators — Mr. Gladstone. My first encounter with him was in the Session of 1902. He piloted through the House of Commons a measure which provoked the most protracted resistance ever offered up to that time to any Bill — the Education Act of 1902. Day after day for the better part of six months Mr. Balfour piloted this Bill through the House against a pertinacious opposition in which I constituted one of the most tireless and tiresome elements. At the end of the struggle we were friends. That friendship I retained and valued to the end of his days.

His weakness as a democratic leader came out in the Free Trade controversy of 1903–06. His mentality was too detached for the zeal that is born of unquestioning faith without facts. He did not believe that tariffs would ruin our commerce. Neither had he any fervid conviction that they would enhance our prosperity. In his heart he thought the protagonists on both sides were exaggerating their case. As fully as 90 per cent. of his party were enthusiastic supporters of Mr. Chamberlain's protectionist proposals, a statesman who took Mr. Balfour's point of view could offer but indifferent leadership in the raging and tearing propaganda which alone could bring victory to the lot of his party in such a cause. The defeat of 1906 was virtually the end of his leadership. He lingered on as a nominal but distrusted leader until the two disastrous elections of 1910 drove him out, with a savage howl from the die-hard jungle at his heels. He then retired gracefully and finally to the honoured seclusion of Elder Statesmanship. In this capacity he rendered more enduring service to his country than in the more dazzling positions he had hitherto held. His achieve-

Photo. by G. C. Beresford

THE EARL OF BALFOUR, K.G., O.M.

ments in this rôle culminated with the Washington Conference of 1922, when he represented Britain at the first (and so far the only) Disarmament Conference that ever succeeded in disarming.

On many an occasion his vast and varied experience coupled with a discerning and mature intellect illumined counsel in dark days. During the war his unfailing courage steadied faltering spirits in hours of doubt and dread. There were times of weariness, many of depression, a few of genuine dismay during that terrible world conflict. When these occurred I have seen men who were reckoned by their public to be inflexible show signs of bending — but never Mr. Balfour. He was never daunted at the worst moments. It was in council that he revealed his strength and his weakness. He listened intently to all that was said, but since his hearing had become dulled by advancing age he failed some times to catch the words of speakers around the table who either pitched their voices too low or articulated indistinctly — a very elementary and painful fault with most English speakers. Mr. Balfour himself was always clear and resonant. Mr. Bonar Law was an egregious example of the first defect. You could hardly hear him at the Cabinet a yard off. Mr. Balfour would rise from his place and stand by the speaker, and when the latter finished his observations he returned to his seat. When his turn came to express an opinion he carefully and lucidly marshalled the arguments for taking a given course, and anyone not accustomed to his methods would have thought he was weighing in heavily on that side. Then came the inevitable "but on the other hand" and the Cabinet listened to an equally logical and well-informed presentation of the case against. He then paused, threw up his head, looked vaguely at the window and in hesitant tones would say, "But if you ask me what course I think we ought to take then I must say I feel perplexed."

Often have I heard him discuss matters on these lines. He saw both sides too clearly to be able to come readily to a clear conclusion. He gave the impression of a man who thought it really did not matter so much which of the two courses you took so long as you stuck to it afterwards. So therefore it was for us to choose and he would abide by the decision. This kind of mentality baffled and occasionally fretted Clemenceau, the man who never had doubts, not even about religion. I recollect at the Versailles War Council in 1918 an important question being relegated to the Foreign Secretaries for decision. They met and placed Mr. Balfour in the Chair. When the time came for them to report to the Council, M. Clemenceau called upon Mr. Balfour. The latter, as was his wont, gave a string of reasons on both sides and then stopped. M. Clemenceau threw up his heavy eyelashes in astonishment, opened his eyes wide, and said, *"C'est fini?"* Mr. Balfour replied, *"Oui, monsieur."* Then Clemenceau retorted snappishly in English: "But are you for or against?" Mr. Balfour had evidently not decided and seemed unprepared for an answer. Ultimately he reported against.

I know nothing of his habit of mind in the days of his prime. At the time of his famous Irish Secretaryship he must have been capable of prompt and relentless decision. He then displayed all the highest qualities of a man of action, not only in his repressive but in his constructive measures. On Land Settlement, Cottage Holdings, Harbours and Rural Development he was a man who did bold things in Ireland, and some of the poorest areas bear witness to this day of his beneficent thought and action. I was an opponent of certain parts of his great Education Act of 1902. There can be no doubt as to the determination with which he drove through a measure which revolutionised popular education in England and Wales. Even in the later days, when he had not supreme responsibility for the direction of affairs, and when he therefore took things easily, he could now and again rise to the heights of great decisions. His conduct of the Washington Naval Conference in 1921–22 affords indubitable proof of his capacity to decide when he was confronted with a dilemma which he also had the authority to solve. But at committees and Cabinets where he was not called upon to act, the picture I have given of him fairly represents his methods of contributing to discussion. It would be a mistake to infer from this that he was worthless in council. You might as well say that the summing-up of an able judge has no value because it is impartial and gives no direction to the jury as to the verdict they should bring in. He often placed before us considerations on both sides which all the rest of us might have overlooked. His summing-up was looked forward to by all his colleagues as a means of understanding the real points at issue and the strength of the arguments for and against any given decision. His was a trained mind of the finest quality, of the ripest experience, of the greatest penetration, piercing and dissecting problems and laying them bare before his colleagues for their examination and judgment.

I can quite understand why the attribute which made him helpful in council completely disqualified him for party leadership. Yet for all these doubts and hesitancies he was a brave man — and a fearless one. In comparatively small things he shrank from conclusions and thus gave a false impression of irresolution, but on fundamental issues he never flinched or meandered. He was through and through a patriot and never lost confidence in the invincibility of his country. He lacked the physical energy and fertility of resource, and untiring industry for the administration of the Admiralty during the Great War, but even the woeful tale of increasing sinkings of our ships by German submarines and the apparent impotence of the admirals to stop the disastrous process did not daunt him. His one comment after hearing the admirals read out the list of sinkings for the previous day was: "It is very tiresome. These Germans are intolerable." He had no notion how the German attack on our shipping could be circumvented. He only assumed that sooner or later it would be done. Meanwhile, the losses were "tiresome." Clearly he was not the man to stimulate and organise the activity of the Navy in a crisis. But he was an ideal man for the Foreign Office and to assist the Cabinet on big issues. His contributions in the war and afterwards in the making of peace were of the highest order. In personal charm he was easily first amongst all the statesmen with whom I came in contact. As to his intellectual gifts I doubt whether I ever met so illuminating an intelligence inside the Council Chamber.

4. Lord Carson

A great advocate — Critical attitude to Mr. Asquith — Opposed to Dardanelles venture — "Agin the Government" — Value of his criticism.

Driving with Lord Robert Cecil from Paris to Sir Douglas Haig's headquarters, amongst an infinite variety of topics out of which we made conversation, we came to the great advocates of the day. Lord Robert had no hesitation in expressing the opinion that Sir Edward Carson was in his judgment the greatest. I asked him if he had heard Sir Charles Russell. He replied that he had but did not think him equal to Carson. I never heard Sir Edward Carson in the Courts, but for nigh unto a generation I saw and witnessed his methods, and felt his personality in the House of Commons. I could well understand his power over a jury. He had the supreme gift of getting to the point that mattered in the formation of opinion and of presenting and of pressing it with the words, voice and emphasis that moved those who heard him in the direction he wished their sentiments to travel. I could also appreciate the terrible force of his cross-examination, the penetration which enabled him to see the real weakness of

Photo. by Press Portrait Bureau

LORD CARSON OF DUNCAIRN

his opponent's case, the weakness of the story told by the witness and the weakness of the witness himself, the grim and relentless skill to pursue until the prey is at his mercy, and the dramatic force which prostrates or destroys.

I saw something of these gifts in his war contribution. As soon as he joined the Asquith Coalition in 1915 he penetrated all the greatest weaknesses of the war administration and was aware of the fatal defects of the two personalities upon whom the potency of direction must descend — the Prime Minister and Lord Kitchener. There was the Prime Minister's lack of initiative and drive, his inability to apprehend the importance of time in a crisis; Lord Kitchener's absorption in comparatively unimportant details, his failure to grasp such of the problems of the war as were not visible to his eye, the waning of the physical and nervous powers that once gave him energy, and his concealment of his limitations under a cloak of professional secrecy. Cabinets, like Boards of Directors, are mostly composed of those who wish to believe that all is going well with a concern as long as they are responsible for the direction of its affairs. Carson's questions cut through complacency and irritated his colleagues of both parties. He exasperated the Prime Minister, whose almost morbid shrinking from unpleasantness was placed in constant jeopardy by the flourish of his deadly scalpel at every meeting of the Cabinet.

Having got rid of the fearfulness of close association with Sir Edward Carson, Mr. Asquith was reluctant to renew the torment of his presence at the same council. This had something to do with his opposition to the proposals for an independent War Committee put forward by Mr. Bonar Law and myself in December, 1916. The name of Sir Edward Carson had been mentioned. From that moment the idea was doomed to immovable dislike.

Carson was very strongly opposed to the Dardanelles Expedition before he entered the Cabinet, and he never changed his opinion as to the unwisdom of having undertaken that disastrous expedition. But once he was inside the Government and found how deeply we were committed to the undertaking, he saw the importance of carrying it right through with all the forces at the disposal of the Allies. He saw clearly that failure would have a very calamitous effect upon our prestige in the East; that it would encourage the Turks to renewed activity against our forces on the Egyptian fronts and in Mesopotamia; that it strengthened the hold of the pro-German forces in Bulgaria and discouraged Roumania. He also realised that now we had lost Serbia and the Bulgarians had occupied the Balkans, our only chance of cutting off the communications between Turkey and the Central Powers was to open up the Dardanelles and give our fleet access through the Marmora up to the Bosphorus. He therefore felt that the best thing to be done was to proceed with the campaign with the forces adequate to the accomplishment of our task. Herein he also displayed that instinct for realities which was his conspicuous mental quality.

As an exposer of shame, humbug and pretension Sir Edward Carson had no rival. But he had neither the natural gift nor the experience to make a good administrator. Even as a member of the Cabinet he had the fatal defect ingrained by centuries of habit in all men of his race — he was naturally opposed to every Government. Whether in or out of office he was always "agin the Government" for the time being. Sir Henry Wilson suffered from the same unmanageable contrariness.

The Irish have become through centuries of misrule a race of "Aginners." It will take a long experience of successful self-government to eradicate this germ from their nature. Sir Edward was in this, as in other respects, a typical

"Aginner." He resigned from two successive Governments during the war — both of them Governments which at the date of his resignation were receiving the full support of his party. He could not help it. The call of the blood was irresistible.

Still, no one outside the Government could have given criticism such effective voice as he did. Men of less authority, courage and oratorical power would have been brushed aside by Ministers. A whisper as to the obligations of patriotism would have silenced them or deprived them of a hearing. Not so with Sir Edward Carson. I doubt whether Mr. Bonar Law would have taken the final step of threatened disruption had it not been for his fear of the lash of Carson's terrible tongue. Lord Beaverbrook knew this well, and made full use of it to persuade his friend to rise to the greatest opportunity of his career.

5. Mr. Bonar Law

Friendships in politics — Work of mischief makers — Similarities in our early experience — Bonar Law and Asquith — "A Glasgow baillie" — Speaking different languages — Bonar Law's pessimism — His value as a destructive critic — His courage — Reluctance to make decisions — Friendship with Lord Beaverbrook — Tragic bereavements — No taste for music — "I like bridge" — A slave to his pipe — Love of tranquillity.

Mr. Baldwin in a recent speech on Bonar Law said that his coöperation with me during the war was the most perfect partnership in political history. This statement must have seemed extravagant to those not intimately acquainted with the facts. I recollect that when I was on the threshold of my official career I was warned by a very shrewd observer, who had been privileged through a long political life to be on intimate terms with some of the greatest figures in the political world, to bear in mind that "there was no friendship at the top." At the time this observation struck me as being the cynicism of a disillusioned man. I wish that after long years of experience I could write with conviction to-day that his comment was unjustifiable. There is rivalry and jealousy in every profession and business. In politics these are stimulated and accentuated by a constant public discussion of the respective and contrasted merits and defects of the prominent figures on the political stage. These discussions are promoted sometimes by genuine interest in a theme which attracts the public — that of the qualities, good and bad, of its well-known personalities — sometimes by sincere admiration for one above all others of the conspicuous political leaders of the day. The virtues and faculties of political leaders constitute an essential item in the assets of the party to which they belong. It is therefore inevitable that exaggeration of the qualities with which their own chieftains are endowed and depreciation of those which characterise the chiefs of rival classes constituted a method of political warfare.

Too often criticisms and panegyrics are instigated by sheer mischief and malice — one of the great ones has had the misfortune to attract the dislike of a critic, and an effective method of retaliation by malignity is not only to detract from the abilities and achievements of the object of its hatred but to laud the personage who is marked for his rival in public favour. All these causes tend to breed intrigues for exalting one or other of the public men at the expense of the others. Friendship cannot thrive in such an atmosphere. For nearly five years Mr. Bonar Law's friendship for me and mine for him not only survived but grew from year to year. When ill-health drove him from collaboration and companionship, I felt the separation more deeply than any I have endured during my political life. At that time the task of government was so absorbing that those who were not working together soon lost sight of each other and thus drifted apart. Immediately on his retirement he left England for a fairly prolonged stay in the South of France. Neither he nor

From a painting by J. B. Anderson *Photo. by Henry Dixon & Sons Ltd.*

THE RT. HON. ANDREW BONAR LAW

Conservative Party Leader, 1911–1921
Prime Minister 1922–1923

I ever revelled in the delights of correspondence. When he returned from his health sojourn on the Continent he had fallen back on other associations which were distinctly hostile to our friendship. Had I enjoyed more leisure and he less, this remarkable political partnership would only have ended with his tragic death, and many a chapter in the history of Britain, maybe of the world, would have been different from those which have now been written in indelible ink by the pen of Destiny.

There never were two men who constituted such a complete contrast in temperamental and mental equipment. We had nothing in common, except a lowly origin — his father was a Presbyterian minister in a humble manse — mine was a school-teacher in times when the pay of that profession was equal to half the wages of a town scavenger to-day. We had the same stern puritan upbringing. These early influences differentiated us completely from the other leading figures with whom he and I had to work — Mr. Balfour, Lord Curzon, Lord Lansdowne, Lord Derby, Lord Milner, Mr. Churchill, and Sir Edward Grey. They had been reared in another planet, and he and I consciously, or rather unconsciously, must have been brought nearer together by that permeating and permanent influence. Although Mr. Asquith had come from similar stock and the like environment, he strove consistently to quit his early past and to surround himself with the appearance of being a native of another world, to which he really never belonged by origin, disposition or pursuits, and to conform as best he could to these new surroundings. Bonar Law would have disdained such contortions to adjust himself to social conditions he detested and despised.

I recollect Lord Morley telling me that a prominent Jew once said to him that he had striven all his life "to get out of the Ghetto, but had utterly failed to do so!" Mr. Asquith strained painfully and patently to get out of "Bethel"; but although he managed to leave it far behind, he was a stranger and a sojourner in any other home. He was ill at ease with either of Disraeli's Two Nations. He shunned direct contact with the people — neither had he the traditions nor the lure of aristocracy. He never appreciated Bonar Law's mental quality, nor the fine but strong fibre of his character. During a gloomy period of the war, I suggested to Mr. Asquith that the leading members of the Cabinet should meet informally one evening to review the situation and consider what could be done to effect an improvement in the Allied position. He acceded to my suggestion. We discussed names. Every peer and aristocrat in the Cabinet was included by him in the list. I suggested the name of Bonar Law, as he was leader of the Tory Party. He snappily answered, "No; he has the intellect of a Glasgow baillie!" So Bonar Law, the trusted leader of the largest party in the British Parliament, was ruled out of an inter-party consultation on events which might decide the fate of the British Empire and the future course of mankind. He was neither a patrician nor an academician. Neither was he troublesome, as some of us threatened to be. So why bring in this common person to such a select gathering?

This represented Mr. Asquith's general attitude of mind towards Mr. Bonar Law. He did not undervalue his abilities; he placed no value at all upon them. His origin, his training, his equipment, his prejudices, his very appearance and outfit excited every antipathy in Mr. Asquith's mind. When Bonar Law joined the Asquith Coalition Cabinet he did little to dispel impressions of his intellectual inferiority. The problems with which he was confronted were new to him, and at first his comments expressed crudely the opinions of a sensible and able business man on propositions with which he was imperfectly acquainted. It took his virile and logical mind some time to acquire an adequate grip of the terrible complexities of the World War. He did not possess a ready command of the conventional and shallow pomposities with which much less able men cloaked the nakedness of their knowledge and the poverty of their faculties. Mr. Asquith, although himself possessing a powerful and illuminating intelligence and a ready command of adequate phraseology, was always too apt to be impressed by traditional ideas garbed in an appropriate jargon. Bonar Law spoke simply and naturally in the language of a Scottish business man. Thus Mr. Asquith and Mr. Bonar Law never came anywhere near friendly understanding.

There was another reason why Mr. Asquith had a fundamental dislike for Mr. Bonar Law. The latter was by temperament a pessimist. He generally took a gloomy view of the world and its ways. Asquith was a temperamental optimist. "Wait and see!" was the natural expression of a mood confident in the immediate future of all the things in which he was concerned. Things might be obscure and unpleasant for the time being, but wait a little longer and you will see for yourself that all is well even now. He could not bear prophets of gloom anywhere around him.

Bonar Law rather liked to dwell on the difficulties of a project or a prospect. Pessimist as he was by nature he, however, never despaired of our ultimate success in the war, provided the Allies made effective use of their resources. When, during the Asquith Coalition, a scare was being attempted by the puckish Keynes as to the approximate collapse of our financial credit, Bonar Law's practical sagacity came to the rescue of the timorous, and steadied counsel.

Bonar's first impulse, when a project or a prospect was placed before him, was to dwell on its difficulties and dangers. I found that idiosyncrasy useful and even exhilarating. When I had any plans I took them around to him to test them on his doubting and unenthusiastic nature. I started work very early, and immediately after breakfast I habitually walked along the corridor from No. 10 to No. 11 Downing Street for a smoke and a talk with Bonar. We surveyed the morning news and the business of the day. If I had been thinking out any schemes I invariably unfolded them to him before placing them before the War Cabinet. His reaction was always to array all the difficulties and obstacles (generally political) in the way of operating these ideas successfully. He had an incomparable gift of practical criticism. When he had finished marshalling his objections I knew there was nothing more to be said against my plans. Sometimes I felt the force of his adverse criticisms was so great as to be insuperable, and I abandoned the project altogether; at other times I found it necessary to alter or modify the idea in order to meet some obstacle which I had not foreseen but which he had pointed out. But if I came to the conclusion that his objections were not sufficient to deter the Government from initiating and carrying out the particular scheme, I went away strengthened in my resolve as the result of our conversation. On those occasions I said to him. "Well, Bonar, if there is nothing more to be said against this scheme, then I mean to put it before the War Cabinet to-day." He usually acquiesced, as he knew that I never failed to listen to his views and to give full weight to them.

Once I had secured his consent I had no more loyal supporter for my plans.

He possessed real courage. It was not the blind dash of the reckless or the buoyant courage of the sanguine. He anticipated trouble everywhere and every time, and mostly exaggerated it. Nevertheless, he faced it without faltering if it came. He was both fearless and apprehensive. His great phrase in beginning and often in ending an interview was, "There is lots of trouble ahead!" Any manœuvring in the House of Commons, especially amongst the supporters of the Government, worried him. On these occasions, when he was more miserable than usual, I used to say to him, "Let us swop jobs. You can take mine and I will run yours." That generally put an end to the discussion. He shrank from accepting the supreme responsibility for decisions which might be right but which would, if they turned out to be wrong, entail irreparable injury to the interests of the country. During those years, almost every day decisions of that fatefulness had to be taken. A reluctance to decide when there was a serious difference of opinion was a curious defect in so resolute and truly brave a man. But there it undoubtedly was. It was probably due to an inherent diffidence which caused him to distrust his own judgment, coupled with a strong blend of conscientiousness and caution which made him fearful of doing the wrong thing.

His attachment to Lord Beaverbrook was largely, although by no means entirely, attributable to this natural defect. He found a support and a strength in this resolute friend whose practical shrewdness gave him confidence and whose personal devotion he knew to be beyond challenge and question. He thus came to rely upon him in every emergency of his public and private life. His remarkable success in so short a time and in a party so constituted as the Tory Party was undoubtedly due to Beaverbrook's prompting and management. Mr. Bonar Law was not without ambition, but this motive was not strong enough to overcome the hesitancies of so anxious a temperament. Mr. Asquith once said of him that he was "meekly ambitious." Lord Beaverbrook's forceful insistence and unfailing backing cured all that. He shoved him almost brutally to the front. He firmly believed him to be the best man to succeed Mr. Balfour when the latter was driven out of the leadership of the Conservative Party. I was certainly of the same opinion at the time and I had no reason to change my view afterwards.

Tragedy deepened the pessimism of Bonar Law's later years. Once it took root it certainly spread rapidly over his spirit, like a parasite, until it hid the strength of the granite underneath. It must have come from the shocks of a succession of great sorrows which shattered the joy of life and even the desire for life. He lost a wife to whom he was devoted, and the war bereft him of two fine boys whom he adored. A placid life of unchecked success is the best climate in which to grow the plant of a hopeful disposition. Such had been Mr. Bonar Law's life until fate intervened to shrivel it all up.

The brightness of his outlook had seemed unclouded by doubts. I remember meeting him in the corridor of the House of Commons soon after I had introduced my Budget of 1909. He said to me, "Well, you are too late to save your party. If you had a General Election now not more than 50 Liberal Members would be returned for England, and once a Government begins to go down it never recovers." He was then almost childishly optimistic as to the chances of any ventures in which he was engaged, so different from the stricken Bonar of 1916, with the nerve of hope paralysed by the lightnings from a dark cloud. Then he said to me as soon as we were installed in joint authority, "In six months Asquith will be the most popular man in England." His face was set towards the sunset, and he never swung round to the end.

He never seemed to me to have any appreciation of the brighter side of life. When he and I paid a visit to Paris to confer with the French Government I took him in the evening to see that joyous comic opera "La Fille de Madame Angot." I have never seen a man so painfully bored at a performance. He continually left the play for the foyer, where I found him smoking his pipe. When I asked him whether he did not enjoy the performance he said: "It would be quite tolerable if it were not for the singing."

I remember before the war, while we were both staying at Cannes, driving with him on a sunny day along the road to the golf course at Cagnes. The sky was cloudless and the sea was blue as only the Mediterranean can be, while on our left was the white-topped amphitheatre of the Maritime Alps. I turned to Bonar and asked him if he did not think it beautiful. "I don't care much for scenery," he replied in his rather toneless voice. The night before I had been to a performance of one of Mozart's operas — I think it was "Il Seraglio." It was the first time I had heard it and I was struck with its exquisite beauty. I mentioned the fact to Bonar Law, but his reaction to my enthusiasm was only to say, "I don't care much for music." As we approached the golf course we saw some extremely pretty women also on the way to play golf. I called Bonar Law's attention to them. "Women don't attract me," was his laconic answer. "Will you tell me," I said, exasperated, "what it is that you do care for? Scenery — music — women — none of them has any meaning for you. What is it that you do like?" "I like bridge," was the reply.

Was he industrious? He was a steady and quiet worker. He took pains to master his case before he expressed an opinion either in council or in public. He read the official papers sent to him carefully, but I never found him searching out extraneous sources of information in order to obtain wider and less official conclusions on the subject under investigation. He was hard-working when the occasion demanded application, but he was not energetic. He loved his armchair and he was a slave to his pipe. He hated a long lunch or dinner, not only because he was an unappreciative eater, but because it delayed the moment when he could pull out his beloved pipe. I believe it helped to undermine his health.

His method of preparing his speeches was to sit in his armchair with his head well back in the chair and his long legs well up on the mantelpiece. He loved quiet and ease. His slogan as Prime Minister was characteristic — "Tranquillity." He hated not only quarrels and tumults but all that demanded a strenuous life or called for a display of energy and vigour. He was not exactly lethargic, and certainly not torpid, but he had no constant urge towards action of any kind. He was in private kindly, good-tempered, genial — nay, essentially gentle. His bluntness of speech was all manner and was not attributable in the least to the temper or cold cruelty of disposition that takes pleasure in inflicting hurt. This impression may serve to explain what follows when I come later on to tell the story of how our partnership began and how it continued unbroken under an unparalleled strain. It is not too much to claim that the effect it had on the events of that critical period is part of the story of the Empire and of the contribution the Empire made to a struggle which must for generations affect the course of civilisation.

CHAPTER XX

1914–1916: A RETROSPECT

The end of an epoch — Allied superiority thrown away — Waste of man-power — What the Germans feared — Sir William Robertson's view of the situation at end of 1916.

AFTER accepting the Premiership from the King's hands, I proceeded immediately to form my administration. How this Government was formed, the conditions under which it was called upon to undertake its task, the problems which confronted it, and the way in which it proceeded to deal with them must be the subject of my next book.

In the foregoing pages I have brought my recollections of the Great War down to the end of 1916. In a succeeding volume I hope to take up the tale, and describe the outstanding events with which I was personally connected during the two concluding years of the world conflict. But the month of December, 1916, forms a fitting point at which to pause in my narrative, for it marked, for reasons which I shall proceed to summarise, the end of an epoch in the progress of the war. So far as my own affairs were concerned, it was the point at which, after serving the State in a variety of secondary offices, I was called upon to shoulder the supreme responsibility for its administration. I carried that burden throughout the remaining years of the war and beyond.

In the story of the war, the end of 1916 found the fortunes of the Allies at their lowest ebb, the outlook dark from the open bankruptcy of both their strategy and their diplomacy. Three of the Allied Powers — Belgium, Roumania,

Serbia — had been completely knocked out; the fourth — and one of the greatest — had also been practically put out of action. On the other hand the Central Power Federation was intact. The prospect facing us at the moment when I became Prime Minister was enough to daunt any man or group of men. By a succession of incredible blunders we had frittered away one advantage after another possessed by the Allies — in material resources and potential man-power and strategic opportunity — until on balance we were on the wrong side in our comparative strength and strategic position as compared with those enjoyed by the enemy. Even our command of the sea was in jeopardy — and daily increasing jeopardy.

The Allies had originally possessed an immense superiority in man-power, and in all the available and accessible means of equipment. We squandered the former and neglected the latter. At the outbreak of the war the men of military age in Russia, France, the British Empire, Serbia, Roumania, Italy and Belgium outnumbered by many millions those which the Central Powers could call upon. How had we used them? Owing to bad strategy and failure to utilise our vast resources for equipment we threw away our overwhelming surplus of fighting men. For this reason we had left Serbia to be overrun and wiped out. More than half her resources of fighting men had been one way or another put out of action, and the remainder, cut off from their own territory, were unable to draw on their potential reserves and reinforcements. Roumania had, owing to the same cause, just shared the same fate, and her army of 900,000 (with reserves) had been written off the account. Russia had entered the war with almost illimitable man-power. It was estimated by General Gourko that up to the end of 1916 she had called 14,000,000 men to the colours. In October, 1916, Sir William Robertson estimated that she still had nearly 5,000,000 under arms, and could draw on reserves of a further 6,500,000. The remainder of her troops had disappeared in the shambles of war or were interned in German and Austrian camps supplying the enemy deficiency in labour. But by the end of 1916, Russia, through lack of equipment which France and Britain could easily have furnished, had almost ceased to be an asset on the balance sheet. Her revolution was only a few weeks ahead, and with it her military value to the Allied cause would disappear altogether. Already her troops, dispirited and disaffected, had ceased to be capable of any serious offensive. On the other hand, Austria, which could have been disintegrated and destroyed in 1916, was so protected and strengthened that she survived as a formidable opponent in resistance and attack for two more years, while Turkey, which could have been finished off in 1915, had beaten us off in Mesopotamia and Palestine and, her armies re-equipped by Germany, was more redoubtable as a military power than she was in 1914.

Two failures on key questions had completely transformed the military position to our disadvantage. The first was the failure to realise that this was a war of machinery, and the consequent neglect immediately to mobilise our national resources to improve the Allied equipment. The second was our failure until too late to appreciate the fact that the weakest point of the Central Powers was in the Eastern and Southeastern fronts. Thus a war of attrition was substituted for a war of intelligence.

Both Lord Kitchener and Sir William Robertson reposed their trust in attrition as a means to victory. How had it worked? I have shown how already we had dissipated our huge surplus of fighting men in the east. What about the west?

The armies of France and Britain were still powerful,

but the course of the war up to this date had witnessed a profligate wasting of some of our finest young manhood. In the offensives of the Western Front we had lost three men for every two of the Germans we put out of action. Over 300,000 British troops were being immobilised for lack of enterprise or equipment or both by the Turks in Egypt and Mesopotamia, and for the same reason, nearly 400,000 Allied soldiers were for all purposes interned by the Bulgarians in the malarial plains around Salonika. Altogether the Allied forces which could still be counted as reliable for energetic campaigning in the future were facing a foe that was now, for effective purposes, just as powerful numerically, and was operating on interior lines with all the best strategic positions in his hands — the Balkans, the Dardanelles, and the high ground in France and Belgium. The silly and bloody game of attrition had already been won by Germany.

With a criminal prodigality we had squandered the superior man-power that had been at our disposal. We had also weakened our resources and strengthened those of the enemy by our failure to gain alliances that would have been ours for the asking, and by manœuvring at least one potential ally to the other side. Our diplomacy was a timid and nervous thing, frightened of America, too shy to tackle Greece, and leaving the Turks and Bulgarians entirely to the allurements of the Germans. Sir William Robertson complained of the undoubted fact that the soldiers had received no help from diplomacy. Bold diplomacy, backed by proper strategy and effective military action, would have enabled us in the early months of the war to call into being a great Balkan Confederation on the side of the Allies, which would have added 1,500,000 to our fighting forces. With Bulgaria, Greece and Roumania, in addition to Serbia, on our side, Turkey would have been cut off and forced to make peace in 1915, or at latest early in 1916. And with these forces pressing up on Austria from the southeast, and with Italy operating from the south, we should have crushed Austria-Hungary, and compelled Germany to make peace particularly if by energetic and early mobilisation of our manufacturing resources we had supplied Russia with the munitions to make her immense armies effective.

Peace with victory might have been ours in 1916 if we had pursued such a course. It would have meant contenting ourselves with holding the Germans on the Western Front, rather than trying to smash through there; it would have meant sending the men, who later on were slain in vain attacks in France and Flanders, to strengthen the forces of a Balkan Confederation for an assault upon the weakest part of the Central Powers' defence; it would have meant sending part of the munitions blazed away in France to assist Russia and the Balkan States. Recently I was told in conversation by a distinguished German who held an exalted position in the government of his country during the war: "That is what we were always afraid you would do!" Nothing pleased them better than to see us mass our forces for attack in the impregnable west while we allowed ourselves to be outmanœuvred and beaten at every turn in the vulnerable east. We hammered at the breastplate of Achilles and neglected his heel. And we called it sometimes "striking at the vital parts" and sometimes "attrition."

Such was the net result of the diplomacy and the war direction and strategy pursued by the Allies during nearly two and a half years of a war in which they had started with overwhelming advantages, and through which they had been supported by unexampled efforts and sacrifices on the part of their peoples.

Such was the situation I was called upon to face when I took up office as Prime Minister. A few days after I became Prime Minister I invited Sir William Robertson to give me a note on any points connected with the war which particularly required my attention and I also invited his candid opinion as to our prospects of winning it. The document with which he furnished me was not an encouraging one. There were such phrases as: "The attitude of the British Empire up to the present time has been lamentable." "We are contributing far more to the war than any Power, and we exercise less general control than any."

Later on he says: "At the present time we are practically committing suicide." Then he goes on: "We must considerably enlarge our ideas as to the magnitude of the war. We do not yet nearly realise the stupendous task confronting us."

He prophesied "an increasing strain in every direction. The strain will become greater and greater as time goes on, and we are undoubtedly in for a bad time for the next few months. . . ." Further on he says, *"We can only expect* just *to win through and no more,* and yet things in England are going on much the same to-day as two years ago. It is upon us more than upon any Power that the final result depends, and *I cannot hold out any hope of winning until we have been strained to the utmost.* If the nation will not stand that, then the chances are we shall not win. . . ."

Later on he says, ". . . some Members of the late Government had no proper perspective of the War. They lived from telegram to telegram. . . ."

He ends, after saying that Germany is also feeling the strain of the war, "We must learn to set our teeth and refuse to be discouraged; *and, generally, put into our task more spirit, soul, courage, and determination to win no matter at what cost, and in any event to go down, if we must, with our colours flying. But there will be no question of going down if we are brave and resolute, and stick to a definite plan once it is made."*

INDEX

INDEX